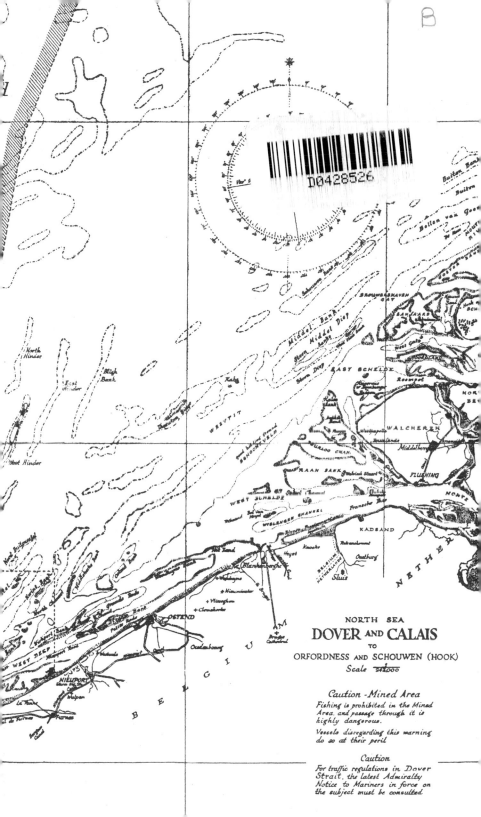

NORTH SEA
DOVER AND CALAIS
TO
ORFORDNESS AND SCHOUWEN (HOOK)

Scale 1/400000

Caution - Mined Area
Fishing is prohibited in the Mined Area, and passage through it is highly dangerous.

Vessels disregarding this warning do so at their peril

Caution
For traffic regulations in Dover Strait, the latest Admiralty Notice to Mariners in force on the subject must be consulted

DUNKIRK

by the same author

*

NAVIES IN EXILE

ROAD TO TUNIS

DESTROYER'S WAR

BEHIND THE FLEETS

THE WAKE OF THE RAIDERS

THE MERCHANT NAVY FIGHTS

DUNKIRK

by

A. D. DIVINE
D.S.M.

FABER & FABER

First published in 1945
by Faber & Faber Limited
Bloomsbury House
74–77 Great Russell Street
London WC1B 3DA

This facsimile edition published in 2018

Typeset by Faber & Faber Limited
Printed and bound by CPI Group (UK) Ltd, Croydon, CR0 4YY

A CIP record for this book
is available from the British Library

ISBN 978–0–571–34257–0

2 4 6 8 10 9 7 5 3 1

A NEW INTRODUCTION
by Nicholas Rankin

The journalist David Divine did more to spread the patriotic legend of Dunkirk than any other writer. He directly experienced Operation *Dynamo* in 1940, getting both a wound and a medal, wrote the first novel about the evacuation, *The Sun Shall Greet Them* (Collins, 1941), and two separate histories chronicling the naval side of the dramatic events of May–June 1940, both published by Faber & Faber. *Dunkirk* was the first to appear in 1945; *The Nine Days of Dunkirk* was released in 1959.

Yet he is largely forgotten today. In more recent narratives, such as Hugh Sebag-Montefiore's *Dunkirk: Fight to the Last Man* (Viking, 2006), Julian Thompson's *Dunkirk: Retreat to Victory* (Sidgwick & Jackson, 2008) and Joshua Levine's *Dunkirk: The History Behind the Major Motion Picture* (HarperCollins, 2017), A. D. Divine does not figure in their notes or bibliographies. But why?

Basically, there are two simple ways of retelling Dunkirk: as tragedy or as triumph. On the one hand, as Winston Churchill frankly declared in the House of Commons on 4th June 1940, it was 'a colossal military disaster'. On the other, in the same speech the Prime Minister also called the evacuation of the British Expeditionary Force 'a miracle of deliverance, achieved by valour, by perseverance, by perfect discipline, by faultless service, by resource, by skill, by unconquerable fidelity'. The inquisitive modern historian finds the disaster more interesting than the dutiful virtues. Twenty-first-century readers understand that not everybody was brave and disciplined, and that service was fallible. We want to know more about the chaos, the cock-ups and the cowardice.

The ignoble side of Dunkirk first emerged in Richard Collier's controversial book *The Sands of Dunkirk* (Collins, 1961). Another revisionist historian, Nicholas Harman, in the source notes of his own provocation *Dunkirk: The Necessary Myth* (Hodder & Stoughton, 1980), wrote that in assembling a day-by-day account of the evacuation, David Divine's *Nine Days of Dunkirk* was 'indispensable. He was there and, more important, he interviewed many participants who are now dead.' But he added: 'It is no criticism of Divine to say that he tended to accentuate what was positive about British actions at Dunkirk.' Harman had known Divine as a journalist colleague at the *Sunday Times* and learned to like him a lot. 'He was always accurate and always intensely patriotic; however . . . although he contributed much to our understanding of how the evacuation took place, he also left things out.'

So how did the writer David Divine come to fulfil this role of semi-official propagandist? He was one of that great generation of journalists from the outer reaches of the British Empire, born in the early twentieth century, who came to London to make their name on Fleet Street or in the publishing houses of the metropolis. Like G. L. Steer, author of the Spanish Civil War classic *The Tree of Gernika*, A. D. Divine was born in South Africa and educated in Grahamstown in the Eastern Cape. In 1922, aged seventeen, he began cutting his teeth as a reporter at *The Cape Times* and, at twenty-five, published his first book, a thriller called *Sea Loot*, for Methuen. He was to become a prolific writer. The British Library catalogue confirms that in a literary career of over forty years, David Divine wrote some fifty books for fourteen different publishers.[1]

In late May 1940, the thirty-four-year-old freelance writer (already with twenty books under his belt) was among the journalists milling around Dover, overlooking the English Channel. On page 24 of this book, Divine describes watching the shelling of Boulogne from the White Cliffs. This determined young man was already an amateur sailor and, through his contacts in the Ministry of Information and the Admiralty, had by 31st May acquired the papers that put him in the navy for thirty days. He told Walter Lord, author of *The Miracle of Dunkirk* (Viking, 1982), that he went to Ramsgate, looked over the commandeered small craft piling up in the harbour, and picked out for himself a 28-foot, Bermuda-rigged yawl called *Little Ann*. With no formal assignment, he jumped aboard and began getting her ready for sea. He was soon joined by a kindred soul – Divine never learned his name – and with a couple of others they set out for Dunkirk early on Saturday 1st June.

At some point, *Little Ann* ran aground on a sand-bar and had to be abandoned. Divine hitched a ride back to Ramsgate, and this time picked out a 30-foot, twin-screw Thames motor cruiser called *White Wing* to steal, before he was told that a senior naval officer also required the craft. So it was that David Divine steered the boat that took Rear Admiral A. H. Taylor, the man in charge of Operation *Dynamo*'s Small Vessels Pool in Sheerness, across the English Channel to organise the evacuations of the last small parties from Malo-les-Bains.

They left at 8.45 p.m. on Sunday 2nd June. They were shelled and shot at and saw 'tragic things', as recorded laconically on page 223. At some point, Divine was wounded in the stomach. He subsequently gained the Distinguished Service Medal (D.S.M.), which is awarded to petty officers and ratings of the Royal Navy (as well as non-commissioned officers and other ranks of the Royal Marines) for 'acts of bravery in the face of the enemy not sufficiently meritorious to make them eligible for the Conspicuous Gallantry Medal (C.G.M.)'.

1 Divine also rewrote the screenplay of the British war film *Dunkirk*, starring John Mills, Bernard Lee and Richard Attenborough. His interventions meant that the British Army was happy to provide 6,500 soldiers for filming at Camber Sands in May 1957, at a cost of £35,000. See S. P. Mackenzie, 'Victory from Defeat: The War Office and the making of *Dunkirk* (Ealing Films,1958)' in *War, Literature & the Arts*, vol. 15, no. 1–2 (2003), a careful examination of the War Office file WO 32/16917, 'Facilities for Ealing Films Ltd "Dunkirk"', in The National Archives, Kew.

A NEW INTRODUCTION

Another *Sunday Times* journalist, Phillip Knightley, wrote a famous book, *The First Casualty: The War Correspondent as Hero, Propagandist, and Myth Maker* (1975, revised 2000), which has a footnote about Divine at Dunkirk on page 253. It reads: 'David Divine, a free-lance, who had written a few navy propaganda books, persuaded the navy to let him watch the evacuation. Divine was wounded and wrote his well-known book on Dunkirk from his hospital bed. Although Divine later became a war correspondent of note, he was not one at that time.' Only the last sentence is correct, however. On page 2 of *Dunkirk*, Divine lists six of his previous books, five of which could be described as 'navy propaganda', while *Road to Tunis* (Collins, 1944) recounted his time as a British war correspondent with the American Combat Forces in North Africa in 1942–3. Nonetheless, all six books were written *after* his experience of Dunkirk. As for what Knightley calls 'his well-known book on Dunkirk', *Dunkirk* was not commissioned until 1944, long after Divine left hospital. He did, however, help the Poet Laureate John Masefield with his pamphlet, *The Nine Days Wonder*, which Heinemann published in 1941.

Whatever revisionists may say, *Dunkirk* remains a good, strong book, most valuable for its vivid contemporaneous accounts from the 'Little Ships', many of which were collected by an eminent barrister, Joshua David Casswell, K.C., and handed over to David Divine to collate. Divine tells their stories well, fitting the individuals into the institutions that co-ordinated them. Without such organisation by the Royal Navy and the Merchant Navy, we clearly come to understand that it would have been impossible to evacuate the 338,000 men who reached England. *Dunkirk* is a book that names many names, giving credit where credit is due.

Appendix B lists the ships that took part and Appendix C contains the full list of all the honours and awards after Dunkirk. First on the list is the knighthood for the great Vice Admiral Bertram Home Ramsay, the Flag Officer Commanding Dover, who went on from the evacuation of Dunkirk to organise the Allied landings in North Africa in 1942, Sicily in 1943 and Normandy in June 1944. David Divine, whose own award appears on page 296, was lucky enough to talk to Ramsay about Dunkirk before the admiral was killed in a plane crash in France on 2nd January 1945.

For anyone impressed by Christopher Nolan's spectacular 2017 film, Divine's *Dunkirk* provides true-life stories. It would take a heart of stone not to be moved by them.

Ramsgate, October 2017

CONTENTS

CONTENTS

INTRODUCTION

The full story of Dunkirk will never be told. The material of naval history lies in the logs of ships, in the reports of captains and of masters, in the records of navigators and the staffs of engine-rooms. For many of the naval vessels, of the merchant ships and of the small craft that took part in the evacuation of the British Expeditionary Force, no such records exist. Some of them were lost when the ships went down in the Dunkirk channel, off Gravelines, in the Zuydecoote Pass; but many of them were never begun. Men worked in the small ships in those days under the spur of a most desperate disaster. They worked, some of them, until they fell exhausted. They brought their ships home and collapsed in sleep. They had not time, they had not opportunity, they had not place in which to write. There were vessels that went to Dunkirk with no more than a series of courses pencilled on the back of an envelope.

Because of these things I am aware that I have done injustice to some gallant ships. There are many which took part in these operations that are not named in these pages. No information exists with regard to them. Of those that are named I am aware that, in spite of exhaustive research, there may be in places error; and again the fault lies in the rich turmoil of the times. In the records that exist there are many discrepancies of date, of time, of place, of names. The captains of vessels in the eye of disaster were not always meticulous in discovering the names of their rescuers or, for that matter, of the rescued; they were not always certain, in the darkness and the difficulty of navigation, of positions; they lost all count of times and days.

None the less I believe this to be a record of Dunkirk, and for that fact I have to thank many people: Mr. J. D. Casswell, K.C., whose collection of small-boat accounts was the springing point of this larger work; Rear-Admiral A. H. Taylor, O.B.E.; Admiral Sir Lionel Preston, K.C.B., and Captain E. F. Wharton, R.N., of the Small Vessels Pool; Captain C. A. H. Brooking, C.B.E., R.N., Deputy Chief of Naval Information; Mr. A. L. Moore, Mr. B. E. Bellamy, Mr. H. C. Riggs, and Mr. J. R. Watkins, O.B.E., of the Sea Transport Department of the Ministry of War Transport; the Press Division of the Air Ministry; Sir Ian MacAlister; the many authors from whose books I have quoted; and Miss S. Downie, who reduced the chaos of the Dunkirk papers to order.

A. D. D.

When I started to collect logs of the Little Ships which went to Dunkirk, my intention was to publish as comprehensive a list as possible of these boats, with a précis of the adventures of each of them and the names of their skippers and crews. This project proved impracticable and I welcomed the opportunity of handing over the material which I had gathered to the far more able and experienced hands of Mr. A. D. Divine. I wish to take this opportunity of thanking Mr. A. L. Moore, of the Ministry of War Transport, Mr. Sydney Elliott, of the *Evening Standard*, to whom I am deeply indebted for their help, and all those who sent me accounts of the cruises of the 'Little Ships'. The right to royalties payable for this contribution to the book has been assigned to the King George's Fund for Sailors.

J. D. C.

Wimbledon
 September 1944

CHAPTER I

WHAT WAS DUNKIRK?

Behind the British Army in May of 1940, as it fell back fighting from the Dyle, lay the sea.

For a thousand years that sea was the great defence of England. For a thousand years it had been called the English Moat. Its bays and its headlands saw the battles that held Britain inviolate from the day the house-carles broke on Senlac Hill and the Saxon power broke with them. And there were years when it was more than a moat. A score of British armies in those centuries fell back upon the North Sea and the Channel, and the sea was to them a refuge; across the narrows the ships of Britain lay like a drawbridge, and by that drawbridge they crossed to safety.

When the British Expeditionary Force in 1940 turned from the line of the Dyle almost as it deployed upon it, there was no longer certainty that the sea was upon our side. New strategies had supervened, new ideas had come to war. The sea that had helped the shattered armies of the centuries that were gone threatened the very existence of this.

It is not easy to make comparisons in assessing the magnitude of Dunkirk. There is nothing new in evacuation. It is a military operation that has been employed as a measure of recovery in a hundred wars. In the course of the Napoleonic campaigns alone, nineteen British forces were withdrawn from various points along the Continental coasts, and the evacuation of the army of Sir John Moore from Corunna—the most important of this long succession—stood for more than a hundred years as the model and the measure of evasive action.

Moore, by his bold thrust in the direction of Burgos, having disrupted Napoleon's expedition against Lisbon and the south of Spain, fell back towards his base at Corunna. Napoleon with an army three times as strong harried him to the crossings of the Esla. Checked there by demolitions, he handed over the command to Soult at Astorga. Moore offered battle at Lugo, but Soult preferred to let the demoralization of retreat do his work for him. Desperately short of supplies, suffering heavily from cold, battered and almost broken, Moore's army reached the port after seventeen days.

The fleet had not arrived.

On the ridge of the Monte Mero Moore established his perimeter of defence. On the 14th of January 1808 Soult attacked. In a magnificent defensive action Moore held his position. Mortally wounded himself, he died before the battle ended—but the ships had come and the French, fought to a standstill, watched his army go.

Twenty thousand men that day went out to the sanctuary of the sea.

Until Gallipoli there was no match to it.

WHAT WAS DUNKIRK?

This was a new century, a new warfare. The Gallipoli evacuation stood for twenty years as the masterpiece of military deception, as it stood as a masterpiece of naval organization. It is the yardstick by which we must measure the Operation 'Dynamo', by which we may assess something of the magnitude, something of the astonishing stature of the nine days of the beaches.

The problem at Gallipoli was to move from two shallow positions served by the main landing places of Anzac, Suvla and the Helles beaches two forces of men, the first (from Anzac and Suvla) numbering 83,000 on December 8th, when the Government's decision to evacuate was received, the second (from Helles) numbering approximately 42,000 at the same date. These men were deployed in perimeters securely held, admirably defended with trench systems, wire emplacements, and a plenitude of artillery that had stood the test of eight months of bitter fighting. Transport difficulties were insignificant, for every man, even in the forward observation posts, fought within walking distance of the embarkation points. On the beaches there were piers and quays. These were rough—improvised, some of them, out of old ships, some of them out of the hard ingenuity of the engineers—but they had served to put an army ashore and to keep it supplied through the long months of the campaign. To add to the strength of the army's defences was the fact that almost everywhere along the perimeters the enemy lines were within reach of naval guns which could give—and did give—an astonishing covering fire. Moreover Monro had two months after his decision was taken in which to prepare for the operation. We had a sufficiency of ships, and we had no danger from the air with which to contend.

Yet of Gallipoli Lord Kitchener could say in a telegram to General Birdwood:

'I absolutely refuse to sign order for evacuation, which I think would be greatest disaster, and would condemn a large percentage of our men to death or imprisonment.'

It is not necessary to detail the unpleasant history of the decisions for the evacuation of Gallipoli. It was an evacuation of policy, not of necessity. The moment for our withdrawal was our own. Before that moment we had time to practise every artifice of deception, every device that might mislead our enemy.

The first phase of the operation was the evacuation of Suvla and Anzac. It was fixed for the night of the 19th of December 1915. By the afternoon of December 18th 44,000 men, 130 guns, and several thousand animals had already been embarked by an intensification of the normal traffic from the beaches. There remained something under 40,000 men ashore. It was considered impossible to lift more than 20,000 of these in a single night. On the night of the 18th the first 20,000 were got clear. On the night of the 19th, without interference from the enemy, the last men left the beaches, the dumps were fired, and the mines exploded. There were no casualties and no losses.

The German military correspondent of the *Vossiche Zeitung* wrote:

WHAT WAS DUNKIRK?

'As long as wars last this evacuation of Suvla and Anzac will stand before the eyes of all strategists as a hitherto unattained masterpiece.'

Three weeks later that summit of achievement was topped by the pinnacle of Helles. Again there was time for preparation, time for deception. The actual movement began on December 28th, and more than half the men were removed in the first period. The enemy knew that it was contemplated and appears to have known early that it was in progress. There was air reconnaissance here, German Taubes flying over the beaches from time to time; and on the 7th of January 1916, the Turks attempted, after a heavy artillery duel, to interfere with the operation. The brilliant covering fire of the naval guns broke that attempt in its own trenches. On the night of January 8th General Davies had 17,000 men and 40 guns left to hold his 8 miles of line. By 8 o'clock in the evening the first flight of ships was in, the first wave of men was filing aboard them. At 11 o'clock the second flight moved in. The wind was rising and the sea with it. At 1.30 the last flight came in, and by 3.30, despite all that the sea could do, the last men were off Gallipoli.

That was Gallipoli, the greatest evacuation in the history of war until Dunkirk.

What was Dunkirk?

It was the rescue of an army. It was not a withdrawal, long contemplated, meticulously prepared. It was not a strategic conception made desirable by extraneous needs. It was a brutal, desperate adventure forced upon us by the most dire disaster, carried out under the eyes of an enemy flushed with victory, elated with the certainty of conquest. It was carried out in defiance of time, of circumstance, of death itself. There was no secure perimeter in the days that led to it, but only an army falling back in hot battle, with its flanks open and its allies broken upon either hand: an army cut off from its bases, lacking the very essentials of modern war: an army outclassed by its enemy, inferior in everything save courage and determination: an army designed for principles of war that were outmoded, facing an enemy who had forged a weapon to fight a strategy unknown.

It came to the beaches after desperate weeks, battered, bruised and infinitely weary. It marched to its evacuation over bitter miles, and every yard of all those miles was challenged by the enemy, and every hour was made brutal by the enormous strength of the Luftwaffe in the air.

And when it reached the tidemark there waited for it the armada of a fantastic improvisation. Here were no troopships long prepared; here was no careful withdrawal. Here was only a fleet of ships' lifeboats and motor yachts, of Dutch skoots and French fishing boats, British coasters and Channel ferries, of drifters, minesweepers, sloops, destroyers: the strangest fleet in the history of war upon the sea; battered from the air and from the shore, bruised, broken, and in ceaseless peril—only these and the spirit of an awakened England.

11

CHAPTER II
PLAN D

1

The first phase of the second Great War ended at 4.30 a.m. on Friday, the 10th of May 1940, when German aircraft appeared over Lord Gort's headquarters at Arras and dropped a load of bombs.

At 5.30 a.m. a message was received from General Georges, commanding the Front of the North East, ordering 'Alertes 1, 2 and 3'. These were the preliminary orders for putting into operation 'Plan D'.

As if the bombers had been a signal, from the estuary of the Ems to the basin of the Saar the whole German front flamed into action. Holland was invaded, Belgium was attacked, Luxembourg was overrun. Over 300 miles of the flat levels of the Low Countries and across the hills of the Ardennes the vast German war machine thundered forward.

Plan D was the counter-move. Long contemplated, long examined, it was believed by the French, with whom it had originated, to provide the answer to a new use of the old invasion route. Pivoting on Longwy at the end of the Maginot Line, the Franco-British forces manning the line of the Belgian frontier were to swing forward like a door slamming in the face of the enemy until they stretched across the line of the Dyle from Namur through Perwez and Louvain to the 'National Redoubt', the vast fortified area of Antwerp and the River Scheldt.

It was a grandiose plan, arresting, compelling, vital—and foredoomed to failure. Its doom was implicit in the fact that the French General Staff—and, for that matter, our own—had failed to digest the lessons of Spain, of Poland and of Norway. It was foredoomed by the pitiful insistence of the King of the Belgians and of his Government on a hopeless neutrality. But beyond all things it was foredoomed by the decadence of France.

The seeds of Dunkirk lay not in any tactical error on the Dyle front, not in any position abandoned or battle lost. They were planted before ever Hitler spoke with a loud voice in a Munich beer hall. Much has been written in condemnation of the Maginot Line. The name of André Maginot has become a symbol of passive resistance. It is perhaps unfair to him: he was the product of his age, the fruit of a nation's irresolution.

But the true measure of France's national and military decadence lies not so much in the Maginot Line as in the astonishing, inexplicable failure to make the Maginot Line complete. It was a strong fortress—by French theory impregnable—and yet it lacked a wall. It was like a box in which one side was open and naked to assault. From the Swiss frontier to Longwy it stood impressive in its power. Whether it would have proved sufficient to withstand a planned and vigorous assault of the whole weight of German arms we do not know. It was never put to the full test. It was never nec ssary to put it to the test!

The classic invasion route into France has always been through the Low Countries. From the line of the Scheldt to the low massif of the Ardennes there is nothing that offers obstacle to a modern army. The rivers are small, low and slow-flowing. There are no hills. The canals offer only momentary obstruction to the engineering genius of the armies of to-day. The first campaign of 1914 demonstrated with a cold clarity that vulnerability. Yet, fifteen years later, the French embarked on the most colossal fortification programme in the history of the world since the building of the Great Wall of China, in a bland disregard of those lessons.

The Great Wall of China was stormed. It may be that the Maginot Line would have been stormed also. But there was no need to climb the wall when the road lay level through the open side.

It is inconceivable that the French High Command believed in the efficacy of Belgian neutrality after the experience of 1914. It is even less conceivable that it could have believed in the efficacy of Belgian fortifications. Belgium was a small power; by many standards she was a poor power; yet it was alleged that the Belgians had built a continuation of the Maginot Line across the Germano-Belgian frontier. No such line existed: there were scattered fortifications only. In the event they delayed the enemy not at all.

In the nine months since the declaration of war against Germany some effort had been made to establish a defence in depth along the Franco-Belgian frontier. Those efforts had been uncertain, irresolute. The theory has been advanced that the French refused to fortify this frontier because of the proximity to it of the vast industrial areas of Lille and its satellite towns. An enormous proportion of the industrial wealth of France lay between St. Omer and Le Cateau. Subsequently in the campaign of 1940 industrial interests were to prove stronger than military necessity. It may be that in the years of the building of the Maginot Line, when the industrialists of France were at the height of their power, those interests overweighted the opinions of the generals.

Plan D had taken no cognizance of a stand between Longwy and the sea. Plan D imagined a successful temporary defence of the Belgian frontier, a successful consolidation across the line of the Dyle, a successful reconcentration of the Belgian Army in its sector between Louvain and the National Redoubt. It imagined—most disastrously of all—a successful stand between armies almost without armour, between troops new-arrived in unfamiliar positions, against the determined thrust of an armoured enemy. Plan D will take a high place in history's list of great strategic misconceptions.

But, misconceived as the plan itself was, there was the seed of even greater disaster in its actual execution. To cover the pivot—strategically the most desirable, as tactically it was the most vulnerable, sector of the whole movement—the French put in troops of doubtful capacity, an army of uncertain merit.

PLAN D

2

Plan D was admirably carried out—too admirably. It is difficult to avoid the suspicion that the Germans refrained deliberately from assaulting its columns on the road, from attempting in any way to assail its wide and clumsy movement. The German commanders could scarcely have asked for more. The French 1st Army, the British Expeditionary Force, the French 7th Army, and part of the French 9th Army had swung creaking on the pivot of Longwy, cheered by the Belgians and wearing lilac in their caps. To the Germans it must have seemed that they came decked like lambs to the slaughter. They had abandoned their prepared positions; they were swinging to the aid of a reluctant ally, whose army was incapable of modern battle, whose frontiers were already broken; and, as they swung, the Germans held their fire.

And on May 14th, only four days after they had moved up the straight and dusty roads of Belgium, Lord Gort says in his dispatches: 'Further serious news came from the south where the enemy had crossed the Meuse between Sedan and Mezières. . . .'

With that news Dunkirk was certain. The hinge was gone and the door hung, for a little, reeling in the archway it was meant to close.

It is not necessary to examine in detail the reasons for the break of Corap's 9th Army along the Meuse. It has been said that the morale of the French troops was sapped by the Maginot Line. This is too easy an explanation of disaster. The Maginot conception was the expression of the morale of France. It preceded the break not by months but by years. The tactical failure on the Meuse front was only a symptom, even as the Line itself was a symptom of the mentality of France.

But that break made impossible the holding of Belgium. This fact was not apparent at the time, nor was it apparent for many days. Belief in the capacity of the French Army died hard. All that the enemy had achieved, as it appeared to those who fought across the plain of Flanders, was that the Germans had forced a salient where the line was weakest. The French High Command had trusted to the natural barrier of the Ardennes and the Germans had partially solved the problem of natural barriers—that was all. The French were believed to have enormous reserves tactically dispersed, and there was no reason to think that this thrust would not be neutralized, that the salient could not be pinched out.

The Belgians were falling back, at times in confusion, from the line of the Albert Canal, and from their fortifications. The Dutch, fighting gallantly and bewilderedly against new tactics and new weapons, were on the point of collapse. On May 15th that collapse took place. The armies of Holland capitulated. The psychological effect on the Belgians was obvious and apparent. The tactical effect of the release of a large proportion of the German armour from the Dutch areas was also obvious. It was becoming clear rapidly that the line of the Dyle would not be tenable.

14

PLAN D

The British Expeditionary Force had from the first, by agreement of the the Governments, been absorbed in the French defence scheme. It was under the French High Command whose authority was delegated through General Gamelin to General Georges as commander of the French Front of the North East. On Sunday, May 12th, at a conference held at Château Casteau, near Mons, that command was further delegated to General Billotte, and it was under Billotte that the uncertainties and co-operational difficulties, which increased as the armies fell back, began. The first signs of the indecision of the French High Command and of the French Government were becoming apparent.

By May 16th it was clear that Plan D had failed and must be abandoned. The position has been described as obscure. Unquestionably it was so in the fog of immediate battle, but it is, in the light of subsequent events, sufficiently clear to-day. The British Expeditionary Force was still in occupation of its line—the line that covered the centre of Belgium. North of it Giraud's 7th Army was being dismembered. Part of it had gone into Holland and was involved in the general debacle. Part of it had been sent across the British rear in an attempt to reinforce the 9th Army. The Belgian Army, which occupied the rest of the sectors of the left, was almost visibly deteriorating. To the right the French 1st Army had lost ground, and to the right of that the French 9th Army had disintegrated—there is no other word sufficient to describe the magnitude of that disaster.

At 10 a.m. on the 16th Lord Gort received orders from General Billotte to commence a withdrawal to the line of the Escaut, the upper Scheldt. This withdrawal was planned to take three days, one day being spent on the line of the Senne river, one on the line of the Dendre, the Escaut itself being reached on the night of the 18/19th.

The first section of the operation was successfully completed, though it involved difficulties with tank units which were to play some part in subsequent events. On the morning of May 17th, as the second phase of the operation began, the full import of the debacle in the south began to manifest itself. Enemy armoured forces were reported to have crossed the Oise. General Giraud, who had commanded the French 7th Army on the British left, had moved down and had been ordered to take command of the force in the area of St. Quentin, but it appeared that no command in fact existed. There was a gap of 20 miles south of the Forest of Mormal. Giraud himself was captured with his staff in the vicinity of Mormal and the last hope of rallying the forces of the gap was captured with him.

The salient had become a breakthrough. This was no longer a sword-thrust—it was a series of axe blows, heavy, sharp, irresistible, cutting with an almost inconceivable speed between the armies of the north and the armies of the south. The rapidity of the German advance from the crossing of the Meuse was almost incredible. Only the slowness and indecision of the French High Command in marshalling its reserves to meet the situation, matched it.

The headquarters of the B.E.F. had been at Arras. The advance bases were all in the area between Arras and the sea, and already the blade of the axe was poised above them. We had three divisions in these areas—the 12th, the 23rd and the 46th. They had been brought to France for training purposes. They had no artillery and their fighting organizations were in skeleton form, but in the desperation of the moment they represented a reserve. Despite the extraordinary failure of General Billotte's headquarters to keep Lord Gort informed, preparations for the utilization of these and of lines of communication troops were put in hand.

But the position of the armies of the north was already untenable in every sense of the word, and it was becoming rapidly and dramatically clear that unless the most drastic measures were taken it would be impossible even to swing back the northern armies into junction with the south.

3

On May 18th the German panzer divisions reached Amiens. On May 20th motor-cyclists in advance of the main German force took Abbeville. The blade of the axe had bitten through to the sea.

There have been many explanations of the failure to cut the German corridor, the pathway of the axe. Not perhaps until many years after the war shall we achieve a proper judgement of the evidence, but the salient facts are clear. Let us consider first the position of the forces in the area. Simplifying the line that in places was indented and battered, the armies of the north occupied a rough semicircle that ran from the estuary of the Somme through Valenciennes and Ghent to the estuary of the Scheldt at a point a little east of Terneuzen. The north of this area was held by the Belgian Army together with remnants of Giraud's command. The B.E.F. held the line of the Escaut with six divisions in the line between Bléharies and Audenarde. South of this sector was the French 1st Army extending as far as Bouchain, 10 miles below Douai. That was the front.

From Bouchain the line bent back in an enormous flank which covered Arras and developed vaguely towards the sea. That flank the generals were now striving desperately to make into a line. Part of it was occupied by the bending back of the French 1st Army with remnants of the 7th and 9th. The rest of it was occupied in the main by the three British 'auxiliary forces'—Polforce, Petreforce, and Macforce. These had been hastily formed out of the 12th, the 23rd and the 46th Divisions. As has been said, they were weak divisions with no artillery and with only skeleton signal and transport organizations.

At midnight on the 18/19th General Billotte visited Lord Gort at his headquarters, and for the first time a comprehensive account both of the situation and of such remedial measures as seemed possible, became available. General Billotte appears to have been in a state of some depression with little faith in the possibility of the restoration of the 9th Army front.

There were three alternatives theoretically possible, and these were discussed. The first, inevitably, was the cutting of the corridor (they still spoke of it at that time as 'the closing of the gap') by simultaneous attack from the north and south. The second was the withdrawal of the entire southern armies through the lower reaches of the valley of the Somme to link up there with the rest of the French. The third was the possibility of withdrawal west and north-west to the Channel ports, with evacuation at the end of it.

Lord Gort says:

'I was unable to verify that the French had enough reserves at their disposal south of the gap to enable them to stage counter-attacks sufficiently strong to warrant the expectation that the gap would be closed.'

In point of fact the gap was a gap no longer.

The second alternative of reinforcement through the lower reaches of the Somme was to be wiped out utterly the following day when the enemy reached Abbeville. There were left two alternatives in fact even as the generals discussed the problems. The first of these was no longer the closing of a gap, but the cutting of a corridor. The second was evacuation.

'I realized,' says Lord Gort, 'that this course was in theory a last alternative, as it would involve the departure of the B.E.F. from the theatre of war at a time when the French might need all the support which Britain could give them. It involved the virtual certainty that even if the excellent port facilities at Dunkirk continued to be available, it would be necessary to abandon all the heavier guns and much of the vehicles and equipment. Nevertheless, I felt that in the circumstances there might be no other course open to me. . . .'[1]

For the first time Dunkirk comes into the picture.

4

Gamelin disappeared unsung on the 18th and Weygand took over— Weygand, the fighting general of France, the heroic figure. Immediately what was known as the 'Weygand Plan' took up the attention of the anxious world. The strange psychological necessity of the French for a formula seems to have found ease in the fact that there was a plan. Of attempts to implement it there appear to have been strangely few. It was a plan founded on misconceptions, and the basic misconception was the fighting spirit of France. Already defeatism had permeated the French body politic. It had permeated the French people, and it had permeated the greater part of the army. The Weygand Plan provided, in the first place, for a grandiose attack from the north of the gap. In that it was nothing more than the elementary strategic necessity which had been discussed and thrashed out already amongst the fighting generals.

Early on the morning of May 20th General Sir Edmund Ironside, the Chief of the Imperial General Staff, arrived at G.H.Q. with instructions from the Cabinet that the B.E.F. was to move southwards upon Amiens, 'attacking all enemy forces encountered and to take station on the left of the French Army'. This decision of the British Cabinet was also founded upon miscon-

[1] Second Gort dispatch, paragraph 30.

ceptions. The B.E.F. was automatically deprived of much of its fighting efficiency when it was deprived of its bases. Sustained operations could not have been undertaken against a strong enemy. It was engaged upon the whole length of its front; any attempt at disengagement would have been followed up immediately by the enemy, and inevitably the point would have been reached where the force was fighting a strong enemy in front and in rear simultaneously. Owing to transport and other difficulties it was improbable that either the French and Belgians on the left or the French 1st Army on the right would be able to conform to such a movement, and the possibilities of successful withdrawal were jeopardized in that fact alone.

But Lord Gort had made preparations already for an attempt at the cutting of the corridor. With the 5th and 50th Divisions he had made his plan to attack on the morning of May 21st south of Arras.

General Ironside met Generals Billotte and Blanchard at Lens, and explained the action that was to be taken. 'General Billotte fully agreed to this plan, and said that the French would co-operate with two divisions.' Returning to Lord Gort's headquarters, the C.I.G.S. telegraphed General Georges at his headquarters to the south of the corridor, and said that it was clear in his opinion that the northern armies would be finally cut off unless the French 1st Army made an immediate attack on Cambrai or unless General Georges launched an attack northwards from Peronne, the most northerly part of the vague line south of the corridor held by the French from the end of the Maginot Line to the sea.

The new force which Lord Gort had concentrated was strengthened by the 1st Army Tank Brigade (taken from Macforce) together with Petreforce and other units. On the evening of May 20th, Major-General H. E. Franklyn, who commanded it, completed his reconnaissances, but at the conference called at 6 p.m. on the evening of the same day at his headquarters no representatives from the French 5th Corps, which was to co-operate, attended.

At 2 p.m. on the 21st General Franklyn's force attacked, with the co-operation of the French 1st Light Mechanized Division. The objectives of the day were captured in one of the most gallant actions of the campaign. But mechanical difficulties with the tanks began early to affect the situation. The French co-operation 'did not develop so widely to the flanks as General Franklyn had hoped',[1] and, with the lack of substantial assistance from the French 5th Corps, it became clear that the momentum could not be maintained.

That was the one attempt to cut the corridor. It failed—but in the measure of its success it indicated what might perhaps have been done with firm purpose on the part of the French High Command. It is still not possible to say that, even if such an attack had succeeded, the position could have been restored, but it remains a tantalizing speculation.

If the corridor had been cut, *if* the German mechanized formations already to the westwards had been cut off and mopped up, *if* the Franco-British-Belgian Armies of the north had been able to wheel back to the line of the

[1] Second Gort dispatch, paragraph 33.

Somme, would France have been saved? It seems improbable. France was defeated not upon the Meuse, not in the battles of the gap, but before a shot was fired.

5

The position now was that the armies of the north had to accept the fact that they were cut off irrevocably from the armies of the south, and that the alternatives facing them were no longer those of continued military usefulness but of escape or surrender. The axe had cut through.

It is time to change the simile. The armies of the north now were contained in a vast misshapen bag with its mouth open along the Channel coasts. There were six ports within the 'mouth'—Zeebrugge, Ostend, Nieuport on the Belgian coast; Dunkirk, Calais and Boulogne along the French. If those six ports could be used, evacuation was possible.

The German High Command had that fact securely in their minds. It is not certain yet how far the plans of the Germans were rigid, and how far the last portion was a masterly improvisation; but at once, as they reached Abbeville, the Germans began the operation for the drawing of the string that closed the mouth. Up the coast roads from Abbeville the panzer columns moved in a brilliant—seemingly irresistible—sweep. Already it was apparent that with the dwindling forces at our disposal we could not hope to hold the Channel coast. The decision was taken to abandon the Pas de Calais, to pull back the troops from what had now become the dangerous salient between Arras and Valenciennes, and to hold a line that ran eventually from the Escaut through La Bassée and along the canals by St. Omer to the sea at Gravelines. The loss of Calais and Boulogne was accepted.

By 8 p.m. on the night of May 21st, when Lord Gort met the King of the Belgians and General Billotte at the Burgomaster's office in Ypres, it was plain that the loss of the Belgian ports was also perilously near acceptance. There was no water in the Escaut. In the head waters the French had closed the weirs to flood the countryside. There was less than three feet of water along the British front—hopelessly insufficient to offer even a momentary check to tanks. Lord Gort recommended—and the meeting agreed—that the Escaut should be abandoned, the army falling back on the Lys to a new line running from Maulde to Halluin on the Franco-Belgian frontier, and thence by the Lys through Ghent and north to the estuary of the Scheldt.

But, says Lord Gort:

'It was evident that sooner or later the Belgian Army would have to swing back to a line in rear, pivoting on their right of Halluin. Accordingly at the end of the conference General Billotte asked the King of the Belgians whether if he were forced to withdraw he would fall back on the line of the Yser. His Majesty agreed, though evidently with some regret, that no alternative line existed.'

Zeebrugge, Ostend, Nieuport were cancelled out. There was left only Dunkirk.

Swiftly the pace of things accelerated. Swiftly, but always steadily, always

19

fighting, the armies fell back. The names of the towns day by day showed the unhappy progress, the names of towns through which the Old Contemptibles had fought, the names of the Flanders battlefields. Over the old trenches the new armies moved—backwards.

The speed of the German attempt to draw the string was almost inconceivable. At 3.30 p.m. on May 21st news reached headquarters that Boulogne was under direct threat. By the evening of the 21st enemy forces were only 9 miles from Calais port. By the 23rd the canal line itself was in desperate peril. The enemy had established bridgeheads at Aire, at St. Omer and near Watten. Calais was isolated.

On the 24th preparations were made for a counter-attack with its objective Plouvain–Marquion–Cambrai. This was an heroic conception. It was never carried out. Already the rear of the armies of the north was in dire danger. We held a corridor only to uncertain objectives. From Gravelines, where our line ended, to Dunkirk harbour is barely 13 miles, and in the north the Belgians were obviously very near the end. Early on the morning of May 25th they were heavily attacked, and for 13 miles between Menin and Desselghem were forced back from the line. There was the desperate danger that a wedge would be thrust between the Belgian Army and the British left. New dispositions had to be made at once to meet the danger. A pincer attack was developing; the left arm of it was already round the whole bulk of the armies of the north and clawing at the canal line, a handful of miles from Dunkirk; the right was cutting along the Menin Road. To ensure the withdrawal of the troops in what was now the bottom of the bag it became essential to swing back the British left flank as far as Ypres. To secure that flank it was necessary to take the last of the British reserves and even to weaken the front-line positions, and it was obvious that, with the Belgian collapse imminent, even more drastic measures would have to be taken in the very near future. The idea of a counter-attack to the south-west was put aside for the last time. The bag was shrinking.

On Saturday, May 25th, General Weygand dismissed fifteen of his generals.

On the morning of May 26th, at a meeting with General Blanchard (who had succeeded General Billotte, after the latter's death, in command of the French First Group of Armies), it was decided that the main bodies were to be withdrawn behind the line of the Lys. The perimeter held now by the French and British forces measured approximately 128 miles of which 97 miles was held by British troops, and inside that perimeter the supply situation was becoming more than difficult. Ammunition already was stringently restricted. It was decided that on the night of May 26/27th a heavy withdrawal, which would have the effect of shortening the total perimeter by 58 miles, must be undertaken.

At 10.30 a.m. Lord Gort returned from a conference with General Blanchard to find a telegram from the Secretary of State which read:

'... I have had information all of which goes to show that French offensive from Somme cannot be made in sufficient strength to hold any prospect of functioning with your allies in the north. Should this prove to be the case you will be faced with a situation in which the safety of the B.E.F. will predominate. In such conditions only course open to you may be to fight your way back to west where all beaches and ports east of Gravelines will be used for embarkation. Navy will provide fleet of ships and small boats and R.A.F. would give full support. As withdrawal may have to begin very early preliminary plans should be urgently prepared. . . . Prime Minister is seeing M. Reynaud to-morrow afternoon when whole situation will be clarified including attitude of French to the possible move. . . .'

Lord Gort replied that the plan of withdrawal had been agreed with the French and that the Belgian position was 'disquieting'. His reply ended:

'. . . I must not conceal from you that a great part of the B.E.F. and its equipment will inevitably be lost even in best circumstances.'

In the afternoon a further telegram was received from the War Office:

'. . . Prime Minister had conversation M. Reynaud this afternoon. Latter fully explained to him the situation and resources French Army. It is clear that it will not be possible for French to deliver attack on the south in sufficient strength to enable them to effect junction with northern armies. In these circumstances no course open to you but to fall back upon coast. . . . M. Reynaud communicating General Weygand and latter will no doubt issue orders in this sense forthwith. You are now authorized to operate towards coast forthwith in conjunction with French and Belgian Armies.'

Every endeavour was made to persuade the Belgian Army to fall back towards the Yser, but a heavy attack developed along its front between Menin and Nevele (8 miles west of Ghent), and late on the afternoon of the 26th a note from General Michiels, the Chief of Staff of the Belgian Army, said:

'. . . To-day, May 26th, the Belgian Army is being attacked with extreme violence on the front Menin–Nevele, and since the battle is now spreading to the whole of the area of Eecloo, the lack of Belgian reserves makes it impossible to extend our boundaries, which were notified yesterday, further to the right.

'We must therefore, with regret, say that we have no longer any forces available to fill the gap in the direction of Ypres.

'As regards the withdrawal to the Yser the idea must be ruled out since it would destroy our fighting units more quickly than the battle now in progress, and this without loss to the enemy.'

The break of the Belgians was, in fact, complete. Once again a flank was utterly open to the enemy. By desperate measures the gap was filled, and on the evening of May 26th Lord Gort began his plan for the final withdrawal. The first reference to actual evacuation occurs in paragraph 47 of Lord Gort's second dispatch:

'The contraction of the B.E.F. area and the shortening of its lines of communication was now making it possible to dispense with a number of rearward units. I had already issued orders for the embarkation of a number of key personnel who could be spared so as to ease the supply situation which was becoming acute. I now ordered the withdrawal of all units which were not required to continue the battle. This policy involved leaving most of the fighting troops until the last, but if full use was to be made of the shipping available, and congestion avoided on the beaches, no other course was possible.'

Even as these orders were issued the first ships of the evacuation were moving in to Dunkirk.

Lieutenant-General Sir Ronald Adam was given the task of organizing the Dunkirk bridgehead and of arranging the details of the embarkation. He took up his duties on the morning of May 27th.

The drawstring was almost closed. There was left only the long, flat level of the beaches from Gravelines to Nieuport. From those two points sprang the arc of what was now to be known as the Dunkirk perimeter, an arc that ran south-east from Gravelines and the Canal de la Colme, along the canal to Bergues, and thence by Furnes to Nieuport. And already even that was in danger. The French were falling back from Gravelines village to the line of the Mardyck Canal, half the desperate 13 miles that held the enemy from the harbour of Dunkirk.

Consider the implications of this thing. The Germans in a vast encircling movement had flung their panzer divisions from the frontier of Luxembourg by Sedan through the Ardennes to Amiens, from Amiens to the sea at Abbeville, from Abbeville to Boulogne, from Boulogne to Calais—300 miles and more of the dusty roads of northern France, 300 miles behind the enemy front line. And they were stopped barely 6 miles from their objective—stopped and held for nine perilous days.

On the northern arc of the encirclement they had thrust across Belgium from Eupen by Liége, Louvain, Brussels and Ghent. As the Belgian Army collapsed and capitulated on the night of May 27th, they raced for the last miles—and they lost the race at Furnes, 170 miles from their starting-point, 13 miles from Dunkirk Mole, checked by the furious defence of the 7th Guards Brigade under Major-General J. A. C. Whitaker. In the words of another British commander who fought on the soil of the Low Countries: 'It was a damned close-run thing.'

Within forty-eight hours the B.E.F. was in the perimeter. With it was the French garrison under Admiral Abrial, who had as his Chief of Staff Rear-Admiral Leclerc, and Rear-Admiral Platon, Governor of Dunkirk. His headquarters were at Bastion No. 32 near the Mole. The situation with the rest of the French Army was so extraordinary that it can be dealt with only by direct quotation from the Gort dispatches:

'Next morning (May 28th) General Blanchard arrived at my headquarters at Houtkerque at about 11 a.m., and I read him the telegram which I had received the previous day from the Secretary of State. It was then clear to me that whereas we had both received similar instructions from our own Government for the establishment of a bridgehead he had, as yet, received no instructions to correspond with those I had received to evacuate my troops. General Blanchard, therefore, could not see his way to contemplate evacuation.

'I then expressed the opinion that now the Belgian Army had ceased to exist, the only alternatives could be evacuation or surrender. The enemy threat to the north-eastern flank appeared certain to develop during the next forty-eight hours. The long south-western flank was being subjected to constant and increasing pressure, especially at Cassel and Wormhoudt, and the arrival of the enemy heavy columns could not be long delayed. These considerations could not be lightly dismissed. While this discussion was taking place, a liaison officer arrived from General Prioux, now in command of the French 1st Army, to say that the latter did not consider his troops were fit to make any further move and that he therefore intended to remain in the area between Bethune and Lille, protected by the quadrangle of canals.

'I then begged General Blanchard, for the sake of France, the French Army, and the Allied cause to order General Prioux back. Surely, I said, his troops were not all so tired as to be incapable of moving. The French Government would be able to provide ships at least for some of his troops, and the chance of saving a part of his trained soldiers was preferable to the certainty of losing them all. I could not move him. Finally he asked me formally whether it was my intention to withdraw that night to the line Cassel–Poperinghe–Ypres.

'I replied in the affirmative and informed him that I now had formal orders from His Majesty's Government to withdraw the B.E.F. and that if I was to have any hope of carrying them out I must continue my move that night. General Blanchard's parting was not unfriendly, and when he left I issued my orders for withdrawal to provide for that change of mind on the part of the French High Command for which I so sincerely hoped and which in fact took place later.'[1]

It is hardly necessary to comment on these paragraphs. Throughout the disastrous weeks of this campaign the French High Command had demonstrated an inelasticity of mind that in itself was the death-warrant of France.

6

This was the story in its bare essentials. It is not possible, nor is it within the scope of this book, to tell the wider story. The British Army was within the Dunkirk perimeter, but its regiments came to it with their honour. The front that they had held from the Dyle through the successive stages of the reverses until they held it now along the perimeter of the ancient town had never broken. They had withdrawn—never to prepared positions—but always conforming to the breaking of the Allies on their flanks. Whether they could have achieved their salvation by some other means has been debated. If at the very start, deserting Belgium and the Belgian Army, the B.E.F. had struck south, there is small doubt that it could have broken across the corridor and reached the French armies of the south. Tactically the operation was feasible: politically it was impossible: strategically it is doubtful whether it would have had any major influence on the sequence of events. France fell when the Meuse was crossed.

[1] Second Gort dispatch, paragraph 52.

PLAN D

There is in the story of the British retreat a saga of heroism and self-denial that will one day receive its full meed of praise. The British Army that reached the perimeter of Dunkirk was a fighting army still. Hungry—it had been put on half rations on May 23rd—short of water, short of ammunition, short of food, short of every essential supply, it retained its valour and its will to fight. When the beach parties were taken off at the end of the nine days the enemy had still broken through nowhere, and in that fight they were helped valiantly by a considerable proportion of the French forces that had garrisoned the port or that had withdrawn with them.

There remain two things only which need mention in this brief account.

The defence of Calais will stand for all time in the history of the British Army as the model for a holding action. It may be that Calais was the key to the holding of the Dunkirk beaches. Had Calais fallen in the first rush, had the two panzer divisions that were held by the heroic handful of the 30th Brigade been free to sweep down the coast through the uncertain French at Gravelines, the beaches might have been cut behind us. As it was the French, even with the forty-eight hours of preparation that were given them by the sacrifice of the Brigade, failed on the Gravelines Canal line. They had to fall back before the thrust of the panzers to Mardyck, less than 7 miles from Dunkirk Mole. The story of that brief battle is long in the telling—long because it is a compound of courage and of resolution, of that superb spirit which can sacrifice self for the general good.

Boulogne is important for another purpose. Boulogne too was defended bravely. I watched the battle for it from the Dover cliffs in the clear light of that hot May afternoon. I watched the shell bursts creep across the town, marking by their pattern the tragedy of that defence; and in the night, by the pricking light of their bursts, I saw the end.

But Boulogne was the pattern for Dunkirk. It set the standard of heroic evacuation. The destroyers that went alongside the old cross-Channel wharves, fired on by tanks from the streets, shelled by field guns, wrecked by pom-poms from those hotels that had held myriads of Channel passengers in the days of peace, were the model for the ships that went in to the Dunkirk Moles.

CHAPTER III

THE ENGLISH SHORE AND DUNKIRK

1

Dunkirk was served from six British ports—Sheerness and Margate to the north of the Foreland, Ramsgate and Dover, Folkestone and New-haven to the south—but Southend and Deal and even some of the beaches saw also scattered groups of men arrive.

Sheerness, at the mouth of the Medway, is a naval port, ancient enough to have been burned by the Dutch fleet under De Ruyter in 1667. While the arrangements for the dispatch of the small boats were proceeding within the area of the naval dockyard, men were working on the ancient fortifications which back the moat that cuts off Sheerness from the mainland in preparation against a new invasion.

Margate has, properly speaking, no harbour. A single curving jetty encloses a narrow inlet from the sea: small craft only can use it. But there is a pier at Margate, one of the spidery iron and timber and gilt filigree piers beloved of the English pleasure coasts; a frail thing—but across its end where the paddle-steamers berthed to land their singing thousands in the summers of the peace, there berthed now sloops and minesweepers, cross-Channel ferries and those same paddle-steamers, grey-coated, grim, and loaded with men who did not sing.

Ramsgate has a harbour. Two curving arms enclose a sheet of water, tidal, drying out in its centre at low water of spring tides, but with sufficient water at all times next to the piers themselves to float small craft. Ramsgate was the harbour of the little ships; so filled with them, so intensely active, that almost all through the operation there floated inside the piers a vast raft of motor-boats and motor-yachts, of ships' lifeboats and naval cutters and fishing craft. At the end of the West Pier there is a floating landing-stage where larger vessels such as the trawlers and drifters put their men ashore.

South of Ramsgate was Dover, Dubris of the Romans, the Continental gateway of England whose gates were open now to take back an army that men thought was lost. Dover was a naval port when Caesar's galleys worked the Channel ferry. Throughout the long history of the Cinque Ports it held a premier place in the marine economy of Britain. But as a modern naval base it came into being with the commencement, in 1898, of the great Admiralty harbour. Three enormous breakwaters, the most important more than 4,000 feet long, enclose a vast protected basin. It was designed to hold the Channel Fleet, but conceptions of naval strategy have changed in recent years. Even in 1914 it was not considered desirable to station a fleet on Dover, and the port was used as a flotilla base throughout that war. Its importance from the point of view of heavy ships was still further diminished in 1939, and, with the movement of the main army bases to the more westerly French ports, its importance even as a cross-Channel ferry harbour had declined in stature.

Yet on the facilities of its peace-time traffic were based the needs of an army in desperation. In twenty years the East Pier had been used only to export odd cargoes of scrap iron and coal while the nearer mines of the Kent field still worked. The Prince of Wales Pier had been used for pleasure-steamers alone. The West—the Admiralty—Pier had been the cross-Channel steamers' terminus. But from the East Pier went out the food, the water, the ammunition, and the stores for the last fight of the British Expeditionary Force. To the Prince of Wales Pier came lame and battered ships. Through the Channel terminus, with its prosaic Customs shed, its dingy passageways to the Maritime Station, its smoke-grimed arches and its blackened roof, came the men of the deliverance in thousands and in scores of thousands.

Beyond Dover was Folkestone, the second of the two great Straits ferry ports. Folkestone's facilities were restricted; they had not been extended for war purposes, and its 500-yard-long harbour pier could handle only a limited amount of shipping at one time. It was used principally by the personnel ships, many of them Southern Railway vessels that had used this harbour in time of peace.

Newhaven, off to the west beyond Beachy Head, was the furthest of all the points used for the disembarkation. There was a special reason for this. The major part of the evacuation of wounded from the eventual Continental battle had been planned to flow through this narrow harbour at the mouth of the Sussex Ouse, with its railway communications with London and the north.

This was the English shore.

2

When on Sunday, May 19th, the first meeting was held in London to consider the problems of the B.E.F., evacuation was regarded as improbable and the meeting was mainly concerned with the possibilities of the mainten-ance of the B.E.F. through the ports of Dunkirk, Calais, and Boulogne. The Allied shore ran through to the coast of Holland.

Four days later the Germans were at Abbeville; Boulogne and Calais were invested, and the Belgian Army was perilously near its breaking point. The coast had shrunk to the stretch from Gravelines to the Belgian ports. As the hours—almost as the minutes—went by that coast shrank. When on Sunday, May 26th, the first ships of the evacuation went to Dunkirk the friendly shore had diminished to the strip of beach that runs from Gravelines to the Belgian ports; and already the Belgian ports were useless, for they lay in the rear of a breaking army. The field of the evacuation was to shrink to the strip from Nieuport town to Mardyck, 25 miles of empty sand.

Dunkirk lies a third of the way along this sector from the west: the rest is open beach. Along the beach lie little villages—Malo-les-Bains, Bray-Dunes, La Panne and Coxyde. They had no piers; they were no more than demilunes of buildings fronting the yellow waters of the North Sea. Their one importance was that by their roads lay access to the hinterland.

The coast itself is low and flat. Most nearly it compares in England with the Lancashire coast: a wide beach, a long shallow foreshore which the receding tide leaves bare for half a mile to seaward, a deep-water channel at the edge of the shallows 800 yards or so in width, and beyond that sandbanks lying parallel with the coast forming a barrier against the North Sea. It is extremely important to remember the seaward aspects of the French coast in the proper evaluation of the operation. Dunkirk could not be approached directly from the North Sea. It had to be approached along this 800-yard-wide deep-water channel, parallel for many miles with the coast either from the east or from the west. Whoever held the coasts commanded the channel.

The focus of all this area was, for obvious reasons, Dunkirk town. It is an ancient harbour. Thirteen hundred years ago in the dunes that fringe the beaches St. Eloi built a chapel—the Dune Church. That chapel became a place of pilgrimage: a fishing village grew about it and enlarged itself. Three hundred years later Baldwin, Count of Flanders, made a fortress of it, ringing it with a moat and walls. By then a harbour was already established. That harbour grew to be the third port of France, a fine modern harbour with seven dock basins, accessible to big ships and amounting in all to approximately 115 acres. It had four dry docks. It had 5 miles of quays, and three of the fine canals of the Low Countries fed into it. The docks were deep set into the town and from them a dredged channel led through to the sea. Long piers protected it against the swirl of the tide along the coast: the West Pier wall that came out from the oil storage area, the East Mole that sprang in a great curve from the ancient citadel and thrust 1,400 yards out into the roadstead.

A fine harbour—had we been able to use it we might have got away the British Expeditionary Force 'horse, foot and guns'. But the docks were useless. Bombed incessantly over a period of weeks they were a mass of battered metal and broken walls; the basins were open to the tide; the gates wrecked and jammed; the cranes stood weakly on three legs or lay like stricken birds along the quays. And over them, all through the evacuation, hung the pall that was lit on its underside by the red flame of the burning warehouses.

There was left for the purposes of the evacuation the East Mole alone.

It is essential to carry in one's mind a clear picture of the Mole. It was not a stout stone breakwater with mooring places for ships along its length. It was a narrow pile plank-way barely wide enough for three men to walk abreast, with on either side a protective railing of moderately stout timbers above which longer piles projected at intervals to make Samson posts by which a ship could be warped in emergency. At the far end was a nose with a substructure of concrete on which a short lighthouse stood. It was not designed for ships to berth against. It was not calculated for the stresses and strains set up thereby. The free movement of the tide beneath the piles made it extremely difficult to bring craft alongside. All these factors were to play intensely important parts in the evacuation.

3

There is no precise record of the bombing attacks upon Dunkirk. They began with small and isolated raids parallel with the opening of the assault on Belgium, and throughout the brief weeks of the campaign they continued on an increasing scale. The greater part of the time the attack was principally upon the harbour and its facilities. The roads leading to it suffered assault. The railway lines were put out of action and the quays themselves received heavy damage.

By the middle of the month the Germans were claiming that the harbour was no longer operable and when, by May 23rd, the enemy had taken Abbeville and threatened the Channel coast as far as Calais, it was admitted on our side that the dock facilities were virtually useless. In the three days that followed before the evacuation began the raids grew steadily heavier.

During this period the s.s. *Spinel*, with a cargo of petrol, arrived at Dunkirk. There were many attacks, and eventually *Spinel* was moved to a new berth in the inner basin. A little after this the bridge at the entrance to this basin was bombed and demolished. The wreck completely blocked the entrance channel, and the *Spinel* was trapped and unable to leave. The vessel was abandoned and her master and crew eventually taken off. Her fate illustrates the general condition.

On the 25th the enemy, leaving the harbour for a brief while, hit and completely wrecked the waterworks which supplied the town with fresh water. On the 26th, even as the first ships were being prepared for lifting the men of the harassed armies, the oil tanks on the east side of the harbour near the entrance were very heavily bombed and set on fire, and the great pall of smoke that was to become the mark of Dunkirk rose for the first time into the afternoon sky.

It was to a broken and battered town that the B.E.F. fell back. It was to a shattered and a useless harbour that the ships came in.

CHAPTER IV

THE PLANNING OF OPERATION 'DYNAMO'

1

' The situation of the British and French Armies, now engaged in a most severe battle and beset on three sides from the air, is evidently extremely grave. The surrender of the Belgian Army in this manner adds appreciably to their grievous peril. But the troops are in good heart and are fighting with the utmost discipline and tenacity. . . .

' I expect to make a statement to the House on the general position when the result of the intense struggle now going on can be known and measured. This will not, perhaps, be until the beginning of next week. Meanwhile the House should prepare itself for hard and heavy tidings.'

(RT. HON. WINSTON CHURCHILL, C.H., M.P.
House of Commons, 28th May 1940)

The story of the week that followed is the story of Dunkirk.
From the hour when the first troops reached the beaches, as Lord Gort's armies fell back within the floods of the perimeter, Dunkirk was a sea battle. Upon the army still remained the urgent necessity of maintaining the perimeter secure; upon the air force lay the necessity of protecting, in so far as it might be possible, the congested demilune that held almost 400,000 men against assault from the air: but upon the navies fell the whole burden of the last retreat—the retreat to safety.

The responsibility for the seaward operations of Dunkirk lies between two bodies: the Royal Navy which, through the Admiralty, the Nore and the Dover Commands, was responsible for the operations, and the Merchant Navy which, through the Ministry of Shipping (now included in the Ministry of War Transport), was responsible for the greater portion of the ships.

Evacuation had started from the Belgian ports as early as May 10th when Sir Lancelot Oliphant initiated the movement of British subjects from Ostend. Simultaneously evacuation was going on from certain of the Dutch ports, but it was not until May 14th that military evacuation began with the attempt to remove a portion of the Dutch Army. These movements were important though comparatively small.

On May 15th the War Office intimated to the Ministry of Shipping that changing circumstances might make necessary the reorganization of the supply lines of the British Expeditionary Force, and an investigation was at once made into the possibility of supply by small vessels through the Channel ports. Within four days our lines of communication were to be cut. With the entry into Amiens and Abbeville the B.E.F. was irrevocably severed from its bases. Even in ancient days lines of communication were a primary charge

29

upon an army's strength. The mechanized army of to-day is more dependent on its lines than any other. To exist at all, to move, it must have petrol in vast quantities. It cannot live upon the countryside: it must have rations in a constant and elaborate stream. The ammunition supply, with the growth of automatic weapons, has trebled and quadrupled in recent years. The increase in size of field guns that has come with mechanized equipment has enormously magnified the weight of munitions to be carried. Lines of communication have become the major preoccupation of a modern army—and these were cut.

On May 16th a further complication arose through a statement from the French Mission to Belgium that the French Government wished to evacuate 300,000 Belgian refugees by sea from Ostend and Zeebrugge. For that purpose they had allocated three cross-Channel steamers! Assistance was asked for.

On the 19th Dunkirk was reported out of action, Calais was damaged and threatened, Boulogne was likewise damaged and threatened. But through the complications of battered ports and refugee shipping it was decided by the War Office on that day that the armies of the north, isolated by the German thrust to Abbeville, were to be supplied by way of Dunkirk, Boulogne, Calais and Ostend.

At a meeting presided over by General Riddell-Webster and held at the War Office this Sunday evening the situation as a whole was examined, and it was determined that, while the decision as to the actual ports to which the ships should go should rest with the Vice-Admiral Commanding Dover, Calais and Boulogne should be used as much as possible as it was more difficult to give air protection to Dunkirk. Various alternative methods, such as barge traffic to Gravelines, Etaples and other small ports, were discussed. In addition to this the meeting considered the question of evacuation of personnel. This question was dealt with under three headings. The first of these was the orderly evacuation of personnel amounting to 2,000 a day from May 20th onwards; the second the possible emergency evacuation of base units, hospital staffs and odd personnel which might amount to some 15,000 in all from the night of May 22nd onwards; and the third 'the hazardous evacuation of very large forces'—this was considered unlikely.

For this purpose at the time the meeting was held there were thirty-six personnel ships based on Southampton or Dover, including railway packet ships, Irish cross-Channel vessels, and Dutch and Belgian ships. It was agreed that control would be delegated completely to the late Admiral Sir Bertram Ramsay, K.B.E., K.C.B., M.V.O., then Vice-Admiral Commanding at Dover; that embarkation would be performed preferably at night; and that, where possible, loading of troops should take place at dispersed points such as coastal piers. In addition V.-A. Dover was to investigate the question of the number of ships that might be able to work from the existing French ports and whether additional loading places could be used in the event of emergency by small craft. The War Office and the Ministry of Shipping were to attach liaison officers to the staff at Dover.

The report of this meeting was the skeleton plan of the evacuation.

2

Perhaps its most significant point was the decision to delegate all authority for the operation to Vice-Admiral Bertram Ramsay. No man in the Royal Navy was better qualified for the task he had to undertake. In the war of 1914–18, as a young commander, he had been captain of a monitor in the bombardment of the Belgian coast. Later he had held the command of the flotilla leader *Broke* in the Dover Patrol. After various appointments he had retired from the Navy in 1937 at the conclusion of his appointment under Admiral Sir Roger Backhouse as Chief of Staff, Home Fleet.[1]

In the Munich crisis he was recalled to the Service and reorganized the Dover Command, which was eventually separated from the Nore. He was in charge at Dover when the British Army crossed to France a year later and his work in the first nine months that followed the 3rd of September 1939 was onerous. It held, however, little of the excitements of the old Dover Patrol; the Straits were a long way from German territory in those nine months, there was in that period no surface attack, no surface enemy to fight. The Dover Command dealt at first only with the possibility of submarine attack, the irritation of sporadic mine-laying. But it was largely in Vice-Admiral Ramsay's area that the first great threat of the magnetic mine developed, and on his shoulders lay much of the responsibility for the initial counter-measures. In his command too developed the first air threat against our shipping.

In this strange warfare his personality achieved a new importance. It was said of him that he was an aloof man, difficult to contact in the human sense, and that he had a dislike for details coupled with a certain ruthlessness. These things may have been true—yet under his command men were inspired to heights that have seldom been achieved in all the long sea history of Britain. Under his authority was carried out the most complex, the most detailed sea manoeuvre in the history, it may be, of the world.

From his staff he selected sixteen men for the immediate purpose of the operation. They worked and had their being—for practical purpose they lived—in a chamber in the Dover chalk that was called the 'Dynamo Room'. The code name for the operation was 'Dynamo'. In that room, and with that tiny staff, the astonishing complexities of the operation were planned, developed and implemented. It was the nerve centre of a vast corporate body that was to stretch before the evacuation ended from Cornwall to the Norfolk coast, from Teddington to Dunkirk Mole.

Over the operation as a whole, therefore, Vice-Admiral Ramsay had complete command. His authority was delegated as far as the surface of the Channel and the waterways off Dunkirk were concerned to Rear-Admiral W. F. Wake-Walker, O.B.E., with the title Rear-Admiral Dover Straits. The responsibility for Dunkirk town and the beaches themselves was rested upon Captain W. G. Tennant, M.V.O., R.N., while at Dover the responsi-

[1] He was restored to the Active List in April 1944 as Admiral commanding the invasion force for the Second Front.

bility for disembarkation and for the ships themselves rested upon Commodore E. G. Jukes-Hughes, R.N., as Principal Sea Transport Officer. At Ramsgate the senior naval officer was Captain W. R. Phillimore, R.N., and at Newhaven, Captain A. A. Lovett-Cameron, R.N., while at Dunkirk Mole, the place of honour, Commander J. C. Clouston, R.N., was appointed Piermaster and served gloriously for six days until his death.

Even as the 'Dynamo Room' came into being the situation changed. It is essential in any attempt to evaluate its work to remember that, as it began its planning, the Germans broke through to the coast and at once, from being an area far removed from the possibility of German naval intervention, the Channel became an intensely vulnerable point. Already the Germans were at the mouth of the Scheldt. Flushing is barely 90 miles from Dover. The Germans held Flushing. E-boats were known to be using the port as they were using others of the Dutch harbours. On the 19th, as the London meeting was being held, the Germans were moving up to Abbeville. On the 20th they had reached the Channel coast. It required small prescience to realize that in a matter of days German guns would be on the heights across the narrow sea from Dover. The home waters of Vice-Admiral Ramsay's own command were under threat.

He had to make dispositions to meet the new problems. Out of the small force of his own ships of the Dover Command he had to provide destroyers to bombard the German columns moving on the coast, to support the Guards as they fought desperately in the defence of Boulogne, to land Marines to assist them, to evacuate them when the defence was abandoned. He had to provide through his command for the landing of the 30th Infantry Brigade for the defence of Calais, and for sea-borne artillery support on its flanks. Escort and anti-aircraft cover had to be furnished for shipping movements connected with the decision to supply the B.E.F. through the Channel ports. Patrols had to be provided against the possibility of E-boats and submarine attacks. And every hour the problems grew in complexity and in urgency.

All this had to be done in these early days with the staff of a command calculated to the necessities of the period when Dover lay far from the enemy. The shifts, the expedients, the improvisations of those days would alone take a book in their telling. Officers were moved from their normal routine duties to a hundred fantastic tasks, but their own duties in the very hour of their removal were become of vital importance. Substitutes had to be found. Wrens, for example, took over the plotting of ship movements; they took over a score of other jobs that they had not before attempted, and in the magic of that hour they succeeded. Petty officers and ratings took on the work of officers, and made good. All over the country naval officers on leave came in voluntarily or were recalled by the Admiralty. Most of them went to the ships of the operation but many of them were detached for the extraordinary duties that arose in every corner of the harbours, on every pier of the disembarkation.

At Dover the command grew overnight from a slender tree to a giant oak and under the shadow of its hundred branches the task began.

Behind Vice-Admiral Ramsay was the whole weight of the Admiralty. There are innumerable facets of Dunkirk of which it may be said that they stand unique in history, but in some ways the most remarkable feature of the whole exploit was the manner in which all those concerned in it dispensed with 'red tape'. This is not an attempt at humour. Modern warfare is primarily a problem of organization. For its very existence organization demands order. No way has been found in modern civilization of producing order without a degree of bureaucracy. With bureaucracy certain restraints, certain restrictions, are not merely necessary, they are inevitable. They are even, despite the endless jibes, desirable when the broad view is taken.

But in Dunkirk, paradoxically, the broad view was no longer possible: only the narrow view, the view of an utter and absolute urgency, could be taken. Everything had to be subordinated to the necessities of the moment, and it is not the least measure of the operation's magnificence that from the Board of Admiralty down to the petty officer storekeepers, regulations were dispensed with; rules, even ancient traditions, were abandoned in the concentration on the one essential .object—the success of the greatest rescue expedition in the history of mankind.

From Whitehall, therefore, as Vice-Admiral Ramsay asked, he was given. As his original destroyer flotilla was decimated by enemy attack, by collision, by damage of one sort and another, he was given fresh flotillas. As his minesweepers were lost, they were replaced from the Nore, from Harwich, from the Humber, eventually even from the Firth of Forth. As he asked for ships, he was given them. As he asked for men and materials, he was given them. And the most remarkable, the most dramatic, of these askings was his demand for small craft to work the beaches.

There is in the Admiralty a department called the Small Vessels Pool. Under the command of Admiral Sir Lionel Preston, it controls the supply and handling of small craft for harbour work and for auxiliary purposes. A fleet of big ships needs another fleet of little ones: ships to take out stores, munitions, water; to take off Liberty men; to take out confidential books and 'hand messages'; to move specialists—the endless specialists required by the intricacies of a modern man-of-war—from one ship to another, to adjust, correct and advise. And where the Fleet goes, these small craft must go also. Admiral Preston's department handles the small craft not for the British bases only, but for new bases as they are established in the Mediterranean, the Indian Ocean, even in the British sectors of the Pacific. It was to this department that Vice-Admiral Ramsay's urgent demand was passed on the night of Sunday, May 26th.

With the wise prevision of a sound organization, the department had already envisaged the possibilities and made its own plans. On May 14th in the 9 o'clock news the B.B.C. broadcast the following announcement:

'The Admiralty have made an Order requesting all owners of self-propelled pleasure craft between 30 and 100 feet in length, to send all particulars to the Admiralty within 14 days from to-day, if they have not already been offered or requisitioned.'

In actual fact this was not a request, it was an Order initiated under Statute, but the framing of the B.B.C.'s announcement led most of the owners who answered to accept it as a request, and in the avalanche of letters that fell immediately upon the Small Vessels Pool it is significant of what was to come that the vast majority made free and unconditional offers of their vessels for any purpose for which the Admiralty might see fit to use them; and with their boats a very remarkable proportion of the owners offered their own services. It is no small tribute to the efficiency of the department that in the twelve days between the broadcast and the opening of Operation 'Dynamo' this mass of offers was digested and the lists prepared and ready.

On the evening of May 26th, when Admiral Ramsay's demand was transmitted to Admiral Preston, all that had to be done theoretically was to communicate with the owners on the lists and issue instructions—but that theory held only for normal times. Vice-Admiral Ramsay asked for the boats 'with dispatch' in the old naval term. The staff of the Small Vessels Pool was very small. Under Admiral Preston, as Deputy Director, was Captain E. F. Wharton, R.N. In all the staff numbered about a dozen. All who could be spared from the office were sent at once to the principal small-boat centres and an immediate request was made for help from H.M.S. *King Alfred*, the south coast training centre for officers for the R.N.V.R., to the Flag Officer Commanding the Port of London, to the Commander-in-Chief, Plymouth, and to V.-A., Dover, for assistance.

This swiftly organized corps began immediately on the department's lists. Up the Thames, at places like Teddington, Kingston, Hampton Wick, Ranelagh, Chiswick and everywhere at the anchorages of the Thames yacht clubs, boats were inspected, passed, requisitioned and provided with the necessary papers. And what took place in the Thames took place also at east coast ports right up as far as the Wash, at south coast ports as far west as Southampton and Poole and Weymouth, and eventually as far as the West Country.

But almost at once it was seen that motor yachts and the small pleasure craft alone were not enough. What was wanted were boats that could be taken on and off the shallow beaches, and the officers of the search were instructed to take lifeboats from ships in the Port of London. Up and down the enormous basins of the port liners and tramp steamers alike were stripped of their lifeboats, tugs were requisitioned, and the boats in vast tows were taken out through the lock gates as the tide served and run down the river to Tilbury. The work that had begun before midnight on the Sunday went on ceaselessly. By Monday the flow had started towards the sea. It was not to stop until the last men were away from Dunkirk beaches.

4

At the outbreak of war the merchant shipping of Britain was placed under the direct control of the Ministry of Shipping. It is not possible here to go into the ramifications of that control, but for practical purposes the Ministry was the overriding authority for all British merchant tonnage that worked out of British harbours. Into its control also, as the debacle of April and May developed, came foreign shipping—Norwegian, Danish, Dutch and Belgian. Throughout the first nine months it had worked with the Admiralty to ensure the proper flow of food, of munitions of war and of men for the prosecution of the war, and it was upon the Ministry of Shipping now that the Admiralty called for the provision of the vessels necessary for the task in hand.

The Minister of Shipping at that date was Mr. Ronald Cross. The work fell principally upon the Sea Transport Department, which was under the direction of Mr. W. G. Hynard (who had as his Deputy Director Mr. D. H. Edwards), and on Captain J. Fisher (now Sir John Fisher), the Director of Coastwise and Short Sea Shipping. The military side of the Sea Transport Department, under Mr. C. E. W. Justice, assisted by Mr. B. E. Bellamy, dealt with the larger vessels and, as need arose subsequently, the smaller vessels were dealt with by Mr. A. L. Moore and Mr. H. C. Riggs.

In peace-time the British Merchant Navy totalled some 10,000 ships. Superficially it would appear as if the Ministry of Shipping had an inexhaustible supply of vessels upon which to draw. In actual fact that supply was small, and most drastically limited by the circumstances of war. The figure of 10,000 in the first place covers Dominion and Colonial shipping as well. Of ships based on home ports a reliable estimate before the war places 1,850 ocean-going vessels at sea on any given day, with a further total of 1,650 smaller and coasting vessels. The number actually in British ports at any one moment is, comparatively speaking, small. Of this residue a proportion at any given time is under repair, and a very much larger proportion is in process of loading or discharging and therefore not available for immediate service.

Owing to the necessities of war and of quick turn-round, that proportion in May of 1940 was even greater than normal. The residue of *available* shipping was, therefore, extremely small, and of that available shipping a considerable proportion was not suited to the needs of the operation. The shallows off northern France, the ever-increasing possibility of air attack, made it quite impossible, for example, to use large ships. Only the extraordinary efforts of the Ministry and its responsible departments made it possible for the final sifting of suitable ships to be brought together at the right place and at the right time.

These, then, were the three main architects of the evacuation: the Dover Command, the Admiralty (with the Small Vessels Pool) and the Ministry of Shipping.

On May 20th the first conference of all parties concerned was begun at Dover. On the agenda for that conference—so much had the situation changed even in the twenty-four hours since the preceding meeting—was 'Emergency evacuation across the Channel of very large forces'. At this meeting (which was continued at the War Office the following day) it was decided that if emergency evacuation became necessary it was to be carried out from the three French ports Calais, Boulogne and Dunkirk, which it was hoped would be available. The estimated capacity of the arrangements, 'allowing for moderate interference', was 10,000 from each port in each twenty-four hours.

Already the first lists of ships available and ready had been prepared. At the disposal of Vice-Admiral Ramsay at Dover were *Biarritz, Mona's Queen, Canterbury, Maid of Orleans, King George V, Queen of the Channel, King Orry, Mona's Isle, St. Helier* and *St. Seiriol*, and at Southampton were *Normannia, Manxmaid, Royal Daffodil, Royal Scot, Archangel* and *Lorina*. From this it will be seen that the authorities had selected the obvious and natural form of shipping for use in these waters—passenger ferry steamers. Most of them had been built for the purpose of using the French and English Channel ports. They were conditioned by years of experience and handled by men who had grown old in the trade. No better selection could have been made.

In addition to this list, and to be ready when the Southampton ships had been called forward, were another fourteen of similar type. To supplement these the navy had twelve drifters, and there were six small coasters.

Captain Fisher, Director of Coastwise and Short Sea Shipping, who attended the War Office meeting, stressed the usefulness of British self-propelled barges, and of Dutch flat-bottomed coasters of which a large number had come to British ports after the fall of Holland. After the meeting Captain Fisher selected some forty-five Dutch coasters to supplement the British coasters which were being rushed to the scene as they completed the discharge of their cargoes, and forty of these were requisitioned in the Thames and at Poole, and immediately manned by naval crews from Portsmouth and from Chatham barracks.

It was proposed that the personnel ships should work the three French ports in pairs, not more than two ships in any harbour at any one time. It is interesting to note that, while the meeting was being held, a French Admiralty signal directed that all shipping in Dunkirk should leave the port and proceed to Cherbourg. Communications, medical supplies, and a score of other details were dealt with by the committee, and the question of reception was debated with the military authorities and with the railways. It was

THE PLANNING OF OPERATION 'DYNAMO'

emphasized at the end that these arrangements provided only for an emergency which might arise.

A representative of the Ministry of Shipping had been appointed to Dover as Liaison Officer, Mr. J. L. Keith, and simultaneously the War Office appointed Captain L. E. L. Wright as War Office Liaison Officer. While the committee was actually sitting and thereafter the work of preparation went on. The Sea Transport Officers at Harwich, London, Newhaven, Southampton, Poole and Weymouth were instructed to obtain records of all the small ships up to 1,000 tons, including paddle-steamers, pleasure craft and so forth, of any nationality in their own or adjacent ports capable of carrying troops, and arrangements were made for obtaining this information when the state of emergency arose and passing it to V.-A. Dover. Simultaneously a complete survey was made of all shipping in British harbours including the recently arrived Dutch merchant fleet.

On this day Captain Digby Best (who, as deputy to the Principal Sea Transport Officer in France, Commodore W. P. Gandell, R.N., could be expected to speak with authority on the situation of the ports) reached England and reported that communication between Boulogne, Dunkirk and Calais was cut off, and that the bombing was constant. With regard to the plan for supplementing the coasters in taking across supplies with self-propelled barges which might be grounded on the beaches, Captain Digby Best raised the objection that both transport and labour were not available at the ports. He himself considered that the best place for sending military stores was Boulogne, and the P.S.T.O. and himself had established their headquarters there.

It is indicative of the swift-moving pace of the times that even at the hour of his arrival in England his news was already out of date. The utility of Boulogne was compromised: the town itself was to be invested within forty-eight hours.

The plan for supplying the army through the Channel ports was, however, still in existence, and work on that plan had to continue concurrently with the bigger scheme. On May 21st it was still hoped that the three ports were available, but it was believed that all were damaged and that Dunkirk was out of action. Already the use of open beaches was in contemplation.

The bombing of the harbours was now becoming a dangerous problem, and on the 21st Vice-Admiral Ramsay made formal request for continuous fighter cover over all three ports. By the 22nd it was obvious—or as near obvious as made no essential difference—that Boulogne and Calais would not be available. Boulogne itself was invested and isolated from Calais. By the evening of that day enemy armoured units had penetrated to within 9 miles of Calais itself.

It is not apparent that the full gravity of the situation was yet completely realized in London. On the 22nd it was said that the War Office did not anticipate any decision to evacuate before Friday, May 24th, nor did it contemplate anything in the nature of 'panic' evacuation, believing that the movement would take place in an orderly manner. It was considered that the flow of ships already arranged for would be sufficient to cover the necessities.

By the 23rd evacuation was upon them. It was small comparatively speaking—the evacuation of Boulogne—but it was vitally important. Approximately 5,000 civilian refugees came through in the last rush, and approximately 250 officers and 2,800 other ranks. The superb work of the destroyers turned what might have been the first great tragedy of the evacuation into a brilliant and seamanlike achievement.

By May 24th the situation was disintegrating everywhere. This was the black Friday. Boulogne was lost. Calais was attacked with overwhelming force, and already the enemy was by-passing it and sweeping on beyond Gravelines, and Gravelines was the end of the perimeter of Dunkirk. This was the closing of the drawstring.

On that day it was realized by the authorities that orderly withdrawal might no longer be possible, that it was necessary—indeed vital—to prepare for a chaotic falling back of small parties of troops anywhere along the coast beyond the line the enemy now held. The flexibility of Vice-Admiral Ramsay's planning was at once apparent. From the stillborn scheme of two ships operating in a sort of shuttle service in each of the three French ports the scheme switched over to the desperate picking up of men from open beaches. It was realized that information, communications, signals, everything might be lacking, and the only possible plan appeared to be the utilization of small craft to shuttle between shoal water and the transport ships in the deep channels that lie along the north French coast. Ports of disembarkation and reception areas were prepared in accordance with the new scheme.

It was to most of those who knew it, to most of those who realized the possibilities of our desperate armies, to those who knew the coast, who knew the ships, who knew the sea, a counsel of despair.

CHAPTER V

THE NAVAL AND AIR PROBLEMS

1

The purely naval problem of Dunkirk had a deceptive simplicity. In its essentials it consisted of the protection of the flanks of a transportation movement which covered a rough quadrilateral whose southern side was the narrows of the Straits of Dover and whose northern side was a line leading from Nieuport to the estuary of the Thames.

The southern side can be dismissed in a few words. It was in the highest degree improbable that attack on a serious scale could come from there. Though the Germans held the coast from Calais through Boulogne to the mouth of the Somme it was impossible that they should yet have been able to bring even mosquito craft to the Channel ports, and the speed of the debacle as a whole had been so great that it was improbable that U-boats in any strength could have been brought up through the Channel in an attempt to attack from the west. But the eastern flank of the movement was intensely vulnerable. The Dover Command was no longer a small enclave separated by 300 miles of neutral coast from the sea bases of the enemy. German E-boats were known to be using the port of Flushing at the entrance to the Scheldt. There was only the narrow fringe of the Belgian coast between us and the enemy's springing place.

To achieve a just balance of the possibilities it is necessary to examine the naval position in the last week of May as a whole. Britain had a big navy, Germany a small one. It is easy to argue from this that no problem should have existed, but the tendency to over-simplification is a dangerous one. For a variety of obvious reasons Dunkirk could not be—on either side—in any way a heavy-ship affair. The shoals off the French and Belgian coasts precluded the possibility of the use of heavy ships, but infinitely more important was the threat of the new air weapon, still in its most doubtful stage. It was not in 1940 thought possible in many places that battleships would ever again be brought within gun range of an enemy's territory. But the very tortuousness of the channels, the alignment of the shoals, the very confusion caused by the use of air power made the quadrangle of the evacuation a paradise for the *schnellboote*. With destroyers, torpedo-boats, motor torpedo-boats and, in a lesser degree, submarines, the Germans could have made the evacuation not merely precarious but impossible.

Since it was a small-boat operation, therefore, it is in the sphere of light craft that any balancing of the problem must be attempted. At the outbreak of war the Royal Navy possessed 189 destroyers. This number was already considerably reduced. The ordinary loss of war was responsible for six

39

destroyers during the period up to the Norwegian campaign. The accelerated hazard of the following month saw another five ships lost to us together with one Polish destroyer. The fighting in Holland saw a further two ships bombed and lost. But this total of fourteen does not represent the whole casualty of the sea war. There were as many ships virtually lost to us through serious damage. There were numerous others in dockyard hands for major repairs. Amongst these were many of the destroyers which had taken part in the Boulogne and Calais operations. *Keith, Venetia, Vimy, Vimiera* and *Whitshed* were all hit at different times, and in point of fact only one of the eight destroyers which evacuated Boulogne on May 23rd/25th was completely unscathed, while *Venetia* and *Vimiera* were so badly damaged as to be unable to take any part in the subsequent operations.

Of the remainder that were fit for service a large proportion were 1,500 miles to the north engaged in the complexities of the last phase of the Norwegian campaign. This was a phase of constant movement; of landing and evacuation; supplied by convoys over a route of 1,000 miles from the north of Scotland—a route subjected to constant U-boat attack along most of its length. Every destroyer of the Home Fleet that could be spared from the actual work of screening the heavy ships was engaged without rest or respite in this task.

But Norway was not the only commitment that we had. Already the Mediterranean situation was beginning to cause anxiety. The few destroyers that we had in southern waters could not be detached from their bases, and in addition to these preoccupations in the far north and the far south there was the deadly preoccupation of the Battle of the Atlantic, then in its first phase. Destroyers in May of 1940 were still the mainstay of convoy escort. The 'Hunt' class escort destroyers were not yet in commission. Only five ships of our huge corvette programme had yet materialized. Over the vastness of our Atlantic sea routes we needed every escort vessel that we could find.

Yet with these three great preoccupations the Admiralty somehow, from some incredible source of its own devising, found forty destroyers to take part in the defence and in the carrying work of Dunkirk. That is in itself one of the major naval achievements of the war—and that it was done in the face of loss that became at one point almost terrifying in the swiftness of its upward curve, demanded a degree of courage on the part of the Admiralty that has not yet perhaps had its due meed of recognition.

The proper measure of this aspect of the operation is to be found in a speech made by the First Lord of the Admiralty nearly two years later when it was stated that in the week after Dunkirk, for all the enormous commitments of the British Navy through a world growing swiftly colder, swiftly more hostile, there were only seventy-four destroyers out of dockyard hands!

2

Why then did the Germans fail to interfere effectively with the evacuation? There was in principle nothing impossible in such interference. The complexity of the operation, the vast number of small craft of every type, the lack of any possibility of a system of identification, of recognition signals in darkness, or of any real 'order', should have made the task of any raiding E-boat almost ludicrously easy. In actual fact E-boats did come through, did take advantage of the conditions, and did sink ships—both destroyers and transports. For submarines the conditions were somewhat more difficult due to the shallowness of the water and the difficulties of the channels. None the less submarines also carried out attacks and secured victims. What was possible for a handful was possible for more. What was the explanation of the failure?

It may be sought perhaps in the Norwegian campaign. It will be interesting to see what verdict historians writing fifty years hence will place upon that brisk and brilliant success. For in securing Norway in a whirlwind month, in seizing a new country whose major use lay in the fact that it provided an exit from the Continent with admirable sea bases for his navy, Hitler and the German Admiralty threw away the balance of that navy. The German loss in the seizure of Norway was heavy by any standard, but in comparison with the total strength of the force at their disposal it was enormous.

The recorded German losses for the Norwegian campaign consist of the armoured cruiser *Blücher* (10,000 tons), the *Karlsruhe* and the *Königsberg* (6,000 tons), eleven destroyers, one sloop, the *Brummer*, one torpedo-boat, and a number of light craft plus submarines. In addition to these sinkings it is known that at least one battle-cruiser, two other cruisers and one of the pocket battleships, with a number of destroyers, were damaged.

Before the Norwegian campaign was over the German Navy had thrown away the possibility of cutting off the sea escape of the Allied armies from the coast of the Low Countries. There was little left in the Fleet bases to carry out such an attack, but there was less courage in high places for the ordering of it.

I have left the French Navy out of this brief summary of the possibilities. At the opening of Operation 'Dynamo' the French had not yet decided either to evacuate or to co-operate in a major evacuation. None the less the French were actively engaged in the removal of scattered units of the French 1st Army from Ostend and Zeebrugge in the days before the final collapse of the Belgian Army; in the evacuation of civilians; and in the removal of shipping and personnel from the other ports—including Dunkirk—to the westward of Brest. In the course of these movements they had suffered substantial loss before Operation 'Dynamo' began.

3

The air problem involved in the evacuation had an equally deceptive simplicity. Briefly it was to provide cover over the Dunkirk perimeter, to prevent the bombing of the appalling concentration of troops within those narrow limits, to protect the perimeter positions and the artillery defending it from air attack, to give cover to the beaches, and to prevent further destruction of the Dunkirk harbour facilities. In addition it had to provide for an air umbrella over the crowded sea lane between the beaches and the English ports.

In May 1940 the radius of effective action of the average type of fighter in use was considered to be approximately 75 miles. The arc of a circle drawn with its centre at Dunkirk with a radius of 75 miles enters the English coast just short of Hastings and leaves it again at Sheerness. It just skims the coast of Essex. Only the east Kent aerodromes, therefore, were properly within fighter range of the Dunkirk perimeter. These were the days before long-distance fuel tanks and long-range fighters, but it was possible for aircraft from the Essex aerodromes to maintain themselves for brief periods over the area. It will be seen from this that the air problem immediately became enormously complicated.

The air component of the B.E.F. had retired down the line of its aerodromes which paralleled the original lines of supply. Of its fighters few returned to England. The losses in the preliminary stages of the campaign were heavy, and despite reinforcements from England there was very little left to fly home.

There remained the metropolitan air force. Its aircraft had to fly at extreme range from limited aerodromes against an enemy who fought at short range from the innumerable landing strips which it was possible to improvise in the flat plains of Flanders in those dry weeks.

Cover was provided over the perimeter, cover was provided (which was even more important) beyond the perimeter, cover was provided over the ships. It was insufficient to prevent loss. Dunkirk was bombed again and again both in the days before Sunday, May 26th, and throughout the Operation 'Dynamo'. Men and ships were lost, but over those days was set up the pattern for the Battle of Britain—that pattern of qualitative superiority that was to save Britain in the second great crisis of the war.

CHAPTER VI

THE WEEK PRECEDING THE EVACUATION

1

The coastwise channels of the North Sea had been dangerous since the very beginning of the war. Aircraft attack was taking its toll of ships long before the avalanche of May 10th. But since that date the danger had increased, and in the week before the evacuation finally began had already reached critical levels.

It is as well to have a picture of this week in mind in considering the problem which faced the authorities in the final planning. Just before the week began H.M.S. *Westminster* (Lieutenant-Commander A. A. C. Ouvry, R.N.), a British destroyer of the old 'V' and 'W' class converted for escort purposes, was bombed. On May 19th the Dover rescue tug *Lady Brassey* was ordered to proceed to Dunkirk for the purpose of towing her back to an English port. Her master, G. W. Blackmore, reports on the evening of this day that the West Hinder lightship was anchored in Calais Roads. There is a certain significance in this. The sea marks were going already. That night, anchored off Gravelines, they watched from the *Lady Brassey* Dunkirk and Calais being raided from the air and saw large fires burning.

At dawn on Monday, May 20th, *Lady Brassey* proceeded to Dunkirk and was bombed off the port. In that raid a French transport was sunk by near misses. At 9 a.m. *Lady Brassey* entered Dunkirk harbour—with instructions to keep 150 feet off the outer moles as a magnetic mine was reported near— to take H.M.S. *Westminster* in tow. Taking the inside passage she appears to have reached Calais Roads without mishap, but 5 miles north-west of Calais her crew saw the London steamer *Mavis* bombed and abandoned. S.s. *Mavis* was one of the small ships concerned in the plan for supplying the British Expeditionary Force through the Channel ports. Much of the traffic during this week was in connection with that plan.

Similarly the French were occupied in their own traffic, supplying the 1st and the remnants of the 7th Army, evacuating civilian refugees and certain classes of army personnel. In covering this traffic they lost the destroyer *L'Adroit* on May 21st to aircraft in the channel off Dunkirk, and there were other losses of small craft.

Meanwhile the work of supplying the B.E.F. according to the new plan proceeded in circumstances of great difficulty and very real danger. This is emphasized by the loss of the store ship *Firth Fisher* with her master, Captain J. O. Roberts, and a number of the members of her crew. She was bombed with her cargo on board, and lost. The account of another of these small ships will serve to underline that danger. The motor-vessel *Sodality* loaded at Deptford Victualling Wharf early on the morning of May 20th. She was off Dover for orders at noon on the 22nd. Her master, Captain R. Roberts, in his report says:

'1.20 p.m. received orders for Dunkirk proceeded on voyage, when entering narrow channel east of Gravelines, saw two steamers on fire in channel, thinking channel being mined kept about ship's length to starboard of channel.

'When some two miles off Dunkirk one of our own destroyers came up alongside and ordered us to stop, asked our speed, speed given 10 knots all out. Was then ordered to follow in destroyer's line as he would be passing very close to sunken wrecks.

'When 1½ miles off Dunkirk destroyer turned back and told us there would be no one to assist us and that we were to do the best we could. We entered harbour and made fast at dock entrance.

'At 8 p.m. one of our naval officers came and told us that we would dock at 10.30 p.m. and 10 p.m. entered locks and before we had time to make fast German planes were over the lock gate. Men went for shelter and left us to make the ship fast ourselves. At 11.30 p.m. went to look for lock gatemen managed to get them to open locks for us to enter dock planes still bombing and kept bombing all night. Midnight made fast in berth.

'The naval officer who spoke to us at 8 p.m. promised to berth us but we did not see him until 5 a.m. on the 23rd, we were on the wrong berth. 5.15 a.m. shifted to No. 7 berth. 8 a.m. commence discharge winches and cranes all through the day we were bombed. The French crane drivers refused to drive cranes. Our own men were put in their place at 8 p.m. discharged. Enter locks 4 a.m. 24th heavy bombing all through the night.

'2.30 a.m. received a note from naval officer to be in locks prompt at 4 a.m. take 240 troops on board and be clear of locks at 4.30 a.m. Entered locks at 3.50 a.m. went ashore to make inquiries about troops but could find no one, took on board 6 men waited until 5.15 a.m. then seeing no one about decided to cast off and proceed on voyage came down narrow channels the same way as we went up.

'When off Calais we were shelled from shore altered course to seaward and got well out of range, when hauling in to No. 5 buoy we were again shelled from shore all dropping a mile short. At noon landed 6 soldiers at Dover by tender and proceeded on voyage. . . .'

This account introduces a new factor. The shelling from the Calais shore was to have a most important effect on the movement as a whole. The Germans had established batteries first of light field guns but later, as their equipment came up, of heavy guns on the rising ground near Calais, from which they controlled to a considerable extent the close route to Dunkirk Roads. The naval authorities were immediately compelled to make possible new routes which involved the sweeping of minefields, both our own and those of enemy origin, and these new routes involved a far greater mileage than the others because of the configuration of the shoals.

There was also the problem of the wounded during this period. Supply had the first priority, but the problem of the wounded was almost equally important and even more difficult. The prearranged system of evacuation had collapsed with the changing situation. The improvised base hospitals that had been set up in the northern area to replace those severed by May 20th from the army were themselves in increasing danger, and together with the normal flow of wounded from the fighting areas the personnel of these improvised hospitals had now to be withdrawn.

An example of what that withdrawal entailed is contained in the work of the hospital carriers *Isle of Thanet* and *Worthing* on May 23rd. They sailed on the afternoon of that day from Newhaven and arrived off Dunkirk in the early evening with an air raid in progress. The Gare Maritime, the old cross-Channel berth, was bombed shortly before their arrival, but the quay still stood and they went alongside. While *Isle of Thanet* took on board 300 wounded and *Worthing* lifted a full load there were enemy aircraft almost continually overhead, and they worked under a curtain of anti-aircraft fire from ships' guns and shore batteries until they pulled out at 11 o'clock.

With them worked cross-Channel steamers taking off civilian evacuees. *St. Helier*, for example, picked up 1,500 British and French this day.

Enemy air opposition was increasing rapidly. The air raid which *Isle of Thanet* and *Worthing* endured was part of an attack that had gone on with brief intervals throughout the day either on the town or on the water. In the course of it the French had lost one old destroyer, *Orage*, and one large new one, *Jaguar*.

2

This was the Dunkirk sector, but while this traffic and this loss continued there was an operation of infinitely more importance to the future in progress at Boulogne. The sacrifice and gallantries of the defence of Boulogne have passed into history. It is impossible to detail them in these chapters. It is the evacuation alone—that long saga of heroism—which has its direct influence upon Dunkirk.

All through this and the previous day the Dover destroyers had worked desperately along this coast attempting to relieve the pressure on the army by bombarding such targets as showed themselves from time to time along the cliffs and on the high ground behind the towns. By the late afternoon the situation had deteriorated so far that the choice before the authorities was not so much between defence and evacuation as between evacuation and surrender. At 5.30 p.m. the destroyers at sea received a signal which stated that evacuation had been decided upon.

Already in the middle of the afternoon H.M.S. *Keith* (Captain D. J. R. Simson, R.N.), the flotilla leader, and H.M.S. *Vimy* were lying alongside at the Quai Chanzy. They had entered under fire and thereafter endured both bombing and shelling at frequent intervals. At 4 p.m., when it was obvious from the progress of the fighting that evacuation was upon them, Captain Simson ordered demolition of the harbour facilities to begin. Shortly afterwards this was followed by an order for the embarkation of the first troops.

This was in progress when the Germans launched the biggest attack of the day in an attempt to overrun the harbour before the withdrawal could be accomplished. A preliminary high-level attack failed under the onslaught of a small formation of British fighters, but immediately after about 60 Junkers-87 dive-bombers attacked the town. Twenty-four of them concentrated on *Keith* and *Vimy*. At the same time mortar fire opened on the destroyers from the hill. The destroyers fought back magnificently and though *Keith* was hit by a mortar shell and much damaged by a near miss which hit the quay three yards away, both ships escaped. With a large number of troops and more than 70 wounded aboard each destroyer, they backed out of the harbour. Captain Simson was dead, his First Lieutenant wounded; the captain of *Vimy*, Lieutenant-Commander C. G. W. Donald, R.N., was mortally wounded; and both ships had heavy casualty lists.

Meanwhile destroyers standing by outside the harbour had also been heavily attacked. H.M.S. *Whitshed* (Commander E. R. Condor, R.N.) was damaged and had casualties, but *Venetia*, *Vimiera* and *Venomous* escaped unscathed. They were joined shortly afterwards by another destroyer, *Wild Swan* (Lieutenant-Commander J. L. Younghusband, D.S.C., R.N.), and a little later nine Spitfires came in to give them some sort of cover.

Immediately two destroyers entered the harbour, *Whitshed* leading, followed by *Vimiera* (Lieutenant R. L. Caple, R.N.). It was now 7.30 p.m., and the destroyers had some difficulty in berthing owing to the state of the tide. Embarkation began at once, and with comparatively little interference from the enemy *Whitshed* picked up 510 and *Vimiera* 500. They could take no more owing to the depth of water.

As soon as they cleared the harbour *Wild Swan* and *Venomous* (Lieutenant-Commander J. E. H. McBeath, R.N.), entered, followed by *Venetia*. When she was within a few yards of the breakwaters there was a sudden sheet of flame on the low hills to the north. This was the signal for a general bombardment in a determined attempt to sink *Venetia* in the fairway and block the harbour. The attempt came perilously near to success. *Venetia* was badly damaged, her captain (Lieutenant-Commander B. H. de C. Mellor, R.N.) dangerously wounded, her navigator killed, and many others wounded. She was grounded, but she was brought out by a young R.N.R. sub-lieutenant stern first, and got clear of the harbour. *Venomous* was also heavily fired upon as she went alongside. The guns of all three ships engaged enemy positions almost at point-blank range, a single shot from *Wild Swan* destroying a tank which was roaring down a side street towards the quay, pom-poms from *Venomous* blowing an armoured car to pieces.

Almost throughout the embarkation the guns maintained their fire, but despite the fusillade troops coming alongside suffered many casualties both from rifle fire and from machine-guns hidden in hotels and pier buildings. By 9 p.m. *Venomous* had picked up 500 men and *Wild Swan* 400, and with superb seamanship the two destroyers, still firing all their guns, worked themselves stern first out of the harbour. *Wild Swan* grounded but got clear; the wheel of *Venomous* jammed and she was forced to steer by her engines; but both ships pulled out and, with the damaged *Venetia*, got back to Dover.

The six destroyers assigned to Boulogne were now all more or less damaged. The destroyer *Windsor* (Lieutenant-Commander P. D. H. R. Pelly, R.N.), patrolling off Calais, was therefore ordered to Boulogne, and arrived at 10.30 in darkness. Though she was fired upon, the confusion of the fires and the smoke saved her from a direct hit. She picked up 600 men and some 30 wounded and in due course got clear of the harbour. But there were still men ashore.

There was only one destroyer now available without damage in the area of Vice-Admiral Ramsay's command, H.M.S. *Vimiera*. At midnight she was dispatched. At 1.30 a.m. she arrived at Boulogne. The inner harbour was a mass of flames and confusion. She secured to the outer jetty and waited. There was no sign of life and her captain was on the point of slipping when he was hailed from the shore. From behind warehouses came a mad rush of Belgian and French soldiers and civilian refugees. The stampede was checked, and immediately after contact was made with British troops. *Vimiera's* captain was told that there were 1,000 men left. 'Could you take them all?' The number was staggering, but she was the last ship. For an hour and a quarter she lay alongside while down the jetty, between the bursts of shelling and machine-gun fire, the men filed, silhouetted against the burning shambles of the town. At 2.45 a.m., with 1,400 troops on board, *Vimiera* slipped her ropes and sailed. It was a magnificent feat, magnificently performed. It was to be the model for Dunkirk.

We lost no destroyers at Boulogne—that is in the sense of total loss—but all save one of that gallant band had to be withdrawn for urgent repairs and two of them were to remain throughout the subsequent operations in dock-yard hands. The tally of loss was growing rapidly, too rapidly.

3

It was to continue to grow. On May 24th the French lost a second ship of the 'Tigre' class, the *Chacal*. She and *Jaguar* were big ships, *contre-torpilleurs* of 2,126 tons, almost small light cruisers. This was in the Dunkirk sector. Off Calais, where the 30th Brigade was still holding out superbly, we lost the destroyer *Wessex* in the course of a bombardment of enemy positions on the flank of the Calais perimeter, to a furious attack from the air. In the course of the same attack the Polish destroyer *Burza* was hit and lost most of her bows. Four destroyers had been lost and six put out of the battle in forty-eight hours. The cumulative effect of this added to the earlier losses was enormous, but the planning for 'Dynamo' went on, its ardour in no way diminished. And with it the ordinary business of the waters continued.

On top of these things a new complication presented itself. In its endea-vours to find some means of checking the desperate situation that now prevailed along the Flanders fronts, the War Office had taken the dramatic decision to throw the 1st Canadian Division into the fray. As the primary object of this move was to strengthen the already tired units of Lord Gort's British Expeditionary Force, the division could only be shipped through the ports that were already intensely occupied with the work which has been described in this chapter—supply, preliminary evacuation and wounded.

On the 24th advance units of the division were embarked on some of the ships. *St. Seiriol*, for example, took on board units of the Canadian Provost Corps. Transport and other ships at the different ports of the south coast were earmarked and held for this purpose. At the last moment, when a number of men were already aboard, the decision was countermanded. The view was taken that the situation was beyond such degree of restoration as could be effected by the throwing in of a new division and that evacuation was now inevitable, in which circumstances an extra 15,000 men would be merely an added embarrassment and a source of confusion to the lines of movement set up by the retreating army. The men who had already been loaded were disembarked.

The traffic was still of the same kind—the evacuation of the wounded. The hospital carrier *St. Julien* went into Dunkirk harbour at low tide and was subjected to heavy bombing, the nearest falling twenty feet away. Her master counted seventeen planes during this attack and, as it appeared impossible to make contact with the shore, he went astern out of the harbour and returned to Dover. Two hours later he was ordered to make a second attempt with the hospital carrier *St. Andrew* (which had made a series of heroic attempts to get into Calais in the course of the morning under heavy cross-fire from the shore batteries) and, provided with air cover, reached Dunkirk without incident. Owing to the shortage of R.A.M.C. personnel in the harbour area the crew had to assist in the loading of patients. On board *St. Andrew* a call for volunteers was made and the entire crew answered it. On their return journey both ships were shelled, though burning the green lights and showing the red crosses obligatory under the conventions.

Simultaneously the ordinary work of supply was going on. As an example the work of the motor vessel *Sandhill* may be cited. On this day she arrived at Dunkirk with a cargo of 940 tons of high explosive. As no electric cranes were available in the harbour, she had to discharge with her own gear, and most of the work took place under heavy raids.

S.s. *Clewbay* reached Dunkirk safely after sighting many floating mines, and was attacked on entering the channel. As she attempted to get alongside the East Pier two more bombs were dropped ahead of her, one of them hitting the pier which was shattered for some distance. As her master could get no information, and as with the darkness the raids had come on even more fiercely, she left and returned to Dover, being attacked by planes on the way and fired at by the Gravelines batteries.

It must not be thought that the ships named represent the whole effort of the day. There were in fact many vessels moving between the English ports and Dunkirk all through these days, even as there were ships moving between Dunkirk and the ports of western France.

4

It is not easy for those who did not see it to picture Dover harbour at this time and in the days that followed. Dover harbour, as has been said, is big, but the actual quays are small and, save for the cross-Channel berth on the Admiralty Pier, unsuited for heavy working. The harbour was designed more as an anchorage for the old Channel Fleet than for a working port.

At the Admiralty Pier there are eight berths for cross-Channel steamers. During the busy days there would be sixteen, eighteen, or even twenty ships at these eight berths. They moored there in tiers two and three deep, and, because of the difficulties of turning space—there is a ridge of rock and shoal between the Prince of Wales Pier and the Admiralty Pier at low water—almost all these ships had to be handled by tugs, and all these ships had to be handled with the utmost expedition. They came alongside, the weary and exhausted soldiers were sent ashore as swiftly as might be, and the ships pulled out again to refuel and return.

In the main harbour there are between forty and fifty mooring buoys. These were constantly occupied with ships taking stores, repairing minor damage, very occasionally resting. At one of the buoys the oil tanker *War Sepoy* was berthed and incessantly alongside her the destroyers and the oil-burning cross-Channel steamers, the pleasure boats and the rest made fast for fuel. Here too they had to be worked by tugs. The great part of the work was done by the four tugs *Simla*, *Gondia*, *Roman* and *Lady Brassey*. They had other duties too—moving ships into the submarine camber at the eastern end of the harbour for repairs, moving them into and out of the inner docks, Granville and Wellington, as the tide served, for work that could not be carried out in the camber.

In his report of this period Mr. G. D. Lowe, the master of *Simla*, says:

'The fortnight commencing the 20th of May 1940 at the time of the evacuation, the tug *Simla* assisted inside and outside of Dover Harbour, 140-odd ships. The crew and myself were practically on our feet night and day. I have great praise for my crew. Never a grumble, but carrying on with the good work, all longing to help as much as possible, to see our soldiers home safe.

'On May 22nd, when attending to harbour work, I received a signal, that a French ship, the s.s. *Themsen*, with refugees on board, had been in collision with a British ship, the s.s. *Efford*, three miles south-west of Dover. On arriving there, the *Efford* had sunk, and the crew on her were in one of her lifeboats which I picked up. I then found out from the Captain of the *Efford* that all his crew were saved, and that the *Themsen* had cut right into his ship.

'The tug *Simla* took the s.s. *Themsen* in tow, and I went on board of her, while my mate took charge of the tug, for the captain of her was in such a nervous condition that he could not take charge of his ship. He had just come from Dunkirk after being bombed all day, and asked me to take charge of his ship. I anchored her off Dover under naval orders. I then landed the crew of the *Efford* at Dover.

'The tugs had orders to shift two destroyers from Admiralty Pier on May 24th, in the early hours of the morning to buoys in the harbour, to make room for other ships to berth. They were the H.M.S. *Whitshed* and *Vimy*, but the crews of the destroyers were so tired and exhausted from their recent experience of Dunkirk that we let them sleep on, and shifted the destroyers without them. I expect that when they turned out from their much-needed sleep, they were surprised to find their ships in a different position, but were all fresh to go to sea again, and carry on the good work.

'During the very dark night of May 24th, the s.s. *Kohistan* (5,884 tons) was outside, waiting to berth at Admiralty Pier. She had about 6,000 troops on board. The naval people wanted her to berth as soon as possible on account of enemy planes coming over. The job of berthing her was not an easy one, for the harbour was full of other ships, no one being allowed to show any light. The tugs *Simla* and *Lady Brassey* decided to do the best they could. It was just like going into thick fog. You could not see the other ships or buoys in the harbour, and it was a great worry trying not to hit other ships. First we would scrape along one destroyer, then just miss another one by a few feet. Well, with great care, I for one was pleased to get that ship on her berth without any mishap, and to know that the soldiers got ashore safely.'

Simla's account may serve to epitomize the work of the tugs which were based on the different ports. They had their share of danger both from direct attack and from the more insidious threat of the magnetic mine; but, for the most part, it was the incessant toil of the work that bore on them. Like *Simla* other tugs went out to rescue work. *Doria* and *Kenia* were at sea almost throughout the period as inspection vessels at the approaches, to the great anchorages. Still other tugs were occupied in the essential work of removing the constantly growing fleet of damaged ships clear of Dover and Ramsgate and taking them to the repair yards of the Thames, of Portsmouth and Southampton.

Complementary to the work of the Dover tugs was that done by other tugs across the Channel. Various British ships took part in this, some of them staying for two and five days at a time. But a little fleet of Belgian tugs— *Elbe*, *Thames*, *Max*, *Vulcain* and *Goliath*—from the Belgian North Sea ports began to work inside Dunkirk harbour on May 25th and continued throughout the whole of Operation 'Dynamo' until the first four were sunk on the last day, and their crews brought to Dover in the surviving ship, *Goliath*.

5

On the 25th much of the recorded activity was again on the part of the hospital carriers, who were now desperately trying to get away the last of the casualties from the base hospitals, together with the rapidly accumulating casualties of the actual fighting and the additional wounded of the air bombardment. The *Isle of Thanet*, *St. David* and other ships were all engaged this day in lifting wounded. *St. David* arrived in Dunkirk in the morning and lay alongside receiving wounded into the evening. All day the town and the quays were subjected to severe aerial bombardment. On her way out, when passing the Gravelines beaches, she came under heavy shelling, one large-calibre shell falling less than a ship's length ahead of her.

The *Isle of Thanet* left Newhaven—where most of the wounded were landed through the whole series of evacuations—and, crossing with *Paris*, arrived at Dunkirk in the early evening and moored at the Gare Maritime outside the s.s. *Canterbury*. She started loading her wounded at 10 o'clock and air raids were frequent during the whole period. One salvo of bombs fell close to the ship, but though she was damaged by splinters no serious harm was done. Fires were raging all round the docks, and her master says that the white-painted hospital carriers showed up prominently. She lifted 608 casualties before she left again for Newhaven.

The transport *Canterbury*, which had been shelled on her way to Dunkirk, carried out this evening one of the first big liftings of men, embarking 1,246 troops from the Gare Maritime. These were mainly base personnel and lines of communication troops who were no longer required, and this was part of the lifting implied by Lord Gort's mention in his dispatches of his decision to reduce the number of troops to ease the supply problem.

St. Helier, crossing in company with hospital carriers, was attacked by two planes, one of the hospital ships having a narrow escape. She arrived at Dunkirk in the early evening, and was immediately attacked by nine planes. She waited until the raid was over to avoid being sunk in the entrance and blocking the harbour and, on attempting to go alongside shortly after, was told to put to sea at once. After waiting in the Roads for some while fresh planes came over and, as it appeared impossible to enter, she returned to Dover.

Meanwhile a new complication had presented itself. The incessant bombing had destroyed the waterworks and mains. There were only wells left within the area that was to become the perimeter, and few of these, and into them the brackish water was seeping from the flooding of the lowland levels. An urgent signal was made to England asking for water, and the water boat *Goldeve* was loaded and dispatched. She was followed by the water boat *Claude*.

6

These examples have been chosen with a view not to providing a record of all the work done in the week preceding Operation 'Dynamo', but of giving a general picture of the conditions which prevailed, of the difficulties and the rapidly increasing danger of the seaward situation. It is a picture of port facilities disappearing in a welter of twisted steel and broken concrete, of torn-up roads and battered quays, of burning buildings and flaring oil tanks. It is a picture of a long channel already littered with ships burning, ships sunk, ships stranded.

THE WEEK PRECEDING THE EVACUATION

It is the picture of a week that from the naval point of view had been disastrous. On the Saturday night Vice-Admiral Ramsay and the Board of Admiralty knew that they had to face a period in which the attacks they had suffered would be not merely renewed, but reinforced with every possible circumstance of ferocity. And the week that was ended had already destroyed —temporarily at least—the destroyer force of the Channel.

But already the decision had been taken to send in reinforcements. The Polish destroyer *Burza*, herself included amongst the casualties of the week, was amongst the first of these. She had come down to Calais from patrol off the Aldeburgh light with the rest of her division to help in the urgency of the Calais situation. Close on her heels were to come fresh reinforcements. They were desperately necessary. Destroyers were almost the only fighting ships that could be used in these narrow and shallow waters, and their responsibility was endless and enormous. From the Belgian coast to the narrows of the Channel they had to fight it out with enemy batteries, to bombard enemy columns, to challenge enemy positions. They had to provide escort for ships moving under constant danger of air attack. They had to watch always against the possibility of assaults by surface craft and by submarine.

Those who had gone through the week were near exhaustion. The report of *Simla*'s master, who moved *Whitshed* and *Vimy* from one berth to another without waking the men on board, is perhaps one of the most vivid indications of the arduousness of the work and of the weariness which supervened as it progressed. All ships—merchant vessels, destroyers, minesweepers, drifters, alike—worked constantly now under the fire of shore batteries, under the ever-increasing terror of a Luftwaffe flushed with victory. This was the basis upon which Operation 'Dynamo' was erected—a basis of near-exhaustion, spiritual and material.

CHAPTER VII

SUNDAY, MAY 26TH

1

At 6.57 on the evening of Sunday, May 26th, a signal from Vice-Admiral Ramsay put Operation 'Dynamo' into motion.

May 26th was considered by Lord Gort to mark the end of what he has called the second phase of the campaign. It is as well to remind oneself of the general picture of this time. By the morning of the 25th it was apparent that the Belgians were cracking. Where their defence zone linked with that of the British the Germans were attacking with four divisions supported by tanks, and at one point they had penetrated for a depth of a mile and a half on a thirteen-mile front between Menin and Desselghem. On the other flank the fall of Calais was inevitable and imminent. With that fall two armoured divisions plus a motorized division would be released to attack the already hard-pressed French on the Gravelines positions.

On the morning of May 25th Sir John Dill (who had succeeded to the command of the Imperial General Staff) visited Lord Gort in response to an urgent request from the latter, and took part in a discussion with General Blanchard. It was clear that the attack south, which was still vaguely hoped for with a sort of obstinate optimism by a French High Command that took no cognizance of facts, could not now succeed. What was imperative was the consolidation of the flanks in order that the contents of what has been called 'the bag' could be brought up to a mouth still open on the coast.

The raids of the last three days and those of the night of Saturday had put Dunkirk finally out of action as a port for handling supplies. Since the 23rd the B.E.F. had been on half-rations. From May 23rd also it had become impossible for airborne supplies to be landed. Petrol, ammunition, were both growing desperately short. Water was non-existent, and already Dunkirk town was burning.

That was the landward side of the necessity. There remained the seaward side. As has been indicated, the last seven days had shown a rapid and dangerous decline in the possibilities of sea transport. Enemy air attack along the channels, the batteries which commanded the inshore route past Calais, an increased degree of mining activity and, on this day, the first signs of attack by motor torpedo-boats, demonstrated that the enemy was beginning to pay attention to the possibilities of evacuation—an intense, an unwelcome and an aggressive attention.

But it was the attacks from the flanks that determined the decision to put Plan 'Dynamo' into being. To many observers who had watched the triumphant sweep of the armoured divisions across the plains it looked as if the end were a matter of desperate hours.

2

Planning for the possible needs of the B.E.F. had begun with the first meeting at the War Office on May 19th. The first-fruits of that planning were the improvised supply lines to the near Channel ports—until they were over-run—and the movement that had taken place thereafter through Dunkirk. Something of it has been described in the preceding chapter, but, important as these things were, they take second place to the fact that in those seven days the necessary supply of shipping for the evacuation was determined upon, organized and provided.

When Vice-Admiral Ramsay made his signal there was sufficient shipping already lying in the Downs or at Dover to carry out his initial movements. There was sufficient waiting in the second echelon at Southampton to supply any deficiencies as occasion called, and throughout the ports of the kingdom there were other ships earmarked and ready to move up as need arose. At no time did the naval authorities call in vain upon the Ministry of Shipping for vessels for the evacuation. At the end of the nine days there were still ships in reserve.

On Sunday morning the distribution of ships available was as follows:

Personnel ships (mainly cross-Channel and Irish Sea packets) at Dover or in the Downs	15
Personnel ships at Southampton	17
Personnel ships at Southampton (Dutch and Belgian)	3
Coasters in the Downs	6
Wooden and steel barges in the Downs	16
Dutch skoots	40
M.T., shore ships, petrol ships, etc.	32

One hundred and twenty-nine merchant ships were thus immediately available for the preliminary phases of the operation. In addition to these the Ministry of Shipping had called on their representatives to the principal ports between Harwich and Weymouth on the south and south-east coasts to ear-mark additional ships and to expedite their dispatch if they should be required. A complete survey of all ships in these harbours had already been undertaken and was available for V.-A., Dover, and a basic survey of all ships throughout the harbours of Britain, with their state as to loading and discharge, was in being and available.

On the naval side Vice-Admiral Ramsay's command had already been very much strengthened. To Dover and the Downs were being sent with increasing urgency the major part of the minesweepers and the minor war vessels on the strength of the south and east coast commands. Elements of the destroyer flotillas which operated out of the Nore and Harwich on the one side and out of Portsmouth and Plymouth on the other were already under his command.

Even on this first day his composite force of destroyers, sloops, Fleet mine-sweepers, paddle-minesweepers, armed yachts, trawlers, drifters and motor craft was a formidable one. It was known as Force 'K'.

There was much for it to do. Calais had still to be supported; German columns along the coast roads had still to be bombarded; anti-aircraft cover for the cross-Channel lanes and for Dunkirk Roads had to be provided; and there was always present the possibility of surface attack from the eastward. In so far as any shape for disaster can be given, it might be said that preparations, when the final signal was made, were in good shape.

But there remained always the fundamental difficulty of Dunkirk—there was no port in working order.

3

Operation 'Dynamo' began with Vice-Admiral Ramsay's signal at 6.57 p.m., but it is impossible to draw a hard and fast line between the work of 'Dynamo' and the work which had preceded it. It was in the beginning similar in character, similar in execution. Evacuation had already been in progress in some degree for the best part of four days. Evacuation of the wounded had been in progress for longer still. So it was that ships which had been sent to Dunkirk on May 25th completed their loading only in the small hours of May 26th and returned to Dover, to Folkestone and to Newhaven to be included in the tally of that day.

For example, the hospital carrier *Isle of Thanet*, with her load of casualties, left Dunkirk quay at 1.15 on the Sunday morning and moored at No. 2 berth at Newhaven at 8 o'clock. There were other ships too which, in continuation of the programme already in being, moved before the 'Dynamo' signal was made. At 3.25 a.m. *St. Andrew* left the Downs for Dunkirk. A little later, however, she was ordered to return as the situation was obscure. *King Orry*, which had left at approximately the same time, reached the port and brought away a number of men. While the morning was still early the *Maid of Orleans* loaded stores and 6,000 two-gallon cans of water. Just prior to leaving a detachment of 250 men drawn from the R.A.S.C. and the Signal Corps were put on board the ship to assist in the organization of the port. At 11 o'clock she set out for Dunkirk using the short route and duly came under fire from the batteries near Calais. Dunkirk on her arrival was, as usual, undergoing air attack and after waiting for some while off the port she was ordered to return to Dover.

Shortly after she had left the Downs *St. Andrew*, in company with *St. Julien*, made a second attempt to get to Dunkirk. Off the Dyck light vessel outside Calais they made contact with the *Maid of Orleans* and immediately came under heavy fire from the shore batteries. The *Maid of Orleans* went through but *St. Julien*, considering it impossible to pass without serious risk, turned back, together with *St. Andrew*, and returned to Dover.

At noon other ships had left Dover, among them *Mona's Queen*. Her master, Captain R. Duggan, in his report says:

'Our route took us about 4 miles off Calais to a certain buoy. On nearing the position I could not see the buoy, but saw a buoy a little further inshore and steamed towards it to make certain. On nearing the buoy I saw it was not the buoy on the instructions and ordered the helm hard a-port. Immediately hell was let loose on our ship. We were shelled from the shore by single guns and also by salvoes from shore batteries. Shells were flying all around us, the first salvo went over us, the second, astern of us. I thought the next salvo would hit us, but fortunately it dropped short, right under our stern. The ship was riddled with shrapnel, mostly all on the boat and promenade decks. Then we were attacked from the air. A Junker bomber made a power dive towards us and dropped five bombs, but he was off the mark too, I should say about 150 feet from us. All this while we were still being shelled, although we were getting out of range. The Junker that bombed us was shot down and crashed into the water just ahead of us (no survivors). Then another Junker attacked us, but before he reached us he was brought down in flames. Then the tension eased a little.

'Owing to the bombardment, I could see that the nerves of some of my men were badly shaken. I did not feel too well myself, but I mustered the crew and told them that Dunkirk was being bombed and was on fire. On being asked if they would volunteer to go in they did so to a man and I am glad to say we took off as many as *Mona's Queen* could carry. Coming back from Dunkirk, I made a route for myself and am glad to say we arrived safely at Dover in the early hours of Monday morning. . . .'

About the same time the hospital carriers *Worthing* and *Isle of Guernsey* left the Downs. In a joint report the master of the *Isle of Guernsey*, Captain E. Hill, and his chief officer, R. F. Pembury, say:

'At approximately 4 p.m. as we approached Calais, which lay in ruins under a heavy pall of smoke, two British destroyers crossed our bows, hove to, and commenced shelling the shore batteries who promptly returned the challenge. To avoid this no-man's land we were forced to deviate, as our proper course would have taken us between the combatants. Whilst carrying out this manœuvre, enemy planes appeared and commenced bombing the convoy but none of the three vessels were struck, although bombs fell very close.

'Arriving off Dunkirk which was under an even heavier pall of thick black smoke than Calais, we manœuvred our way inside through the various wrecks of vessels which had been struck by bombs and the *Worthing* having been made fast to the quay we moored alongside her. A few moments after our arrival streams of motor ambulances arrived threading their way through the columns of troops who were not so seriously wounded and were able to walk. Loading was commenced immediately and every member of the ship's crew assisted in stretcher-bearing so as to facilitate the loading. By 9.55 p.m. both hospital carriers were loaded with as many as they could take, the *Isle of Guernsey* having 346 cases on board, and as her number of cots is only 203, many of these cases were accommodated in between the cots on the deck along corridors, in fact wherever it was possible to put a stretcher. The voyage back to Newhaven via Dover passed without incident. . . .'

In the late afternoon still further movements were initiated. *Maid of Orleans* made a second attempt and this time berthed. *Canterbury* left about 6 o'clock and ran the usual gauntlet of the guns off Calais. At Dunkirk she berthed outside *Maid of Orleans* and loaded 1,340 troops under continuous bombing, leaving again about midnight, while *Maid of Orleans* took off 988.

4

This is not a complete record of the movements of the first day. The lifting of the ships that have been named was supplemented by that of smaller ships. Naval vessels also began on this day to embark troops in great numbers. The destroyers too worked endlessly; two lay off Calais almost throughout the daylight hours bombarding the columns moving on the roads wherever they were visible from the sea, others gave such support as was possible to the hard-pressed garrison, yet others worked escorting the troop-carriers and providing anti-aircraft cover for shipping in the narrow channel off the beaches.

But even as *Canterbury* was making ready to return at midnight it was clear that the first day's operations were perilously close to failure. Ships were turning back from the danger spot off Calais and it was obvious—. certain—that this danger spot would grow more dangerous still, for, in the last hours of this day, Calais was falling.

That desperate and most gallant defence was coming to an end. At 8 o'clock in the morning Brigadier Nicholson had received the German demand for surrender and to it had given his curt, heroic 'No'. At 9 o'clock the general bombardment that had gone on all the night began again. From 10 o'clock low-level bombing started and never ceased. It was done in relays —one squadron overhead, one waiting to attack, one returning for more bombs. The streets were filled with the debris of ruined houses, the defensive positions were wrecked; the whole force was gravely short of ammunition— the Rifle Brigade was already near its last shot.

At 5 o'clock the Germans captured the Citadel and with it Brigadier Nicholson. The fall of the Citadel made Fort Risban untenable. It was almost over. In the darkness—that was not dark because of the fires of the burning town—what was left of the little garrison surrendered. Their work was done. They had given time for the right flank of the perimeter of Dunkirk to be made secure.

But now the whole weight of the two armoured divisions that had been held by Calais town was free to thrust. The Belgian Army was being attacked with extreme violence on the front Menin–Nivelle, and a note from General Michiels, Chief of Staff of the Belgian Army, declared that his army could not fulfil its promise to withdraw to the Yser. 'On this evening', says Lord Gort, 'I put in hand my plans for a final withdrawal.' Lieutenant-General Sir Ronald Adam was appointed to the task of organizing the bridge-head of Dunkirk, and with Admiral Abrial, General Fagalde, General Prioux, General Blanchard, and General Koeltz (representing General

Weygand), a conference was held to decide on the organization, the areas of responsibility, and the frontiers of the perimeter.

Brigadier the Hon. E. F. Lawson was instructed to lay out the defence of the perimeter and to utilize such troops as were on the spot or entering it.

5

The difficulties and dangers of the air are indicated tersely enough in reports like those of the masters of *Mona's Queen* and *Isle of Guernsey*. They were, in fact, growing rapidly. Every day now the Germans were putting new landing strips close in to the Dunkirk area into action, while the British Expeditionary Force was now totally divorced from the air component whose co-operation had been an integral part of its economy. The substitute defence provided from the Kentish aerodromes on this day met with much success; but it was apparent even then that it was quite impossible to maintain daylight cover over the area, or to maintain cover at any time in sufficient strength to give the protection necessary to prevent loss.

None the less on this day the qualitative superiority of our aircraft began to manifest itself in no uncertain manner. Two of our squadrons met and soundly thrashed an important attack on the shipping channel off Dunkirk. It consisted of Junkers 88's and Junkers 87's covered by masses of Messerschmitt 109's flying high above them. In four hours between dawn and 9.30 more than twenty bombers and fighters were shot down. In the course of the day approximately forty enemy planes were destroyed for the loss of seven of our own.

Meanwhile Bomber Command was doing what it could to relieve the pressure. In a series of widespread attacks it had bombed during the night railway junctions in north and west Germany, south Belgium, and north-east France. On the Friday night it had attacked Flushing and canal bridges in the south Holland areas.

The numerical victory of the fighters was spectacular. It was even more important in consideration of the smallness of the number of Spitfires engaged. But it was not enough: attacks continued at intervals throughout the day.

6

Even as the shore defences took shape the first plan for evacuation—the first sketch for Operation 'Dynamo'—was in ruins. It had envisaged the use of Boulogne and Calais as well as of Dunkirk. It had been based on a shuttle service that would have provided two ships loading every six hours from each port, each ship lifting between 2,000 and 3,000 men per trip: 10,000 men per port per day: 30,000 men in all. The B.E.F. numbered almost a quarter of a million men. It would have needed eight days on this basis with three ports working continuously day and night, and under nothing more than—to use the terms of the report—'moderate interference'. On this Sunday evening we were reduced to one port and that in ruins; the approaches to it harassed by shell-fire from the shore, by endless bombardment from the air; the loading berths themselves under a rain of bombs; the town behind them shattered and burning; the army short of food and short of water; and a movement on either flank threatening to cut off even what pitiful hope remained.

It was time for the second plan.

CHAPTER VIII

MONDAY, MAY 27TH

1

On the morning of May 27th the great movement into the perimeter began. It is difficult even now to appreciate precisely what this movement meant.

The vast tide of refugees which had swept through Belgium from the German frontier by way of Brussels, by Mons and Arras, by Courtrai and Lille, had met with the swifter-flowing river of the German encirclement along the Somme and had recoiled upon itself. The congestion of the roads in the great circle which has for its centre Armentières and which reaches to the coast on the one hand and Valenciennes on the other, was beyond description. It was a whirlpool of frightened humanity, a maelstrom of the terrified. Harassed from the air, frightened by the sound of guns, by shell bursts, by the sight of the enemy, and above all by rumour that ran through them like an electric current, they milled up and down the narrow highways—and through them the armies had to pass. The armies were foodless, but these people were beginning already to starve. Swiftly it became necessary to take drastic action. Whole mobs of refugees had to be turned off the roads into the fields to let the army columns through. Every movement that was made was hindered appallingly by this problem.

In a desperate effort to simplify in some degree the question of the roads within the area of the perimeter it was decided to abandon all vehicular traffic outside its line. This was agreed to both by the French and by ourselves. It was not adhered to by the French. It was impossible to spare sufficient men for military police duties, and a certain proportion of our own vehicles in addition came through what should have been the cordons; but the western side of the perimeter became jammed with French lorries, tank vehicles, buses, armoured cars and the like.

An extract from the diary of a French officer[1] at this time gives some indication of the state of mind of the French Army on this Monday. Up to then the officers appeared to have been buoyed by hopes of some form of counter-attack. On May 27th he writes:

'Alas! All the information is false. Frère's army had no other mission than to obstruct the formidable German advance towards the south. The High Command appears to have given up all hope of saving us. We must reach Dunkirk at all costs.'

---

[1] D. Barlone, *A French Officer's Diary* (Cambridge University Press).

2

This was the position on the land. At sea the problems were as difficult. With the fall of Calais the Germans had mounted batteries on Fort Risban at the entrance to the harbour. They had mounted another battery on the dunes close to the Gravelines road. It was clear that a new route must be developed at once.

There was a possible short route across the sandbanks, but it was blocked almost solidly with our own defensive minefields. The only immediate alternative was the route by the channel past Dunkirk, which continued out through what was known as the Zuydecoote Pass to the north-eastward of the roadstead, and then followed tortuous swatchways almost to Ostend, where it came out through the sandbanks into the open sea. As a temporary expedient this had to be adopted, though the route was not yet swept of enemy mines. Sweepers had to be organized and dispatched at once to deal with it.

These were the first preoccupations of Vice-Admiral Ramsay, but the greatest preoccupation of all now was the necessity for organizing some method of lifting men from the beaches. To those who had watched the bombing of the port, who had seen the gradual deliquescence of its facilities under the hail of the bombs, who had seen the quay walls crumbling under high explosive and lock gates wrecked and jammed by splinters and by blast, it must have seemed impossible that ships could go on loading in that shambles. Even where the walls still stood square to the water's edge warehouses and stores and ships were alight behind them. The heat from these, from the burning town, from the oil wells on the western bank was so great that there was no question of the use of the inner harbour.

There were left only the outer piers. That to the westward had a facing of piles sloping so that no ship could lie alongside to load. There was only one length of jetty here that could be of continued service. That to the east was the great Mole, with its five-foot plank-walk. It was impossible to place faith in that!

The major problem for 'Dynamo Room' and the Dover Command was to plan and provide for the lifting of an army off the open beaches.

3

All through the night the staff of the Small Vessels Pool had worked in the Admiralty building in Whitehall getting their scheme into operation, while up London River and in the ports the officers had continued their search for craft.

At Dover complementary preparations were in being. Rear-Admiral A. H. Taylor, O.B.E., who had been working for most of the war in the office of the Economic Warfare Division, received final instructions from Vice-Admiral Ramsay, and proceeded to Sheerness to take up the duties of 'Dynamo' Maintenance Officer. His staff consisted of Commander H. R. Troup, R.N., and Lieutenant-Commander D. E. Holland-Martin, R.N. Admiral Taylor's headquarters were in the gloomy and ancient Admiralty House under the shadow of the ramparts of the sea-wall in Garrison Point.

The 'staff' was exiguous and in the highest degree fluid. Various officers came to it from time to time, served with it for a day or two—some of them for no more than an hour or two—and, as a sudden emergency arose, disappeared to sea in command of a vessel or a flotilla, and were next heard of on the Dunkirk beaches. But with the constant aid of H.M.S. *Wildfire*, the Sheerness depot (which was commanded by Captain Coleridge, R.N.), with the admirable services of the Fleet Engineer-Officer, Captain T. E. Docksey, R.N., Paymaster-Captain E. C. Annaheim, R.N., and Commander V. P. Freeman, R.N., the work of handling the stream of small craft that came flooding down the Thames went forward swiftly and efficiently.

Perhaps the most important movement of the day was that of the first Dutch coasters (to be known hereafter as H.M. Skoots, an anglicized form of the Dutch *schuit*). These were from the forty selected by Captain Fisher of the Ministry of Shipping. The forty had been divided between Poole and the Port of London. Manned entirely by naval crews, the first two, *Hilda* and *Doggersbank*, crossed to Dunkirk on this Monday. Meanwhile the Poole division was moving up-Channel.

And working with the Small Vessels Pool was the small craft section of the Ministry of Shipping under Mr. A. L. Moore. Mr. H. C. Riggs of this department had been warned by telephone during the night of the urgency of the situation, and with the early morning he began to get in touch with Ministry officials in various ports. Up the Thames Messrs. Tough Brothers, boat-builders of Teddington, were approached to act as agents for the collection of small craft in their area, while all through the Port of London officials of the Authority were warned to expedite the passage of small craft in every possible way. The Ministry of Shipping undertook the whole responsibility towards crews and towards the small craft themselves in regard to financial problems. Payments for runner crews, for travelling expenses and for necessary stores were undertaken by Mr. Moore's department, and by that department eventually all responsibility for craft damaged and lost was assumed.

With this department, as with the responsible Admiralty departments, the story is precisely the same. Everywhere they were met not merely by a dumb acquiescence in the requisitioning of the little ships, but by an almost importunate desire to help. And here, as in the Admiralty, the whole of these days is marked by a complete and utter absence of red tape—a swift, deliberate and absolute abandonment of any rules or restrictions which might tend to hamper the mighty effort that had sprung so swiftly into being.

In addition to these efforts the army itself proposed to assist directly with landing craft (A.L.C.s), with pontoons from the bridge-building supplies of the Royal Engineers, and with its own collapsible boats. Early on the morning of May 27th at Southampton, s.s. *Clan MacAlister* began loading the A.L.C.s, carrying eight altogether on her shelter deck and upper deck hatches and on her after deck. Accommodation was also arranged for forty-five naval ratings to man the landing craft, and the whole party was placed under Commander Cassidi, R.N., with two R.N.V.R. lieutenants in charge of the landing craft themselves. At 6.30 p.m. the ship left for the Downs.

4

Meanwhile it was essential to maintain the flow that had already begun. It is never possible to draw a hard and fast line between the ending of one day's operations and the beginning of the next, but at 4 o'clock in the morning fresh ships were already under way for Dunkirk. At this hour two coasters, the s.s. *Yewdale* and the motor vessel *Sequacity* sailed from the Downs. The report of Captain J. MacDonald, the master of *Sequacity*, is an admirable essay in objectiveness. He says:

'All went well until we arrived off Calais, then I noticed some shells falling in the water ahead of us. I then thought it was land batteries ashore firing at some mines, but soon after the shells started dropping all round my ship, and one came through the port side, at the water line in the main hold and went out the starboard side.

'I sent my mate down in to the hold with some of the crew to try and patch the hold up. The next shot came through the port side of the engine-room and smashed up the auxiliary engines that drove our dynamo, etc., put our switchboard out of action, and went out the starboard side.

'This put our pumps entirely out of action for pumping water out of the hold.

'Another shot came through the wheelhouse and went through the hatches, down the forehold, and right through the ship's bottom.

'We then shaped our course away from the shore and the *Yewdale* which was outside of us did likewise.

'In the meantime eleven German planes appeared overhead and bombed both the *Yewdale* and ourselves. Another shell burst over our fiddley and put the Bren gun out of action, and wounded the chief engineer.

'Meanwhile the wind increased and caused a nasty chop on the sea, which allowed a lot of water to come through the hole in our side, and as we were unable to pump our hold out the ship began to take a nasty list.

'I blew for the *Yewdale* to stand by us, but he did not appear to notice our signal. A British plane then appeared and saw the trouble we were in, and flew ahead to the *Yewdale* and dropped some red flares.

'The *Yewdale* then returned to us, and we launched our lifeboat, and then after we got aboard the *Yewdale* she went down by the head and sunk.

'I should add that in addition to the two soldiers that worked our Bren gun, before we left the Downs we took on a young naval rating named Evans with Lewis guns. We had to fix these on the open bridge, and all the time we were being attacked by the planes he kept up incessant fire with the Lewis guns and stuck his job manfully.

'The *Yewdale* landed us at Ramsgate. . . .'

The report of the master of the *Yewdale*, Captain Edgar Jones, is equally unimpassioned, but it explains his brief failure to come back to his sinking consort. He was engaged whilst still under fire in picking up 'five men on a raft who said they were soldiers who had left Calais in the dark. They informed me that they believed that Dunkirk had been captured by Germans.'

The s.s. *Yewglen*, which left some time later, was also attacked. A wireless message at 8.30 stated that she was being bombed by ten aircraft and was making for the Downs.

The transport *Biarritz* left Dover about half an hour after *Sequacity* and *Yewdale*. While steaming along the French coast 6 miles east-north-east of Calais the batteries opened fire on her. She was at times surrounded by shell splashes, and in another extraordinarily factual account her master, Captain W. H. Baker, says:

'While passing Gravelines en route to Dunkirk we engaged the attention of enemy artillery on shore. The first shell entered the forward boiler room, piercing first a large-diameter oil fuel vapour and overflow pipe and then the auxiliary steam pipe to forward. The nose passed through the further side of the hull on the water line while various minor damage was done by fragments, one entering the starboard wing fuel tank and another passing through the left thigh of Fireman A. Phillips, severing the main artery, and causing great loss of blood.

'Steam at full boiler pressure was entering the boiler room in great quantities. Further shells were hitting the region of the first hit and danger of severe scalding and of an outbreak of fire were the conditions under which Fireman Phillips then found himself. Notwithstanding, he made efforts to close the oil fuel supply to the furnaces of the two forward boilers. That he was unable to do so will occasion no surprise. As it was, he retained sufficient strength to climb two flights of ladders out of the boiler room where he was met by myself and he reported that he had been unable to shut off the fires. He then collapsed.

'Fireman A. Phillips died on the night of May 27th as a direct result of his wound. In this connection it must be stated that Fourth Engineer E. Terry, who was in charge of the forward boiler had left the room in pursuance of his duties only a minute or two previous to the event.

'Meanwhile in the after boiler room Mr. Crockhart in charge, on hearing the explosion of the shells and the subsequent escape of steam, sent his two firemen on deck to ascertain the happenings and to assist if required. He closed the supply of fuel to the forward boilers and then began to encounter very great difficulty in maintaining steam pressure and water level in boilers.

'Due to the necessity of keeping way on the ship to get out of range and to avoid stopping in the minefield into which the ship had to be turned, it was imperative to keep fires under the three after boilers in spite of the fact that at times the water could not be seen in the gauge glasses. It was impossible for a time even to locate the damage in the forward boiler room. . . .

'In addition Archibald Crofts, 2nd steward, received a wound in the back and John Groves a slight wound in the leg. . . .'

At approximately the same time *Archangel*, very close to the same position, came under heavy attack and was damaged and compelled to return.

At 6.30 the hospital carrier *Isle of Thanet* made another attempt, still trying the short route, but at 8 o'clock off Calais she was shelled by the usual batteries. A vessel a little ahead of her was fired upon by a new battery apparently from the heights above Les Hemmes. The Germans had been swift to put their new gains to advantage.

At 11 o'clock a convoy of four ships—the transports *St. Helier* and *Royal Daffodil* and the hospital carriers *St. Julien* and *St. Andrew*—left for Dunkirk escorted by two destroyers. They took the outer passage. The new route involved a round trip of 172 miles; the old route through Calais Roads had made a round trip of 80: the loss of time had to be accepted.

The convoy was attacked—inevitably. There was no shell-fire on the new crossing, but bombers picked up the ships off the Middlekirk Bank buoy. The first stick of bombs fell close to *St. Andrew*, the second on *St. Julien*'s starboard quarter. The Germans were dropping heavy bombs now, and most of the ships were more or less severely shaken. On the way down the inner channels through the sands they were under constant attack, and when they reached Dunkirk pierheads there were enemy formations overhead. *St. Helier* and *Royal Daffodil* entered at 4.20 p.m., and, as if this were a signal, the harbour was immediately subjected to very heavy bombing. The other ships lying in the roads were also severely attacked, and when *St. Helier* was sent out again and passed a signal to the effect that owing to the danger of blocking the harbour it was impossible for ships at present to enter, the convoy re-formed and returned to Dover. *Royal Daffodil*, however, picked up 900 men before she herself came out.

5

In the early afternoon the transport *St. Seiriol* left in company with the motor vessel *Queen of the Channel* by the long route. They began lifting troops at once, but when *Queen of the Channel* had about fifty men on board she and *St. Seiriol* were ordered to move out and lie off the beaches, picking up troops from the sands with their boats. This is important, for it was the virtual beginning of the new policy. During daylight hours a start had been made: first the destroyer *Sabre* (Commander B. Dean, R.N.) had picked up men, using her small boats, then drifters and Dutch skoots had joined in the work; but this was the first time large transports were employed in this manner.

The beaches were not yet organized, but skeletal arrangements were in being, and La Panne, Bray-Dunes and Malo-les-Bains were each allotted to one of the three British corps, while military beach parties were improvised at those points to work with the naval parties. Lord Gort says in his dispatches that during daylight hours on the 27th no more than 200 men were embarked from the sands. Before darkness set in, however, this number was being considerably augmented. *Queen of the Channel* herself picked up 200 men, sending four of her boats away for the purpose. *St. Seiriol* had sent her boats away when she received fresh orders to return to the Mole as by this time large concentrations of troops had assembled there. This was at 10 p.m. Her master, Captain R. D. Dobb, says:

'I got alongside the Mole in a very short time and embarked 600 soldiers and left the Mole at about midnight. I went back to look for my lifeboats but as they were being used to convey troops from the beach to other craft I proceeded to Dover via the Calais route as ordered by a destroyer. During the voyage I was again attacked by aircraft but got away without being hit.'

This coldly matter-of-fact statement gives very little of the actual picture. *St. Seiriol* was a peace-time passenger ship. She carried normally thousands of holiday-makers to the North Wales holiday ports. All this night, still with many of her peace-time crew on board, she was working under heavy bombing and in darkness on a strange and dangerous coast, working in and out of a narrow harbour entrance already impeded with sunken wrecks, with dangerous cross-currents swirling across it, with destroyers moving off it and through it at high speeds. She was doing boat work for which her men had never been trained on difficult and dangerous beaches, and everything she did was underlined and underscored by the note of urgency. Her chief officer, Mr. J. McNamee, is a little—only a very little—more explicit, but his picture is by that little a clearer and more graphic one:

'There was an air raid in progress as we arrived alongside. Our guns with others were in action. We landed a man on the pier to hang on to our ropes. About 8 p.m. Lieutenant-Commander Williams, R.N., came on board and told the captain to proceed out of the harbour, lower his boats, and get the men on board from the beach. We got to the anchorage. I lowered the first boat in charge of the second officer and the second boat in charge of R. Thomas, A.B. The third boat was taken by the crew of a trawler.

'When I was about to lower the fourth boat we received information that there were a number of troops arriving at the pier. With the remainder of the crew we still had on board we proceeded alongside the pier. We got about 600 men on board, they were arriving in batches, about 11 p.m. we were told there were no more men in the vicinity, so we cut our mooring ropes. On hearing more men running along the pier we got the ship alongside the pier again and got about 80 more men on board. During our stay alongside the pier we had four air raids. While we were leaving the pier the enemy dropped illuminated parachutes which lit up the whole sea front. Our captain backed the vessel up the harbour under the smoke screen made available to us from the burning town of Dunkirk.

'We then proceeded to try and pick up our boats and crew, but were ordered by a destroyer to proceed to Dover via Calais. When off Calais we were attacked by bombs and machine-gun fire, the plane coming down to the level of the navigation bridge, but fortunately for us a destroyer was passing at the time and came into action and the plane was destroyed. . . .'

St. Seiriol got away early on the 28th and returned without incident.

Queen of the Channel, leaving at approximately the same time, was lost. Her loss properly belongs to the story of Tuesday.

An hour after *St. Seiriol* and *Queen of the Channel* had left, *Canterbury* sailed again. Arriving almost simultaneously with the others she picked up 457 troops, the majority of them wounded, including 140 stretcher cases, and left within an hour. As she left she was given orders by the Senior Transport Officer to turn back ships as conditions were becoming dangerous again. Meanwhile *Isle of Thanet* had made a second attempt. Leaving Dover at 5 o'clock, she was in the Dunkirk East Roads at 9.15 p.m. accompanied by the hospital carrier *Worthing*, who had joined her on the way across, having no charts. *Canterbury* passed this signal to *Maid of Orleans*, which had sailed shortly after her from the Downs, to *Isle of Thanet* and to *Worthing*, and her master reports that throughout the return journey enemy aircraft were dropping flares over the route.

Isle of Thanet followed her, reaching Dover just after 2 o'clock. *Isle of Thanet* then received orders to proceed to Newhaven, and immediately afterwards she was in collision with the examination vessel *Ocean Reward*. *Ocean Reward* heeled over and sank at once, and though *Isle of Thanet* lowered her boats to search, and the tug *Lady Brassey* came out from Dover to assist, no survivors were found. *Isle of Thanet* was badly damaged and made no further runs.

6

While these things were happening across the corner of the North Sea the armada of the little ships was getting under way. The first area dealt with was that of the River Thames, but the calls on the Essex yachting centres and along the south coast ports were simultaneous. Perhaps the easiest way of describing what happened is to quote once again actual experience. Dr. B. A. Smith, in his description of the work of his motor yacht *Constant Nymph*, says:

'At 12.10 in the early morning of May 27th the Admiralty rang up to confirm that my boat was ready for sea, and arranged for four hours' notice.

'At 8.45 the Admiralty rang up again and asked me to go to the boat. Having already put a few things in a bag I went to Isleworth as soon as possible and arrived there between 10 and 11. It was obvious that some form of permit would be required as my own permit only carried to Middle Blythe Buoy, and my instructions were to take the boat to Sheerness. I found at the boathouse that a naval officer was expected who would issue the permits and was requisitioning other boats in the same yard.

'He wanted the boats to go down together, but separate permits were issued by the afternoon so that I was then ready to start at any time, and the others did not look like being ready for several hours.

'At about 5.30 p.m. I tried to ring up the "Mate" as I felt sure he would want to be in on this game and might at least be able to help me work the boat down to Sheerness. Luckily he was home early and put such a jerk into things that he got his things together and arrived from Tulse Hill to

Isleworth before 7.30, and we started at 8.30 without waiting for the other boats. . . .'

This was the spirit of the small boats—the spirit of urgency that ran through every movement that was made. *Constant Nymph* was ready—'we started without waiting for the other boats'!

7

Meanwhile Vice-Admiral Ramsay's naval force was increasing steadily. On May 27th more of the 1st Flotilla, which had been screening across the area of the North Sea out of Harwich on the latitude of Yarmouth, was sent down to replace ships already damaged.

The second of the Polish destroyers, *Blyskawica*, went this day. Her captain says that even from his patrol line off Yarmouth on the 26th he could see in the night the red glare of Dunkirk to the south. On the 27th, with the British destroyer in whose company she was patrolling, *Blyskawica* went south and established a new line along the swept channel which had been cleared towards the Dunkirk shallows. All through the day she helped to shepherd the increasing flotillas of the evacuation. That night, with two of her British flotilla mates, she received orders to go into Dunkirk. At midnight, and in a heavy bombing attack, they reached the entrance to the harbour. One plane of the attack detached itself from its formation and came down to less than 1,000 feet, spraying *Blyskawica's* decks with machine-gun bullets. The Pole opened fire in reply and the plane crashed shortly afterwards. Still under desultory attack she put her boats in the water to pick up men from the beaches in obedience to instructions, but at 1.45 a.m. these orders were cancelled and she was sent back to work on patrol, this time in the vicinity of the North Goodwin light vessel.

On this day the destroyers began to act as transports themselves. They had carried small numbers of men before, but it was on the 27th that serious loading began. Those loads were one of the most astonishing features of the evacuation, for a destroyer is not built to carry men. Below decks there is little space; in the after-section only the small wardroom and the officers' cabins; amidships nothing save the ordered confusion of the engines and boilers; for'ard only the mess-decks, small even for the crew. Most of the men then had to be carried on deck: but a destroyer is built with a comparatively narrow margin of stability, and most of these ships were old destroyers on to which much top-weight of new gadgets, conceived since their designing, had been added. With the weight of guns, ammunition lockers, depth charges and the heavy superstructure there was little margin of safety. Men who stood on the quays at Dover were horrified at the shape in which some of these ships limped in, heeling at fantastic angles. But in Dover they were in the calm of harbour waters. In the channels off Dunkirk they had had to fight their guns, to return the fire of shore batteries and of aircraft, and to take the violent avoiding action that alone means safety from falling bombs, with these loads on board. It is a strange and wonderful story.

Vivacious (Lieutenant-Commander F. R. W. Parish, R.N.), for example, was attacked on passage by twenty-five aircraft. More than a hundred bombs were counted falling close to her. She brought down two of the attackers, very severely damaged a third, and came safely through.

This day is notable too by reason of the fact that the old destroyer *Sabre* made her first crossing, picking up—as has been said—a load of men from the beaches. She was destined to set up the Dunkirk record of ten successive passages. One of the oldest destroyers in service, she was built in 1918, a 900-ton ship of the Admiralty 'S' class, intended originally for minelaying operations.

Gallant (Lieutenant-Commander C. P. F. Brown, R.N.) and *Greyhound* (Commander W. R. Marshall-A'Deane, R.N.) were also amongst the destroyers who made the crossing.

The naval losses this day, despite the difficulties and the increasing number of ships engaged, were not heavy. The worst incident took place on board H.M.S. *Mona's Isle*, one of the Isle of Man pleasure steamers, which was in commissioned service as an armed boarding vessel. Returning with a full load of troops, she was bombed a little after she was clear of the narrow channels, and had some forty men killed on her upper deck and seventy wounded. She was left out of control, but the prompt action of destroyers in the vicinity broke up the attack, and she was still afloat when the tugs *Lady Brassey* and *Simla* reached her from Dover and towed her in to safety.

Though *Mona's Isle* was the only important casualty of the day, attacks from the air were numerous, not only on shipping but on the town itself, the harbour, and on the roads where the troops were streaming back into the perimeter. Once again we scored a qualitative victory, the figures this time being approximately 50 German planes destroyed for the loss of 14 of our own: 29 more Germans were seriously damaged. The first plane to be destroyed was a Messerschmitt 109 at 6 a.m., the last was a Dornier 215 at 9 p.m. For fifteen hours air cover of a sort was maintained, but once again it was not sufficient. Attacks continued throughout the day, and our loss was heavy.

8

Despite the tremendous work of the destroyers and minor war vessels, despite the efforts of the personnel carriers, the day was a failure. The beach loading during the first three-quarters of the day was pathetically inadequate in its results. Partly this was due to the fact that strings of ships' boats being towed over in the early hours had been cut down and the boats scattered in accidental collisions. The drifters and trawlers, the minesweepers and destroyers that were to take the flow from the beaches had to lie in the deep water. Their own boats, with their crews working themselves to utter exhaustion in the ferry, could lift only at a tragically slow rate. From the harbour five troopships which got in lifted between them 3,952 men, but from the beaches all the minor war vessels and the destroyers lifted less than 2,000 and the day's total was under 6,000. There were still more than 300,000 men of the B.E.F. apart from the French to lift.

MONDAY, MAY 27TH

And now another factor was threatening to enter the already complex and difficult situation. The weather, which had been excellent all through the first two days, was threatening to break up. There was a depression of ominous dimensions in the Atlantic. Its general movement was north, but there was a possibility that it might shift a little to the eastward. Its fringe would pass over the western portions of the British Isles and the slightest alteration would bring it over the Channel and the North Sea.

CHAPTER IX

TUESDAY, MAY 28TH

1

At midnight on May 27th the King of the Belgians capitulated. Lord Gort in his dispatches says:

'While at the Bastion (in Dunkirk), General Koeltz asked me, shortly after 11 p.m., whether I had yet heard that H.M. the King of the Belgians had asked for an armistice from midnight that night. This was the first intimation I had received of this intention, although I had already formed the opinion that the Belgian Army was now incapable of offering serious or prolonged resistance to the enemy. I now found myself suddenly faced with an open gap of 20 miles between Ypres and the sea through which enemy armoured forces might reach the beaches.'

The hours that followed are amongst the most dramatic of the whole evacuation. Despite the efforts he had made the previous day to counter the possible defection of the Belgian Army, Lord Gort, away from his headquarters and without information, could not know what measure of success had been attained, and now in this critical hour, partly owing to the breakdown of the attempt to keep the perimeter clear of traffic, he was unable to get back to Houtkerque where his headquarters were. For five and a half hours he was struggling through the crowded madness of the roads. No one who has not driven against the retreat of an army can imagine that return. In darkness, driving through blind columns of men, through jammed vehicles and broken-down transport, past bomb craters and damaged bridges, he got back eventually to Houtkerque—and the dispositions he had made stood! His prevision and the admirable work of Sir Ronald Adam and Brigadier Lawson had closed the gap. The beaches were safe.

There has been much discussion of the action of the King of the Belgians. This is no place for an examination of his decision. It was a disaster, but it seems clear from the Gort dispatches that it was—in principle at least—an inevitable disaster. The Belgian Army was already defeated. Whether it might have held on for another twenty-four hours, whether a section of it could have retreated towards the Yser as was originally agreed, are questions which cannot be decided here.

The main failure of Belgium, however, came long before King Leopold's request for an armistice. That failure lay in the blind clinging to an impossible neutrality, in the refusal to face the obvious facts of German aggression, in the failure to provide against possibilities. The Belgians are not to be blamed for the major disaster of the Flanders campaign. But to the failure of Belgian preparations, the obstinate refusal to provide information to the

Allies or to attempt anything in the nature of staff talks, must be attributed much of the speed and the completeness of the collapse—at least upon the northern flank.

The collapse was to have no immediate effect on the evacuation. By the foresight of the British High Command much of its harm was discounted. But inevitably it would bring the Germans, as swiftly as they could move their artillery, within range of the beaches and of the Zuydecoote Pass. The sands were running out.

2

And, matching the urgency of the hour, across the North Sea the little ship flotillas were gathering. From Deal and Dover and Ramsgate they were beginning to move across.

'I am writing the letter on behalf of myself, Harry Brown, and Fred Hook who were the crew of the *Gipsy King*, a small motor-boat. We went to Dunkirk on May 28th. We stayed there about forty-eight hours. We were under shell-fire and machine-gun fire. We stayed there till every British soldier was off the beach. I should like to mention Harry Brown who did a brave action. We just loaded boat with troops. We saw a pontoon with soldiers in, being swamped with waves. Brown, being the swimmer, decided to go over the side with a rope, he tied it to the pontoon and saved the soldiers from being drowned. I am writing this letter as Fred Hook and Harry Brown are in the minesweepers.

'If this letter is satisfactory please would you give me a reply.

'A. BETTS.'

Gipsy King was a Deal beach boat: her crew were lineal descendants of the famous Deal hovellers. These simple facts need no elaboration.

All along the south coast the little ships were moving. Mr. Button of Littlehampton was working in the shipyard that lines the Littlehampton quay when he was asked to stand by to take *Green Eagle* to sea after dark. With him went *White Lily* and *Hilda*.

Down London River from Hampton Wick, Kingston, Teddington, at the end of the tideway, from Richmond and Hammersmith and the river below bridges, they were moving out.

'The hall porter of the flats handed us a message, received by telephone, which requested us to immediately get in touch with the boat-yard at Teddington at which the motor-yacht *Advance* was temporarily "laid up".

'On doing so we learned that the Admiralty had taken over the ship, together with ten other privately owned craft and "would we please remove all our gear".

'Arriving at Teddington we found that the boat-yard people had already taken ashore most of our personal gear and all that was left for us to do was to go on board for a final farewell, we not knowing her final destination or fate.

'*Advance* was a 40-footer, with a beam of 11 ft. 6 in., an open bridge, and a 140 h.p. Thornycroft engine. We found that all the boats taken over by the Admiralty were to be away by 7.30 on the following morning, May 28th, and we also learned that there was an acute shortage of crews and volunteered to take her ourselves to Sheerness, this being her first call.'

Messrs. Dick, Hamilton-Piercey and McGuffie took her to Sheerness and by sheer persistence took her on again from there.

From the Docks the ships' lifeboats that had been stripped from cargo boats, liners and tramp steamers were already on the way. The Southend boats were ready to sail, the Canvey Island boats—'Round the Nore lightship for a shilling!' . . . 'Out to the Mouse and back!' . . . 'Cruise to the Chapman Light!'

3

The plans that the Small Vessels Pool had worked out in the brief hours at its disposal were well in hand. To the lay eye the movement of these little ships might have seemed ragged in these early hours. The professional eye knows that something of a miracle was achieved by this handful of naval officers and the officials of the Ministry of Shipping.

And at Sheerness Rear-Admiral Taylor's organization was beginning to function with a high degree of speed and efficiency. All through Tuesday the work in the ancient tidal basin of Sheerness dockyard and outside it went on. By five minutes after noon the tug *St. Clears* was got away in company with *Sun V*, towing between them twenty naval cutters with half crews, seventy of these being on board *St. Clears* under Commander Hayward, R.N.R. In the course of the afternoon further small craft were sent away, amongst them the motor-boat *Reda*. One or two Thames river steamers also left on this afternoon, one of them at least breaking down and having to return. A little later the motor-boat *Vera* sailed, but broke down twice during the night and did not reach Ramsgate until Wednesday afternoon.

These breakdowns have a simple explanation. It lies in the fact that neither private motor-yachts nor public pleasure boats function normally off the coast of England in the winter period, and this was the end of a war winter. Most of these boats had been laid up for seven or eight months, many of them for more than that. A marine motor, however carefully 'put to bed' for the winter, needs an overhaul again in the spring: parts rust up, wires corrode, the inevitable deterioration of idleness affects everything that moves. The spring 'fitting-out' season is one of the most important periods of the yachting year. Most owners take from two to three weeks to get their boats ready for the quiet pleasures of a summer's cruising.

These boats had been got ready in two to three hours, and they left their moorings not to cruise gently to the next quiet harbour, but to thrust straight out to the difficulties and dangers of the long cross-sea passage to Dunkirk. Rear-Admiral Taylor's staff at Sheerness and the maintenance officers at the other ports did all that they could in the brief time at their disposal. But some of the craft did not survive even the run down the river. Most of them left Sheerness and went into that sea of danger in a condition that would have horrified their owners in times of peace. Some of them broke down between Sheerness and Ramsgate, some of them broke down on the way across; but the eternal marvel of the small boats is that so many of them survived to keep their engines running for days on end, to carry loads that would have appalled their designers, to work in foul water that was a mass of fuel oil, stirred-up sand, ropes' ends, discarded clothing and floating wreckage of every kind, size and shape. Enough of them survived to achieve a miracle.

4

It was the working of fate that even as the small boats began to cross the weather broke. The depression that was reported on the Monday sweeping up the Atlantic, moved as predicted to the north. Off the west coast of Ireland the gale blew. In the Irish Sea there were strong winds, but across southern England and up the Channel there came only the fringes of the secondary. It blew—not hard, but hard enough. Over the shoals the sea was breaking. The long sandbanks that edged the Dunkirk channel were white with surf and in the channel itself a vicious chop set up and drove in on the shallows of the beaches. They were not big seas. To a swimmer they would have been no more than a joyous surf, but to men handling waterlogged craft over-weighted with exhausted soldiers, to men rowing heavy ships' boats for the first time, handling long sweeps without previous experience, they meant something only a little short of disaster.

A legend has arisen that through the evacuation the weather was on our side. Much of it was. One great gale at the height of the beach work would have cost us 30,000 men. But, though we were spared the great gale, we had the lesser ones; we had fog; we had haze that made the crowded channels in the hours of darkness a grim and furious nightmare. Hour after hour as the fog held, as the haze drifted up and down the channel, as the smoke came roaring out of Dunkirk, the list of collisions mounted—ships sunk, ships damaged and out of action, men drowning in the thick obscurity of night.

5

The first casualty of the day was not actually a Dunkirk ship, but she was on the Dunkirk route—the northern route as it was called—and her loss is the first recorded sinking during the operation of an important ship by E-boats. On May 25th the s.s. *Abukir* had sailed for Ostend. She arrived there to find the sea front in ruins and the town in flames following heavy air raids. The pilot who berthed the ship informed her master, Captain R. M. Woolfenden, when the ship was alongside, that apart from a few French naval officers there was no one of any authority in the port. In his report her master says:

'I interviewed these officers who apparently had no knowledge of my ship, but suggested that I should start discharging at daybreak.

'On the way back to the ship I met a British Army lorry driver who told me that a Lieutenant Harris with thirty-eight British troops who were adrift from their units were standing by at a farm about 5 miles outside the town. We went out and brought them in but on our arrival back at the ship we were bombed so intensely—the quay being the target—that I decided to abandon the ship until daylight. At 2 a.m. on May 26th I managed to get into telephone communication with the British Mission at Bruges, who instructed me to commence discharging, which I did with the assistance of the troops and the ship's crew. We were bombed off and on throughout the day. Later on the British Mission informed me that a British bomber had made a forced landing at Ostend and would I try to make contact with her crew. Lieutenant Harris and myself located these men at the Stane aerodrome. After firing the machine, the two officers and two men who formed her crew joined my ship later on in the afternoon, bringing with them the machine-guns and instruments of the destroyed bomber. On the way back from the aerodrome we picked up another twenty-five British troops who had also been separated from their units, also two wounded R.A.F. men.

'At 8 p.m. on May 26th the bombing became so intense that once again we abandoned the ship until daybreak, resuming work with the assistance of Dutch Army men. Throughout the day German aircraft were continually bombing us and at 3 p.m. they started dive-bombing and machine-gunning us so heavily that once again I decided to abandon the ship, having had two casualties, one being an R.A.F. gunner shot in the arm and a Belgian civilian shot in the left eye. Getting through to Bruges again they instructed me to cease discharging and to load what army vehicles I could, the rest to be destroyed, also the British Mission had decided to evacuate by my ship that night.

'I suggested sailing after dark at 10 p.m., to which they agreed. The Mission boarded me and at the stated time I cut my lines and sailed with approximately 220 people on board including crew, soldiers and Belgian refugees. I was followed out of the port by the British s.s. *Marquis*. On clearing the entrance enemy aircraft flew over dropping Very lights and bombs. A call for assistance was sent out as Mr. Newman of the British Mission had previously informed me that an escort consisting of two destroyers would be waiting for me off the port. This attack lasted for half an hour when the aircraft returned to Ostend.

'Avoiding the regular channel, I steered direct for the North Goodwin Light Vessel hoping to miss any enemy craft that may have been waiting for me off the buoys. At 12.15 a.m., when approaching the North Hinder Buoy, I heard the second officer, Mr. Rust, give the order hard a-starboard and I saw a torpedo crossing our course about 50 feet ahead of the ship. The machine-gun was manned immediately by R.A.F. gunners whom I ordered to fire immediately on sighting the craft, while the ship's gunner, Church, was sent aft to stand by the smoke boxes. An S.O.S. was sent out and we commenced zig-zagging, no sign of the escort having appeared.

'About half an hour after the first attack we avoided a second torpedo which was fired from the port side and passed about 20 feet astern, followed almost immediately by a third which also missed us. Five minutes after the third attack I sighted the enemy craft which turned out to be a coastal motor-boat about 300 feet on the port beam. The order was passed to the gunners to fire immediately they got the enemy on their sights and I went hard a-port to try and ram the craft. Our machine-gun got a burst of fire in but the motor-boat withheld her fire until we were about 150 feet off her when she fired her fourth torpedo which I was unable to avoid, being so close. This torpedo struck us at an angle underneath the bridge on the port side.

'The concussion was terrific and I had a vague idea of the bridge collapsing and finding myself down the fore hold, fortunately floating out and clear when the ship settled by the head. After the ship had foundered, which I reckon she did in a minute and a half, the E-boat turned her searchlight on us and machine-gunned us. There must have been quite a few killed then.

'At daybreak three or four ships passed us without seeing us, but at 7 a.m. a flotilla of H.M. destroyers picked us up. The kind treatment we received on board is beyond all praise.

'As you can see from this report, there was no time to lower the boats, but A.B. Carrol managed to slip one of the life rafts which was later on filled by Belgian refugees. This raft, I regret to say, received the brunt of the enemy machine-gun fire, wiping out nearly all the occupants.

'As to what caused the death of the chief officer I am unable to say. He appeared to be all right after the action as I was speaking to him in the water, but did not see him after daylight.

'I would like to say a word in praise of my officers and crew. Throughout the intense bombing in Ostend they carried out their work with extreme coolness and cheerfulness, and during the three-quarters of an hour engagement with the E-boat there was at no time any sign of panic. I would like to mention in particular L. Tanner, sailor, who was at the wheel during the engagement. Although only a lad of barely nineteen years of age, he carried out my orders with precision and coolness. . . .'

The E-boats were coming in, hanging on the outskirts of the movement like jackals on the flanks of a migration. The destroyers had a new and arduous addition to their task.

The loss of the *Abukir* was followed by the sinking of the *Queen of the Channel*.

'After sailing at about 4.15 a.m., half an hour before sunrise,' says Captain W. J. O'Dell, her master, 'an aeroplane was observed approaching on the starboard bow about 2,000 feet up, distinguishing marks not being decipherable, this plane circled and dived when on the port beam. Lewis-gun fire was then opened from the ship, but three or four bombs had then been released which straddled the ship a little abaft the mainmast. The slight delay action of these bombs caused an upward explosion which broke the vessel's back, the starboard propeller shaft and rudder, the stern dipping into the water. The wireless aerial had also carried away and No. 5 boat was blown across the deck.

'Lewis-gun fire was continued as guns were able to bear, the aeroplane again circled and approached the port bow, dropping more bombs which fell about 100 feet away and, after apparently passing through two lines of tracer bullets from the forward two guns, the plane flew away to the eastward.

'Meanwhile the aerial had been rehoisted, and an S.O.S. sent out, the four remaining boats swung out, and the troops [she had picked up 920 off the beaches and the Mole] ordered on the loud speakers to vacate the after end of the ship and walk forward, in order to lift the after end as much as possible.

'A slight electric wire fire was extinguished in the after dining saloon.' Pumps were started on the two after lower saloons. Reports from carpenter showed that water was making rapidly in the after four compartments, therefore orders were given to lower away boats and fill them. This work proceeded in good order.

"The s.s. *Dorrien Rose* (Master, Captain William Thompson), a store ship proceeding to Dunkirk, was standing by and, as the weather was fine, was requested to come alongside forward and the two vessels were secured port bow to starboard bow to prevent troops all going to one side and listing the *Queen of the Channel*.

'The troops were then ordered over the rail to the other ship, this work proceeded smoothly, the lifeboats meanwhile making an extra passage, having discharged their troops into the *Dorrien Rose*.

'By 5.20 a.m. all troops had been transferred. A further inspection was made, and water was found to be gaining in the steward's store-room and engine-room and by this time the bow was out of the water. It was therefore decided to abandon ship. Confidential papers were collected and final transfer was completed by 5.25.

'The *Dorrien Rose* let go and proceeded to Dover, arrival being at 2.30 p.m., and the passage being without further untoward incident, and during part of it the destroyer *Greyhound* acted as escort. The four lifeboats were towed for extra security in case of further attack, but during the passage two broke away and were lost.'

E-boats and air—the pace of danger was quickening.

6

This day the beaches were worked again, largely by drifters, minesweepers and destroyers with assistance from some of the personnel ships and the coasters. There exist a number of accounts of the beaches at this time from both points of view—those of the soldiers and those of the seamen. One of the best of the soldiers' accounts is given by Sir Basil Bartlett.[1] He reached Dunkirk in an air raid on the morning of the 27th, at a time when raids were coming in every ten minutes and, endeavouring to get information in the shattered town, learned for the first time that the only hope was to destroy his matériel and make for the harbour.

By the afternoon, when he brought his men in, it was impossible to get to the Town Major's office where he had picked up his first instructions. Leaving

[1] *My First War* (Chatto & Windus).

some of his men in the town with orders to make a dash for any ship they saw, he took the rest out to Malo-les-Bains and thence to the sandbanks along the beach. For the first time he learned here that the navy was coming in with small boats and, on investigation, found that his own corps staff had already been taken off in a destroyer an hour before. All through that night, as the boats came in, he helped to load parties aboard. The French, he says, were very worried and kept demanding passes and papers.

The following day he describes as 'unpleasant', bombing and machine-gunning continuing at intervals from daybreak. On this day, the 28th, he went to Dunkirk and found it impossible to move in the town except on foot, the streets being blocked with the ruins of the houses. Again and again in his dispassionate, factual account he pays little tributes to the navy.

'In spite of the shelling and the bombing, however, I'm told that the Navy achieved the impossible and took off a number of troops from the one remaining jetty during the night.'

And again:

'On the other hand, everyone was much more optimistic than I'd expected. The whole B.E.F. has a blind faith in the Navy.'

All the way through the military accounts of the evacuation there are to be found similar tributes. In his excellent account of the retreat 'Gun Buster'[1] describes his final experience on the beaches.

'We tacked ourselves on to the rear of the smallest of the three queues, the head of it was already standing in water up to the waist. Half an hour passed. Suddenly a small rowing boat appeared. The head of the queue clambered in and were rowed away into the blackness. We moved forward, and the water rose to our waists.

'Our only thoughts now were to get on a boat. Along the entire queue not a word was spoken. The men just stood there silently staring into the darkness, praying that a boat would soon appear, and fearing that it would not. Heads and shoulders only showing above the water. Fixed, immovable, as though chained there. . . .'

Eventually the boats came in. Weighed down by the weight of water in his clothing and equipment, 'Gun Buster' had found difficulty in climbing over the side. In the end he was hoisted in by the crew of the boat, falling on his head on the bottom boards.

'From the instant I landed on my head in that lifeboat a great burden of responsibility seemed to fall from my shoulders. A curious sense of freedom took possession of me. All the accumulated strain of the last few hours, of the last day or so, vanished. I felt that my job was over. Anything else that remained to be done was the Navy's business. I was in their hands, and had nothing more to worry about. There and then, on that dark and sinister sea, an indescribable sense of luxurious contentment enveloped me.

'Again the hearty voice of our helmsman:

'"A little bit more to the left, Mr. Jolly. Little bit more to the left. Or we'll hit her in the backside."

[1] *Return Via Dunkirk* (Hodder & Stoughton).

TUESDAY, MAY 28TH

'The unseen Mr. Jolly so contrived as to avoid this disaster, and the grey flank of H.M.S. *Medway Queen*, paddle-steamer, loomed in front of us, her shadowy decks already packed with troops from the beaches. . . .'

There was no embarkation from the beach areas in which Bartlett moved during daylight hours. At noon he describes Malo as becoming congested with men coming out of Dunkirk and at that time he moved his men to Bray-Dunes. Shortly after he reached this he saw a Messerschmitt shot down and, as if to celebrate the occasion, a number of the men stripped and began to bathe. Fresh machine-gun attacks, however, put an end to frivolities.

At 4 o'clock, he says, the navy turned up again. In his sector the loading was being done with destroyers' boats, and it took almost six hours to fill the destroyers to capacity. The two ships working off his beach (one of them was H.M.S. *Grafton*) took about 1,500 men between them. He helped to get the walking wounded from a hospital near the dunes and eventually went off with one of the loads to *Grafton* himself.

From his account much emerges. For the first time, it seems, the B.E.F. was realizing actually what it was up against. Out of his quiet sentences it is possible to assemble a picture of the inchoate mass that was Dunkirk town at this time: the impossibility of getting orders, the breakdown of communications, the blocking of the roads, the incessant shell-fire, bombing and machine gunning. In any assessment of Dunkirk these points must be remembered for because of them it happened over and over again that men came down to the beaches when no ships were there, and that conversely ships went in to the Mole and the jetty under fire or under bombing and found them empty. These things played their inevitable part in making worse the intolerable conditions of the time.

But though the outward flow from the beaches was still inadequate to the task at hand, the total of the liftings was increasing rapidly. By Monday afternoon, as has been stated, the total number lifted from the beginning of the retreat amounted to only 18,000. With the rising crescendo of the lifting over the remainder of Monday afternoon, Monday night and Tuesday, the total was brought by Tuesday midnight to 45,000: 27,000 that is, were lifted between Monday afternoon and Tuesday midnight.

The heaviest loads for the personnel ships throughout the evacuation appear to have been those of *Tynwald* which, according to the official figures, carried 7,500 men in five trips. This figure of 1,500 per trip is greatly in excess of the general average, even for the personnel ships, and the figure of 27,000 over thirty-six hours at this period indicates a very large number of ship movements.

The work, as on the previous days, was heavy, incessant and dangerous. The scale of the enemy attacks was increasing. Where previously planes had been reported in flights of as many as forty, on this day ninety were counted in a single attack. The beaches were strafed from high level, by dive-bombers and by low-flying fighters. The remnants of the harbour and the Mole with the ships berthed alongside were attacked endlessly. The narrow channel—so narrow that in it ships could not dodge aircraft attack, so crowded that any abnormal movement meant collision—echoed throughout the day with the thunder of the bombs. The approaches to the channel east and west were searched relentlessly by the enemy. Gallantly the handful of R.A.F. planes tried to mitigate the fury of the onslaught. There are stories of single planes attacking enormous enemy formations, of small patrols breaking up whole squadrons of bombers, of ships rescued in the very penultimate minute of a bombing attack. The destruction of twenty-two German planes for the loss of thirteen of our own is recorded.

But courage was not enough. The tally of our losses mounted. The incessant mining of the enemy and the dangers of sweeping the new passage across the shoals cost us two trawlers. We lost another minesweeper by collision in the height of a raid, and we lost three drifters to bombing. In addition to *Abukir* and *Queen of the Channel* the Southern Railway Company's *Lorina*, a ship of 1,600 tons, was attacked by dive-bombers and a hit amidships broke her back. An attempt was made to beach her, but she sank in shallow water with her top-sides still above the tide. Eight men were lost in the course of the attack.

7

The hospital carriers were busy again this day. The report of *St. David's* voyage says:

'The weather was very misty, and navigation made very difficult owing to the lack of the usual aids to navigation and the fact that many vessels had been sunk in the fairways since her last leaving that port. At 8 o'clock that evening she entered Dunkirk, where she remained until the next morning.

'During the whole of the night the town, quays, etc., were subjected to terrific bombardment by air and land, and it became necessary, owing to the lack of R.A.M.C. ashore, for the seamen, firemen, stewards, etc., to load the wounded themselves, carrying them down the quay as required, with the medical staff on board receiving the wounded and placing them in the cots, etc.

'This work was exceedingly difficult, as the whole area was in a bad condition, and there were not even any gangways available for passing the stretcher cases on board. However, the engineers constructed a wide and useful gangway, which was used during the whole time of the embarkation. . . .'

These accounts are almost more valuable for the general details they give of conditions within the perimeter than for the description of ships' voyages, magnificent as these were. It is difficult to conceive of the ordinary, the routine troubles with which these ships had to deal. The first of these was unquestionably the almost fantastically perilous navigation. The channels were quite inadequate to the amount of traffic they had to carry. They lay between some of the most dangerous shoals off the coast of Europe. In peacetime these shoals are admirably marked, but now the marks could no longer be depended upon. Some of the light buoys had been sunk by the enemy, some had been sunk by ships swinging wildly to avoid aircraft attack. There was no way of conveying information swiftly to all the vessels involved as to these changes. The weather for a great part of the time was hazy. It was difficult to pick up unlit buoys even in daylight. The black smoke blew at times off the beaches and was ten times as bad as the haze. Added to these things was the constant accretion of new wrecks in the fairways: ships sunk by bombing or by torpedo or by collision. All these the navigators had to contend with, and added to them was the stream of small craft moving at different speeds without lights. These little ships had to be avoided, and somehow for the most part they were avoided. Without machine-gun fire, without shelling from the shore, without bombing, these things alone were enough to shake the nerve of the stoutest seaman.

The account of *Dinard*, which had crossed in the afternoon, underscores these things:

'We had difficulty in finding the channel as several of the light buoys were not functioning. We managed it, however, without any harm coming to us.'

Against Dunkirk Mole itself these 'ordinary' troubles were magnified. The Mole was in no way suited for berthing. Mooring bollards were few and far between. It was difficult to secure ropes. During the period of heavy bombing there were long spells when there was no one on the wooden decking to take the ships' lines as they came alongside; and with the tide running, with unfavourable winds, with sunken ships against the wall, with small craft moving continually, with every circumstance of abnormality in bringing ships alongside, they had to be brought close enough for their own crews to jump to the pier decking and take the lines with them.

And even when made fast there were still difficulties. *St. David* says that her engineers constructed 'a wide and useful gangway'. In other ships men came aboard over mess tables and benches, over single planks, over every possible kind and degree of substitute for gangways. And even when gangways had been provided the shortage of R.A.M.C. personnel ashore rendered it necessary for the weary seamen, stewards and the like, to carry the wounded on board themselves. And it must be remembered always that from this day onward the Mole was not only the target for every German bomber that could be brought to bear, but for the batteries that the Germans had swiftly installed outside Nieuport.

8

It is not to be wondered at that by this time signs of exhaustion were beginning to manifest themselves amongst the crews of some of the ships. The first serious instance of this occurred with the transport *Canterbury*, which from May 19th had been ceaselessly on the move. She had worked at the Hook of Holland, Cherbourg, Boulogne, Calais and now Dunkirk, carrying first refugees and then military personnel. Much of the time she had worked under almost continuous air attack, latterly under shell-fire as well. Her crew were worn out and, on the evening of the 28th, having had no orders since he had oiled the ship at noon, her master decided to shut down steam and give his crew some rest. He granted partial leave. On the following day his chief officer and his chief engineer were instructed to report sick by a naval doctor.

On the 28th also some members of *St. Helier*'s crew protested against the lack of armament and left the ship. Her master applied for a naval crew, and a party of ratings together with a military detachment manning Lewis guns for anti-aircraft protection, embarked on the ship.

St. Seiriol's case is in a slightly different category. Exhaustion was not perhaps the dominant factor here, but her one trip had taken place in extremely severe conditions, and the element of shock on those who had not previously played a part in the acerbities of the Channel in war-time was a very considerable one. An armed guard with a reinforcement of naval stokers under a naval officer was placed on her and she sailed in due course.

These signs of strain were to show in one ship after another as the evacuation proceeded. They were conditioned by physical and nervous exhaustion.

9

The coasters and the personnel ships were also working throughout this day, but a tendency was becoming apparent to move as much as possible in the hours of darkness, a tendency that was inevitable as the daylight loss to bombers grew.

Royal Daffodil was among the many who made trips and brought back full loads during the daylight hours. In the late afternoon *Prague* weighed and proceeded in company with *Manxman* and the hospital carrier *Paris*. Again the question of navigational difficulties arises, and it is essential that this point should be stressed. The account of her master, Captain B. Baxter, is admirably clear:

'During the forenoon the Examination Officer visited the ship and gave me two small charts of the district, and promised to return with a large-scale chart of the Dunkirk district when he had obtained one but this was evidently not possible and the ship made all her passages to and from Dunkirk on small-scale charts only. . . .

'The weather was drizzly and misty, the visibility shortening as the coast of France was approached. The draught of the ship was something over 16 feet and in view of the meagre information about the Zuidcoote Pass which was procurable from the small-scale chart, it was decided to allow the other two ships, both of considerably less draught than *Prague*, to keep ahead, the ships being roughly in single line.

'The great majority of the buoys were unlit, and as remarked above the visibility poor and when very near to the Zuidcoote Pass *Manxman* and *Paris* ran aground on the Smal Bank and *Prague* touched starboard side. *Paris* came off immediately, but *Manxman* stuck for some hours. Meeting one of H.M. sloops, whose Captain very kindly sent a boat with advice of the district and a chart marked in better detail than our own, I realized that it was hopeless for a ship of my draught to attempt the pass at that state of tide and accordingly returned to the vicinity of the Nieuport Bank Buoy and anchored to let the tide rise a few feet. *Manxman* joined us here a few hours later and afterwards acted in concert with us.

'May 29th, 3.55 a.m. Got under way again and proceeded via the pass to Dunkirk and when ordered to enter the port made fast just inside the end of the eastern jetty. Embarkation started almost immediately, the Naval Beachmaster realized our difficulties and loaded us up in time to return through the pass before the tide fell too much as our draught when loaded with troops was estimated to be about 17 feet 6 inches. . . .'

The *Lochgarry*, sailing at 9 o'clock in the evening, was in difficulties before she cleared the Goodwins, and almost rammed the North Goodwin light vessel, which was unlit. She anchored close to the lightship and was shortly afterwards passed by 'five destroyers at full speed without taking the slightest notice'. A little later the *Clan MacAlister* passed her and, as the night was now a little clearer, she heaved up her anchor and followed.

Another of the late convoys to leave consisted of the *Yewdale* (which had taken in stores and water after landing the *Sequacity's* survivors) and the motor vessels *Beal* and *Bullfinch*. They sailed at 10.30 p.m. for La Panne.

The difficulties for all these ships began actually in Dover harbour. To negotiate the appalling crowding of the anchorage in darkness was in itself a feat of seamanship; but outside Dover there was another anchorage, up the Downs and in the Small Downs ships of all sorts were clustered, and the Downs themselves in those days were still full of the wrecks of the bad period of the magnetic mining and of the early days of the bombing. This night too the enemy made an attack on the shipping there—a weak attack, not pressed home and with very few planes. Amongst the major omissions of the Germans during the evacuation was the extraordinary failure to attack Dover, Ramsgate, Margate and the anchorages. But despite this the areas between the Admiralty Pier and Dunkirk Mole were then and after a seaman's nightmare.

10

The naval work increased on this day in the same ratio as the general difficulty. Destroyers were early to the eastward of Dunkirk investigating the changes inevitable upon the fall of the Belgian Army.

Fresh reinforcements in this class of ship were once more clearly necessary, and in point of fact the prevision of Vice-Admiral Ramsay had already arranged them. The remainder of the 1st Flotilla was already on its way south. One division of the flotilla—H.M.S. *Codrington* (Captain G. F. Stevens-Guille, D.S.O., R.N., who commanded the flotilla), H.M.S. *Grenade* (Commander R. C. Boyle, R.N.), H.M.S. *Jaguar* (Lieutenant-Commander J. F. W. Hine, R.N.) and H.M.S. *Javelin* (Commander A. F. Pugsley, R.N.) —was deep in the North Sea on a four-day patrol designed for the protection of the extreme outer flanks of the evacuation area. They were ordered south to lift troops, and on their way in they sighted the survivors of the s.s. *Abukir* in the water. *Codrington* herself picked up thirty-two men. When the rescue was completed they went straight on to Dunkirk, reaching the harbour in the latter part of the morning heavily attacked from the air. For nearly two hours the bombs continued to fall, groups of planes numbering half a dozen at a time coming over the area. *Grenade* berthed at the West Mole, *Codrington* at the East, and each picked up a heavy load of men, *Codrington's* numbering approximately 700, mostly base troops. They returned to Dover at 22 knots, the shallow water preventing any higher speeds.

Codrington, with the others of her flotilla, landed her men, had a brief hour or two of rest, and crossed again that evening. Once more the flotilla's loads were heavy, *Codrington's* being close on 900 men.

Destroyers were everywhere throughout the day—helping the s.s. *Dorrien Rose*, thrusting in to shell the Calais batteries, nursing, advising, cajoling, sometimes bullying the stream of traffic in the swept channels, rescuing airmen from the water, bringing their guns into action every time enemy aircraft swept across the traffic lanes, and in between these things, during them, throughout them, picking up cargoes of khaki-clad men from the beaches and the Moles.

The first heavy cargoes of troops carried by them had reached Dover in the small hours. *Gallant* landed at 4.15 in the morning 900 men. *Greyhound* came in shortly afterwards with 681. *Codrington's* division in the early afternoon landed an average of 700 men per ship. Amongst other destroyers which crossed and picked up men were *Malcolm* (Captain T. E. Halsey, R.N.), *Scimitar* (Lieutenant R. D. Franks, R.N.), *Wolsey* (Lieutenant-Commander C. H. Campbell, R.N.)—which had her degaussing gear put out of action at 1 a.m., but continued to work in these intolerably dangerous waters—and *Harvester* (Lieutenant-Commander M. Thornton, R.N.).

The case of *Harvester* is interesting. She had only just been recommissioned; her crew had been with the ship barely three days; there had been no time to work up. She reached Bray-Dunes on the night of the 28th and sent ashore a party under Sub-Lieutenant E. C. Croswell, R.N., in her motorboat. They remained ashore throughout the night and succeeded in sending off more than 700 men, of whom 100 were wounded. In this area the Sub-Lieutenant reports that discipline among the troops was bad.

These crossings were not accomplished without loss. The 'W' class destroyer *Windsor*, which had performed magnificent service at Boulogne, was hit after repeated attacks from the air by a bomb and seriously damaged.

On this Tuesday (28th) Vice-Admiral Ramsay's heaviest ship, H.M.S. *Calcutta*, the only cruiser to take part in Operation 'Dynamo', came into the news. *Calcutta* was an old light cruiser of the 'C' class of 4,200 tons, built in 1918. In 1939 the ship, too old for normal cruiser duties, was refitted and given a new lease of life as an anti-aircraft cruiser. Under the rearmament she mounted eight 4-inch anti-aircraft guns, one multiple pom-pom, and a number of lighter guns. As anti-aircraft armament went in the early days of the war, this was formidable, and she made a most valuable addition to the anti-aircraft defence of the narrow waters off Dunkirk itself.

Sailing about midnight, she reached La Panne at 2.48 in the morning, worked off the beaches for about four hours, and went to Dunkirk at 6.15 a.m. An hour later she left for Sheerness, carrying 700 men. She was back again off La Panne before midnight.

The work of the Fleet minesweepers was becoming increasingly important. These, in the main, were ships of two types—the 'Halcyon' class and the 'Albury' class. The first were ships of a little over 800 tons, shallow-draught (they only drew a maximum of 8 feet) with a speed of 17 knots, and armed with two 4-inch anti-aircraft guns and five smaller ones. In general appearance they were not unlike small destroyers and are frequently spoken of as such in accounts by the masters of merchant ships and soldiers. The 'Albury' class was similar but rather smaller, carrying only one 4-inch gun, and with a displacement of just over 700 tons. They were capable of 16 knots. Owing to their very shallow draught they were able to work closer in than the destroyers, and throughout the operation until the very last day their work was of the highest importance.

The 'Albury' class were the oldest Fleet sweepers in the navy and the only class of coal-burning ships on the Navy List. Almost inevitably their nickname was the 'Smoky Joes'. This day they made their first crossing, H.M.S. Pangbourne (Commander D. Watson, R.N.) berthing first in the late afternoon. From the Mole she picked up 200 unwounded British troops, and later moved under shell-fire to the quay on the west side where most of the wounded were handled, and lifted a tremendous load of wounded. Cot cases had to be stowed on the open deck, and it is recorded that there were fifteen men in each of the officers' cabins and that some of them even occupied the baths. She left Dunkirk in darkness and headed for a green light buoy, which was one of the principal sea-marks of the homeward passage. Unfortunately the buoy had been bombed, and Commander Watson made his course on what afterwards turned out to be the starboard navigation light of another ship, and ran aground on a sandbank. There was a rising tide, however, and after two hours Pangbourne managed to get off the bank and got to Ramsgate in safety.

With the Fleet minesweepers the paddle-minesweepers were also hard at work. The first paddle-sweepers to reach Dunkirk were those of the 10th Flotilla, which had been working out of Dover. They had been employed on preliminary sweeping operations, but, as the need grew desperate, they were ordered to start lifting men. This flotilla consisted of H.M.M. Sandown (Commander K. M. Greig, R.N.), the new paddle pleasure-steamer H.M.M. Gracie Fields, H.M.M. Medway Queen and H.M.M. Brighton Belle.

The Brighton Belle (Lieutenant-Commander L. Kaye Perrin, R.N.R.) was the oldest paddle-sweeper in service. She had swept mines throughout the first Great War and, had there been mines laid in the Boer War, she could have swept them then; but she crossed valiantly to do her part with the others. She picked up a load of some 800 men on her broad decks and turned to go back to England, but on the return passage she struck the uncharted wreck of a ship that had been sunk by a magnetic mine a couple of hours previously and lay in the middle of the fairway, completely hidden. The impact tore the bottom out of the old paddler, and she sank rapidly. Fortunately *Medway Queen* (Lieutenant A. T. Cook, R.N.R.) was in sight of her as she began to settle, and reached her in time to take off both her crew and her troops. Everybody, including the captain's dog, reached England safely.

The minesweepers, with the bigger naval vessels, with the personnel ships, and with the increasing host of small craft, achieved admirable results this day. By midnight 45,000 men—more than a sixth of the British Expeditionary Force—had come to safety; and at Nieuport and at Furnes, at Bergues and Mardyck the lines were holding. Even in the destruction of the hour there was hope.

CHAPTER X

WEDNESDAY, MAY 29TH

1

The wind had changed on the 29th. There was still through most of the day a surf running on the beaches, but now the smoke was coming off the town and from the burning oil tanks, and it was at times impossible to see the roadstead from the harbour. Finding the harbour entrance was a matter of great difficulty at various periods throughout the day, and over the beaches there hung a choking cloud.

None the less 38,000 men were lifted during the twenty-four hours. It was an incredible achievement—the fruit of courage, of endurance and of sheer brutal toil that is almost without parallel in history. From a score of aspects it was a fantastic day. The nightmares of the night seemed somehow to have extended themselves into the daylight hours.

Ashore, inside the perimeter, the major problem was working itself up with dangerous speed. The French were flooding in over the eastern half, superimposing their dispositions on ours, bringing in vast quantities of transport: for two days the road from Dunkirk to La Panne was blocked with a solid mass of vehicles two and three deep. Regiments were heading down to the beaches between our troops; their men expected immediate succour: yet neither the French Government nor the French High Command had made any decision as to evacuation. There existed still in the French High Command that strange refusal to consider realities. As late as the evening of May 28th, when the columns released by the defection of the Belgians were smashing already at the canal line in the neighbourhood of Furnes, when German troops were beginning to thrust across the great bridge at Nieuport which had not been blown, when Mardyck Fort was on the point of falling and the new line that the French had just established to the west was in immediate danger, Lord Gort received a message from General Weygand appealing personally to him 'to ensure that the British Army took a vigorous part in any counter-attacks necessary; the situation,' he added, 'made it essential to hit hard'.[1]

This was nothing but the French love of a fine phrase. In the military sense, as in the moral sense, it was empty and meaningless. If Weygand did not know, and could not conceive, the position that prevailed in this last stretch of the Low Country territory that we held, he had no right to the title and style of General. Here was an army still holding a front infinitely too long for its strength, hammered on every side by strong formations of armour in the very heat and passion of victory; an army that already for days had been on

---

[1] Second Gort dispatch, paragraph 54.

half rations, that was waterless, that had its one inadequate base in flaming ruins, that was short of ammunition for its guns and even for its rifles, that had lost most of its scanty armour and was almost denuded of petrol for the rest, that had no hope whatever save in the stubborn courage of a last defence, that had no life except that which a hardly contested sea might give to it. Overwhelmed from the air, overwhelmed from the land, this was no hour to make heroic gestures over counter-attacks. There was choice here only between a desperate evacuation bought by the courage and the lives of seamen, and a shameful surrender.

The decisions of the British Government had throughout been communicated to the French Government, but they had apparently not been transmitted by the French Government to the generals. This is in keeping with much that was done in this strange hour of France's history.

In a previous chapter I have given in full Lord Gort's impassioned appeal to General Blanchard with regard to General Prioux and his army. On the 28th orders were issued for the withdrawal of a part of this force. This was in addition to the French troops that were already coming into the perimeter and, as Lord Gort says with some restraint:

'Meanwhile, the French troops were expecting to embark along with their British comrades, notwithstanding that no French ships had so far been provided: the beaches were becoming crowded with French soldiers, and difficulties might have occurred at any time. I urged the War Office to obtain a decision as to the French policy for embarkation and asked that the French should take their full share in providing naval facilities. However, to permit embarkation of the French troops to begin at once, I decided to allot two British ships to the French that night, and also to give up the beach at Malo-les-Bains for their sole use.'

One of the immediate results of this decision was a signal from the Admiralty to Admiral Darlan through the British Liaison:

'French troops are beginning to arrive at Dunkirk and on the beaches but at the moment there are only three French destroyers and one French vessel to evacuate them. Please impress on Admiral Darlan the necessity of a large number of destroyers and passenger ships for Dunkirk and something in the nature of a hundred small craft for evacuating the beaches.'

2

The military situation was not materially altered save that the line to the south-west (the bottom of the bag, as it were) was shortening as French and British alike poured into the perimeter. But over in Nieuport the enemy had established a bridgehead across the unblown bridge, and guns behind Nieuport and on the outskirts of the town were beginning to bombard the beaches and to range on the channels that led through the Zuydecoote Pass. To the west Mardyck Fort had fallen to the enemy.

The destroyers had a new responsibility. All through this day they were engaging the Nieuport guns and German formations close to the coast along the roads. Over the perimeter the bombing went on, not diminishing but growing in fury. In an unfortunate and early error, personnel of a considerable part of the anti-aircraft units which had been intended for the defence of the perimeter had already been evacuated, and the guns were silent. From the south-west also the enemy artillery was ranging on the town, and everywhere damage was increasing, more and more roads were being blocked. There was no water to fight fires, no equipment even if water could have been made available.

3

The ships of the night movement began to leave for Dunkirk early. The transport *Scotia* sailed by the northern route. Coming in through the narrows, she passed destroyers already engaged with the shore batteries and enemy positions at Nieuport. She was told by them to proceed to Dunkirk and, following the *Malines*, moved past the entrance to the port. No pilot was available and dense clouds of smoke obscured the entrance. The ships continued to the westward for some time. *Malines* was then fired on from the shore somewhere near Mardyck, and both ships turned just before 1 a.m. and headed back for Dunkirk. During this manoeuvre, while going astern, the *Scotia* was struck abaft the engine-room on the port side. Soundings were taken in all compartments, but the ship was found to be not making water. Captain W. H. Hughes, her master, says in his report:

'This proved afterwards to have been a torpedo, which had struck the bilge keel and failed to explode. We hailed a small sloop which was proceeding towards the end of the Eastern Channel and asked if Dunkirk was clear. On being told what ship we were he told us to proceed cautiously towards the entrance. He added, "You are very badly needed." On this I decided to go on and do our utmost to relieve the situation. The small craft all along the pier were shifted so as to enable us to berth. We berthed at about 1.30 a.m. close to the lighthouse, East Pier. Immediately the vessel was alongside the Embarkation Officer requested that I should take as many troops as possible. This I did. The count showed 2,700, but many more had been taken aboard of whom no account could be taken. The *Scotia*, I estimated, had fully 3,000 troops on board, as every available space had been taken up. The troops (British) were very exhausted and many of them could hardly walk along the pier. The Embarkation Officers' duty was a very strenuous one, and in passing, I should like to express my admiration of the manner in which this difficult work was carried out by them. I gathered that some of these officers had been on duty unceasingly for thirty-six hours. . . .'

Her return journey was without incident.

Here were three fresh complications—shelling at either end of the narrow waterway off Dunkirk (the running of the Calais gauntlet had extended now to the Dunkirk channel) and torpedo attacks off the port itself. These things were disregarded. There is little evidence anywhere of ships failing because of them.

The guns themselves had comparatively little success in this opening phase, but some of the escapes were narrow. H.M. Tug *St. Clears* (W. J. Penny, master), which had left the previous day with eleven naval cutters and seventy ratings from Sheerness, was fired on, for example, when passing Nieuport. She had first attempted to make the western passage but had had two cutters sunk by the guns from Gravelines. Coming past Nieuport shells again fell very close to her and she lost two more cutters and had a third adrift. French destroyers then engaged the battery and seem to have got her out of an unpleasant situation. With her six remaining cutters she went in to La Panne, and Commander Hayward, R.N.R. (who was in command of the party) and his men helped to load *Beal* and *Bullfinch* and the bigger ships which lay off the beach.

While the big ships like the *Scotia* were doing a superb job the little ships also were working magnificently. *Yewdale* had left Dover at dusk in company with the motor-vessels *Beal* and *Bullfinch* for La Panne. Her master says:

'We anchored to await orders but as we received none I decided to move down the Channel to where a large number of troops were gathering. When shifting we picked up two boats with ten soldiers in them. We took the men on board leaving two men in each boat to take them ashore again for more troops. We also put our boat out which A. Flett, G. A. Sutherland, and G. A. MacKenzie (sixteen years old) manned. MacKenzie took charge of one of the other boats and directed the soldiers who were rowing, himself steering the boat. W. Watterson (mate) and J. Runcie (second engineer) also took charge of their boats and made several trips to the beach. The rest of the crew, including the chief engineer and firemen, were employed in bringing the boats alongside with lines. Army Captain Fred Williams kept count of the men and at 12.30 p.m. he reckoned we had 500 men on board. As we were at that time being assisted by several motor-launches and other small boats, counting became almost impossible. Another officer who also assisted a great deal counted twenty men boarding in five minutes. This we maintained until 2.30 p.m. when I decided that we were too tightly packed to hold any more.

'The soldiers, numbering about 1,000, were put into the cargo hold of the vessel and in addition every available space on the deck (which being a self-trimming vessel was very limited) was covered with men. Every room and space on the ship including the engine-room and stokehold was packed with men.

'At 2.35 we hove up and closed a destroyer for advice and we were told that we could travel in company with her.

'There had been a few air raids during the day but no bombs had dropped, at least not close to us. At 4 p.m. several German planes were seen overhead, and bombs dropped close to this ship. We then hove up and proceeded on our passage to Downs with m.v. *Beal* about 1 mile ahead and a destroyer about 1 mile astern. At 4.50 p.m. several enemy planes appeared overhead and began dive-bombing; several bombs fell very close. This continued off and on for about three-quarters of an hour with one final attack shortly before 6 p.m. During the third attack shrapnel struck the steamer and five men were killed

WEDNESDAY, MAY 29TH

and 78 wounded (two I believe died later). Our mate, W. Watterson, was struck in the leg and seriously injured.

'About six soldiers who apparently thought the ship to be sinking jumped overboard. These men possibly were picked up by the destroyer astern. It would have been dangerous to all those on board for us to turn back for them. In the next raid a dive-bomber was hit by our guns and appeared out of control, it lost height and as it passed close over the ship our gun kept firing and each tracer bullet was seen to enter the plane until it got out of range. Several soldiers actually saw it striking the water about half a mile on our port bow. At 6 p.m. the raiders were driven off, we believe by our own planes. . . .'

The *Bullfinch*, working in company with *Yewdale*, arrived at the same time. A report on her activities says:

'The beach was crowded with troops but there were only a few boats bringing off small numbers. The master (Captain H. Buxton) received orders to beach the *Bullfinch* and accordingly he let go the kedge anchor and headed slow for the beach. The vessel grounded about 5.45 a.m., but owing to the kedge anchor not holding, her stern swung to the eastward and the ship was aground fore and after with the beach.

'After the first boatload came aboard one of the troops swam ashore with a line. Two 5-inch ropes were run ashore and hauled boats off and back to the beach. When the tide receded the troops waded off and embarked up the ship's ladders. Embarkation proceeded until the ship had about 1,500 on board, during which time the ballast tanks were pumped out. The ladders were then pulled up, as the ship could take no more.

'The troops had two Bren guns with them, which were mounted one each side of the boat deck. The troops also manned the ship's Lewis gun. Bomb attacks were taking place all day and after a very anxious time from 5.30 p.m. until 6.15 p.m. the vessel floated and proceeded.

'German aircraft attacked the ship repeatedly. When passing Dunkirk several bombs dropped close to the vessel's stern, the concussion from which caused the circuit breaker to come out and put the steering gear out of action. The engines were stopped whilst the engineers effected repairs, and the ship then proceeded.

'Three dive-bombers then attacked the *Bullfinch* from aft. One of the Bren gunners, Sergeant Cook, shot one down into the sea. Shortly afterwards three others attacked from forward and the sergeant again shot one down. Further attacks were made at frequent intervals until a formation of Spitfires drove the enemy off. . . .'

Beal had difficulty in getting her small boats off the shore and A. D. C. Hall, one of her A.B.s, swam a considerable distance from the ship to the shore with a line in order to get a rope passed for the boats.

Remember these were little ships—less than 1,000 tons, without the wide decks of the personnel ships, in no way suited for carrying large quantities of men. These facts must be considered in judging their performance.

The *Royal Sovereign* began a splendid day by anchoring off the East Jetty

91

just before 3 o'clock in the morning. At 4.45 she berthed, and before 5.45 she was clear of the harbour with a full load on board. At 9.25 she was ordered in to Margate pier, went alongside at 12.15 p.m., and an hour and a quarter later had disembarked all her troops and cleared. By 5.30 p.m. she was back off La Panne in time to see the tremendous attack on the harbour. At 6 o'clock she found *Bullfinch*, loaded with troops, ashore and went to her assistance. At 6.20 her master, Captain T. Aldis, says briefly, 'Commenced embarking troops from beaches.' A superb day's work.

The Clyde steamer *King George V* made her first run to Dunkirk about the same time, and brought back a full complement of troops. Her chief steward, Mr. George L. Weir, says:

'We got filled up very quickly with troops (all the time we were at the quay we were being bombed and shelled). Those brave fellows whom we took on board were weary and tired; some of them had been on the beach for several days, without sleep and little to eat, being bombed and machine-gunned, besides being under shell-fire almost continuously. We were only about five minutes away till most of them were sound asleep, and their troubles forgotten. There were a good few Scotch chaps among them, several of whom I knew, and it was quite nice to hear someone shout out, "Hey, Mac, when do we get to Rothesay?" It was fine to hear a Scotch tongue and to see a "kent" face. One of them proudly showed me a souvenir pencil with our ship's name on it—*King George V* (one of those we sold in the ship), which he had bought last summer while on a trip to Staffa and Iona. He was so proud of it, and as I happened to have one or two on hand I gave his pals a present of them, and they were delighted and said they would show me them when they were on holiday and we were back on our own run again. . . .'

The hospital carriers were still continuing in the same indomitable spirit. *Dinard* picked up 271 stretcher cases and 13 R.A.M.C. personnel with the usual difficulties, and, cutting her moorings, came astern out of the entrance. Captain J. Ailwyn-Jones, her master, writes:

'At about 1 a.m. on the 29th we were attacked by torpedoes, two being fired at us from the starboard quarter. The water being very luminous that night, it was very easy to see and avoid the attack, one torpedo passing ahead and the other astern. Some minutes after this we heard a heavy explosion astern of us, and saw what appeared to be smoke and steam well back in our wake. This took place between Kwinte Bank Whistle Buoy and West Hinder Whistle Buoy.

'We had several narrow escapes from collisions as we were meeting dozens of ships coming along without lights, and the weather misty. One destroyer actually touched our belting on the starboard side, going very fast. We arrived back at the Downs at 4.30 a.m., and on to Newhaven, berthing at 8.35 a.m.'

Maid of Orleans went alongside about 4.30 on the ebb tide, and three times, as the falling water made her berth untenable, she had to shift further down the pier. She was alongside for about five hours picking up 1,372 troops including a number of stretcher cases. On leaving her master, Captain G. D. Walters (who had replaced her original master, Captain A. E. Larkins, when the latter collapsed through exhaustion) reports a submarine hunt in progress. Shortly after he left by the Zuydecoote Pass, and off Nieuport town he stopped the ship to pick up two French officers who were attempting to cross in a small boat. Though attacked from the air on several occasions *Maid of Orleans* got through without difficulty.

Clan MacAlister had sailed from Southampton on May 27th. Early on the morning of the 29th she was ordered to proceed with the motor landing craft that she had loaded to Dunkirk. Her master, Captain R. W. Mackie's, account is amongst the most interesting of the many that have been written, for it describes admirably the almost intolerable difficulties under which an ocean-going ship worked in the maelstrom of the traffic. He says:

'I was to proceed at once as near Dunkirk as possible, there discharge the A.L.C., and their crews, and then it was suggested that I might make a rendezvous with Commander Cassidi where the boats, if damaged, could come and be repaired. These were verbal orders. I was given a route through the Downs to Dunkirk also the position of some dangerous wrecks. I did not like proceeding in the dark through the Downs among those wrecks and so many ships at anchor without lights, and I told Commander Cassidi that I should have had a pilot. The naval officer had departed by this time. I laid down on the chart all the route and the wrecks and I told Commander Cassidi again that I did not like the job in the dark. He then said, "If you don't like to go, Captain, give me a course to steer and put the boats in the water and I'll take them across." I felt that was a challenge to our ability, so started to heave up right away and was under way by 1 a.m. on the 29th. I picked our way through the Downs, narrowly missing one of the wrecks to the westward of the Goodwin Sands. At 3.30 a.m. we heard an S.O.S.—"Unknown steamer torpedoed at Kaempfe Buoy"—and, as our route was to pass south of that buoy, I wanted to avoid the area and asked permission from a patrol vessel to steer direct for Dunkirk across a "Forbidden to Anchor" area, but he said "No." I spoke to Commander Cassidi and he said, "You can take me as close as you can, Captain, discharge my craft and then go back home. . . ."'

Captain Mackie accepted the challenge a second time and took his ship safely in to the vicinity of Dunkirk entrance.

'We started to discharge the craft and had just lifted our first into the air when the destroyer *Vanquisher* dashed past at full speed and set up so much wash as to cause the ship to roll so heavily that the men lost control of the guys and the craft swung violently from side to side with the crew on board.

'The second officer then lowered the craft down a little to try to get control of it but it damaged itself and the other one on deck so they became unfit for service. Commander Cassidi left in the third boat and his two lieutenants in the fourth and fifth boats. That was the last I saw of them. We discharged the six sound craft, then asked a destroyer which was closer inshore embarking troops if he had any fresh orders for me. He replied, "Carry out your original orders." As I had no definite orders I asked if I could assist them by taking any more troops back, some having already come on board uninvited. (By the time the third boat was in the water the first boat was back with troops from the beach.)

'Then a signal was passed which we understood to be that the destroyer *Ivanhoe* would put his troops on our ship, then return for more, and I could sail thereafter. *Ivanhoe* stopped ahead of us and then we received a signal to cancel previous orders and await further orders. *Ivanhoe* then dashed off for home. I then shifted my anchorage a little further east, then I was told to stop, so dropped anchor just south of No. 6 buoy, leaving a channel between our ship and the buoy.

'About 3.45 p.m. an air raid was made over the ship and when it had passed we found our vessel on fire aft in No. 5 hold, on deck and on the gun platform. No. 5 hatch beams had been cut and twisted. The combings burst out and the hatches all dropped below and were on fire. On the port side there was a large hole in the deck, the plates being pushed downwards at the after end of the hatch abreast of the tonnage opening, also another large hole in the wooden sheathed deck further aft and the crew's quarters were a mess of twisted beams and wreckage. On the starboard side of the deck about the same distance aft, there was another hole where a bomb had penetrated the deck and burst, as the hatch combings on that side were full of holes and most of the dead were lying on that side as far as I could see. When we were seen to be on fire H.M.S. *Malcolm* came alongside and started taking the soldiers off and some of the crew that were injured. Two lines of hose were passed on board and started playing into No. 5 hold, but could not reach the gun platform which was alight. The ship's hose was brought into use, but as the deck service pipe had been broken and holed in places, we did not get much pressure. While this was going on a party were dumping the petrol out of the two damaged A.L.C. also the ammunition from around the gun platform. (The high-angled gun breech-block was seen to be wrenched off.) While the wounded and troops were being transferred to H.M.S. *Malcolm* some of the native crew had got on board and the commander intended to put them back on the ship, but the aeroplanes were coming at us again so she cast off, her commander giving me a new course to steer. We continued with the hose aft, but the fire soon gained on us and, as we had to take cover again while the raid was on, it soon got a good hold. Rifle ammunition was also popping off every few minutes, so it became too dangerous to go near. When we found the engines and shafting were all right and that the steering gear seemed to work I decided to try to put to sea. We had no sooner started to heave away, when the aeroplanes came on us again and dropped bombs, one of which just missed the fore end of the bridge on the port side, stopped our gyro compass and shook the ship from stem to stern. The chief officer had left the windlass running and took cover under the forecastle head. When the raiders had passed, we tried our telemotor but found that it was broken, so we stopped the windlass. I called the engineers up and told them our position. It was hopeless to get aft to see if the steam gear was intact for no one could stay aft and steer owing to the fire and there was the danger that our spare ammunition in the tonnage opening would explode at any moment. Just as I suggested going aft (but was stopped by my chief officer) the first of the big shells went off.

'As it then seemed to me that we could not get to sea and steer through the sandbanks and that we seemed to be a ship marked for destruction by the enemy who were dive-bombing at us frequently, we signalled a destroyer which was embarking troops inshore from us that we wanted assistance. He did not answer, but H.M.S. *Pangbourne*, a minesweeper, which was entering the roads, came alongside and, when I told the commander that the telemotor was broken and that I could not get out clear, he agreed to take us on board. He pressed me to say that I wanted to abandon the vessel, but I would not use that word, so the commander said, "Well, temporarily abandoned."

'In the interests of the human beings left on board, I consented to this. The chief and fifth engineers went below and drew the fires as much as possible. The natives would not go down below a second time. We mustered the natives and found only twenty-three on board, eight of whom belonged to the saloon, eight were engine-room men and seven were deck men, and there were also twelve European members of the crew.

'When we left the vessel she was burning fiercely aft. . . .'

Clan MacAlister became one of the great sea-marks of Dunkirk. She sat more or less on an even keel, and was therefore bombed endlessly by the Luftwaffe whose pilots thought from her level position that she was still afloat and still busy. The mistake was made equally by some of the men of the little ships, who time and again went up to her in the darkness and tried to put soldiers on board.

As will be seen, these reports of the masters and officers of the ships vary both in method of expression and in emotional content. None the less they preserve throughout that curious reticence, that understatement, that is one of the traditions of our sea services. Few, however, have reached such heights of understatement as that of Captain A. Holkam, the new master of the *Mona's Queen*, who says:

'I joined the *Mona's Queen* on May 28th. On the evening of that date I received orders to leave Dover in the early morning of the 29th to carry fresh water to Dunkirk and return with troops. Everything was uneventful until we reached to within about half a mile off Dunkirk, when the ship was mined and sank within two minutes, the survivors being rescued by the destroyer *Vanquisher*.'

There is a succinct brevity in this that defies comment.

A report from another ship gives slightly more detail. The s.s. *Killarney*, finding herself unable to proceed owing to heavy mist, anchored off Gravelines. In the morning, when she arrived off Dunkirk, the very limited space along the Moles was full of vessels loading and she lay to off the entrance. Captain R. Hughes, her master, says:

'We were keeping a lookout for the *Lochgarry*, one of our Company's ships, which was also on the same mission.

'We saw a steamer much resembling her come up astern of us, using the daylight route. Whilst we were watching her, trying to ascertain who she was, there was a terrific explosion, and the centre part of her disappeared in a cloud of smoke. When the smoke cleared away, her stern portion from the mainmast aft had vanished, and in about two minutes the forward part heeled over and sank. So passed the *Mona's Queen* as a result of a magnetic mine.'

The chief cook of *Mona's Queen*, Mr. H. Crane, with great gallantry, went back while the ship was sinking to rescue the chief steward, Mr. Morgan, and a second fine effort was made by Gunner J. Osborne, who rescued the purser, Mr. R. Gallagher, and swam with him to *Vanquisher*. Unfortunately Mr. Gallagher died on the passage home.

About an hour later *Killarney* went alongside and embarked 800 troops. Her report says that she had extreme difficulty in preventing what appeared to be the whole canine population of France and Belgium from taking passage with her. These animals had attached themselves to the Tommies, and hundreds were shot on the quays to prevent their starving to death.

On her return journey, with her decks covered with men, she came under fire from the Gravelines guns. It was estimated that three batteries of 6-inch guns were firing. Heavy smoke was made from the funnel in an endeavour to set up some sort of smoke screen, and, despite the narrowness of the sand-banked channel and the known minefields, she zig-zagged violently. The ship was not degaussed. During forty minutes about ninety shells were fired and one hit on the after end of the boat deck, killing eight men and wounding thirty. A little later they were attacked by machine-gun fire from enemy aircraft.

'But,' says her master's report, 'to our great delight a Spitfire came right out of the clouds on to the German's tail, and giving him a good burst of his guns sent the enemy crashing in flames into the sea, on our port side, about 600 yards away. We did not dally any further to look for survivors.'

A little later they sighted a raft, made of wood and an old door, bearing one French officer and two Belgian soldiers.

'The commissariat of the raft was most complete—two tins of biscuits and six demijohns of wine. Also, carefully lashed on the raft was a bicycle of ancient vintage.'

Lochgarry, which had set out the previous day, saw a submarine hunt in progress as she was nearing the French coast. The berths were filled when she arrived off the head of the Mole and she waited to watch *Killarney* out. The tide was low and falling, and her master, Captain Ewen MacKinnon, had considerable anxiety as to whether there would be sufficient water for him to go alongside. *Killarney* drew roughly as much as he did and he hoped to take her berth, but it was taken by a shallow-draught vessel before he could reach it and he was forced to go further up the harbour.

'There we met two very brave and cheerful men—the Commander and the Lieutenant-Commander, who were carrying on their work and directing operations as if no danger existed. There was no bustle or commotion, but everything was orderly and well regulated. The Jerry shells were dropping in the harbour about fifty yards from the bow of the *Lochgarry* at 11.25 a.m.

when we were fixed in our berth, but they did not appear to explode, and all of them could be heard coming, screaming through the air, through the smoke and haze, and dropping in the very centre of the harbour. They had the range perfectly. Well, it was all right so long as they did not alter it a degree the one way or the other. There was nothing but thick black smoke and fire everywhere round the harbour, and parts of several sunken vessels were projecting in the inner harbour at low water. . . .'

Lochgarry loaded through air raids and shell-fire with a destroyer berthed alongside her and loading across her decks. Astern of her were three destroyers loading, and she had some difficulty in getting out. A drifter, trying to assist, cut her degaussing wires and started a small fire, but that was soon put out. When she cleared the harbour she waited for a short while for her escort, the destroyer *Greyhound*. *Greyhound* closed her, and they were discussing which route to take when they were heavily attacked from the air and *Greyhound* was hit.

They passed the blazing *Clan MacAlister* a few moments later and a little after that were attacked again. In the course of this new attack the minesweeper *Gracie Fields*, crowded with troops, was hit. *Lochgarry* was attacked almost all the way back to the North Goodwin light vessel, but came through in safety.

Normannia, sister ship to the *Lorina* which had been sunk earlier, was also lost to aerial attack at this time, settling in shallow water near No. 9 buoy off Mardyck on an even keel with her flags flying.

Canterbury, with a small naval party in addition to her crew, picked up 1,950 troops. She was bombed in the Zuydecoote Pass and again near the Nieuport Bank buoy. One salvo burst so close to the port quarter that the ship suffered considerable damage and on her return she had to be sent into the Granville Dock for temporary repairs.

4

The day was passing in a steady and dangerous increase in the rate of loss and somewhere about 5 o'clock there developed the most vicious air attack on the harbour itself in the whole period of the evacuation. An unfortunate shift of wind had suddenly driven the smoke inland, and the thin protection that it had given up till then disappeared. In the harbour there were at least ten ships loading, approximately equal numbers of destroyers and personnel vessels. The rate of loading had been admirable up to now, something like 2,000 troops an hour being embarked, and though outside there had been a steady proportion of loss among the returning ships, the tide of return was in full flow to the English coast.

Alongside the Mole amongst other ships were the s.s. *Fenella*, H.M.S. *Crested Eagle*, H.M.S. *King Orry*, s.s. *St. Seiriol* and s.s. *St. Julien* endeavouring to berth. The destroyer *Grenade* was loading, so was *Verity* of the 'V' and 'W's' and the old destroyer *Sabre*.

Fenella was berthed on the east side of the East Mole at the seaward end. Captain W. Cubbon, her master, says in his report:

'We had between six and seven hundred troops on board when the enemy dive-bombers scored a direct hit on *Fenella's* promenade deck, doing considerable damage, at about 5 p.m. They also scored a hit on the jetty causing it to split in two, parts of the concrete being blown through the ship's side below the water line and into the engine-room which immediately began to flood with water. Another bomb fell between the ship and the jetty, the force of the explosion blowing out the oil cooler from the ship's side and completely wrecking almost every pipe and pump in the engine-room, rendering the engines useless.

'I inspected the damage in company with the Chief and Second officer—the ship was listing badly—fortunately inclining towards the jetty—and was rapidly making water. Our examination of the damage proved that the ship was doomed and the only course open was to disembark all troops and abandon ship. I instructed the O.C. troops to this effect.

'As the jetty abreast of gangways had been blown away, the only method of disembarkation was to climb over the rails on the forecastle head which fortunately was level with the jetty. The enemy was particularly active at this time and several times his bombing and machine-gunning held up the disembarking of the troops, but owing to the skilful handling of my Chief and Second Officers, all troops and stretcher cases were safely disembarked, the only casualty on board the *Fenella* being Engineer Roy Motion, who suffered leg injury through bomb explosion. I must mention that throughout all of these raids our Lewis gunners, F. Garrett and J. Cowell, who were members of the crew, and two Bren gunners appointed to the ship by the military authorities at Southampton, all remained at their gun posts in very exposed positions and continued firing at the enemy aircraft.

'On going through the ship and making sure that every soul on board had been safely landed, I reported the fact to the Embarkation Officer in charge of the jetty. I then suggested to him that if he could obtain tugs or trawlers, we were prepared to tow *Fenella* away from the jetty to render the berth available for other ships and beach her before she finally sank. He was in favour of this suggestion and tried to get tugs, but no vessels capable of towing were available. All the troops and the majority of *Fenella's* crew had by this time been embarked on board the steamer *Crested Eagle*. The Embarkation Officer then suggested, as nothing further could be done with regard to *Fenella*, that I and my officers should proceed home in this steamer. Unfortunately, this ship was herself bombed and set on fire within ten minutes of leaving the jetty and had to be beached. I regret to say this caused a number of casualties, among them sixteen of the *Fenella's* crew who lost their lives.'

H.M.S. *Crested Eagle* (Lieutenant-Commander B. R. Booth, R.N.R.) already had part of her complement of troops on board. As soon as she had taken the troops and the majority of *Fenella's* crew on to her decks, she pulled out. *St. Seiriol*, unable to berth, received orders to pick up men from the beaches and proceeded to follow her. Immediately afterwards *Crested Eagle* was bombed and set on fire. *St. Seiriol's* chief officer says:

'We lowered the dinghy in charge of the Second Officer with other men, and I took charge of our remaining lifeboat with four naval stokers. We proceeded to the rescue of the men from the burning ship and brought them aboard. After we got everybody that it was humanly possible from the burning ship we went to the shore.'

Through the late afternoon with its raids, and through the early evening, the work of the personnel ships and the coasters went on. *Royal Daffodil* picked up 750 men. The s.s. *Roebuck* was ordered to La Panne, which she reached after a minor collision with a destroyer, but, when making arrangements to pick up from the beach, she received an urgent order to proceed to Dunkirk. Arriving there she waited until the *St. Julien* left her berth and then went in to load over 100 wounded and about 400 troops. *Roebuck* was not degaussed, and she ran a very high degree of risk in facing these narrow and much-mined channels.

St. Helier picked up 2,000 troops 'without incident'—without, that is, more than the normal incident of mines, artillery fire and incessant attack from the air.

St. Julien (Captain L. T. Richardson, master) was heavily attacked from the air north of the Nieuport buoy as she approached the Zuydecoote Pass and subsequently, as she went up past Nieuport, she was shelled and then machine-gunned. The ship was damaged, but by zig-zagging in the channel (this was one of the stretches which was a bare 150 yards wide) she managed to escape without serious hurt. She reached Dunkirk as the big air attack developed and, entering the harbour, found no berth vacant. While she waited a berth was vacated, but before she could reach it the armed boarding vessel *King Orry* (Commander Jeffery Elliott, R.D., R.N.R.) slipped in ahead of her. Almost immediately afterwards *King Orry* was bombed. She was taken in tow in a sinking condition and foundered a short distance from the end of the Mole.

The *Isle of Guernsey* left Dover in the late afternoon, and a little after 7 o'clock watched an engagement between enemy aircraft and a British destroyer. British fighter planes intervened and one of them was brought down. Her pilot came down by parachute ahead of the ship and J. Fowles, one of the *Isle of Guernsey*'s A.B.s, went down a rope ladder to try to pick him up. Before he had reached the bottom of the ladder ten enemy planes attacked the ship with bombs, cannon, and machine-guns. None of the bombs hit, but the ship was badly shaken by concussion and suffered much damage. Fowles was wounded by machine-gun bullets and splinters, and fell from the ladder. Captain Hill, her master, was compelled to go ahead and abandon him in an attempt to save the ship, and Fowles was given up for lost. By admirable fortune, however, he was picked up still alive by another ship a little later.

5

The personnel ships, some of the coasters, and a large proportion of the destroyers all through this day were using the Mole. That frail pathway, disregarded in the first appreciations of the port, hardly considered in the early days even as a possible berthing-place for ships, had grown in these last hectic days to be the main roadway of escape. Along its 5-foot causeway an army was marching to safety.

But on this day the beaches began to play a major part in the extraordinary lifting rate of 2,000 men an hour. For some days men had been taken by small boats from the beaches (in the accounts of ships that have already been quoted there are numerous instances of this), but it was not until the evening of the 29th that the traffic became fully organized.

All that afternoon and all the evening flotillas of small boats were setting out from Ramsgate and from Dover. To replace them fresh flotillas were coming down from Sheerness, Southend, from the east coast ports and from the little harbours of the west. Reinforcing the motor-boats, the little pleasure boats, the beach boats and the like, the naval yards were sending out everything that would float: picket boats belonging to the old steam era when a brilliantly polished funnel was the way to a commander's heart, 'liberty boats', canteen boats and ammunition barges and dockyard launches, harbour craft of a score of kinds, lighters—'X' lighters many of them, that had taken their part in the Gallipoli withdrawal. Everything that would float at Chatham, at Portsmouth, at Plymouth, was moving along the coast.

The first boats from Sheerness were mostly navy-manned. Those that carried a proportion of civilians in their crews were commanded for the most part by sub-lieutenants R.N.V.R. One small convoy was towed by the skoot *Jutland*. In this convoy were *Johanna* and *Chantecler*, converted Dutch eel boats, and *Golden Lily*. The motor-boat *Triton* left with a convoy of nine, including the *Silver Queen*. The motor-boat *Reda* (Sub-Lieutenant P. Snow, R.N.) sailed from Ramsgate at 10 o'clock in the morning with five other small craft and, reaching the beaches at 5 o'clock, worked for three hours taking out men to the destroyers and the minesweepers, and came back to Ramsgate with twenty-one soldiers on board. She was bombed on departure, one salvo falling within 20 yards, but beyond having several planks loosened escaped serious damage.

Pauleter, a 35-foot motor-boat, went over also. She was commanded by Stoker D. T. Banks, who had as crew two Ordinary Seamen, with a Bren gun, a Lewis gun and a compass which he did not know how to use. Like many others he steered by the blaze from Dunkirk. On his arrival some forty British and French soldiers, including several wounded, waded and swam off. As he could not see any large craft near him, Banks brought them home. On the way *Pauleter* was attacked from the air and there were several hits, but no serious damage was done.

Elizabeth Green and *Viewfinder*, *Glitter II*, *Bobelli*, *Sceneshifter*, *Frightened Lady*, *Black Arrow*, *Minikoi*—the names crop up in the accounts of ships they worked with, in brief reports at Sheerness; little three-line stories that are part of the mosaic of history. With them are other names, names of little ships that started and broke down half-way across to be towed back or abandoned, names of other little ships run down by destroyers and fast-moving craft. *Bobelli* (Sub-Lieutenant W. G. H. Bonham, R.N.) was broken up by a destroyer which went full ahead to dodge aircraft attack while she was made fast alongside. *Sceneshifter* was swamped by a French troopship and lost. *Frightened Lady* (Sub-Lieutenant S. C. Allen, R.N.V.R.) fouled her screw, ran aground and was abandoned. *Glitter II* (Sub-Lieutenant J. W. Culham, R.N.) ferried until 2 o'clock the next morning when she lost her rudder on wreckage and had to be towed home. *Black Arrow* went aground and was abandoned. The litter of small craft that was to line the Dunkirk beaches by the end of this incredible week was beginning.

But the loss was not only on the beaches. *Mary Rose* (Sub-Lieutenant H. McClelland, R.N.V.R.) broke down on the way over. The ship was taken in tow but became unmanageable, filled and sank, and her crew was picked up by H.M. Trawler *Strathelliott* (Sub-Lieutenant W. E. Mercer, R.N.V.R.). *Skylark*, a Brighton beach boat (Sub-Lieutenant E. C. B. Mares, R.N.V.R.) also sank under tow. *Ellen Mary* was in collision with a lifeboat and had to be abandoned. *Minikoi* was run down and sunk by M.A./S.B. 6 as she was leaving the Downs a little before dawn. The litter of craft of all sorts that lined the bottom of the Channel was already well begun.

With the ships that were manned by the navy the ships of the volunteers were going out. From Southend sailed *Shamrock*, *Princess Maud*, *Canvey Queen* and *Queen of England*—Southend pleasure-boats. Off Shoeburyness *Canvey Queen* developed engine trouble and had to be towed almost to Margate before she could make good her defects. They had orders to make their 'utmost speed direct to the beaches eastward of Dunkirk'. When they were 10 miles to the westward Allan Barrell of *Shamrock* says:

'Ahead everything was blazing, oil and petrol tanks were continually exploding near the coast, the noise and flames were beyond description. I was feeling a bit weary about the feet, cramp through cold was aggravating me, it was about sixteen hours since we left Canvey.

'Brown took the wheel while I had a sip from a lemonade bottle, a matter of seconds, when I noticed one of H.M. ships (H.M. Skoot *Tilly*) bearing down on us.

'Then came the crash; I could see the *Queen of England* being sliced in two.

'There was not time for words, in my effort to gain control poor Brown was knocked to the deck, but I managed to open the throttle and swing her round and so miss the same fate by inches. We heard the cries of "Come on, Canvey" in the darkness and by bawling "Where are you? Where are you?" we located and grabbed them into our boat as the remnants of their beautiful craft were just disappearing. We came alongside the big dark ship, an officer after making inquiries about the condition of the three men, dropped a rope ladder down and took them on board, we didn't even say "Good night".'

The motor-boat *Advance*, which had left on May 28th from Sheerness, reached Dunkirk about 12 o'clock on the 29th, and the detailed report of her owner, C. P. Dick, gives an excellent picture:

'1 p.m. Approached a large merchant ship (on fire) with a destroyer alongside, for more detailed instructions. Told to get as many men as possible from the beach to the waiting ships. Proceeded to do so.

'Took *Advance* as close in as seemed safe, Piercy and McGuffie away in whaler. Whaler broached to and swamped on reaching beach; as two men only not enough to handle her in slight surf caused by other ships' wash and bombs.

'The troops at this time rather disorganized, not only units, but nationalities being mixed. Saw a French officer, on a horse, making great efforts to obtain order (later "the Frenchman on the horse" seemed to become almost a landmark).

'Eventually Piercy and McGuffie, assisted by a French interpreter officer (Captain de Gailis) succeeded in getting whaler partially emptied of water, loaded, and under way. Taken in tow by Dick in *Advance*.

'Proceeded alongside destroyer, and troops embarked therein.

'Returned to beach for more. Shortly after we left this destroyer appeared to be hit by one or more bombs.

'Troops in rather better order by now, so got second boatload off without much trouble.

'On third trip managed to get *Advance* close enough in for men to wade or swim out, in addition to those picked up by whaler. (Some naval ratings in this party.) On the way out, the whaler fouled some submerged obstruction, was holed, overturned, and sank. Picked up all but three men, who were rescued by a motor pontoon.

'Took our men out to a drifter. (Two ratings remaining with us.)

'On the way back to the beach, picked up another whaler, empty and abandoned, but apparently intact. Piercy and two ratings took it in, filled up, and returned. Took it in tow and went alongside a destroyer to unload.

'While we were there, and troops were climbing up nettings hung over her side, aircraft dived from behind clouds, and the destroyer suddenly went ahead, presumably on orders, carrying away our lines and also the whaler's two ropes. Three or four men were seen to fall overboard, some being crushed between the destroyer's side and *Advance*'s port quarter.

'After getting *Advance* under control again we could only see one man floating, so went to pick him up; McGuffie remaining in whaler, in charge of her and the remaining troops. Piercy and a gunlayer who had remained with us (name unknown) had some difficulty in getting this man on board, as he was wearing full equipment and a greatcoat; so Dick left the wheel temporarily to help. The man turned out to be a middle-aged infantry captain, and appeared to have a broken thigh. He fainted after we got him on board.

'Went alongside an escort vessel and got the man on to a stretcher and on board her, assisted by two ratings who remained with us afterwards.

'McGuffie had also got the whaler alongside this vessel, and had unloaded his men, so took him in tow, and returned to the beach to fill up again. Did not take *Advance* close in, as we had touched several times previously, and were worried about possible damage to propeller, etc.

'As we got clear again great aerial activity began, so decided that it would be safer to keep clear of all ships for the time being. Stood out.

'A bomb fell close to our starboard side, shaking us considerably; when we had got to our feet again, we saw that, though there were no casualties, the whaler's seams had opened up, owing to the concussion, and she was sinking rapidly. Stopped and took the men out of her and abandoned.

'Without the tow, we could make better speed away from the bombed area, and were able to investigate the damage to *Advance*.

'She appeared to have been considerably strained, and was making a certain amount of water but the only hole found was about six or eight inches above the water-line.

'After things had quieted a little, returned and got our men into a transport.

'After this we made no attempt to use a boat of our own, but picked up anything we could find near the beach, whalers, pontoons, rafts, shore boats and even bathing floats and canoes; taking the men from them to the nearest ship of any sort that we could find. (Including a heavily laden motor-boat (broken down) from one of H.M. ships.)

'After several trips of this sort, we realized that we had drifted rather far to the east, i.e. into Belgium, so we picked up several pontoons with a view to towing them further west, to where they appeared to be more needed.

'While we were doing this, we were hailed by a destroyer and came alongside. We were instructed to take on board a portable radio transmitting set and two operators, and to land them at a certain place. (Signal Station at La Panne, not marked on our chart, but readily visible on land.)

'Embarked signalmen and equipment.

'Cast off pontoons, etc., so that they would, as far as possible, drift on to beach near troops and so be of further use.

'Picked up another whaler, and while doing so, passed close to a transport using her remaining boat to evacuate troops from a crowded paddle steamer recently bombed; aground and with her after part on fire.

'Went as close to beach as possible, transferred signalmen and radio to whaler, and slipped them near "the Frenchman on the horse". Their plan was to get a volunteer party of soldiers to carry their gear, and to leave the boat to be used by troops. . . .'

After this, with her electric circuits gone, most of her instruments damaged, and her fuel short, *Advance* reported to the R.N.V.R. lieutenant under whose command she had been placed, and both craft decided to make for Ramsgate. The damage *Advance* had sustained caused her to leak rapidly, and eventually she had to be beached to save her from sinking alongside the quay at Ramsgate.

6

With the small craft reinforcements new ships were promised. To the signal made to Admiral Darlan by the British Admiralty came a reply which said:

'All small ships in Channel requisitioned by French. Twenty-eight of these already left for Dover under Admiral Landriau and have been ordered to co-operate with Admiral Ramsay. They should arrive at Dover to-morrow, May 30th, about 10 o'clock. More are following.'

Some of these ships began to arrive at Dover the following afternoon. They had to come from Cherbourg and ports far to the west, and the faster naval vessels were the first to arrive.

7

If our loss from the air this day was heavy, that of the Germans was heavy too. The Boulton-Paul Defiant, a new type of fighter, which afterwards proved unsatisfactory, achieved this day an extraordinary success. A squadron of twelve planes had been in action on the Monday and Tuesday, shooting down six of the enemy on the Monday and seven on the Tuesday. On this Wednesday, presented with greater opportunity by the increasing weight of the German attack, they began by bringing down seventeen fighters and a dive-bomber on their morning patrol. On their second patrol, in the afternoon, they brought down nineteen bombers with possibly two others. It was an extraordinary achievement for a small force of twelve planes, and for the moment it raised amazing hopes.

Meanwhile the Hurricanes and Spitfires of the other squadrons were achieving like results. Altogether the day's total reached seventy-seven for the loss of seventeen.

Not all our pilots were lost. The story of one of the survivors is typical of the spirit, if not perhaps of the fortune, that prevailed amongst our airmen:

'I was in a formation of nine aircraft patrolling Dunkirk. Towards the end of our patrol we sighted about nine Messerschmitt 109 fighters. A dog-fight ensued.

'A Messerschmitt 109 started climbing away from me. I opened fire at 100 yards and the second burst set him on fire. I then turned right and attacked another Messerschmitt 109 firing one burst from astern. His port wing folded up.

'As I levelled out a Junkers 88 flew across my path. I did a quarter attack. His starboard engine emitted black smoke and he half-rolled into the sea.

'I was then hit underneath by a cannon shell. As I did a complete turn to the right, I saw a Messerschmitt 110 flying past. I did a beam attack on him. His starboard engine smoked and he turned on his back and fell into the sea.

'I then turned to the right and saw a large number of enemy aircraft so I turned sharply to the left and saw at least eighty enemy aircraft proceeding in the direction of Dover. A number of them immediately turned on me, so I headed for home, twisting and turning to avoid the attack. Whichever way I turned I ran into fire. My Hurricane was hit a number of times. Two shells smashed the instrument panel and three more struck underneath. The engine stopped and flames appeared over the wing roots.

'I was at 400 feet and tried to get out but couldn't, so I pulled the stick back from a crouching position on the seat.

'As the Hurricane stalled, I got over the port side and took a header off the main plane. I was being fired at, so I delayed pulling the ripcord as long as possible above the sea. I left the fighter at 800 feet. The parachute worked perfectly. My lifejacket held me up well with one deep breath in it.

'I was picked up by a paddle steamer and landed at Margate.'

8

Magnificent as was the work of the personnel ships on this day, it was matched in every particular by the work of the destroyers. Over and over again the accounts of the masters of the personnel ships stress the difficulties of going alongside the East Mole. But these ships, designed as they were for the Clyde passenger service, the Isle of Man ferry, for the North Wales pleasure piers, for the cross-Channel routes, were built for going alongside piers and quays and jetties of a dozen different constructions at speed, for quick loading and quick discharge. They were built with their sides specially stiffened for the purpose. They were built with thick rubbing strakes from bow to stern to take the shock of barging up against granite and concrete and steel piers. One of the very first considerations of their design was this necessity for 'going alongside'.

Destroyers are built for speed. They are light craft, fragile, difficult to handle at low speeds. Their side plating is astonishingly thin. They have no rubbing strakes, no extra stiffening. And these destroyers were working themselves alongside Dunkirk Mole, slamming up against wood and concrete, jamming themselves into berths between other ships, sandwiching themselves against paddle steamers and turbine steamers alike. The sheer ship handling of the destroyers in Dunkirk harbour is one of the most astonishing facets of the whole operation.

The price they paid was a heavy one. As has already been indicated, the first part of it was paid in damage. The list of collisions and collision damage alone amongst the destroyers of the operation is tremendous. No single ship escaped scatheless. But on this day there were worse things than collisions. The naval losses of the 29th were amongst the heaviest of the entire operation.

They began very early in the small hours. At 3 o'clock the destroyer *Grafton* (Commander C. E. C. Robinson, R.N.), which had lain throughout the early night off Bray-Dunes beach picking up men from the small boats, was attacked by an E-boat on her return passage. There is an admirable account of that brief action in Sir Basil Bartlett's book:

'. . . there was a terrific explosion as a torpedo hit the destroyer. I suppose the force of it must have knocked me unconscious. First thing I knew I was stumbling about in the dark trying to find the door of the cabin. The whole ship was trembling violently. The furniture appeared to be dancing about.

There was a strong smell of petrol. I heard someone scuffling in a corner and just had the good sense to shout:

'"For God's sake don't light a match."

'With the greatest of difficulty I found the door and managed to get it open. . . .

'I pushed my way out on deck.

'Someone said:

'"Keep down. They're machine-gunning us."

'I huddled against a steel door and watched the fight. Two dark shapes in the middle distance turned out to be German M.T.B.s. The destroyer and another British warship were giving them hell with shells and tracer-bullets. The M.T.B.s were answering with machine-gun fire. But one by one they were hit. We saw them leap into the air and then settle down into the water and sink. Everyone sighed with relief. . . .

'The deck was a mass of twisted steel and mangled bodies. The Captain had been machine-gunned and killed on the bridge. The destroyer had stopped two torpedoes. She'd been hit while hanging about to pick up survivors from another ship, which had been sunk a few minutes before.

'She was a very gruesome sight. . . .

'Wounded men began to be brought up from the bowels of the ship. I learned that one of the torpedoes had gone right through the wardroom, killing all thirty-five of our officers who were sleeping there.

'It's pure chance that I'm alive. If I'd gone on board a little earlier I should have been put in the wardroom. I only slept in the Captain's cabin because there was no room for me anywhere else. . . .

'There remained only one job to be done. We had to transfer our cargo. The men showed wonderful discipline. There was no ugly rush. They allowed themselves to be divided into groups and transferred from one ship to another with the same patience that they had shown on Bray-Dunes beach. It must have been a great temptation to get out of turn and take a flying leap for safety. But no one did. . . .

'The sailors didn't come with us. They rowed off in a little boat to a cruiser[1] which was standing by and went back to Dunkirk to do more evacuation.

'The cruiser put two shells into our destroyer.

'We watched her sink, carrying with her her load of unknown dead.'

While *Grafton* was sinking, another destroyer was in process of rescue 20 miles to the westward, off Calais. H.M.S. *Montrose* (Commander C. R. L. Parry, R.N.), coming back with a full load of troops, had been in trouble earlier. At midnight she was lying within range of the Gris Nez searchlights, helpless, with her bows blown away. At 12.30 the tugs *Lady Brassey* and *Simla* were ordered out of Dover to her assistance. They picked her up at 3 o'clock and she was towed stern first into Dover.

This was not the end of the loss even as it was by no means the end of the work of the destroyers. All through the day their names crop up in every

_____
[1] This was probably a heavy destroyer.

account by the masters of the merchant ships, in every story from the troops they rescued.

A little after dawn a division of four destroyers, hurrying across, was attacked by a U-boat. The torpedo was sighted by the leading destroyer, which made an emergency turn to starboard. The second destroyer in the line was the Polish ship *Blyskawica*, and from her bridge they saw the track of the torpedo cross the wake between their bow and the stern of the next ahead. She carried out an immediate depth-charge attack and the leading destroyer, circling, attacked in her turn. While they were taking up position to drop a fresh pattern of depth charges they were attacked from the air; a bomber dived on *Blyskawica* out of low cloud, dropping a stick of bombs and machine-gunning the destroyer's decks. The hunt did not cease. Some minutes later a periscope was observed for an instant in line with the West Hinder buoy. Both ships attacked rapidly in turn, and a little after five British aircraft appeared and joined in the hunt. There was no observable result, but submarine attacks in the area ceased for a time.

Submarine attacks ceased, but not the endless air attacks. *Gallant* was dive-bombed and damaged; *Intrepid* (Commander R. C. Gordon, R.N.), a little later, was also bombed and damaged; *Saladin* (Lieutenant-Commander L. J. Dover, R.N.) suffered slight damage from a near miss; *Icarus* (Lieutenant-Commander C. D. Maud, D.S.C., R.N.), coming through the crowded channel, was attacked by ten aircraft, one of which came in persistently at low level, but by using smoke and zig-zagging violently, she got clear. *Sabre*, whose boats had been left on the beaches, steaming through a position where another ship had been sunk ahead of her, manœuvred the ship to pick up individual survivors. While she was doing this she was attacked from the air, but continued until every man in the water had been picked up. Every ship that crossed seems to have had some experience with enemy aircraft. *Scimitar*, *Wolsey* and *Malcolm* all reported attempts at bombing.

The destroyers were mainly working the beaches. One of them, *Vanquisher* (Lieutenant-Commander C. B. Alers-Hankey, R.N.), moving at high speed under air attack, accidentally interfered with *Clan MacAlister*'s operations at this time. Reference has been made before to the danger to small craft of the wash set up by the destroyers. It is possible to measure something of that danger. *Clan MacAlister* was an ocean-going ship of 6,900 tons—nearly twice the size, that is, of any other ship that took part in the operation. She was loaded and she was stationary, yet the swell set up by the destroyer's wake moved her so violently that the landing craft on the derricks carried away and became uncontrollable. The difficulties of the little ships along the beaches, overloaded as they always were, are not to be wondered at.

H.M.S. *Harvester*, which had been working off Bray-Dunes in the earlier part of the night, moved at 5 o'clock to La Panne. Sub-Lieutenant Croswell landed again and, by organizing a line ferry from a stranded paddle-steamer to the shore, was once more responsible for sending off a large number of men.

Harvester lay off La Panne throughout the morning. At 2 o'clock in the

WEDNESDAY, MAY 29TH

afternoon a very heavy bombing attack developed, and a supply ship close to her was hit, set on fire and destroyed. There were no naval beach parties other than that under Croswell in the area, and during the bombing something approaching a panic developed on one part of the beach. Boats were crowded in the rush, and in one case seven men were drowned in four feet of water.

Sub-Lieutenant Croswell, realizing the difficulty of getting small boats afloat once they were heavily loaded, suggested that an attempt should be made to build piers. Late that night the first pier at La Panne was begun under the direction of Colonel Porter.

H.M.S. *Ivanhoe* (Commander P. H. Hadow, R.N.) was also loading off the beaches at this time. The destroyer *Jaguar* lay off Bray beach for sixteen hours while her boats' crews, foodless, wet through and incessantly bombed, brought off parties of men to her till she was fully loaded. All day there were destroyers alongside the Mole and at the west quay. *Vanquisher*, which had made one of the earliest loadings, returned to Dover, discharged her men, came back and picked up a second load, discharging that in turn within the twenty-four hours, and found time in the course of this to rescue survivors of the s.s. *Mona's Queen. Codrington, Verity, Greyhound, Sabre* and many others also loaded at the Mole this day.

Shortly before 2 o'clock the personnel ship *Lochgarry* pulled out of the harbour as has already been recorded, and waited for destroyer escort which had been arranged. This escort was *Greyhound*, which had been loading further in. *Lochgarry* was receiving a signal from *Greyhound* when, according to her master:

'The destroyer jumped, as it were, and made a series of twists and zig-zags in front of us. Well, I thought to myself, if you are going at that speed there's damn little hope of me keeping up with you! The next moment there was a terrific explosion close to the destroyer on her port side, but it was a miss. Another moment and a column of water shot up ahead of us about fifty yards away. No. 1 salvo for the *Lochgarry* also a miss! But the third salvo caught the destroyer fair amidships and ripped her side open, causing many casualties, I would say, but the Commander was still on the bridge and her guns were active peppering away. It was apparent the vessel was out of action. I heard the telegraph to the engine-room ringing but could see no response from the engines. I passed by the destroyer close to. The Commander shouted, "Carry on"; we then tore away full batter with a double ring on the telegraph, and zig-zagged so far as the channel would allow us. . . .'

Greyhound was much damaged in her engine-room and badly holed, but she kept her guns in action throughout this and subsequent attacks. By supreme efforts her engine-room staff got some sort of order going below and after a long interval she limped away under her own power. In the early evening *Blyskawica*, still working her patrol somewhere near the West Hinder buoy, sighted her and took her in tow to Dover. Even off Dover she was by no means safe for German planes dropped magnetic mines about 3,000 yards

108

ahead of the ships on their course. They avoided the dangers, however, and the cripple was taken safely in.

There was variety enough in their work. The story of the *Clan MacAlister* gives a graphic description of one of the most fantastic efforts of the day when H.M.S. *Malcolm*, in the midst of heavy bombing attacks, fought off Junkers 88s, as it were, with one hand and with the other passed fire hoses on board the burning steamer in a magnificent attempt to put out the flames.

Still the story of the loss went on. H.M.S. *Grenade* which had come in with a division of the 1st Flotilla only the previous day, was alongside when the tremendous air attack on the harbour developed about 5 o'clock in the afternoon. With other ships there she was hit and set on fire. She swung into the fairway out of control, and for a few desperate minutes it seemed likely that she would sink and block the harbour. By excellent seamanship, a trawler under way in the harbour managed to get a line on her and tow her clear, and she sank a little outside the harbour, close enough inshore for a good many of her complement to swim in to land. Others were picked up by a drifter which in turn was sunk, and the survivors of this reached home on a third vessel.

H.M.S. *Verity* (Lieutenant E. L. Jones, R.N.), which was in the harbour at the same time, hit a sunken drifter as she came out and narrowly escaped complete disaster.

These losses ended, for practical purposes, what might be called the day phase of the operations, but there was more to come. The destroyers' work never stopped. The night period might be said to have begun with the arrival of *Esk* (Lieutenant-Commander R. J. H. Couch, R.N.). At 8 o'clock Rear-Admiral Wake-Walker (Rear-Admiral Dover Straits) with his staff embarked in H.M.S. *Esk* and sailed from Dover to take command along the beaches. With her *Esk* also took fresh naval beach parties to superintend the beach and the embarkations at La Panne, Bray-Dunes and Malo-les-Bains. These parties were put ashore in the destroyer's boats at the three points named. *Esk* was followed by other destroyers both for the beaches and for the harbour.

H.M.S. *Jaguar*, which also left late in the evening, picked up 800 men. She was ordered to provide escort for a heavily loaded personnel ship, and while engaged in this work she was attacked in succession by fourteen dive-bombers. She escaped the main dangers, but a near miss caused serious damage, and she was compelled to call for assistance. H.M.S. *Express* (Captain J. G. Bickford, D.S.C., R.N.) and H.M. Skoot *Rika* closed her and managed, despite the threat of further attacks, to take off her troops. Working magnificently, her engine-room staff repaired the disrupted connections and damaged gear, and managed to raise steam again. Under her own power *Jaguar* made good most of the passage back across the Channel, but in the small hours, making water rapidly, she was compelled to call for help, and the tug *Simla* went out from Dover to her and, getting a line aboard, towed her in to safety.

The cruiser H.M.S. *Calcutta* had returned, as has been said, late in the evening of the 28th. Until 4 o'clock on this afternoon she lay off La Panne with her boats in the water working the beaches and taking cargoes of men from small craft. While these things went on her anti-aircraft armament was constantly in action. At 4 o'clock she left for Sheerness with slightly more than 1,000 men on board.

9

Fresh reinforcements of minesweepers reached Force K from Harwich at midnight—the 12th Flotilla. This consisted of *Waverley, Marmion, Duchess of Fife* and *Oriole*, all of them paddle-minesweepers, ships of the Clyde ferry in peace-time. Owing to the darkness and confusion they were unable to do anything until daybreak, but from then on they acted with a remarkable resolution.

Oriole, having no motor-boat and realizing the tremendous difficulties of taking men off with the inadequate boats she possessed, solved the problem by empirical means. Boldly and deliberately her captain, Lieutenant E. L. Davies, R.N.V.R., put his ship on to the beach, trusting that when the tide ebbed far enough men would be able to wade out and climb aboard and, using his ship as a pier, pass out to other ships in the deeper water astern of him. The account of her sub-lieutenant, Sub-Lieutenant John Crosby, R.N.V.R., gives a striking picture of the method used:

'We still had about two hours flood so when we got off a busy looking part of the beach, her head was brought slowly round until we were facing dead on to the beach, everybody went aft to raise the bows as much as possible, and we went lickity-slit for the shore and kept her full ahead until we jarred and came to a full stop. As we went in we dropped two seven-hundredweight anchors from the stern, to kedge off with. The men waded and swam out and many of them had to be hauled over the rails. The snag was that when a rope was thrown to a man, about six grabbed it and just hung on looking up blankly with the water breaking over their shoulders, and it was a hell of a job getting any of them to let go so that the rest could get pulled aboard.'

In this way some 3,000 troops passed over *Oriole* to safety. The ship was attacked at intervals throughout the day, frequently being straddled by sticks of bombs, but she was never hit, and in the evening, during another severe raid, Lieutenant Davies took *Oriole* off the beach with a load of 700 soldiers and nurses from the last of the field hospitals, and got safely back to England.

There is a sequel to this action that is not without significance. Lieutenant Davies was too busy for the next couple of days to bother much about official correctitude, but on May 31st his official conscience finally pricked him to action, and he sent the following signal:

'Submit ref. K.R. and A.I. 1167. Deliberately grounded H.M.S. *Oriole* Belgian coast dawn May 29th on own initiative objective speedy evacuation of troops. Refloated dusk same day no apparent damage. Will complete S.232 when operations permit meantime am again proceeding Belgian coast and will again run aground if such course seems desirable.'

There is a superb spirit in this message, a sort of blunt defiance of conse-quences that is the very essence of naval forthrightness. And in the official response there is much also of the essential spirit of the Royal Navy. Lieutenant Davies had deliberately hazarded his ship, a proceeding that is theoretically looked upon with much disfavour, but the reply that came to him read simply: 'Reference your telegram of May 31st. Your action fully approved.'

Oriole was fortunate in her boldness. Her flotilla leader, *Waverley* (Lieu-tenant S. F. Harmer-Elliott, R.N.V.R.), was not. *Waverley* had also been waiting for dawn, and when dawn came procceded to ferry with small boats, rowing them out from the beach despite an insufficient crew. By 3.20 in the afternoon she had loaded some 600 troops and lifted her anchor in the middle of an air attack. Half an hour after she had begun her homeward journey a near miss sent big splinters through the generator and left the engine-room in total darkness. She was being attacked by a force of twelve Heinkels which concentrated on her from a height of about 8,000 feet. For half an hour she dodged and twisted about under the rain of bombs, but another near miss ripped off the rudder and smashed in the side plating at the deck level and finally a direct hit wrecked the wardroom flat and, passing through the bottom of the ship, left a hole six feet in diameter. Four soldiers were killed and a number wounded. For another fifteen minutes the attack went on, but *Waverley* with her one 12-pounder, with Lewis guns, and with massed rifle fire from the troops, fought off low-flying machine-gun and bombing attacks, and no further bombs hit. Gradually, however, the ship became unmanage-able, she ceased to answer her wheel, and finally began to sink rapidly by the stern. The order to abandon ship was given and within a minute after it she had disappeared.

Lieutenant Harmer-Elliott had no time to get clear of the bridge and was still holding on to the rails when she went down, but he managed to kick himself free of obstructions. When he surfaced the water was thick with troops, but gradually the concentration thinned. The first ship to arrive on the scene of the disaster was a French destroyer which picked up many men. Subsequently H.M.S. *Golden Eagle*, together with drifters and a tug, was guided by aircraft to the scene. Lieutenant Harmer-Elliott himself was rescued after three-quarters of an hour, but many of his ship's company had perished, and with them between 300 and 400 of the troops which they had had on board.

Marmion (Lieutenant H. C. Gaffney, R.N.V.R.) and *Duchess of Fife* (Lieutenant J. Anderson, R.N.R.) both passed through the day unscathed, taking off heavy loads of men with their own boats.

Meanwhile the 'Smoky Joes' were back again. *Pangbourne*, having dis-embarked her troops in the morning, turned straight back for Dunkirk. She reached there in the late afternoon just as the master of the s.s. *Clan Mac-Alister* decided to 'temporarily abandon ship'. After the rescue *Pangbourne* went in to the beach, and Commander Watson sent away his whaler and motor-boat. There was a horde of Junkers 87s over the harbour by this time

—and one of these turned its attention on *Pangbourne*. Five bombs dropped close to her and the explosions lifted her out of the water. The men in her boats on the edge of the shallows thought that she had gone, but when the spray cleared she was still afloat. Four of the gun's crew, however, had been killed and the gun was damaged and would no longer train. The First Lieutenant and the Sub-Lieutenant had been wounded. A few moments later a second aircraft bombed the ship from the beam. Splinters from a near miss tore her degaussing gear and holed the ship in over a hundred places above and below the water-line. The boats had already brought off a number of soldiers and the other small craft had brought off a number of French and Belgians, many of them wounded. In view of the damage Commander Watson determined to get under way, and the engineers and all men who could be spared set to work to plug the holes with pieces of wood. It was now 7 p.m., and Commander Watson decided to return.

As he ran back for Dover he sighted H.M.M. *Gracie Fields*. She was one of the ships of the 10th Flotilla. On the previous day she had made a successful run, but this day disaster took her as well. When *Pangbourne* sighted her she was listing and out of control with her rudder jammed. A bomb had hit her in the engine-room, wrecking her engines. *Pangbourne* took off her troops and the majority of her crew, leaving a skeleton staff on board, and, passing her sweep wire, commenced to tow her. But the *Gracie Fields* made a bad tow. The jamming of the rudder sent her fetching out on the starboard quarter all the time and, as she was making water steadily, it became clear after an hour that there was no hope of saving her. *Pangbourne* closed her again and took off her captain and the remainder of her crew.

It was by this time dark and, her compass having been destroyed by the bombing, *Pangbourne*, with the hundred holes in the thin plating of her sides, limped back to England, feeling her way 'by hand' from buoy to buoy. Her difficulties were not quite over, however, for off Dover she was forced to steam in circles—her degaussing gear being out of commission—while minesweepers cleared a passage through freshly laid magnetic mines into the harbour.

Other ships of the '*Albury*' class, including the *Albury* (Lieutenant-Commander C. H. Corbet-Singleton, R.N.) herself, were also hard at work in the lifting this day, and with them the '*Halcyons*' picked up a heavy load. *Hebe* of this class was acting for a while as policeman-cum-traffic director off the Mole, and when at dusk it was decided to divert personnel ships to the east beaches, she did the necessary interceptions. From this she graduated to the general control along the beaches when the destroyer *Esk*, having filled up with troops, left for England.

H.M.S. *Skipjack*, a sister ship, towed over two Belgian launches *Ambleve* and *Sambre*, and with these two picked up a full load of men. *Ambleve* ran aground and was lost when her crew (under Sub-Lieutenant R. E. Blows, R.N.V.R.) were having a stand-easy and were being relieved by another crew.

In addition to these big sweepers there was 'Vernon's Private Navy'. This was a flotilla of five East Coast herring drifters—*Lord Cavan, Silver Dawn,*

Fisher Boy, Jacketa and *Fidget*. These ships had been taken up at the end of 1939 when wooden ships were desperately needed for the work of counteracting the magnetic ground mine. They were equipped with special gear and in May the flotilla was operating from Ramsgate under Lieutenant-Commander A. J. Cubison, D.S.C., R.N., with Lieutenant R. S. Armitage, R.N.V.R., as second in command. The ships themselves were commanded by R.N.R. skippers from the Grimsby and Hull fishing fleets.

They were sent over to Dunkirk to ferry from the harbour to larger ships lying outside. On this evening they picked up loads of 150 men apiece and stood out into the roadstead. Two of them attempted to discharge their troops into a large vessel which was lying outside only to find after angry efforts that she was abandoned and aground. It was then decided that the *Lord Cavan*, with Lieutenant-Commander Cubison, should remain at Dunkirk while the rest took their second loads of men back direct to Ramsgate, and this was done.

10

The complexity of Vice-Admiral Ramsay's force had grown incredibly in these last days. Sloops, gunboats, armed boarding vessels, Thames special service ships had all been added to his command, and one by one they come into the news this day. The sloop was H.M.S. *Bideford* (Lieutenant-Commander J. H. Lewes, R.N.), which went in to Bray to take off ferry loads from the small craft. The gunboat *Locust* (Lieutenant-Commander A. N. P. Costobadle, R.N.) was working the boats similarly, while the two auxiliaries, *King Orry* and *Crested Eagle*, were working from the Mole.

King Orry had a curious history. In 1918 she had represented the Merchant Navy at the formal surrender of the German High Sea Fleet. In this war she was recommissioned as an armed boarding vessel. After her first voyage to Dunkirk, early on the morning of May 26th, she was heavily shelled off Gravelines with the loss of eight soldiers killed and forty-eight wounded and considerable damage to the ship. This damage was repaired. The excellent account of her First Lieutenant, Lieutenant J. Lee, R.N.R., gives a clear picture of her end:

'We were able to leave Dover again on May 29th about 4 p.m. This time on our way up the fairway at Dunkirk we were bombed. Three bombs dropped just ahead of us, two dropping on the port bow and one on the starboard, and as we were proceeding at about twenty knots we were almost on top of them when they exploded, and the ship caught fire forward, the result of electric shorts caused by the explosions. No other damage was apparent, and we extinguished the fire and entered the harbour, intending to do the same as we had done on the previous occasion.

'However, we had to wait whilst a hospital ship came away from the berth, and whilst waiting were bombed by three aircraft. We only received one direct hit, on the stern, which blew the rudder off, and we just drifted alongside the Mole. The *Fenella* was alongside the same Mole only on the outside, the *Grenade* was blazing away furiously, and whilst we were drifting both her (*Grenade's*) magazines blew up. After drifting alongside we moored up, and the C.O. and myself carried out an examination of the ship, and found so many holes from shrapnel that it was considered impossible to do anything, and it was only a question as to whether or not we could get her away from the Mole. We eventually decided that we must make the attempt, because, if the ship sank, she would be certain to turn on her starboard side and thus block the entrance with her funnel and masts. This was all about 8 p.m. The tide was low and the ship resting on the bottom, so we had to wait for about two hours. Then when we came to shift we found that the rubbing strake on the port bow was actually resting on the Mole and the Mole was virtually carrying the whole weight of the ship. It took a tremendous effort of the ship's engines to get the rubbing strake clear and about two hours for us to get the ship out of the harbour stern first, just using the two engines. Our intention was to beach her out of the way, but she suddenly took a heavy list to starboard and sank almost without warning. This was at about 2 o'clock on the morning of May 30th. We all took to the water, my watch stopping at 1.59 a.m.'

The sinking of the *Crested Eagle* has already been detailed. She was a paddle-steamer and had been working in the Thames together with *Golden Eagle* and *Royal Eagle* as a flak ship. Known to uncounted thousands of Londoners as one of the favourite vessels of the Ramsgate run, she had a tremendous capacity, and would have been a most valuable vessel in the later stages of the evacuation.

Golden Eagle, as has been said, picked up survivors from the paddle-minesweeper *Waverley* and returned to Margate to land them. *Royal Eagle* (Lieutenant-Commander E. F. A. Farrow, R.N.R.) reached La Panne at 9 a.m., lay off the beach throughout the day, and at dusk weighed anchor with between 800 and 900 troops on board, returning to Margate during the night.

These were the bigger ships. There was a host of small naval craft, a host so large as to be nameless—anonymous in gallantry, magnificent in achievement. Trawlers, drifters, dockyard craft of all sorts, they worked superbly with their bigger sisters, and they too suffered loss.

It is as well to count up something of the total of this day. The loss was very heavy. Destroyers, as has been indicated, were of the very utmost value to our naval economy. Vital as they were in these operations, the need for them in the wider seas was even greater. Now in one day two were sunk, four were so battered as to be out of the war for a long time and others had suffered more or less damage. Fleet minesweepers, paddle-steamers. special service ships and auxiliaries of one kind and another had to be added to this total as lost or badly damaged.

Yet the reply of Vice-Admiral Ramsay and of the Admiralty which backed him was to send more and still more ships in to the dangerous beaches. There is an exhilaration about the decisions of these days that will put them amongst the great moments of history.

CHAPTER XI

THURSDAY, MAY 30TH

1

On Thursday, May 30th, Lord Gort estimated that only 80,000 British troops remained within the area of Dunkirk, and on that day he began his plans for the final withdrawal of the force. His instructions from England were definite and unequivocal. The telegram from the Secretary of State for War read:

'Continue to defend the present perimeter to the utmost in order to cover maximum evacuation now proceeding well. . . . If we can still communicate with you we shall send you an order to return to England with such officers as you may choose at the moment when we deem your command so reduced that it can be handed to a Corps Commander. You should now nominate this commander. If communications are broken you are to hand over and return as specified when your effective fighting force does not exceed equivalent of three divisions. This is in accordance with correct military procedure and no personal discretion is left to you in the matter. . . . The Corps Commander chosen by you should be ordered to carry on defence and evacuation with French whether from Dunkirk or beaches. . . .'

The problem now facing Lord Gort was intricate and difficult. The successful completion of the evacuation depended on his being able to remove his last flight in a night, since already daylight evacuation was becoming so hazardous as to be almost impossible. But shipping capacity was limited not so much by the number of ships available as by the fact that loading facilities on the single pier with its five-foot gangway had a definite and obvious mathematical limit, and that limit, as the evacuation continued, declined steadily.

The reasons for this are obvious, but it is desirable to state them once again. In the first place the approaches to the pier on the landward side were difficult. Streets were blocked by fallen debris and by burning houses. Communications were broken, even the field telephone arrangements were almost out of action by now. It was never possible to maintain a steady and unbroken flow of men without establishing highly dangerous concentrations in an area that was under almost continuous shell-fire.

It is clear at once then that the theoretical discharge rate of the Mole could never be maintained even from the landward side, but from the seaward side the factors were immensely more important. The Mole was long, very long, but the inshore end of it was extremely shallow. Report after report from the masters of the personnel ships stress this point. Ships sometimes had to change berths, dropping down towards the mouth of the harbour as many as

115

three or four times during a single lifting. Ships inshore were continually grounding, setting up difficult problems for the handful of tugs and small naval craft available. For practical purposes only the seaward half of the Mole was really useful, and not all of that at all states of the tide.

On the seaward half then depended the evacuation. But by now berths along the seaward half were occupied in many cases by immovable wrecks. Ships had been damaged alongside and had sunk with their mooring lines still fast to the flimsy quay. The superstructure of the Mole itself had been damaged, and had had to be bridged with every possible material from planks to mess tables. Moreover, on the bad-weather nights, and with the necessity for the destroyers to use speed in dodging shellfire, many of the masters speak of their ships as ranging heavily—lifting up and down, that is, as the swell came in from outside. When it is remembered that gangways in most cases did not exist and that men came aboard over single planks, over structures made of oars lashed together, over a score of improvisations, it will be seen that the theoretic rate of loading was cut down to the lowest of the bare essentials.

Always it must be remembered that there was no peace-time estimate of the number of people who could be embarked from this pier, for always it must be remembered that no one had *ever* embarked from this pier—that in peace-time no one would ever have considered it possible. It is as well throughout these days to recall this single fact.

And now Lord Gort had his problem made infinitely more difficult by the Government decision to take off French and British troops in equal proportions. Fresh French ships in answer to the urgent signal of the 29th were beginning to take part in the operation, but the dominant factor in every calculation that Lord Gort had to make was the capacity for embarkation of the pier and the beaches. He had to reckon in with this factor the increasing enemy interference from shell-fire. He had above all, for the purposes of his last 'flight', to remember the possible increase of this interference when the perimeter had shrunk to the outskirts of Dunkirk town itself. The Government decision to embark equal numbers of French and British—magnificently disinterested, magnificently generous as it was—virtually halved the number of British troops whom Lord Gort could hope to get away on a single night. The arrival of French ships at this stage of the proceedings could not materially increase the flow of evacuation except in some degree along the beaches, and it remains an acknowledged fact that throughout the operation British ships carried not only all but a handful of the B.E.F., but also the vast majority of the French armies which came through to safety.

In relation to Lord Gort's problem then the position was that since the flow could apparently not be accelerated beyond a certain point, and since, as the operation progressed, there must be a considerable downward curve from that point the question resolved itself into one of time. Thirty-eight thousand troops had been embarked on the Wednesday. With every possible effort, therefore, it seemed reasonable to expect that the remaining 80,000 men could be withdrawn in two days, but if the British were to be almost wholly responsible for the evacuation also of 80,000 Frenchmen, the time factor was inevitably doubled. Instead of holding the perimeter for an additional forty-eight hours, it would have to be held for at least four days.

2

The picture of Dunkirk on this day is one of the strangest in the long history of war—strange, terrifying, almost shattering. One of the best descriptions comes from an officer of Rear-Admiral Wake-Walker's staff The Admiral had transferred from H.M.S. *Esk* in the small hours of the morning, hoisting his flag in H.M.S. *Hebe*, a Fleet minesweeper, off Bray-Dunes, and it was hoped to keep *Hebe* as a sort of permanent flagship off the beaches.

'Dawn found us still there,' says the report, 'and it brought with it one of the most astounding and pathetic sights I have ever seen. Almost the whole ten miles of beach was black from sand dunes to waterline with tens of thousands of men. In places they stood up to their knees and waists in water waiting for their turn to get into the pitiably few boats. It seemed impossible that we should ever get more than a fraction of all these men away. The immediate and urgent need was for more boats—both small pulling boats for inshore work, and power boats to tow them seawards to the ships. These we asked for, and as the day progressed many more arrived. . . .'

In the town conditions were worse. The steady shelling, the incessant bombing, had ruined more streets, more houses, more stretches of the quays. The smoke was worse this day, the flames higher.

But once more the weather had turned in our favour. There was low cloud, visibility was poor, there was little wind and the sea was calm. These things are of the very first importance. They were to play this day, and subsequently, an increasing part in the success of the lifting. The poor visibility meant that the German guns at Nieuport and near Bergues and at other points in the perimeter could not see to mark the fall of shot in town and in harbour. At times, when the visibility fell even below the general level of the day, they could not see to bombard ships in the channels. The low cloud cut out almost entirely the dive-bomber and the enemy's fighters. Neither of these things meant that there was a complete cessation either of artillery or of air action; that went on throughout the day, and there were times when it went viciously: but, broadly speaking, accuracy of all types of attack was considerably hampered on this Thursday by the weather.

The absence of wind—during part of the day it was a drift from the eastward—and the calmness of the sea were as important along the beaches. The absence of a serious swell meant easier handling of the ships alongside the Mole, but, infinitely more important, it meant easier boat work on the open sands.

Again it must not be taken that this statement means there was no difficulty in handling boats. There was difficulty in every boat trip that was made from the ships offshore to the edge of the tide-mark. Throughout the day, despite the calm, there was a slight natural swell which alone was enough to give tired and exhausted men a heavy task. But ship movements added heavily to the weight of this task. The destroyers' main protection against enemy air attack lay in their manœuvrability and in their speed. It is true that there was little full-speed work in the Dunkirk channels, for the water was too shallow for destroyers to go flat out at 30 knots and more. But even at 20 knots, which was roughly the average speed they used, a destroyer throws up a very considerable wash. Pictures of destroyers taken from high in the air are familiar to everybody. Invariably they show enormous chevrons spreading from the bow and the stern of the ship wide over the sea's surface. Dunkirk channel was narrow, and though the actual dry beach lay perhaps three-quarters of a mile from its centre, the shallows where the boats grounded were sometimes more than a quarter of a mile out. There was here a slight but distinct bar that, at most states of the tide, impeded progress, and here the wash from fast-moving ships threw boats up and beached them broadside on, flooded small craft, and put out of action the motors of open dinghies and lifeboats.

But on this day the army, and particularly the men of the Royal Engineers, ashore made every effort to turn the advantages of the weather to our purpose. At La Panne and again at Bray and at various points in between them, new piers were improvised by driving vehicles and lorries—even Bren-gun carriers—into the water nose to tail. On the top of these they made causeways of planks, and some of these causeways; coming out far beyond the edge of the low-water mark, made piers at which, when the tide rose, motor-boats and lifeboats could come alongside and load afloat. These piers at once became a target for extensive bombing, but they survived notably throughout the day.

3

The lifting from the beach this day was heavy but, as throughout the operations, the bulk of the troops were carried in the destroyers, working ceaselessly under a strain that is beyond description, and in the personnel ships. *St. Helier* brought back one of the earliest loads. She had crossed in company with two French troopships and picked up, according to her report, over 2,000 troops. She had the usual bombing attacks and claims to have brought down one plane. That night she was back in Dover. Again her master's report is a masterpiece of understatement:

'On coming out H.M.S. *Sharpshooter*, a minesweeper, went across the *St. Helier*'s bows and there was a collision. At the request of the captain of the *Sharpshooter* the *St. Helier* did not withdraw but steamed into her at half speed on one engine for forty minutes to ease the pressure on the bulkheads. It was not quite dark and enemy planes came over dropping flares to locate the ships. A tug came to attend to H.M.S. *Sharpshooter*. Enemy planes were continually around the ships and in the confusion the *Princess Eleanora* struck the *St. Helier* on the starboard bow. After ascertaining this vessel required no assistance the voyage was just proceeding when the *St. Helier* ran over a wreck, but fortunately without doing any underwater damage. The troops were landed at Dover. . . .'

The one important thing in this quotation is the last sentence: 'The troops were landed at Dover.'

Royal Sovereign, which had made two crossings the day before, completed her loading at 5.30 a.m. and with the vessel full (and her master's laconic statements mean precisely what they say) returned to Margate. Again she allowed herself no time at all. At 11.35 she was alongside Margate pier disembarking. At 1 o'clock she was heading for Dunkirk again—an hour and a half occupied with the turmoil of coming alongside and with the disembarkation of tired troops as a substitute for rest! At 6.20 she was anchored and once more embarking troops.

Royal Daffodil crossed about the same time and picked up 2,000 French troops.

Princess Maud left at 11.30. At 1.30 she rounded the green buoy off Calais and, approaching Gravelines, observed and reported a large French steamer beached near the shore. Her master, Captain H. Clarke, reports: 'Two or three objects resembling tanks were visible close to the stranded steamer.'

'At 1.57,' he says, 'an explosion occurred aft. Clouds of smoke were in the position of No. 5 lifeboat on the poop. It was thought the poop ammunition had exploded, but this idea was soon expelled a few seconds later when a salvo of four shells straddled our stern, one scoring a direct hit on No. 5 lifeboat. Course was altered away from the shore so as to present a smaller target. Before this was completed another shell scored a hit at the water line into the engine-room, starboard side; several other shells fell all around us.

'When out of range, course was set again for Dunkirk.'

Four men were injured and first-aid was given them while officers inspected the damage. It was found that the shell in the engine-room had made a hole in the skin plating more than a yard square. Working desperately, her people plugged it with mattresses, which checked the flow, but they were unable to stop it entirely. As it was clearly impossible to carry on with the passage, Captain Clarke listed the ship by draining tanks and hoisting out his boats on the port side, and turned back for Dover. 'All hands,' he says, 'were disappointed at being thwarted.' By 4.30 she had moved into the inner dock at Dover to effect her repairs. Her four wounded men died subsequently.

Prague anchored off Folkestone at noon in what her master describes as dense fog. At 5 o'clock she left for Dunkirk, and her master, Captain Baxter, says blandly: 'Certain minor departures from the official route were made necessary by the draught of the ship.' Since the official route concerned itself as much with wrecks and mines as with what might be called normal navigational necessities, the remark is interesting. She experimented with a new berth well inside the outer harbour along the eastern jetty, and embarked what she describes as 'a full load of troops'. A thousand men with equipment, rifles and ammunition, weigh very little under 100 tons. By the time she had her load aboard *Prague* was hard on the bottom. 'It took the combined efforts of two tugs (*Lady Brassey* and *Foremost* 87) and both engines working at full power to get the ship afloat', and this was done under shell-fire with 'several projectiles bursting in the water close to the ship'.

King George V made her second run on this day, but reports no particular trouble.

During the course of the early night the Mole was again heavily damaged, so much so that when *Maid of Orleans* arrived a little after midnight her master says: 'The only berth now usable was the one at the extreme end as the pier had been subjected to heavy damage from shell-fire and bombs.' None the less she embarked 1,253 officers and men, including a number of wounded.

Once again it must be remembered that these were not all the personnel ships which sailed for, or reached, Dunkirk on this day. It is improbable, even with these big ships, that every detail of the movements will ever be described. With the little ships it is impossible.

Alongside the personnel ships the hospital carriers continued their admirable work. They suffered from the same disabilities as the personnel ships. Their draught was too deep for the difficulties of that narrow harbourage. They lifted up and down with the swell, with the wash of the ships outside, with the waves set up by bursting shells and bombs .Their improvised gangways parted, broke as the ship ranged, carried away.

In the very early hours the *Isle of Guernsey*, which had had to return empty owing to the appalling bombing of the previous afternoon, reached Dunkirk again. Her master, Captain Hill, speaks of the whole place being brilliantly lit up by fires. There were many periods when the Dunkirk flames helped us in the darkness of these nights, taking something of the confusion from the crowded harbour. By 2.15 a.m. she had taken 490 wounded on board,

'. . . although the ship was shaken every few minutes by the explosion of bombs falling on the quay and in the water. Just outside we found the sea full of men swimming and shouting for help, presumably a transport had just been sunk. As two destroyers were standing by picking these men up, we threaded our way carefully through them and proceeded towards Dover. It would have been fatal for us to attempt to stop and try to save any of these men, as we made such a wonderful target for the aircraft hovering ahead with the flames of the burning port showing all our white paintwork up. Everything was comparatively quiet on the way across, except that just before we got to Dover a patrol boat headed us off as we were heading straight for a recently laid minefield.'

This was the *Isle of Guernsey's* last trip. In this and previous voyages she had sustained copious minor damage. The sum of it was such that she had to lay off now for repairs. By the time her repairs were complete the evacuation was over.

Dinard went in under orders after dark.

'During the whole of this time,' says her master, 'shells were bursting about us, enemy planes were continuously overhead, and bombs were dropped all round us, but none near enough to damage us. Whilst alongside, shellfire was very intense, and planes overhead were giving the range by Very lights. The pier was damaged, and men coming along the pier to destroyers to seaward of us were being wounded and killed. Shrapnel from bursting shells was continually coming aboard. We found great difficulty in making contact with those in charge of wounded, the same conditions prevailed regarding gangways, having to use planks and skids as best we could. The range was getting very close at this time, shells falling and bursting not more than 20 yards from our vessel, causing her to rock and range. It was with difficulty we kept our improvised gangways intact. The water was falling, and our draught being 13 feet 6 inches we decided, when 14 feet 6 inches was reported to me, to prepare to get out. We still found difficulty in contacting the wounded, and at 11.45 p.m., the water being under 14 feet 6 inches, we cut our moorings and backed out.

'We made our way down the channel by steaming close to the buoys and using an electric torch to identify their markings. We had no idea what wrecks we should find in our way. We steamed cautiously, however, to the end of the channel and eventually made our way back to the Downs. We were under shellfire to the end of the channel 3 W. buoy.

'During both these expeditions I cannot speak too highly of the conduct of the crew; officers, engineer, sailors, firemen, and stewards did everything in their power to assist me in every way, getting the wounded aboard over these improvised gangways, with the disturbed water causing the ship to shake and range continuously, carrying stretchers, standing by to sound our depth, carrying men wounded alongside, aboard, and a dozen and one things. They were splendid, I cannot draw attention to any special case.

'The engineers deserve great credit, giving us all we asked for from carrying stretchers to giving us the last ounce in manœuvring. With one or two exceptions, every man was ready to go over again, but circumstances were such that we were not required.

'I trust that the devotion and loyalty of these men (and one woman, a stewardess of fifty-nine) will not be forgotten.'

As always, her master writes without passion and without heat, but there are points in this brief statement that cannot be forgotten. One of them is his reference to his engine-room staff.

There is a special grimness about the duties of the engine-room in times like these. On the deck it is possible to see at least something of what is happening. There may be moments when to see is terrifying, but there is, on the deck, always at least the illusion of freedom and of space. But the engine-room staffs worked deep in the ships at the bottom of long, frail ladders that had a tendency to jar off or to smash when bombs hit. They worked in absolute blindness for all the brilliance of their electric light, feeling only the shaking of the ship, the concussion of the bombs outside, the thud and clang of the splinters against the plating. There could be no illusion of shelter in their working place. No one knew better than the engineers the thinness of the skin plating, the ease with which those sides could open to the slash of steel, to the blast of high explosive. No one knew better than they the instant consequence of such opening; the furious anger of steam from the broken pipes, the crash of machinery wrecked at high speed, the rush of scalding water that overwhelms. Throughout the operation the courage, the self-sacrifice and the devotion of engineers and stokers is beyond praise, as it is beyond description.

There is one other point—the mention of the stewardess. This was Mrs. Goodrich. She had been one of the ship's stewardesses on the peace-time runs when *Dinard* carried her loads of cross-Channel passengers. She had carried on. Dunkirk was 'carrying on'. Mrs. Goodrich's name is the only woman's name in the list of Dunkirk awards. She received a Mention in Dispatches. Besides her there was a handful of nurses. They too worked magnificently.

Again, as with the personnel ships, this is not a complete record of the work of the hospital carriers on this day, but it will serve for example. Always it must be remembered that these ships were without even the exiguous protection of Bren guns and Lewis guns and light ack-ack that the transports and some of the others carried. The red cross of Geneva, the white paintwork, and the lights should have been their protection. Against another enemy they would have been enough, but not against the German.

By this day some of them were beginning to show signs of strain. At Newhaven the crew of *St. David* protested against sailing unless the ship were armed or escorted. If either of these alternatives was adopted, they were ready to sail instantly. At Newhaven the naval sympathies were entirely on their side. The naval officer in charge there recommended at once that escort should be provided, but from the Commander-in-Chief at Portsmouth came the reply regretting that he had 'nothing left' with which to escort them!

4

But great though the work of the hospital carriers, of the little coasters, of the paddle-steamers, and the cross-Channel boats was, it is the work of the little ships that on this day captures and holds the imagination. Thursday was the day on which the little ships came into their own—the first day of their glory. Once again the few will have to speak for the many. It will never be possible to gather the record of every ship in this incredible armada, but in the accounts which follow may be read the story of them all. It is a story that needs no comment. In the stark, unimaginative writing of the men and the skippers of these tiny craft may best be read the immensity of their service, the grandeur of their task.

In addition to the tremendous numbers of new motor boats, launches, ferries, and the like that came in this day, there were still the 'veterans' of Tuesday and Wednesday. *Shamrock*, after the running down of the *Queen of England*, searched for her convoy mates and found *Canvey Queen* with her engine broken down again. She took her in tow and anchored for a little close to a burning troopship.

'Dawn soon came, we stared and stared at what looked like thousands of sticks on the beach and were amazed to see them turn into moving masses of humanity. I thought quickly of going in picking up seventy to eighty and clearing off, with the sun behind me I calculated I should find some East Coast town. We got our freight, so did the *Canvey Queen*, when I realized it would be selfish to clear off when several destroyers and large vessels were waiting in deep water to be fed by small craft, so I decided what our job was to be.

'We could seat sixty men and with those standing we had about eighty weary and starving British troops, some without boots, some only in their pants, but enough life left in them to clamber on board the destroyers with the kind hand of every available seaman.

'Again and again we brought our cargo to this ship until she was full, the *Canvey Queen* and the *Maud* were doing likewise.

'The destroyer moved off whilst we were still made fast and we were carried to a very awkward position under her stern and saved from anything more serious by the quick work of an A.B. who set us adrift.

'By this time I was numb to anything else that was taking place, aeroplanes, guns, and flames. It was not bravery but just a will to snatch those boys away from the hell which might overtake them at any time.

'Our next load, nearly all north-country lads, had an officer (a captain I believe), who demanded that his men be taken to a destroyer and not a troopship as I had been ordered. I regret having to tell him to shut up but having done so the whole crowd were silent and well behaved and were put aboard the troopship.

'Navigation was extremely difficult owing to the various wreckage, upturned boats, floating torpedoes, and soldiers in the water trying to be sailors for the first time, they paddled their collapsible little boats out to me with the butts of their rifles, and many shouted that they were sinking, we could not help them. I was inshore as close as I dare. "Stop shouting and save your breath, and bail out with your steel helmets," was the only command suitable for the occasion. Scores offered me cash and personal belongings which I refused, saying, "My name is Barrell, Canvey Island, send me a postcard if you get home all right". They have all forgotten—no wonder!

'Frantically we kept running in front of the large red brick building which will be familiar to thousands, the remains of the white-hot *Crested Eagle* still smouldering just eastward and still they marched column after column through the gaps in the sand dunes.

'Whilst serving the destroyer, H.M.S. *Anthony*, I could not get a volunteer from the soldiers to take the three or four ships' lifeboats back to the shore. They were all done up.

'I ordered Roy Brown to do so; he did this without hesitation and continued this work for a considerable time, while his place on the *Shamrock* was taken over by a seaman lent to me by the destroyer commander. The *Princess Maud* ventured in too close and was aground, scores waded out and climbed on board her, but it was obvious she was to be another souvenir for Fritz.

'I was ordered by an officer of this destroyer not to bring any more wounded but my very next trip found me helping aboard a badly wounded young lad, for this I was shouted at by the same officer. My reply was a rude army one which could not be withdrawn.

'The officer was right, there was no room for medical attention on his ship; but what could you do?

'I took in two or three large Carley floats one behind the other. These were filled to capacity, about fifty men in each standing up to their waists in water in the net inside.

'My craft was well loaded too, we were just making for our destroyer when I was brought to a standstill; my engine stopped, the propeller had fouled, I believe a human obstruction. There were many in the shallow water. I signalled the *Canvey Queen* to take me in tow, and with a struggle against the tide she got us alongside and every man got aboard O.K. One of them took my revolver from under my nose—it's a way they have in the army. Naval men came down and tried to free the obstruction but without success. I was too weak to dive under the thick black oil which surrounded us, so rather than be left sitting on our useless craft I asked to be taken on H.M. ship. This was the last straw, having to leave my vessel which constituted my life savings.

'My spare fuel was taken off by a small naval motor-boat, the fire extinguishers were taken on the destroyer. Roy Brown followed me up quickly on board as she was about to leave. I took one more glance at the beach.

'I sat down beneath a gun with my hands over my face and prayed.'

Bonny Heather was one of the up-river Thames motor-yachts. She left Ramsgate at 6.45 on Thursday evening under the command of Lieutenant C. W. Read, D.S.C., R.N.R., as leader of a convoy of ten motor craft all towing ships' lifeboats. On the way across the convoy lost one boat, the *Wolsey*, a motor-yacht from Hampton Wick, which broke down owing to dirt in the carburetter and had to make fast for the night to the North Goodwin lightship.

It is as well to record some of these failures. They were not failures of the spirit. The condition of these boats has been stressed before this, but it must be borne in mind in considering the passages made by every single one of the little ships. *Wolsey* was a well-found, well-equipped craft, but Mr. A. Malcolm, her owner, says in his account:

'In the meantime I had got the engine in running order, and the water-tank filled, but had no time to clear out the filters and carburetters or to attend to other details which would have been seen to in ordinary circumstances.'

No time—that is the keynote of all this strange effort. Every movement, every sailing was made under the compelling necessity of speed.

Bonny Heather reached Dunkirk safely. This was the first of seven complete round trips which she made between Ramsgate and Dunkirk, in addition to incessant work in filling up transports and destroyers lying off the beaches. Normally she carried sixty men, once she carried eighty.

THURSDAY, MAY 30TH

Bonny Heather came from the upper Thames. Side by side on the beaches working with her were two of the ferry-boats from Sandbanks at the mouth of Poole harbour. At 11 o'clock on the morning of May 29th, when *Southern Queen* and *Ferry Nymph* were busy moving backwards and forwards across the harbour entrance, their owners, Messrs. J. Harvey & Son, received a telephone message ordering them to have the boats ready to proceed to Dover. At 11.30 they were instructed to proceed with all possible speed. At 1 p.m. on May 30th they were off Dover. At Dover the boats were taken over by naval crews, and by the middle of the afternoon were on their way towards the great column of the smoke. Mr. C. H. Harvey says:

'Eventually *Ferry Nymph* came back to Ramsgate, and early in July was towed back from Ramsgate to Poole. Examination revealed many scars in her woodwork, and aboard her were a large number of empty cartridge cases, sundry other relics, and a good quantity of Dunkirk's sand. The boat was reconditioned, and is now in service again.

'The *Southern Queen* did not return. We have since met an army officer, when on leave, who stated that a bomb fell close to the boat shortly after he had been taken off the beach in her. She collapsed and slowly sank. He remarked that he had been in the boat many times whilst it was on the Sandbanks ferry, and little expected to be in it again on the other side of the Channel. He stated that the boat made two more trips inshore after rescuing his party before being sunk.'

Motor-yachts, ferry-boats, the types were becoming swiftly more varied. From Burnham-on-Crouch came another little convoy.

'On Wednesday, May 29th,' says L. W. Salmons, her skipper, 'returning from a day's oyster-dredging with the oyster-dredging smack *Seasalter*, we were hailed by the oyster-dredging vessel *Vanguard* and informed that a naval Commander wished to see the *Seasalter*.

'We immediately went ashore and were introduced to Commander Bowles, R.N., who told us the *Seasalter* was required to attempt to help bring back some of the soldiers off the beach at Dunkirk. I volunteered to take the *Seasalter* and asked for a crew. Dick Cook, the engineer, and Bill Bridge, one of the hands, also volunteered.

'The Commander said there would be two other boats, the oyster-dredging vessel *Vanguard* (Albert Grimwade, skipper, Joe Clough, engineer, Dick Woods, deck hand) and M.Y. *Ma Joie* (whose crew consisted of George Harvey, Walter Amos and Bertie Payne, a youth of seventeen). We were required to leave the following morning at 5 a.m. Our particulars were taken and the Commander wished us luck. We spent the rest of the evening taking aboard stores, water and refuelling. We did not have a boat on deck as the Commander had said it would be in the way. Not altogether liking the sound of this, I took a small pram dinghy. (Incidentally this provided sleeping accommodation for a couple of soldiers on the return.)

'At 4.45 a.m. the next morning we all mustered and got aboard and got the engines running. It started to come in foggy and by 5 a.m. it was thick, which delayed our start until 6.30 a.m.

125

'It was decided between us that M.Y. *Ma Joie* should be leading ship, *Vanguard* second and *Seasalter* in the rear.

'We started in this order, passed down the river out of the Whittaker Channel, through the Barrow swatch across to the North Foreland. By now there wasn't a ripple and the tide was running to the west.

'From the North Foreland we shaped our course for Goodwin light vessel. We passed close to this and shaped our course to Dunkirk.

'After about two hours' steaming it came down foggy. We had no charts and our compasses were not of the best. Roughly half-way across we spoke a patrol ship, asking if we were all right. This was at the West Buoy. Weather still calm. We could just begin to hear the guns and some aircraft which we couldn't see because of the fog.

'It was 6 p.m. when we spotted the coast and picked up Dunkirk lighthouse right ahead.

'We could still hear aircraft above. Then the fog lifted altogether and the A.A. guns lct loose at the planes, one of which spotted us, dived low, and machine-gunned us, but missed. He was so low I could see the crosses, undercarriage stowed away, and the dirty oil marks. He didn't waste a bomb on us. Another plane made a dive but couldn't get in position to fire.

'We were now getting close to the shore, and by 6.45 p.m. were at the harbour entrance. We asked someone on the breakwater where we should go and were told "Get out of the harbour".

'We then approached a destroyer to ask what to do. When we got near the destroyer opened fire at the aircraft, so we sheered off. After this we steamed up towards the east beach. No one spoke to us or took any notice at all. We thought this strange as we had been told there would be hundreds of boats and someone to tell us what to do. Instead of that we were the first three small craft there. By then we didn't want any telling.

'The soldiers were coming off the beach clinging to bits of wood and wreckage and anything that would float. As we got close enough we began to pick them up. We saw a rowboat coming off loaded right down with troops and with this we went to and fro bringing off as many as it would dare hold, and in the meantime we went round picking up as many as we could. When we had got a load we would take them off to one of the ships lying off in the deep water. Some were Dutch coasters flying the White Ensign and the armed yacht *Grive* [commanded by Captain the Hon. Lionel Lambert, R.N. (Ret.), a magnificent veteran, and subsequently lost with all hands].

'Unfortunately the *Ma Joie* had got into difficulties and had to be towed off the beach. We went alongside and were told the rudder was broken and the propeller fouled. It was decided they should come aboard us as their ship was useless.

'All this time the din was deafening, aircraft flying around, A.A. guns banging, and all over the place fountains of water would fling into the air. We went on getting loads and taking them off to the ships. When the two boats came off next time the *Ma Joie*'s crew and a soldier took over and these three men rowed back and forth all the rest of the time we were there.

'If it hadn't been for this soldier we shouldn't have done much good. He was a man of roughly forty, born at Tollesbury, Essex, and before the war was a barge skipper. This man worked like a hero. He marshalled the men into the boat and out again. Where he got the boat from we don't know, as along the whole length of the beach there was no more than eight or nine rowboats. He could have gone aboard one of the ships but he wouldn't leave the rowboat.

'About ten o'clock it began to get dark. The ships got their anchors up and got out of it. We were still getting soldiers aboard and could find no ship to put them on. By 11 there we were with ninety men aboard. We didn't know what to do with them, so we put twenty aboard the *Vanguard*. We gave them some beer we had, and Bill made tea and gave them biscuits and the remainder of our stores. We didn't know whether we were doing right or wrong. Bombs were falling and shells bursting all round, so we decided to make for Ramsgate.

'How we got out without seeing or hitting anything I don't know. Any rate we did, and by 12 o'clock we were clear. We then shaped our course for Ramsgate. We hadn't gone far when we met a convoy of small ships going in. They had no lights, as we had no lights. Jerry was flying around dropping parachute flares and bombs, but they fell nowhere near us.

'We kept coming across and all kinds of navy ships came and had a look at us. At nearly 4 a.m. (Friday) the wind started to freshen and some of the soldiers on deck got a wetting. We heard no more aircraft and steamed into Ramsgate with the *Vanguard* in the rear at 8.30 a.m. The soldiers went ashore. All seemed very happy, if they had been a bit sick. We lay alongside the quay. No one spoke to us until the afternoon when we were told with the other small craft to disperse immediately. We made for Burnham and arrived home at midnight Saturday, dirty and tired but glad to have brought a few chaps across.'

Tigris I came from Kingston. She passed through Sheerness in command of her owner, Mr. H. Hastings, proprietor of the 'Gloucester Arms' at Kingston. She arrived at Ramsgate and left there at 2.30 on Thursday morning with a convoy of little ships.

'We still had no pilot but were told to follow a pilot-boat. Owing to the engine of the pilot-boat breaking down we were asked to tow her but we found that our boat was not powerful enough for towing as the sea was very rough. We had to leave the pilot-boat and were told to steer for the burning flames at Dunkirk which would take us about two hours.

'We arrived at Dunkirk but found we could not get in close enough to get the troops off the sands, so we got the *Lansdown* to go in and we pulled her off ground after the troops were aboard. We also used the *Princess Lily*. We were told to proceed to La Panne which is about nine miles further round the coast. Owing to the engines failing we had to leave with only a few troops. We proceeded back to Dunkirk where we took five more loads off the shore which we were now able to do owing to the rising tide. Whilst these operations were being carried out we were being bombed and we were under machine-gun fire. We took the troops off to the nearest vessels which were larger ships.

'On the fourth run back to the shore I was blown overboard by the blast from a bomb. After I got back aboard the vessel we proceeded to take more troops but our boat became disabled and I was told to abandon her as she was in a sinking condition. Eight hundred troops were taken off the beaches during the period and we were then taken back to Ramsgate in the same boat as the troops.'

Constant Nymph, which had got away amongst the very earliest of the up-river boats from Isleworth, reached Sheerness on the 28th.

'The other boats from Isleworth were nearly all present by the time we got back from breakfast. We were informed that we could sign on for one month but did not then know for what purpose we were required, although I had been told by the pleasant-voiced man who spoke to me from the Admiralty that it was dangerous.

'Of the boats which had come down from Isleworth, mine was the only one in charge of its owner so far as I know, and at that time we had rather thought that there was nothing very urgent in the wind and most of the men who had brought boats down from up-river had done so without any previous knowledge that they would be doing so and had had no opportunity of making arrangements with employers, etc., so that few of them felt able to sign on for a month and went back to town very regretfully by train.

'The opportunity of playing boats for a month with the navy seemed to me too good to miss in any case, and I had been able to warn my partners that I should be away for a bit, but there was some difficulty in getting signed on and I toured Sheerness Dockyard interviewing numerous people until late in the afternoon, and by about 5 p.m. had formed a pretty accurate idea what the job was and was quite determined not to be put off, so I appealed to the Commodore himself, who was supervising the fuelling and victualling of the motor-boats at the basin. Within half an hour I was signed on and back at the basin, and by 6 p.m. was making my way out of the basin with a crew of two young ratings, a full tank, and deck cargo of petrol, water breaker, and enough provisions to last my little gang for about a week, including a large lump of raw beef, and two small sacks of potatoes—raw. The boat seemed very overcrowded.

'As we passed out of the basin the Commodore hailed us and told me that we had got to tow a navy cutter to Ramsgate. These were brand-new boats, fully equipped and weighing pretty nearly as much as my own little craft, and had very thick new tow ropes. I must admit that I regarded this idea with considerable misgivings and was truly grateful for the fact that my boat had Samson posts and not cleats.

'Orders being orders, we took the cutter in tow and dug out for Ramsgate, having our own chart of the estuary and trusting to luck for the rest. The faster boats, which were also the bigger and less burdened by their cutters, got out of sight about dusk and another motor cruiser about the same size as my own and an open launch were the only vessels left in sight. The launch was having continuous engine trouble, and the other motor cruiser was also having a little trouble, so I turned back and closed them at 10 p.m., so that we could keep together, taking the launch in tow. Before it became quite dark a drifter turned up from Sheerness and informed us that she had been sent out to look after the motor-boats. Her captain decided to anchor for the night and we tacked on to him. The occupants of the open launch went on board the drifter for the night but my crew and myself remained on my boat and slept between the intervals of popping up on deck to be sick. It was by no means a comfortable lie for a 24-foot boat under five tons in weight. . . .

'Our instructions were to get fuel from a tanker which could be found in the roads off Deal and we spent until 12 noon getting to Deal and chasing round innumerable tankers, all of which dealt in heavy oil only. At 12.10 we found a drifter with some petrol. At 12.40 we left in tow to a drifter for the Belgian coast with other motor-boats. One tow parted and *Maid of Honour* was very nearly sunk by the rope from *Isa* crossing her. The rope was cut just in time and we were fairly well over in the mix-up. About 2.20 we were ordered to return to Ramsgate under our own power and tied up there at 3.10 p.m. We arrived at Ramsgate and got tied up in the outer harbour in time for a late lunch and I then made inquiries about the job in hand.

'I found that the course to Dunkirk then in operation had grown to be a round trip of from 140 to 150 miles, and as such a trip would take me the best part of twenty-four hours, since I could not count on doing maximum speed and should have to consider petrol in any case, it seemed to me that a mere dash over to rescue about fifteen men, all my boat would hold, was not good business. The Commander whom I saw on the point, like all the naval officers with whom we had dealings, was just as helpful as was possible and agreed with me that the best use for my boat was to go over with two navy rowing-boats in tow to a ship so that we could operate on the beach and fill the ship. After a few inquiries I was told to rendezvous outside the harbour at 9.30 a.m. on Thursday, May 30th, and accordingly had a good night's sleep with my crew, the first since Sunday night so far as I was concerned.

'We turned out on the morning of May 30th and by 9.30 a.m. were lying in tow to H.M.S. *Jutland* with a navy whaler and cutter. *Jutland* was one of the Dutch diesel-engine cargo boats taken over by the navy and flying the White Ensign, and would carry about 450 men; H.M.S. *Laudania* was a similar ship. Both these ships carried Lewis guns fore and aft for A.A. defence.

'I do not know what delayed our start, probably alterations in the mine-fields, but we lay on tow to *Jutland* until 3.30 p.m. outside Ramsgate harbour with occasional intervals of casting off in order to carry officers from one ship to another lying outside the harbour. At about 3.30 we got going and, with our own engines running at about 6 knots, were towed to Dunkirk in about six hours (an average of about 12 knots). This was a very uncomfortable trip, destroyers kept crossing and passing at high speeds making a heavy wash and we had to try and keep my boat sheered off to port while the cutter and whaler were sheered off to starboard. Sometimes we came together in spite of all effort, but no damage was done.

'*Constant Nymph* and the pulling boats were secured to a curious vessel of

Belgian extraction called *Johanna*, and she was on tow to *Jutland* by a wire rope. This wire parted about 4 p.m., but *Jutland* was stopped in time to ease the strain before the last single strand went, thus saving some injuries and possibly lives. *Johanna's* crew fell on her deck and I crouched behind my cabin trunk as that wire spun and strand after strand parted. *Johanna* was like a heavy old scow and at the rate we were going the wire was like a banjo string and the whip back if the last strand had gone would have been terrific. At 4.50 p.m. a new manilla rope had been passed and we got going again.

'We arrived at Dunkirk about dusk and turned along the beach eastwards for a few miles before *Jutland* dropped anchor. We cast off tow at once and I took the whaler and cutter in tow myself and set out for the beach. It was slightly misty as well as dark, but it was not really a dark night and visibility was not too bad. As this point had not been worked before, we did not know whether Jerry was there or our men. Being quite unarmed we had to be canny about hailing until we knew who was there. At first we could find no life on the beach, but after a short time were hailed by Frenchmen and for a little while found Frenchmen only, and made one or two full journeys back to the ship with them. The procedure was to tow the whaler and cutter to the beach and swing them round and cast off tow in about 3 feet 6 inches (my draught being 2 feet 6 inches). The cutter then dropped her grapnel and went in as close as she dared without grounding the whaler, and troops waded out to board them. As soon as the two boats were full they called for the motor-boat and pulled up on the cutter's grapnel; I would come past and take the cutter's bow rope in passing and swing out towards the ship which had to lie about three-quarters of a mile to a mile out.

'While the whaler and cutter were loading I patrolled parallel with the beach, keeping as close as I dared without grounding, it being essential that the motor-boat should not take ground as it was the only motor-boat in that area and the cutter and whaler had only three men apiece aboard so that they were not in a position to row out to the ship, except at a great loss of time.

'While patrolling my job was to pick up any swimmers or waders and any odd craft which had put out from the shore. There were several of these. After the first few loads had been taken to the ship, all Frenchmen, a British officer waded out and was picked up by me and reported that a whole division of British were waiting to be taken off a little nearer Dunkirk town than we had been working.

'I took him aboard, went back and picked up the full cutter and whaler, and took them all back to the ship, reported to the captain of *Jutland* that the British were further up the beach, and that I was going there, a big fire just inshore was my leading mark as the British were just to the east of this. From then on we worked to this point and the French came down the beach and mingled with the British: *Jutland* was filled roughly half and half British and French.

'After we had been going to this point for about three or four trips, a German bomber most inconsiderately dropped a large bomb on our large fire and blew it out like a candle, this did not matter very much as I had other leading marks and the mass of troops had increased so that they were quite visible on the beach.

'By about 3 a.m., May 31st, *Jutland* was full, and she sailed at once to avoid the dawn bombing, Jerry was trying to bomb the ships as they left loaded, but his efforts throughout the ten to eleven hours that I was working on the beach were very poorly rewarded. . . .'

Stoker Banks (whose exploits with *Pauleter* have already been described) had transferred at Ramsgate to the motor-boat *Marasole* with his crew. Going alongside the Mole at Dunkirk *Marasole* was damaged. She was taken in tow by a trawler but sank subsequently, and Banks and his crew were brought home in the trawler.

Sub-Lieutenant E. T. Garside, R.N.V.R., who had been ferrying in *Elizabeth Green* the previous day, had also transferred to another ship. This Thursday he took over the R.A.F. launch *Andora II*, ferried for some while, and then brought back twenty-three Frenchmen.

Lady Sheila (Skipper G. H. E. Brooks), a small motor-coaster, arrived at Dunkirk at 9.30 p.m., and in an hour and twenty minutes had picked up nearly 400 men; she left immediately for Dover.

Yachtsmen, oyster-fishermen, ferrymen, publicans, doctors—to the infinite variety of the little ships, the infinite variety of trades and professions, the types of Englishmen were matching themselves.

And with them the men of other nations were working. *Lydie Suzanne* was a Belgian fishing vessel, part of the great fishing fleet of 450 ships that left Belgium as the enemy swept down to the coast, carrying refugees. They had moved west straight through the Channel to Dartmouth, to Milford Haven, to Brixham and to the French western ports across the Channel. When the urgent signal to Admiral Darlan was made, many of them turned back in company with French vessels. *Lydie Suzanne* was one of them. On May 30th, on her first trip, she lifted just over 100 officers and men. With her was the *Gilda*. Returning on the 30th with a large number of British and French troops on board, she was attacked, and a Belgian naval officer, Commander Ghesselle, who was in charge of her, was seriously wounded. These little ships ranged from 217 to 23 tons. Some of them were so small that, for example, the *Maréchal Foch*, lying alongside the quay in Dunkirk harbour, was actually sunk by the weight of the men who crowded into her. That story has a sequel for her gallant crew were determined not to be defeated, and on the following day at low tide they salvaged their ship, reconditioned her and eventually brought back no fewer than 300 men.

And with these oddly assorted ships there were three little fleets belonging to organizations so vastly different in character that only a cataclysm of this kind could bring them together.

One belonged to Messrs. Pickford, the great firm of general carriers. Built for transport trade between the Solent ports and the Isle of Wight, they were to carry across the Channel new freight. There were five of them— *Bee*, *Bat*, *Chamois*, *Hound* and *M.F.H.* Their crews varied from four to two, and with only two exceptions all their people insisted on going with their ships.

Bat (J. T. Butchers, master), on her first trip, picked up fifteen of the crew of the French destroyer *Bourrasque* and took them back to Ramsgate.

Chamois (A. E. Brown, master) made two attempts before she actually reached Dunkirk, being beaten back each time by air attack.

' *Chamois*, making her third attempt, succeeded in getting within two miles of Dunkirk where she encountered two transports who were being heavily bombed. She went to the rescue of the survivors, who were French and Belgian troops. The clothes of many of these were on fire and the ammunition in their pockets was exploding. The crew managed to rescue 120 men, whom they transferred to a French trawler for medical attention.'

The second fleet consisted of the splendid craft of the Royal National Lifeboat Institution. At all the salient points of the British coastline the motor lifeboats of the R.N.L.I. have worked to save men from the fury of the sea. Now, from the strategic points that faced the new-conquered coasts, the lifeboats came in to save men from the fury of the enemy. From Great Yarmouth to the north, from Poole to the south, from all the harbours and headlands in between, they came to Dover and to Ramsgate.

Louise Stephens	Great Yarmouth and Gorleston
Mary Scott	Southwold
Michael Stephens	Lowestoft
Abdy Beauclerk	Aldeburgh
Lucy Lavers	Aldeburgh
E.M.E.D.	Walton and Frinton
Edward Z. Dresden	Clacton-on-Sea
Greater London	
(Civil Service No. 3)	Southend-on-Sea
Charles Dibdin	
(Civil Service No. 3)	Walmer
The Viscountess Wakefield	Hythe
Cyril and Lilian Bishop	Hastings
Jane Holland	Eastbourne
Cecil and Lilian Philpott	Newhaven
Rosa Wood and Phyllis Lunn	Shoreham Harbour
Lord Southborough	
(Civil Service No. 1)	Margate
Prudential	Ramsgate
Guide of Dunkirk	From building yard at Rowledge; crew from Walton and Frinton
Thomas Kirk Wright	Poole and Bournemouth

There were difficulties with the lifeboats. They are big craft, specialized for their work of sea rescue. Two generations back lifeboats were beach boats. To-day they draw, for their size, a fair amount of water. They are motor-driven and they are, with their elaborate cellular construction, heavy ships. They are not fit 'to take the ground'. When the coxswains and crews of the first of the fleet arrived at Dover and were informed that their task was to take men off the beaches, they demurred on the ground that, on a falling tide, they would inevitably be stranded and lost. There was no time for argument, and the Admiralty immediately took over completely the three boats which had raised the objections, manning them with naval crews; and, considering that what applied to some might apply to all, they—to the considerable indignation of the boats which came after from Yarmouth, Lowestoft, Southwold, Aldeburgh, Walton and Frinton, Clacton, Southend, Hastings, Eastbourne, Newhaven, Shoreham and Poole, and the new *Guide of Dunkirk* —announced that naval crews would take over, and that they were only prepared to utilize the services of mechanics. This decision was a difficult one, but in these days hours counted. There was no time for discussion, little for explanation. It was acknowledged that there was substance in the objections, but the situation demanded every possible effort and every possible degree of speed. The decision stood.

The crews of the two ships nearest to the disaster, however, had already volunteered *en bloc*, and the Dover lifeboat had also volunteered but was retained at Dover for service in the neighbourhood of the base. They did magnificent work. The coxswains of the Ramsgate and Margate boats have each made reports that are worthy of the very finest traditions of the Institution.

Edward Drake Parker, coxswain of the Margate lifeboat, says in his report:

'On May 30th in the forenoon, an Admiralty official rang me up on the telephone asking if I would go to Dunkirk in the lifeboat and take as many small boats as I could. I said I would and was told to report to the Senior Naval Officer at Margate which I did, and got instructions to proceed in company with a Dutch barge, naval officer and ratings in charge. Boats were taken from the foreshore and put on board of various craft that were also going. The weather was very fine with a light southerly breeze and we left Margate about 5.30 p.m. The lifeboat was towed by the barge to save petrol and make sure we should not lose company as the commander knew where best to pick the troops up. We arrived at Dunkirk about midnight when the barge ran aground on the sand, with the lifeboat also bumping, but afloat, I tried to tow the barge afloat but could not, but at the commander's request I laid out an anchor on a long length of wire (which on the flowing tide was a great help to the barge as the wind veered to the N.W. blowing fresh, making a lee shore). We could by then, out of the darkness, hear someone calling out so we went as close as we could to them, and when they waded out to us up to their armpits in water, they proved to be French soldiers, these we took on board and transferred them to the barge. The commander then asked us to get some British troops; we again went in, and this time found some men of the Border Regiment. By now it was low tide so we loaded up with the troops (how many I could not say) and they said they had got a couple of stretcher cases, could we take them if they carried them off, and we told them yes. The weight of the troops had put the boat hard on the sand and we had to wait for the tide to flow. After putting this load on the barge we again returned to shore, dropping stern anchor to help us get afloat. We were joined this time by a whaler from a destroyer and we asked them if they would bring off the two stretcher cases, which they did, and we again loaded and returned to the barge with them. By this time it was getting daylight and we could see the troops east and west of us stretching along the sands as far as we could see. We again went in, getting a very heavy load and returned to the barge, when he told us to take them to a destroyer which was lying some little distance away. This we did and returned for more. The wind by this time had veered to the N.W. and was making a nasty surf on the shore. We continued to make further trips to the destroyer—how many times I do not know.

'By this time things were getting bad, troops were rushing out to us from all directions and were being drowned close to us and we could not get to them and the last time we went in to the shore it seemed to me we were doing more harm by drawing the men off the shore, as with their heavy clothing on the surf was knocking them over and they were unable to get up. The whaler from the destroyer which went in to the shore with us on our last trip was swamped, so was the motor pinnace that was working with the whaler, and so it was all along the sands as far as I could see, both sides of us and there was not a boat left afloat. All this time we were working very near to Nieuport and as I could not see that I could do any more good I decided to return, and we left about 8.30 a.m.'

This was the *Lord Southborough's* first trip.

H. Knight, coxswain of the Ramsgate lifeboat *Prudential*, says in his report:

'Proceeded to a given position at Dunkirk; accompanying boats discharged water and rope as instructed, as also did lifeboat, found seas breaking in the shoal water approach to beach; had to lay off on account of the deeper draft of lifeboat; found naval ratings who manned wherries were not skilled at handling small boats under such conditions; members of lifeboat crew took their boats and places, and although an intensely dark night managed by shouting to establish communication with officer in charge of troops on beach; arranged for men to take to the water in batches of eight which was the capacity of the small boats, and each boat conveyed them to the lifeboat, thence to the awaiting craft in attendance: about 800 were safely transported on Thursday night and when the last three boatloads were being taken from the water, the officer called, "I cannot see who you are; are you a naval party?" He was answered, "No, sir, we are members of the crew of the Ramsgate lifeboat." He then called, "Thank you—and thank God for such men as you have this night proved yourselves to be. There is a party of fifty Highlanders coming next." When the last of the first party were safely aboard the *Rian*, a motor craft of some 500 tons, the captain received instructions to proceed to Dover; his engines were in poor condition and the engineer feared for their holding out during the passage; two members of the crew of the *Prudential* were taken aboard to assist with their local knowledge of tides and currents, thus enabling the vessel, now with engines running on two cylinders only, to make Ramsgate with her valuable freight: had these men not been deputed for this job the possibilities of the vessel grounding on the Goodwins and becoming a casualty would in my opinion have been great. . . .'

She towed small craft, including the punt *Carama* (belonging to her Acting Second Coxswain, A. Moody), to ferry troops through the shallows of the beach.

This was the beginning of the lifeboats' efforts. It was by no means the end. Whether towing other craft in convoy, or by themselves, the rest of the little fleet, with their crews of naval ratings, made the passage.

And behind them at Dover the District Surveyor of Lifeboats, Commander J. M. Upton, R.D., R.N.R., reaching Dover from Brightlingsea, organized a petrol-engine repair party, adding to it Mr. J. A. Black, District Engineer for the East Coast, Mr. J. Hepper, District Engineer for the South Coast, and Messrs. James, Cavell, Stock, Lister and Foster—all mechanics of the Institution. For the next three days they rendered invaluable service in making doubtful small craft serviceable, in coaxing balking engines to the heavy needs of the Dunkirk run.

There was yet another fleet, not belonging to a single body but joined by a community of work and of interest—the fleet of the Thames tugs. As the work went on more and more tugs were sent out of the Port of London. Before the evacuation was over there was left in the whole confines of this, the greatest port in the United Kingdom, only one tug capable of handling a deep-sea ship. Up the coast Harwich and even the Humber sent tugs. Down the coast Dover, Newhaven, Portsmouth and Southampton sent their complement. In a previous chapter something has been told of the work of the Dover harbour tugs. Their record by no means stands alone. Tug after tug of the great fleets—Suns, Watkins, Gamecocks, United Towing Company and many others—came up to Ramsgate and to Dover with a white bone in their teeth and the steam pluming at their exhausts.

The tug *Java* had left in the afternoon of the previous day in company with three drifters and four motor-boats. At daybreak on the 30th she went as far in to the beach as she could go and lowered her boat. This was manned by the mate and one deck-hand, who rowed to and from the beach transferring troops to motor-boats, who again transferred them either to *Java* herself or to the drifters. After working in this way all the afternoon, she went into Dunkirk and berthed alongside the Mole, taking off a full complement of troops. Leaving Dunkirk she moved up the beaches to La Panne, transferred her troops to destroyers, and returned to repeat the work all through the evening, filling a minesweeper as well as other craft in the vicinity.

'After filling ourselves up again,' says her master, W. Jones, 'there was no other vessel in the vicinity to transfer these other troops to, so decided it would be best to return to England with them. (During these operations we had been violently attacked from the air by dive-bombers and machine-guns, attack lasting for an hour and a half.)

'It was 5 p.m. on May 30th when we left Dunkirk, and when five miles off we observed a plane in the water. Had a hard job to prevent troops from firing at it as they took it for granted it was German. It proved to be British and we succeeded in saving the two airmen in her. After proceeding another mile we ran across troops clinging to wreckage and swimming about. We lowered the small boat again and also placed the tug so that some of the men were able to climb on board, the mate and deck-hand also bringing them on board with the small boat. I remained and did all that was possible, saving everyone that could be saved, and then carried on to Ramsgate. . . .'

The tug *Persia*, which had already done admirable work in bringing in a damaged destroyer, left Dover on the Wednesday, towing the dumb barges *Sark* and *Shetland*, loaded with food, ammunition and water, across the Channel. The supply situation was rapidly becoming critical in Dunkirk, and as a desperate measure it had been decided to strand barges laden with these commodities on the beach at high water, so that they could be discharged by the troops themselves as occasion served and as need arose. *Persia* took her barges with some difficulty to a point 4 miles east of Dunkirk, arrived there at dawn on the 30th, and at 12.45 p.m. anchored the barges as close in to the beach as was prudent, so that motor-boats could tow them in on the flood tide.

'Then,' says her master, H. Aldrich, 'left Dunkirk at 4 p.m. with soldiers and equipment, anchoring in the Downs at midnight.'

Foremost 87 picked up *Sark* and *Shetland* from their anchorage and ran them in to the beach 100 yards apart off Malo-les-Bains.

'Heavy aerial bombing and ground gunfire going on while doing this job,' says her master, J. Fryer, 'shrapnel splinters hitting deck very hard. Finished this and steamed inside harbour again. Things getting worse but everybody happy. Troopship *Prague* unable to get away from eastern arm Dunkirk harbour, loaded with troops, so took same in tow and towed out clear to Dunkirk Roads. Told to stand by and assist in any way. One or two little jobs leading destroyers to berths in the dark rendered—heavy shelling and air raids still in progress. At 12 midnight told to return to Dover. . . .'

Foremost 87 had crossed in company with the Dover rescue tug *Lady Brassey*, who was searching for the sloop *Bideford*, which had been bombed and was aground. Off Dunkirk she reports a large oil tanker settling by the stern. She closed it, but found that her crew had already taken to the boats and disappeared. *Lady Brassey* failed to find *Bideford* and throughout the early part of the night assisted *Foremost* 87 between the Dunkirk Moles.

The work of the tugs this day, as throughout the operation, was beyond praise. It is essential always to remember in the sober sparsity of their words the amazing achievement that these reports represent. Piloting ships in that traffic jam of big craft and small, working under fire with small boats manned by amateurs and enthusiasts, passing their tow to one damaged ship after another, seeing ships sunk on tow and gone aground in the narrowness of the sandbanks—their work was incessant, breathless and often bitter. They performed it superbly.

5

In Sheerness the work of the Small Vessels Pool and of Rear-Admiral Taylor's staff was now in full spate. It is difficult to picture the complexity of it. Captain Docksey was making the converted motor-car engines of week-end yachts run well enough to take them to Dunkirk. Captain Coleridge of *Wildfire* was producing stores and accommodation for a constant stream of officers and ratings out of reserves that were already extended to the utmost. The Chief Constructor of Sheerness dockyard, Mr. S. R. Tickner, was building rafts small enough to be manhandled, large enough to carry men. The shipwrights of the yard were making ladders with which to load small ships from the high decking of the Mole or to pick up men who had waded out to ships grounded off the shallows of the beaches. The whole yard was working in a complete abandonment of official formulae, of paper work, of red tape.

And the boats were going away. Convoy after convoy was pushing out to sea: ships' boats still and service boats, dockyard launches and 'X' lighters, Dutch craft of one kind and another, Belgian (the Belgian Government issued a statement on this day authorizing the use of all suitable Belgian ships for evacuation purposes, but many had been working since the start). The total of small craft sent out from Sheerness is extraordinary. There were more than 100 motor-boats, 10 lighters, 7 skoots, 1 oil tanker and 6 paddle-steamers in Admiral Taylor's division—this, of course, is quite apart from the naval craft under the Nore Command.

The *Johanna* was over again on this day under Sub-Lieutenant Carew-Hunt, R.N. She was working with *Constant Nymph*, whose story has already been told, and Carew-Hunt tells of the curse of Babel that fell on the beaches—the enormous difficulty in making the first French troops, who in the main were not fighting troops, understand the dire necessities of the evacuation. There were many cases in the first hours where, away from the scattered naval beach parties, boats coming in were rushed by bodies of these troops.

One of the worst was that of the open motor-boat *Eve*, a 24-foot craft in charge of Leading Seaman Norman Furse, R.N.R. Furse had as crew one A.B. and a stoker. At Dunkirk *Eve* ferried six boatloads from the beaches, but on the seventh trip she was rushed by a party of French soldiers, and neither Furse nor the others could make them understand that the boat was overloaded. She had barely left the beach when the men moving in her so altered the trim that she flooded at once and sank. Furse himself started to swim ashore, but he was caught in the swift tidal current and it was several hours before he reached the beach. As far as he knew he was the sole survivor.

There were other cases of boats being swamped. But there were some like Carew-Hunt who, producing a revolver, got the elements of discipline into demoralized men. The inland Frenchman is infinitely less accustomed to the ways and possibilities of the sea even than the inland Briton. He could not understand that twenty crowding into a grounded boat would set it so firmly on the sand that nothing on earth could move it. He had neither the patience nor the self-control to wade out with the boat until it was safe to clamber aboard. Many Frenchmen, standing in the shallows, shouting wildly for help, worked themselves into a passion of something like panic.

Lieutenant Irving, R.N.R., took over *Triton*, a motor-boat, as leader of a convoy of eight small craft. He had lost three to engine trouble by the time he made the North Goodwin light. The convoy was ordered to a point between Bray-Dunes and the Moles. On the way across they had low visibility with showers of heavy rain, and navigation became almost impossible. Just at dawn they fell in with a heavy destroyer, loaded with troops, and damaged by shellfire aft. She confirmed the course that Lieutenant Irving was steering and all five of the remaining boats reached the beaches safely near the cupola at La Panne.

From 5 o'clock until noon *Triton* worked at the towing of small boats from the edge of the surf to the destroyers, the trawlers and the Dutch skoots. At midday she was hailed from a desttoyer and boarded by Vice-Admiral G. O. Stephenson, C.B., C.M.G., R.N. (Ret.), (serving as Commodore, 2nd Class), who asked to be put ashore as he wished to make contact with Lord Gort. *Triton* dropped him as close in as she could, and the Commodore waded ashore up to his neck in water. Commodore Stephenson returned subsequently and carried on in *Triton* until the small hours, when she ran aground for a while.

Silver Queen, which sailed with her, began her work by ferrying to the destroyer *Esk*. Like *Triton* she worked desperately throughout the day ferrying, and estimates that she carried off about 1,000 troops in some eleven trips. Eventually she was told by a trawler to go into harbour to find another ship. After searching the harbour she was unable to make contact, and decided to take back her load (about 100 French soldiers) to England. They had neither charts nor compasses on board, but decided to trust to a sense of direction. When they estimated that they were about half-way over they found a soldier's compass and used that, and after some little while sighted land. Assuming from the compass bearing that this was Ramsgate, they closed the land but, when they were about half a mile off, shore batteries opened fire on them, and they discovered that they had come close in to the German-occupied coast near Calais. For over twenty minutes they were under fire, and the Belgian launch, *Yser*, which was in company, was hit and started to make water badly. *Silver Queen* was hit in the stern by a single shell, and both ships were in a position of extreme danger when a destroyer came up in response to a Very light fired by *Yser*, and gave them covering fire.

At 9 o'clock in the evening *Silver Queen* reached Ramsgate. It was a very close thing. As she tied up to disembark her troops it was obvious that she was slowly sinking, and very shortly afterwards she was awash.

Sub-Lieutenant T. K. Edge-Partington, R.N., sailed (with the convoy which included *Golden Lily* and *Johanna*) in command of the Dutch eel-boat *Chantecler*. He had engine trouble—the words are almost unnecessary—and, only able to make good 4 knots, he continued by himself with a compass that, situated directly above the engine, revolved slowly round and round. *Chantecler* picked up thirty men and came back with them, and all the external trouble she reports in the round trip was creeping past a floating mine at night.

Sub-Lieutenant Lawrie, R.N.V.R., took over the Thames pleasure steamer *Maldon Annie IV*, one of the queer little double-enders that used to run from Westminster Pier to Greenwich. She was towed over half the distance by *Strathelliott*, but, working off the beaches, her engines finally broke down, and she was last seen drifting in an unseaworthy condition.

The list can be continued indefinitely. These few names, taken almost at random, are a fair cross-section of the whole. There were many scores of these little ships run by youngsters who had come up at speed from H.M.S. *King Alfred*, the great R.N.V.R. training school on the south coast, by men from contraband control work at Torbay, by sub-lieutenants on leave who had snatched at the wings of opportunity, by gunners training at Whale Island, by torpedo experts doing their courses at H.M.S. *Vernon*, or the Signal School. They worked with and among civilian volunteers. Crews were mixed: sometimes a civilian volunteer commanded a crew of naval ratings; sometimes a sub-lieutenant captained a crew of bank clerks and stockbrokers. It was haphazard, it was methodless, it was improvised—and it worked superbly.

6

The naval effort as a whole on this day was on an unprecedented scale. If measure is wanted for it, it lies in the reply from the Commander-in-Chief at Portsmouth, the greatest of all the peace-time bases of the Royal Navy, to the urgent appeal from the hospital carriers at Newhaven for escort. The Commander-in-Chief at Portsmouth regretted that he had 'nothing left' capable of the task of escort!

This is an astonishing commentary. Chatham, Portsmouth, Plymouth and the little auxiliary bases between had been swept bare of naval craft. Nothing was left in them that would float or fight. Into the narrow waters, into the channels between the sandbanks, had been poured every single armed ship that the navy could command between Land's End and the Firth of Forth.

Already the destroyers were lifting more men than the personnel ships, the passenger ships that were built and adapted to that task of carrying men. Alongside the Mole they were enduring the same bombing, in the narrow waters of the approaches they were undergoing the same enormous difficulties of turning and manœuvring their ships in shoal waters already crowded with wrecks, obscure and macabre under the smoke pall of the burning oil wells. Off the beaches they were sharing with the minesweepers, the Dutch skoots and the other ships, the task of lifting men, fed by the endless gallantry of the small boats. It meant lying stationary or backing and filling in the swift-running tide for five, six or eight hours at a time before they picked up a full cargo. It meant dodging in those hours as much sometimes as

a dozen air attacks; shorn of manœuvrability, shorn of speed, shorn of everything save the matchless judgment, the unwearied skill of their captains.

Only figures can indicate the immensity of this work. There were seven
destroyers each of which in a single period of twenty-four hours landed more
than 1,000 men. All of them carried out two trips in the period. *Wolsey*, with
amazingly quick 'turn rounds', managed to carry out three, lifting 1,677
men. The old *Sabre*, in spite of slight damage from a bomb, and in spite of
coming under the fire of the shore batteries, lifted 1,700 men. *Vimy* (Lieutenant-Commander M. W. Ewart-Wentworth, R.N.) brought back 1,472;
Express, 1,431; *Whitehall* (Lieutenant-Commander A. B. Russell, R.N.),
1,248; *Vanquisher*, 1,204; *Vivacious*, 1,023. These are the heaviest of the
liftings.

And lifting men was only a part of their duties. They had other arduous
work. There were destroyers flung right forward almost to the coast of
Holland as a screen against the E-boats that were thrusting through. There
were destroyers patrolling all the while against the submarines that were
beginning to be used. On either flank of the perimeter, off Nieuport and off
Mardyck and Gravelines they were bombarding the German guns that tried
to close the channels, they were wrecking the newly established German
positions from which tanks and infantry were trying to approach our hurried
line. Throughout all the days of the evacuation that strange, independent
battle of shore bombardment went on; two—three—sometimes four destroyers moving up and down the shallow water blasting the enemy with every
gun that would bear.

And on the homeward channels they kept the same endless vigil—guiding
the small craft and the bewildered large, keeping them from the danger areas
of fresh-sown mines, fighting off E-boat attacks, gathering in the lost, picking
up survivors, hurtling forward at high speed to put a barrage between a
threatened convoy and the endless onrush of the bombers.

The Norwegian campaign is to the destroyer men who took part in it a
tangled memory of incessant action, but never in naval history have small
ships worked so ceaselessly, so utterly without rest, so continuously in the
very eye of the enemy as at Dunkirk.

This day is full of destroyer names. Once again in almost every account
from the big ships and the small craft the names crop up. There is an almost
humble gratitude in most of these brief mentions: ships were put on the right
course here—the destroyers came between them and the guns there—the
destroyers' fire broke up this bomber attack or beat off that E-boat. In the
last resort the destroyers picked up survivors from the water.

H.M.S. *Esk* had been the flagship for the night of the 29th, but destroyers
were needed so urgently at a dozen points that in the small hours Rear-
Admiral Wake-Walker transferred his flag to the Fleet minesweeper *Hebe*.
It was intended, as has been said, to keep her as a floating headquarters, but
once again the need was too insistent. There were too few ships in the area.
She filled with men and left. Admiral Wake-Walker transferred to a
destroyer filling up with men off the beaches, waited till she was full and

transferred to the next. His flag stayed afloat, but surely no flag has ever had so many changes in so short a time.

At dawn a report spread that the East Mole was no longer serviceable, but just before 4 o'clock H.M.S. *Vivacious* (Commander E. F. V. Dechaineux, R.A.N.), which was lying temporarily disabled off the harbour, signalled to Dover that a survivor of H.M.S. *King Orry*, who had just come off, stated that it was still perfectly practicable but that no troops were near it.

Immediately after the destroyer *Vanquisher* (Lieutenant-Commander W. C. Bushell, R.N.), temporarily in control off the beaches, signalled Dover that more ships were urgently required east of Dunkirk. A little later *Vivacious*, under way again, moved to the beaches herself and made a similar signal. It was essential to have more ships and boats. Between them they picked up many men, and other ships, coming in in answer to the call, took off fresh loads despite the breaking day. H.M.S. *Anthony* (Lieutenant-Commander N. J. V. Thew, R.N.) worked the Bray area. Other destroyers were in at the Mole, once again picking up heavy loads—*Icarus*, *Malcolm* and *Codrington* among them. *Codrington* picked up her usual complement of about 900 men.

The day was costly. The French had sent in their first reinforcements of craft, and *Bourrasque*, one of the older French destroyers (she had been built in 1925) set off a mine, and sank while heading back to Dover with a load of men on board. She sank in daylight and craft near her picked up the majority of her survivors, but approximately 150 men were lost. She was the first French destroyer to be sunk during the actual Dunkirk evacuation. Nor was this the only destroyer loss. A little later H.M.S. *Wakeful* (Commander R. L. Fisher, R.N.) was heavily attacked by dive-bombers. She was hit and sunk.

Wakeful was one of the old destroyers known colloquially in the navy as the 'V and W's'. The oldest ships of the class were laid down in 1916 (*Vivacious*, who was herself working the beaches this day, as early as July of that year) and the great majority were completed before the Great War ended. They were the oldest important class of destroyers in service, and it is a most remarkable testimony to British shipbuilding that, when this war came with its stringent demand for destroyers, they were able to take their place beside ships that had been built in the twenty years between. Fifteen of the class took part in the Dunkirk operation. The 'V and W's' are reputedly lucky ships. Their luck held at Dunkirk save in the case of *Wakeful*. She was the only one of the fifteen to be lost, joining *Wessex* which had been sunk on May 25th during the Calais bombardments. *Wakeful's* sinking brought the number of British destroyers already totally lost during 'Dynamo' to three or, with the addition of *Wessex*, to four; but it must be remembered always that besides these there were, as has been indicated, a very much greater number of destroyers put out of action for the foreseeable period of the evacuation by severe damage.

Perhaps the most remarkable story of the day, however, belongs to the one sloop that was at Vice-Admiral Ramsay's disposal during the operation— H.M.S. *Bideford*. She was a ship of the 'Shoreham' class with a displacement of 1,105 tons. She had been working, as has been described, off Bray beach close to H.M.S. *Jaguar* in the later part of May 29th. While men were being brought off to her from the beach—she had already loaded something like 400—a bomb struck on her quarterdeck. Forty feet of her stern was blown away, and she suffered heavy loss of life amongst her crew and the men who were crowding her decks; twenty-five were killed. Some fifty others were badly wounded, and Surgeon-Lieutenant John Jordan, R.N., her doctor, though his sick-berth attendant had been seriously wounded, dealt magnificently with the casualties, assisted by George William Crowther of the 6th Field Ambulance, who had embarked with the troops. The unwounded survivors were moved to another ship, but Crowther volunteered to stay with Lieutenant Jordan on board *Bideford* although by this time she had been run aground and seemed 'unlikely to reach England'.

The tugs *Lady Brassey* (F. J. Hopgood had now replaced G. W.Blackmore as master) and *Foremost* 87 were sent from Dover to see what they could do about H.M.S. *Bideford*, but meanwhile the wreck had refloated and had been taken in tow by H.M. Gunboat *Locust*. *Locust* was half her size, a shoaldraught gunboat built for river work, drawing only 5 feet of water, mounting two 4-inch guns, and looking rather more like a pleasure yacht than a man-of-war. She was theoretically capable of 17 knots, but not with an unwieldy tow like *Bideford* astern of her. The story of that voyage back is among the epics of Dunkirk. For thirty-six hours she towed the helpless ship—all through May 30th and into the 31st. The tugs passed them in the fog that came down at intervals during the day. Grimly she clung on to her damaged consort. All through the night she kept on, yawing wildly from side to side through the stream of traffic, and by the following morning she was off Dover. There *Bideford* was taken in tow by the tugs *Simla* and *Gondia* and brought safely in to the submarine camber in Dover harbour.

The work of the sweepers on this day was of the high standard that had already been established. Fleet sweepers' names recur along the beaches and in the harbour. Trawlers and drifters put in magnificent work. 'Vernon's Private Navy' was there again; so were the paddle-sweepers, *Marmion*, *Duchess of Fife* and *Oriole* prominent amongst them, with *Sandown*, *Medway Queen* and many others. The Thames special service ships were again at work. *Royal Eagle* reached La Panne at 1 p.m., having been shelled by the shore batteries during the last stages of her passage. She lay off the beaches for the rest of the day, picking up forty wounded and between 1,800 and 1,900 troops, and at dusk took them back to Sheerness.

And there was a second magnificent salvage job on this day. It arose not out of enemy action but out of the extraordinary hazards of the night navigation, and a brief account of it has already been given in the report of s.s. *St. Helier*'s proceedings. The credit belongs to the tug *Foremost* 22, which had left Dover at 1.35 p.m. with five small vessels in company and had arrived at Dunkirk a little before dusk. Frederick Mafeking Holden (who was acting master owing to the illness of her regular master, C. Fieldgate) says:

'I took the *Foremost* 22 to the harbour entrance following a destroyer which was going in. The destroyer commenced firing at the entrance to the harbour, and as other destroyers and a large troopship were endeavouring to enter, I decided to get out. I ordered the engines astern, backed out of the harbour, and proceeded along the coast in the direction of Ostend.

'We proceeded along the coast for about two miles, and as it was getting dusk and there were no small boats to bring the troops out to my vessel (her draught was 13 feet aft), I decided to go back to the harbour entrance to see whether I could be of any assistance there.

'There was some confusion owing to the heavy bombardment from the shore and the activity of hostile aircraft.

'Just after 11 p.m. I heard the sound of a heavy collision close to my vessel. I went to the spot and found that the *St. Helier*, owned by the Great Western Railway Company, had been in collision with H.M. Minesweeper *Sharpshooter*. The weather was fine, sea smooth. There was very little wind, and visibility was fairly good. The *St. Helier* struck the starboard bow of the minesweeper with her stem.

'When I arrived at the scene of the collision the two vessels were together. The officer in charge of the minesweeper hailed me, and asked me to take hold of his vessel as quickly as possible. I at once ordered my crew to get out the tow ropes, and then made fast. I backed my stern close up to the stern of of the minesweeper and passed the end of the wire aboard. The tow rope consisted of sixty fathoms of 16-inch manilla rope, shackled to fifty fathoms of 5-inch wire. The end of the wire was made fast to the stern of the minesweeper, and the manilla was on our towing hook. I had to use care in passing the tow rope because I could see the minesweeper had a number of depth charges on her stern.

'As I passed the tow rope to the minesweeper, the *St. Helier* backed away and carried on with her business. I made fast at about 11.20 p.m. and at once commenced towing in a westerly direction. . . .'

H.M.S. *Sharpshooter*, with the eventual assistance of the tug *Empire Henchman*, was got safely into Dover after a tow of fifty miles that took the tug thirteen hours. *Empire Henchman* herself had been towing small boats from the deep water immediately off the beach out to a destroyer.

It was a day of mingled disaster and success. The loss and damage to destroyers and the bigger ships was important, but to counterbalance it there was the fact that those ships which got back brought with them 45,955 men, much the heaviest total of the evacuation to date, a total that was the equivalent of a fifth of the whole of the British Expeditionary Force in France. Despite the losses it was a notable advance on the previous day, and round Dunkirk the perimeter was holding out.

CHAPTER XII

FRIDAY, MAY 31ST

1

Friday, May 31st, was the sixth day of Operation 'Dynamo'.
Almost precisely in the centre of the long, flat beach between Nieuport Bains and Dunkirk, the Franco-Belgian frontier comes to the sea. This was the end of the so-called extension of the Maginot Line, the frontier on which the B.E.F. had lain for the first nine months of the war. But in this coastal sector it was more than that, for along the last segment of the frontier ran the outer works of the fortified area of Dunkirk. These were old, permanent works improved and adapted to some extent during the previous nine months for the purposes of modern war. They were not the defences that to-day we know are necessary to stand against the modern conception of war, but they were, in comparison with the line we had been holding, strong for defence in the hands of resolute men.

Approximately a quarter of a million men of the British Expeditionary Force fell back upon Dunkirk. In the last stages of the retreat and in the defence of the perimeter many died and more were captured. Precise figures are not possible. This applies to all day-to-day figures given throughout the period of the operation, but it is probable that approximately 230,000 men of the B.E.F. reached the evacuation points. Of these 150,000 men had already been lifted by first light of this morning. In addition to them a large number of men of the French 1st Army and the remnants of Giraud's 7th Army—men who had been fighting in Holland or with the Belgians of the right flank—had already been embarked in British ships. The numbers available for the defence of the perimeter were shrinking. It was essential, in view of the enormous strength of the German thrust in armour and in infantry, that the line of the perimeter should be drastically shortened. The old defences made the obvious line. They had from the very first been calculated in all the plans for the defence of Dunkirk as the inevitable line of the first major contraction of the perimeter.

'I judged that it would be imprudent', says Lord Gort, 'to continue to maintain our position on the perimeter outside the permanent defences of Dunkirk for more than twenty-four hours longer, and I therefore decided to continue the evacuation by withdrawing 2nd Corps on the night of May 31st/June 1st.'

The 3rd, 4th and 5th Divisions were ordered to withdraw to the beaches and to Dunkirk town for evacuation by small boats and from the Mole. The 50th Division was put under the orders of 1st Corps to man the French defences on the frontier. These moves began on the morning of this Friday and, says Lord Gort again:

'... by this time there had been a general thinning out of the whole force, and I felt that, however the situation might develop, valuable cadres had been withdrawn which would enable the fighting units of the B.E.F. to be quickly re-formed at home.'

Even in the very midst of disaster the cool, clear note of an essential optimism sounds through these steady words.

The changes of the 31st were many. The British Government had stated definitely, and in terms that brooked no discussion, that Lord Gort should hand over the command of the B.E.F. to a Corps Commander when its effective fighting force was reduced to the equivalent of three divisions. On this Friday morning that point was very near to achievement.

Meanwhile the withdrawal inside the frontier fortifications made inevitable severe changes in the conditions of the beaches. La Panne is in Belgian territory—the wrong side of the fortified line. When the withdrawal was complete La Panne passed out of the picture. Of the beaches there were left only Bray-Dunes and Malo-les-Bains. Bray-Dunes was only just inside the new line, and from the point where the wire ran down to the sea it was approximately $8\frac{1}{2}$ miles to Dunkirk Moles. The whole line of the beaches came under direct artillery fire and observation of that fire was rendered easier by the use of a captive balloon.

2

But on the beaches this day the most serious factor was the weather. By dawn there was a fresh northerly breeze blowing and at once a heavy sea—heavy, that is, in relation to the small craft that were affected by it—rose. Boat work became intolerably difficult. At high water about 8.30 in the morning the wind was at its worst and in the vital hour immediately after high water a disastrous proportion of the pulling boats, dinghies and motor-craft broached to or were forced by the surf on to the beach and stranded. It was impossible to get them out. The troops, for the most part, were too tired to refloat them; their own crews too exhausted. To get heavy boats off the sand on a falling tide is a task for fresh men in the very best of circumstances: but here, as the tide fell swiftly, it was not a matter of pushing for a few feet to get them into water deep enough to float; by the time a boat had been beached for ten minutes it might mean carrying or pushing for a hundred yards. The task was impossible.

At the same time the piers, which had been improvised out of lorries and vehicles of one kind and another with so much labour the day before, were damaged and in some cases destroyed. They had already suffered from shell-fire. What remained of them now was to suffer increasingly from enemy shelling throughout the day as the other tide of our withdrawal drew back inside the line of the frontier defence. The rate of flow from the beaches was cut down to a minimum.

But not all the beaches were put out of action. The crew of the indefatigable *Triton* had clawed off the sand again on the rising tide at 4 o'clock and despite the strong northerly wind and heavy swell, which made going along-side ships extraordinarily difficult, was still hard at work ferrying. Commodore Stephenson transferred now to an M.T.B., but Lieutenant Irving remained on board. They worked all through the morning, but at 1.30 p.m. a violent bombardment of the beach began. About this time they noticed that the destroyers had moved off and the beach itself had emptied. This was the moment of the German advance which took advantage of our withdrawal to the line of the old frontier fortifications.

Triton moved along the beach close inshore, taking in tow a heavy boat loaded with troops on the way, until she reached the position the ships were now using. A strong air attack developed about this time, and while she still had the boatload of troops in tow *Triton* saw the pleasure craft *Prince of Wales* bombed. Lieutenant Irving closed her and took off two badly wounded officers and two ratings. About this time one of his seamen fell over the side from exhaustion. Immediately afterwards a heavily loaded boat capsized fairly close inshore, leaving a number of soldiers struggling in the water. *Triton* thrust her way into the centre of the group and managed to get them on board, but while she was towing the boat a rope fouled her starboard screw and put her rudder out of action. Lieutenant Irving managed to get alongside a lifeboat that was attached by a grass rope to the gunboat *Mosquito*. From her, hauling hand over hand along the rope, he brought *Triton* with a full load of soldiers (six of them wounded), with men hanging on to her stern in the water, and the full boatload that he had been towing, alongside. An attempt made by *Mosquito*'s people to clear the fouled propeller failed, and Lieutenant Irving took his lame ship across to the yacht *Caleta* for a tow home.

Caleta was already drawing the fire of the German shore batteries, but her commanding officer wanted one more load of troops before leaving and asked Irving to close the beach and get one. He was heading for the shore when he saw *Caleta* signalling him. The fire of the shore batteries had become too hot, and the yacht was pulling out, so *Triton* turned and went back to her. She was made fast for towing and *Caleta* pulled out. Unfortunately the tow rope parted and *Triton* had to be abandoned about 6.40 in the afternoon.

But though the stranding put out of action the greater part of the small-boat force that had worked along the beaches through Thursday night, the tremendous efforts of the Small Vessels Pool, the naval dockyards and the Ministry of Shipping had guaranteed a growing rate of reinforcement. That flow never stopped, though there were inevitable intervals.

This morning, for example, at 3 a.m. a convoy of four fast War Department launches—*Swallow, Marlborough, Haig* and *Wolfe*—left Ramsgate. They went in line ahead at 18 knots, and despite damage to *Swallow* on the way over (she hit a piece of floating wreckage and lost a blade off one propeller), the whole flotilla was off Dunkirk very early. The other three launches entered the harbour and filled up with troops from a paddle-minesweeper, with the intention of returning direct with them to Ramsgate. Major J. R. L. Hutchins, of the Grenadier Guards, who was in command of

Swallow, considered this something of a wastage of effort, and decided that his boat would be of more service ferrying men off the beaches to the larger craft.

Major Hutchins' account of the situation and of his subsequent work is of very great interest. He saw the circumstances of the army as a soldier not as a sailor (despite very extensive yachting experience), and it is with a soldier's eye that he describes the scene.

'The situation at 6 a.m. was as follows:

'Dunkirk was under a pall of smoke from fires which appeared to be mainly to the south and west of the port. There were numerous wrecks outside the harbour and along the beaches. There were large numbers of troops on the shore as far as it was possible to see to the eastward, and the beach was strewn with all forms of motor transport. Along the foreshore were a very large number of pulling boats, aground, capsized, or damaged, and abandoned. There were also a considerable number of motor-boats, motor-launches, and yachts aground and, in most cases, abandoned, and several wrecks close inshore. About one mile out in the Dunkirk Roads were numerous destroyers and other vessels waiting to embark troops, but scarcely any boats were running between the shore and these ships.

'There was a light onshore wind, which unfortunately freshened considerably later, and caused a ground swell which made embarkation more difficult. The tide at 6 a.m. was setting fairly hard to the eastward. There was a heavy bombardment going on on shore, but the beaches were quiet except for occasional shelling and intermittent bombing which did not become heavy until late afternoon.

'On arrival at the beach I saw one small motor-yacht, which was aground, but which appeared capable of being refloated, and I passed her a towline and pulled her off. This yacht subsequently signalled for further assistance and reported her steering gear or rudder out of action. I took her out and laid her alongside a small coasting vessel which was at anchor.

'There was a Service cutter lying astern of this coaster, and I took it over for use in embarking the troops. At first, I could see no British troops on the beaches, and in my first three or four trips I conveyed only French troops whom I took to H.M.S. *Impulsive* from whom I borrowed two, and later two more, hands to man my cutter. For the rest of the day until my last trip I carried only British troops.

'Owing to the ground swell and the fact that *Swallow*'s propellers were unguarded and below the hull, we considered it unsafe to go into less water than five feet, and it was necessary, therefore, to run inshore at some speed, check my boat's way, and allow the cutter to shoot in towards the beach, and when it was nearing the end of its tow (50 fathoms of grassline bent on to 30 fathoms of 3-inch rope), the cutter's bows were turned to seaward and the boat was backed in to the shore.

'Crowds of soldiers immediately rushed into the water and clambered over the stern and quarters of the cutter. I instructed them by megaphone how to distribute their weight, and when I thought enough had been embarked, I went ahead so as to take the cutter out of reach of the remainder; subsequently stopping while hangers-on were pulled inboard.

'With the British troops the loading was easier, but in all cases the men were very weak and very helpless; for instance, on one occasion when the tow parted, both the cutter and the whaler, which were fully loaded, were blown in broadside on to the beach, and in the case of the cutter, the combined efforts of the four naval ratings and the soldiers were unable to refloat her, so that I was obliged to send a line in to them, using *Swallow*'s dinghy. The tow parted again and it was only with great difficulty that we reestablished it and hoisted in the half-swamped dinghy.

'Each time after loading, I proceeded alongside *Impulsive*, which had a "jumping ladder" rigged. In order to avoid waste of time in shortening in my 80-fathom towline, I passed the end of it to *Impulsive* and requested her to haul the boats alongside, which was done by part of the ship's company doubling along her deck. After the first trip, I borrowed *Impulsive*'s whaler and two more hands, and made a number of trips from shore to ship, towing both boats. There were at this time very few boats working between the shore and the ships, but there were some boats full of troops broached-to on the beach and unable to get off. One motor-boat belonging to a destroyer, one whaler and a small motor-yacht were the only boats working on two or three miles of beach, and in view of the target presented to enemy aircraft by destroyers and other ships waiting to embark troops, I requested *Impulsive* to transmit a signal from me to Admiralty, repeated V.-A., Dover, requesting more cutters and power boats to speed up the embarkation. There was some shelling on the beaches, and a good deal of A.A. fire from the ships as German aircraft appeared overhead at frequent intervals.

'At about midday, *Impulsive* hoisted two black shapes, and when I next came alongside she reported that she had struck some wreckage and damaged her port propeller (this happened, I think, while she was taking avoiding action during an attack by aircraft).

'As *Impulsive* had to proceed for docking, I returned her whaler and the borrowed ratings who had manned my cutter, and proceeded to work with *Winchelsea*. Up to this time *Impulsive* had taken some 400 soldiers, nearly all British. Before she left, I obtained from her fifty gallons of fuel for my boat.

'I should like to mention here the ready co-operation of the captain, the first lieutenant, and many others of H.M.S. *Impulsive*; everything possible was done to assist me both by the handling of the ship to provide a lee, by hauling the low towline, and by providing petrol, lending a whaler, and hands to help in working my cutter and also by providing food for me and my boat's crew during the short periods when we were alongside.

'I later received much assistance and co-operation from H.M.S. *Winchelsea* who lent me a signalman and ratings for my cutter and gave me all her available petrol.

'In the early afternoon, the wind lightened and conditions became easier. Observing that there were boats at the davits of a wreck (the Southern Railway Company's s.s. *Lorina*) close inshore, I borrowed some hands from

Winchelsea to lower and man them, and ordered a R.A.F. launch which was lying astern of a neighbouring vessel to take over these boats ex the wreck and embark troops.

'Soon after this, on the suggestion of the captain of *Winchelsea* (Lieutenant-Commander W. A. F. Hawkins, R.N.), I boarded *Keith* to discuss with Rear-Admiral Wake-Walker the possibility of making all remaining troops march to Dunkirk for embarkation. The Admiral concurred in the suggestion and asked me to try to get into touch with the military commanders on shore and to give orders for the troops to march to the piers, on contradiction of previous orders. I landed for this purpose a young yachtsman (whose name I never learnt) who had come off in one of my boatloads and had asked if he might join me, his own craft having been put out of action. He succeeded in his mission.

'By 5.30 p.m. there were few troops waiting to embark at this part of the beach and the remainder were making their way along the beach to Dunkirk, and at this time *Winchelsea* signalled proposing that this should be the last trip; I concurred. In the last trip only about thirty soldiers embarked in the cutter, and I transferred them to the cabin and engine-room of my boat, handing over the cutter to the R.A.F. launch. During this last half-hour, several dive-bombing attacks were made on *Winchelsea* which appeared to be straddled by the first salvo. A transport further to the eastward was hit about this time, and enemy air activity was intense. *Swallow* was hit by a few small splinters, presumably of anti-aircraft shell, but was undamaged.

'After the last trip inshore I proceeded direct to Ramsgate, and arrived there at about 9.50 p.m. The engines of the boat had been running since 3.15 a.m., and when outside Ramsgate first the port, and a minute later, the starboard engine failed; the port engine was restarted.

'The master (Mr. Clarke) and the crew of the *Swallow* worked extremely well throughout and I would like to bring to your notice the work of an Able Seaman, Peter Johnson, of the Patrol Service at Lowestoft, taken over with the cutter. This man was working in the cutter single-handed for some of the earlier trips to the beach and was untiring in his efforts and showed great initiative and resource. I put him on board *Impulsive* before she left, and obtained his name, as I wished to draw attention to his very good work.

'I estimate the total number of troops embarked from the beaches and transferred to H.M. Ships by *Swallow* as between 700 and 800.'

In many ways this is the clearest account that exists of the work along the beaches during this day, and it gives a most admirable picture of the magnificent co-operation between the destroyers and the small boats, and of the almost incredible difficulties of the work.

3

Admirable as was the work of boats like *Swallow*, however, it was patent on every hand that the flow of reinforcements in small craft and big had to be accelerated.

Four of the 'X' lighters left Sheerness on this morning and, sailing direct for Dunkirk with the motor-yacht *Marsayru*, reached the beaches about the middle of the afternoon. By weaving his dinghies in and out Sub-Lieutenant R. A. W. Pool, R.N., who commanded the party in 'X' 217, collected more than forty or fifty French soldiers, whom he transferred to a motor-yacht. Subsequently, using *Marsayru* and a cutter, he collected 250 more Frenchmen. His lighter could not go astern, and the whole operation was fraught with quite extraordinary difficulties, but she got back safely to Ramsgate with her load.

Marsayru, which was commanded by Skipper G. D. Olivier, towed across a whaler and, herself keeping in deep water, sent it in to the beach. It was immediately stormed by a group of about fifty French soldiers and capsized. The rating in charge of it, Leading Seaman Brown, with some difficulty escaped being drowned. Coming away from the beach, *Marsayru* picked up the cutter and, going to an area where the French troops were calmer, worked for five hours loading 'X' 217, s.s. *Foam Queen* and s.s. *Jaba*. With them worked the motor-boat *Jong* (Sub-Lieutenant I. F. Smith, R.N.V.R.).

Again, inevitably, there were losses. The motor-boat *Janis*, working off Dunkirk pier, was demolished by a direct hit from a bomb. Sub-Lieutenant Bell, R.N.V.R., in command of her, was killed, together with a stoker rating. Three seamen who survived the hit were picked up by the *Queen Boadicea II* (Lieutenant J. S. Seal, R.N.R.).

By this time reinforcements of French ships were beginning to come along in increasing quantity. Mainly they took off their own countrymen but, as with the British ships, there are frequent cases of mixed loads and occasionally of French ships carrying entirely British cargoes. They varied from the large French personnel ships like *Rouen* or *Newhaven* to little coastwise cargo boats. Two of these, *Keremah* and *Hebe* (not to be confused with the British minesweeper), ships from Quimper, worked the west quay this night, taking their loads to Dover.

The part of the tugs now was tremendously important. What might be called their 'normal' work went on day and night—the work of searching for disabled vessels, of pulling stranded ships off the sandbanks and off the shoals of Dunkirk harbour itself, of rescuing boats that had gone adrift. And with that there was still the task of victualling the remaining men within the Dunkirk perimeter and of supplying them with ammunition, and now with the necessary explosives for demolitions.

The tug *Crested Cock*, for example, had brought three barges—*Glenway*, *Spurgeon* and *Lark*—to Dover. At 4 a.m. she took in tow a lighter loaded with fresh water and food together with an army working party.

'I steamed to a given position,' says her master, T. Hills, 'and anchored with the lighter about 60 feet off the beach, and putting the troops aboard the lighter, we worked her in towards the beach where the troops ashore were waiting to receive her. After seeing the lighter in the hands of these troops ashore, I was then ordered by a naval officer to proceed to a destroyer further up the roads which needed assistance. I steamed at full speed and found the

destroyer *Basilisk*, which had troops on board, was unable to turn round owing
to a damaged propeller. The commander requested me to take hold and turn
her round, and having done this, *Basilisk* was able to proceed with one propeller, and at 2.10 p.m. I was ordered to let go my tow rope, and I escorted
her as far as Dunkirk pier heads, where the commander informed me he was
going to proceed alone at 15 knots. There were heavy bombing raids going
on at this time, and the town was being heavily shelled. We then proceeded
to Dover, passing Gravelines under cover of *Basilisk*'s guns. . . .'

At 5 a.m. *Ocean Cock*, her sister ship (A. V. Mastin, master), left with six
motor-boats from Dover, reaching Dunkirk beach about 1 p.m. He slipped
his tow off the beaches and steamed back to Dover for orders.

Towage, salvage—it was all the same to them; and the *Crested Cock*'s
report, incidentally, gives an insight into the resourcefulness and the determination of the destroyers.

In the same convoy the *Sun VII* was sent off with five R.A.F. motor-boats
in tow. These were tenders from the R.A.F. station at Calshot. As a small
indication of the difficulties of even a theoretically simple operation like this,
G. Cawsey, her master, says laconically:

'Six times the boats broke adrift, and were picked up again, and eventually
arrived at destination.'

Under command of Pilot Officer C. Collings they did excellent work on the
beaches, ferrying troops out to deeper-draught ships. Two of them were lost
in the course of the work—S.T.254 (under Leading Aircraftman E. Price)
and A.M.C.3 (under Corporal C. Webster). S.T.254 became overcrowded
and was caught by the swell, broached to and sank. A.M.C.3 damaged her
propellers on the bottom and fetched up on the beach. But between them the
launches rescued at least 500 men on this day, and the three remaining
returned safely to Dover with the crews of the lost boats.

Sun XI left Dover at approximately 10 o'clock with a barge loaded with
stores and cans of water, with orders to beach it two miles east of the pier-
heads. She was at Dunkirk by 5.30 p.m. Her master, J. R. Lukes', account is
human in spite of its terse officialese.

'Got barge alongside and steamed in to 2 fathoms, a small motor-boat
took barge and beached her. Jerry bombing beach and ships anchored off.
Left Dunkirk 6 p.m. 7 p.m. bombed by Jerry, two incendiary close to tug, one
drifter went up. Tug *Contest* picked up crew. 7.30 p.m. passed *Sun XV*, *VIII*
and *IV* going in, sorry for them, glad to get out.'

, The little procession of her sisters that *Sun XI* passed coming in were
ships of the biggest convoy of the day. *Racia* with twelve lifeboats, *Foremost* 87 with two sailing barges, *Tanga* with six boats, *Vincia* with three
boats, *Sun IV* with nine boats, *Sun VIII* with twelve boats, *Sun XII* with
two barges (*Tollesbury* and *Ethel Everard*), *Sun XV* with six boats, were part
of the great flight of small craft that was sent across to make good the
damage of the morning's wind and to replace the craft lost in the hectic work
of the Thursday and in the dark hours of the night. There were other ships in
that convoy, other tugs and other strings of lifeboats; there were drifters and

FRIDAY, MAY 31st

Dutch skoots. Clearing Ramsgate at 2.30 on the afternoon, they made a continuous stream nearly five miles in length along a narrow channel. They were bombed, they were machine-gunned from the air, and they went on.

One of the best accounts comes from a typographical designer, Robert Harling, writing under the *nom de guerre* of Nicholas Drew.[1] His experience throws light on the manner in which some of the crews of the little ships were brought together. Like many other yachtsmen he was taking a course in navigation with Captain O. M. Watts. He describes how Captain Watts came into the lecture-room and said:

'Well, gentlemen, it's quite true. I've just had word from the Admiralty that they'd like as many of you as possible to go off right away to help on a job. I'm not allowed to tell you what the job is, but I think it's fairly certain it's to help take off some of those poor devils from Dunkirk. How many would like to give me their names?'

The volunteers (there were a score of them immediately) went to the Port of London Authority building on Tower Hill. There they were given instructions.

'We arrived at Tilbury after passing some meticulous sentries. There we were passed into the care of a middle-aged R.N. commander. He was moving quickly amongst a strange collection of humans. He stopped and asked us where we came from. We told him. He summed us up pretty quickly, and I cannot think he had other thoughts than that we seemed an odd gang of dilettantes. Around us were tougher-looking members of society, men of the Thames itself, odd-job men, lightermen, dock labourers and scores of others. They looked as if they were adrift and waiting to be directed, but they did at least look ready for action. Our party, I thought, looked more like a handful of young men who could be picked out from any crowd at a varsity rugger match. They looked as if they too were adrift, but also as if they were completely unperturbed by the fact; they began immediately to take a curious interest in everything that was going on around them.

'Stolid Thames tugs were moored fast against the quayside. In mid-river there were scores of ships' lifeboats. They seemed sound enough but were obviously old; several, I thought, had that "parched" look about the timbers and paint which any wooden vessel gets after it has been out of the water for very long. I hoped I should have a baler ready if I were unlucky to get pitched into one of them.

'The commander came back and told us the arrangements. Each tug was to tow twelve lifeboats across the North Sea; each lifeboat, powered by an auxiliary engine, would carry a crew of four; one charge hand, one engineman and two deck hands; pulling-boats would carry one charge hand and three deck hands. We were told no more. When we got to "the other side" we would receive further instructions. . . .'

They were signed on under the T.124 agreement.

'We returned to the quay's edge. Our turn was imminent. The bearded lieutenant was still collecting crews, marshalling them into what he probably

[1] *Amateur Sailor* (Constable).

158

hoped were reasonably efficient units, instructing them in getting their boats shipshape, supervising their disposition of stores, criticizing their knots for towing ropes, and pacifying the tug masters, anxious to be away. Each was a full-time job, but he carried on as if he had been accustomed to this multiple command all his life. . . .'

Eventually they joined the 2.30 convoy.

'With eleven other boats in charge of Thames tug *Sun IV* we moved off down river, a strange cortege, nestling in the wake of the fussing tug with its two small white stern lights. Midnight donged on one of the riverside churches. The river and the night were wholly merged.

'In the first ten minutes the tug was stopped twice for adjustments to towing ropes; two of the boats had swung round, broadside on to the tug, and had almost capsized. There were shrill calls and curses in the darkness from huddled shapes at the tillers. The throb of the tug's engines died; ropes were moved to more precise positions; "O.K.," shouted somebody through the night and the procession again moved into life.

'We divided ourselves into watches; one hour on, three hours off. . . .

'All through the afternoon we passed our own ships returning with men. British and French destroyers, sloops, trawlers, drifters and motor-boats were on their way back. They were packed tight with masses of khaki figures lining the decks, crowded to the ropes of bulwarks. The destroyers slit the calm seas as if this were a journey against time and "the quicker back to Dover, the quicker back to Dunkirk written all over 'em", someone said.

'In the middle of one of the discussions which started from time to time, our starboard companion-boat swung round, crashed into us at what seemed terrific speed, forcing us far over, so that we lay dangerously upon our beam. The other boat buried her port side completely under water. Three ratings were hurled into the sea. The fourth yelled and hung on to a thwart. I saw two go clean under our boat; the other was caught as he was swept past a boat astern. I looked to port, two white faces were carried astern very swiftly.

'One still wore a tin helmet, and the other yelled fearfully. I think he yelled "I can't swim", but he went down once and was gone. Voices cried frantically to the tug. She swung round quickly to port; as skilful and as swift a turn as a London taxi-driver's. Engines were slowed for the search. One was picked up. The other had gone. The tug cruised around for about ten minutes, but it was a vain search and we turned once again to our course. . . .

'An hour later we were nearing the French coast. Subtly the feeling in the boat changed. There was a nervous tenseness amongst us; we no longer talked, but stared ahead as if looking for a reef. We were moving up the coast with a stranger miscellany of craft than was ever seen in the most hybrid amateur regatta: destroyers, sloops, trawlers, motor-boats, fishing boats, tugs, Dutch schuits. Under the splendid sun they seemed like craft of peace journeying upon a gay occasion, but suddenly we knew we were there, for someone said, "There they are, the bastards!" My eyes followed the line of his pointing arm, but I could see nothing; but not for long this blindness.

There were over fifty German planes. I counted them swiftly, surprised to find how easy it was to count them. We did not get so many at a time in Norway. I imagined that they were bombers with fighter escorts, but my silhouettes were never very sound. They were like slow-flying gnats in a vast sky, seeming to move deliberately and with simple purpose towards us, flying very high. I got a heavy sick feeling right down in the stomach. The bombs dropped out of the cloudless sky. We watched them fall as the planes directed their principal attack upon two destroyers. The destroyers seemed to sit back on their buttocks and spit flames; the harsh cracks of their ack-ack guns were heartening. Then we got the kick from the bombs as their ricochet came up through the sea. Our little boat rocked and lifted high out of the water. One, two, three, four . . . we waited, counting them and held tight to the gunwale. . . . The bombers seemed to be dispersing. Our own fighters suddenly appeared. It was quite true, I thought, all that I had read in the newspapers: our pilots really did put the other chaps to flight. Far above us the German formations broke. Some came down in steep dives. From the 15,000 or 20,000 feet we had computed they were down to 2,000 or 3,000. One came low, machine-gunning a tug and its towed lifeboats. Then came another. We knew it was coming our way. It was crazy to sit there, goggle-eyed and helpless, just waiting for it, but there seemed singularly little else to do. The seconds were hours. "Wait for it and duck!" shouted someone above the roar of the engines. "Now! and bale like bloody hell if he hits the boat." We ducked. The rat-a-tat of the bullets sprayed round the stern boats of our little fleet; the two Lewis guns in the tug answered gamely as the plane zoomed up. . . .'

The convoy arrived off the beaches according to orders a little after dark. Some of the tugs with their tows were sent to the extreme eastern limits of the beaches and at once the work of ferrying began again. The lifeboats, towed by the motor-boats, brought out their loads of troops for the destroyers, the minesweepers and the personnel ships, and eventually for the tugs themselves. The numbers loaded in this way were amazing considering the intolerable conditions of the task. They formed a tremendous share of this day's, the second-highest, aggregate of the liftings.

At 10 p.m. there was another convoy. *Sun VII*, which had returned after slipping her tow of R.A.F. motor-boats during the morning, was ordered to steam back to Dunkirk. She joined six other tugs and the seven of them were ordered to rendezvous off Dunkirk 'to render any assistance to any craft in need of it'. The orders were comprehensive: they were carried out comprehensively.

4

With the tugs and in independent groups both earlier and later in the day went the Thames barges. Amongst the loveliest survivors of the days of sail along our coast, the Thames barges were eminently suitable for one aspect of the work they had to do. Broad-beamed, shallow-draught ships, they carry for their sail area the smallest crews known to the sea. In harbour they are squat and chunky, but no one who has seen a line of them moving along the flat levels of the Thames estuary in the evening light, their canvas red against the eastern sky, their great spritsails soaring up like the point of a flame, can deny their beauty. It is the essential, fundamental beauty of craft absolutely suited to their task. And on this day a fleet of them went in to Dunkirk. Many of them failed to return, but they went gallantly, and their work is not least in the records of Dunkirk.

Lady Rosebery, loaded with stores, went over with the big convoy. The report of her journey says abruptly:

'Arrived Dunkirk 10.30 p.m. Craft and tug blown up before stores could be unloaded. Ordinary Seaman Cook and J. E. Atkins missing.'

Atkins was a boy of fifteen. Her skipper was W. F. Ellis, and her mate A. W. Cook.

Pudge (Skipper W. Watson) picked up the survivors of this tug and of another barge, and was towed back to Ramsgate.

Glenway (Skipper W. H. Easter) was towed in to the beach with stores, and beached on naval instructions. She was to have other adventures.

Duchess (Skipper H. J. Wildish) somehow managed to ferry ninety soldiers out to a destroyer. On her last trip to the beach she had to be abandoned.

Ethel Everard (Skipper T. Willis), in company with *Tollesbury* (Skipper R. Webb), went over with the convoy, loaded with dynamite, small-arms ammunition and food. Skipper Willis says in his account:

'About 1 a.m. on Saturday morning when about a mile east of Dunkirk we shortened tow rope and the tug-master informed us we were to steer for the beach and await orders.

'We sailed on to the beach, and it was now about half ebb, and the small swell which was on knocked us round broadside, and by this time we were being continually attacked.

'We had a sergeant and five soldiers on board, and he hailed the troops that were on the beach thinking they were the working party to discharge us, but they turned out to be troops waiting to be evacuated and they soon swarmed on board. They were suffering badly from thirst so they soon emptied our water tanks, and a naval cutter from the gunboat lying off then took them on board the gunboat.

'Shortly after an army officer came on board and asked me to allow my crew to row him off to the gunboat, and we were still being badly bombed. About thirty minutes after a naval pinnace came up to us, and instructed us to go back to the gunboat with the crews of the other barges that were on the beach.

'On boarding the gunboat a naval officer informed me they had decided to abandon our vessels, and were going to fire them. . . .'

Ethel Everard was blown up eventually. *Tollesbury*, which had worked in company with her, managed to get most of her stores ashore.

Barbara Jean (Skipper C. Webb), *Aidie* (Skipper H. Potter) and *Doris* (Skipper F. Finbow) were all run ashore and abandoned. It was the only way to make certain that dumps of water, of food and—most vital of all—of ammunition, now dangerously low all along the line of the perimeter, should be got ashore. To discharge in the confines of the harbour was impossible. Even to discharge on the beach was fraught with the very gravest difficulty and danger. But these barges took the ground upright. They were built to lie on the barge beds of the Thames foreshore, of the estuary banks, of a hundred creeks and mud flats in Essex; and, grounded, they became dumps that for a considerable proportion of the tide were available to working parties from the dunes. They and the Thames dumb barges and the lighters were sacrificed, but their sacrifice was by no means in vain.

Spurgeon (Skipper Haisman) was bombed on the passage over and damaged by splinters from a near miss. *Beatrice Maud* (Skipper L. Horlock) crossed and was anchored off the beaches. *Ena* (Skipper A. G. Page) was also anchored in deep water. The subsequent history of these two ships and of *Glenway* was remarkable, for *Ena* at the end of the evacuation came home by herself. She was found stranded on the Sandwich Flats practically undamaged and quite empty. *Beatrice Maud's* career was almost more remarkable still for on June 5th she was picked up in mid-Channel, long after the operation was over, with 260 men on board. *Glenway* was boarded by 190 soldiers on Malo beach, refloated, and on their courage and resource brought half-way across the Channel under sail. Here a tug found her and towed her to safety. *Lark* (Skipper J. F. Filley) was abandoned on the beach. The motor barge *Seine* (Skipper P. W. Cogger), under the orders of Lieutenant-Commander Filleul, R.N., on this day brought back 352 and on two subsequent trips brought back roughly the same number each time.

Other barges were to follow them the next day.

5

The pattern of this day is of an impossible complexity, yet there is a pattern. Nowhere in this stupendous movement are the details unrelated. It was a theme of many variations, but within it always an essential simplicity. It was concerned with the rescue of men, and in every move, every dispatch that was made that day the work of rescue was the dominating motive. Whether the convoys were of lifeboats or of paddle-minesweepers, whether the stream of shipping was made up by motor yachts or by destroyers, whether the ships left from Margate or Ramsgate or Dover, they all came together off the beaches in a tremendous surge of rescue.

On this day the great tug convoys and the barges were a new variation, but all the while, even as they were crossing, the work of the other ships, the earlier variations of the theme, continued. While the barges were under way the little ships of the previous day were still working the beaches where they could. All through the small hours *Constant Nymph* had carried on, but she too was to become a casualty of the morning.

'Jerry,' says Dr. B. A. Smith, 'also had some big guns for which aeroplanes were spotting, and they dropped Very lights over the ships, but here again Jerry wasted ammunition without hitting anything that I saw. One of the crumps came as a nasty shock, the explosion actually stopped my boat for a split second, and I thought I had grounded, as she quivered all over, but in the next moment she went on again and the noise of the crump followed the air push so that I knew it was nothing serious. At least two bombs shook the boat but nothing stopped it. When *Jutland* left, about 3 a.m. on May 31st, I turned over with the cutter and whaler to *Laudania* and by about 8.30 she too was full, making a total of about 900 men brought off. *Laudania* was filled about three-quarters British, quarter French. By this time I had used up all my deck cargo of petrol and the engine wanted more oil and the grease cups refilled, also there was a certain amount of rotten rope round the propeller shaft, this I had not been able to cut in time. My two crew were both stoker ratings of four months' service in the Navy only and being stokers were not issued with clasp knives, on my sternman shouting at me that an odd rope was getting round our propeller, I had to leave the wheel and cut it with my own sheath knife, if he had had a clasp knife he could have done it in time. I was a moment too late.

'About 7.30 a.m. the captain of *Laudania* told me to come on board with all my crew to get some sort of meal, and we were to be replaced by a naval petty officer and ratings from *Laudania* to carry on the embarkation till the ship was full; I had to do two trips with the petty officer to coach him in the handling of the motor-boat. Having done these trips and left him to it, not too easy in my mind about the *Nymph* as it was choppy by then, a breeze having sprung up at dawn, and he was bringing her alongside in a way that boded ill for her side lights and covering boards, I had just settled down to a lovely pot of tea and bread and butter and jam when the captain came for me. The petty officer had somehow let his tow get adrift and had lost control of the cutter which had gone aground—would I be good enough to take over again and rescue the cutter's crew, even if I could not get the cutter itself off. Cocking my tin hat like Captain Kettle, I went on deck and hailed my own boys, Allen and Meikle, who shed their reluctance at leaving their breakfast on learning that our "expert" services were required to put things right—I think we all felt very old salts for the moment.

'The cutter had gone aground under a stranded lighter on the windward side of it, a N.W. wind having got up a bit in the morning, and as I could not get near enough to get the cutter off and the crew, also very young sailors, did not know how to get off, I rescued the crew and brought them off to *Laudania* in accordance with the captain's instructions. The engine had been stalling, probably on account of rope, and the self-starter now refused service. My boat only just managed to get alongside *Laudania* with the last whaler load that she could take, and the captain ordered me off with my crew and the crew of the whaler, the crew of the cutter being already on board, and turned over my boat and the whaler to a naval drifter which was said to have petrol and mechanics on board so that they could be of further use.

'The whole of us who had been on the beach work then had our first stand-easy since 9.30 p.m. the day before and my crew and I had not had anything to eat since 5.30 p.m. the day before, and nothing to drink since

8.30 p.m., and had been continuously employed, as had the two naval ratings who remained on each of the naval rowing boats during the tow across.

'Jerry started his usual effort when the ship left between 8.30 and 9 a.m. on the 31st, but with no results, and plenty of hot tea and bread and butter and jam and a chance to light a pipe had made me perfectly indifferent to anything Jerry did. Feeling pretty good and the pipe doing well I went on deck to have a look round and see how the troops were faring. Almost at once I came across an elderly man wearing the 1914 Star and looking pretty tired, greeted him cheerfully and remarked that I had understood that this was a young man's war. He gave me a quick look and replied, "Well, you're no bloody chicken!" As my tin hat covered my bald head, I was rather pained at this; but on taking an early opportunity to look at myself in the captain's mirror found that my beard of a few days stood out all round my face in pure white stubble, I looked like an aged tramp.

'On the way back to England we avoided a drifting mine, but the two officers' pistols and the A.A. Lewis guns were unable to pop it, so we informed another ship that was outward bound and it was popped in due course.

'The troops on board *Laudania* evinced no interest whatsoever in the drifter, nor the popping of it; it was first sighted on our starboard bow and as the tide was running that way we sheered off and passed behind it. The troops evidently regarded this as entirely a naval matter and I do not think any of them even got up to see what happened to it.

'I had brought my own pet rug off the boat and told my two boys to bring one each; these we lent to the tiredest or wettest-looking men we found on the ship, who fell asleep at once. Just before we tied up at Margate all three rugs were brought to me on the bridge and placed carefully folded by my tin hat and binoculars on the little platform just outside the combined bridge and chart room. The 1914 veteran had my rug and never stirred from his sound sleep on the hatch cover in full view of the bridge for the whole trip—neither A.A. fire nor mines interested him. Both on the beaches and on the ship, and also on the quays at home the troops struck me as not only disciplined in a steady, reliable, and unostentatious style but also as most courteous and considerate—it must be a great privilege to have had a command in that crowd; they had been through enough to bring out the weak spots if there had been any. The whole course from Ramsgate to Dunkirk was like a main street in a busy town, traffic several abreast going each way.

'Off the Foreland we inquired of the local policeman, a gentleman in his shirt-sleeves on a drifter, as to which port would take us, and were sent to Margate. Three other ships and two destroyers also had loads for Margate and we eventually tied up outside two destroyers and landed the whole issue across each other about 5.30 p.m. on May 31st.

'On the trip the captain very courteously allowed me to act as his relief watch—keeping the bridge for about thirty minutes, in fact he invited me to do so.

'I reported to the naval office with my crew of two and we were promptly put in a taxi and sent back to our own port at Ramsgate, a matter of a few minutes which might have been a dreary journey by train. As throughout, there was no red tape in the navy at all, they had ready everything that was necessary and our general instructions were that if we were in any sort of trouble we could close any ship we saw as it would be one of ours.

'Both on the ship and while walking off the pier at Margate, we were repeatedly stopped by troops and thanked for getting them away—and those men were dog-tired. . . .'

Despite the disasters at the top of the flood tide, there were still boats working, but the flow from the beaches was cut now to a thin trickle, and it was essential to hurry from the English side as many small craft as could be got across with fresh crews. Within an hour or two reinforcements were under way. Again the prescience of the Admiralty had made preparations in time. The previous afternoon and the previous night fresh requisitioning had brought in a flotilla of new craft.

Once again there were new types among them. In contrast to the swift, slender R.A.F. launches that had gone over at dawn there sailed a little after 10 o'clock from Leigh-on-Sea six cockle-boats, the familiar old cutter-rigged cockle boats of the estuary of the Thames with their splendid names— *Renown, Reliance, Resolute, Defender, Endeavour* and *Letitia*. Off the Nore lightship it was decided that the more powerful boats should take the weaker in tow and, the little convoy having re-formed, they made for Margate. Passing Margate pier they received orders to shape a course straight for Dunkirk, and off the Foreland they saw the long line of that much-travelled sea road. By the evening they were off Gravelines, and at 7 p.m. they were attacked by some forty German bombers. Zig-zagging wildly, they escaped the bombs and, moving now independently, they reached Dunkirk. As the swell was too heavy for them to go in to the beach, they began to ferry off troops from the outer end of the Mole. They were working in conjunction with H.M. Skoot *Tilly*, and swiftly filled her. A. J. Dench, *Letitia*'s skipper, says:

'On going in for the third time, a shell burst in between the last boat of them, and us, we turned back, to go out, but the signaller that we had on board, and had only been "out" for about six weeks, and never been under fire, said "We've got to go in again" so we went in.

'We passed the others going out for their last journey and then a voice hailed us from the docks, we loaded up again, and also towed a lifeboat full of soldiers as well. These, as we couldn't find the *Tilly*, we put on board a trawler, which was towing another, and that in turn was towing two life-boats, one sunk and the other with sailors in. We didn't know our course home, so we also made fast.

'Soon we saw another boat coming up behind us. It was the *Renown*, and yelling that they had engine trouble, they made fast to our stern and we towed them, about $3\frac{1}{2}$ fathoms of rope being the distance behind us. That was at 1.15 a.m., and tired out, the engineer and seaman and signaller went to turn in, as our work seemed nearly done. We were congratulating ourselves

—when at about 1.50, a terrible explosion took place, and a hail of wood splinters came down on our deck. In the pitch dark you could see nothing, and after the explosion we heard nothing. And we could do nothing, except pull in the tow rope which was just as we passed it to the *Renown* about three-quarters of an hour before, but not a sign of *Renown*. . . .'

The story of the little ships and of the big at Dunkirk is underscored with many tragedies, but there is in this unlettered, unadorned narrative a curious poignancy. These were fishing boats. Only the day before they had been busy at their quiet task. They knew nothing of war: they went not to fight, but to save. They had done their work, and now, suddenly, on the way home, there came annihilation. It was a small tragedy in the great disasters of these days, but it has in it a deep and humble bitterness. The crew of *Renown* consisted of W. H. Noakes, skipper; L. V. Osborne, mate, and F. W. Osborne, engineer. The tragedy was heavy, but these six cockle-boats between them rescued 1,000 men.

The skoot *Tilly* did excellent work in this period. The skoots, in fact, were one of the most successful pieces of prevision in the whole Dunkirk operation. Small, squat-looking ships with their Diesel engines astern and living quarters for their Dutch captains and their families next to the engines, they were admirably suited to this work, for they were built for the coasts of the lowland sea. They had been selected by Captain Fisher of the Ministry of Shipping, and throughout the operation until the very last night they worked strenuously and well. *Aegir* (Lieutenant W. B. Whitworth, R.N.), for example, made six trips; *Reiger* (Lieutenant A. Tyson, R.N.), made five. *Bornrif*, *Gorecht*, *Doggersbank*, *Java*, *Jutland*, *Pascholl*, *Besta*, *Twente*, *Princess Juliana*, *Hilda*—the names crop up endlessly. They were lucky ships too. Only one was lost in the whole course of the operations—*Horst*, which had to be abandoned after damage from a near miss—but a number of the others were damaged in varying degrees.

From Ramsgate about the same time went four hopper barges. By no means can a hopper barge be considered as a passenger-vessel. They are large, self-propelled steel barges, with a sludge hold amidships built to take the spoil of dredgers and capable of being opened to the sea. *Foremost* 101, the 'flagship' of the little flotilla, had been damaged already by a near miss. Her sludge hold was full of water. Her maximum speed was about 5 knots.

Cadets of the R.A.S.C. Officer Production Centre had been ordered to Ramsgate harbour to take part in the defence of the harbour, and from this little force, some of whom were cleaning Bren guns and other weapons that had been brought back from France, twelve men asked permission to cross with the ships as gunners. They were told that no authority could be given, that if they went they might have to stay, and the officer who informed them ended his warning with the words, 'The school can accept no responsibility. Good luck!'

The four naval officers who were in command of the hopper barges selected parties of three, and a little after 10 o'clock the flotilla sailed. They reached Dunkirk in the middle of the afternoon, and motor-boats, which they had towed with them, were sent in to the beaches. For six hours the work went on, load after load of men being brought out. The hoppers were shelled and bombed during this time, and their improvised armament went into action against low-flying aircraft. But by 10 p.m. they were loaded, and *Foremost* 101, the leader, started for home. Her lifeboats were waterlogged, and one of her motor-boats had to be left behind (she had started with two). In one of the other hoppers the R.A.S.C. gun crew were actually credited with a German plane. *Foremost* 101, after heading direct for Calais and being shouldered off by the watchful destroyers, reached Ramsgate safely with 400 British, Belgian and French troops. The rest of the little flotilla acquitted themselves equally well.

The motor-yachts were still pouring across, many of them in tow of the great flotilla of H.M. skoots. One of the biggest of these tows was taken over by H.M. skoot *Hilda* (Captain R. P. Pim, R.N.V.R.). Formerly Assistant Secretary to the Ministry of Home Affairs in the Government of Northern Ireland, Captain Pim was on leave when the evacuation began, but, immediately offering his services, was given the *Hilda*. She left Ramsgate in the middle of the morning towing *Britannic*, *Golden Spray*, *Gipsy King*, *Lady Haig*, *Moss Rose*, *Rose Marie* and four lifeboats from the Belgian steamer *Flandres*, which had been sunk in collision in the Downs some months previously.

These ships were the result of a fresh sweep of the Dover, Deal and Walmer areas on the afternoon of May 30th, when the increasing need for craft of this type was already urgently apparent. They were requisitioned by Captain G. Fraser, D.S.O., R.N., of Dover, inspected, and manned almost entirely by volunteers of their own crews. They were assigned to La Panne and Bray-Dunes, and reached their positions in the late afternoon.

The motor-boat *Reda* crossed at the same time on her second trip to ferry off fifty Frenchmen to waiting ships. She brought back twenty-three to Ramsgate.

The further portions of the La Panne beaches were already virtually no-man's-land. By noon the minesweeper *Hebe*, working off La Panne, reported that owing to increasing shelling from comparatively close range, she was compelled to fall back to the westward nearer to Bray. This was the shelling which was directed from the enemy observation balloon a few miles eastward of La Panne, and the movement of the enemy artillery was due to our abandonment of the old perimeter positions at Nieuport and our deliberate withdrawal to the frontier line.

Captain Pim, on arrival, having collected some other craft on the way, found what was apparently evidence of fifth column work. Trawlers and drifters, which had been standing off these eastern beaches, were getting under way to return to England on orders from unidentified craft. There appears to have been more than one occasion on which contradictory orders were given to small ships, and it is possible that a certain number of these contradictions were deliberate. But with the enormous number of craft, and the confusion and difficulty of the whole operation, it is equally possible that they arose out of genuine misapprehension and the inevitable herd instinct of small ships. If one ship pulled out suddenly (and the impulse to pull out must have been intolerably frequent as shelling, machine-gunning and bombing increased) there was always the possibility of other ships following her in the belief that orders had been given for a withdrawal.

Hilda dropped her tow off the beaches and at once her boats went in. Captain Pim himself landed and interviewed as many senior officers as he could find. As a result of this he assumed the duties of beach master and remained ashore controlling the use of the pontoons and improvised piers until midnight.

Britannic, one of the Deal beach boats, did excellent work for a long while, but was eventually lost. *Golden Spray,* crewed by J. O'Neill and N. Cohen, both Deal boatmen, lifted six boatloads of troops before she was caught by the wash of a destroyer taking violent evasive action during a bombing attack. Heavily loaded, the wash of the destroyer roared over her side, filled her and she sank. Mr. A. G. Crothall, who had sailed from Deal as one of her crew, had transferred off the beaches to one of the *Flandres'* lifeboats. She too was lost, but Crothall swam in to the beach in safety. *Gipsy King,* the third of the Deal boats, was making her second trip across. She had already put in forty-eight hours of strenuous work along the sands. The first engineer of *Lady Haig,* Mr. Reginald Walter, earned a Mention in Dispatches for the excellence of his work throughout this night. *Moss Rose* and *Rose Marie* also did magnificent work.

From Ramsgate, following the same Thursday afternoon search, sailed three trawlers—*Kestrel, Tankerton Towers* and *Provider,* all Ramsgate boats. Walter W. Cribbens, skipper of *Kestrel,* pays an excellent tribute to the destroyers.

'We had had a quiet, uneventful crossing in very fine weather on this particular morning, and orders were to enter Dunkirk Roads, by the South Channel. This channel runs very close to the shore, to the southward of Dunkirk, and part of this shore was in enemy hands. As we entered this channel a destroyer came to meet us, and got between us and the shore, escorting us for some distance, and letting out a smoke screen, shielding us from the shore. All the time the destroyer's guns were blazing away, and his anti-aircraft guns were in action with many enemy planes that were overhead.

'The destroyer went ahead, and as he passed us, we got a cheery wave from the officers on the bridge, and most of the crew. It was the cool efficiency with which those chaps were doing their job that drew the admiration of myself and crew. Their action made our work easier, and we filled up with troops in no time.'

Jack Hannaford, skipper of the *Tankerton Towers,* says in his report:

'During the afternoon of May 31st, after taking aboard some boatloads of soldiers, we decided to steam inshore to pick up some more, when we came across a motor-yacht disabled. This we took in tow. After about an hour her tow rope fouled our propeller, which we could not free. I knew we should be seen by a patrol ship at some time or other so we went on with our work, getting as many soldiers aboard, which at this time proved a mixed lot, British and French.

'Every available space aboard was taken up by a soldier, cabin, fish hold, wheelhouse, decks, even in the engine-room. Some time in the evening, I cannot give the correct time, a patrol ship did arrive, and took us in tow.

'It has since occurred to me that no one thought of the predicament we were in, and the only concern of everyone was to get the troops aboard. In between times we were kept amused by the way our men of the navy were shooting down the dive-bombers, just like rooks.'

Frederick Hannaford, skipper of the *Provider*, has equally lively memories.

'One incident which stands out vividly in my mind was the action of part of my crew on the morning of May 31st. The naval officer in charge of my ship had asked a few motor-boats which were laying about, if they were going to get some troops off the beach, and the reply he received was that there was not sufficient water to get in close enough. On hearing this four of my crew, the mate, boatswain, and two deck hands, all volunteered immediately to take a chance and go themselves. Of the two deck hands one was aged fifty-eight and the other twenty years. It was only possible for three to go, so the younger man insisted that the other deck hand should keep aboard the *Provider*. The young deck hand's name was Penn.

'The three pushed off, arrived at the beach, and picked up a load of soldiers. A motor-boat then went alongside to tow them back. Unfortunately, the motor-boat in starting off with its load pulled too hard, and swamped the small boat. All were thrown into the water. Only two of my men were found and brought back to the *Provider*. The young deck hand Penn had lost his life.'

The Belgian fishing vessels were working in increasing numbers. *Lydie Suzanne* crossed again and brought back 105 men; *Zwaluw* brought back 58; *Cor Jesu* brought back 274; *Jonge Jan*, 270; and the A.5, 234.

About the same time the ex-naval steam pinnace *Minotaur* left Ramsgate. She had been converted to serve as a Sea Scout training craft. Normally she moored at Mortlake, ten miles above the London bridges. With a Scout crew she was brought down to Southend. Then, with a Rover Scout as engineer, she carried on to Ramsgate, took on stores and fuel, and, picking up two naval ratings, made her crossing. Her skipper, Mr. T. Towndrow, Scout-master of the 1st Mortlake Sea Scouts, gives an interesting sidelight on the flow of rumour and what the lower deck calls 'buzzes' at Ramsgate during this time.

'Of the whole of our operations this six hours' crossing was the worst as we had nothing to do but contemplate the job ahead of us and had been foolish enough to listen to the idle talk of naval ratings in Ramsgate before we left, who assured us that very few of the boats that had gone across had come back and that, now that Jerry had captured the harbour and had mounted machine-guns covering the beaches, our chances of coming through were very slender indeed. Of course, such was not the position. The whole of Dunkirk was still very much in our hands, but we did not know this. . . .'

She reached the beaches safely, and proceeded to ferry out troops and to tow out loaded small boats to transports lying off the beach. She was working in a French area and all her troops were French soldiers, and Mr. Towndrow says:

'We were astonished at the way they refused to discard any of their gear. We got some out of the water who still had their full uniforms on complete with blankets in a roll on their backs. It often required all the strength we had got to haul them on board.

'We were working near to a group of destroyers and conditions were fairly quiet until suddenly we heard the roar of twenty-five German bombers and about the same number of escorting fighters overhead. The destroyers' anti-aircraft guns and the batteries ashore quickly opened up. Adding to the already deafening noise the air-raid sirens started wailing ashore. The realization that there were civilians living ashore in that inferno who needed warning to take cover seemed strange. The destroyers quickly got under way and started circling to elude the salvoes of bombs which were loosed at them. Shell splinters and flaming onions soon started dropping all round us. We steamed away from the unhealthy spot, but one destroyer singled out for special attention by the aircraft persistently made circles round us, giving us a pretty warm time.

'Two aircraft were hit and dived in flames into the sea, no distance away, their crews baling out. One destroyer was sunk with a direct hit. After the raiders had passed we rather shakily resumed our job. Eventually our fuel running low and the engine making ominous noises, we took on a final load of soldiers meaning to run back with them. Some way out, however, a trawler took off our soldiers and we returned to our East Coast base, refuelled, and turned in for a few hours' sleep. . . .'

Pickford's fleet was carrying on. *Bat*, returning for the second time, 'put in close to shore on the west side, but found that all the remaining troops had been taken off in a destroyer, so proceeded to the east side, being machine-gunned and shelled on the way. On this occasion they got on board in small boats about 100 men. These they brought safely back to England, having been without sleep for ninety-two hours, and the engines having been running continuously all the time.'

Bee (W. E. Trowbridge, master) reached Dunkirk on the 31st and 'after lying three miles off the shore all one night, was placed alongshore and took 360 British troops aboard. These were later transferred to a tug. Later ten British and five French troops were taken from small boats and brought back to England.'

Hound (W. H. Knight, master) arriving there about 6 o'clock, 'sent two of the crew to the shore in a small boat to help the troops get away. It was dangerous owing to the number of men who got into the boat, but eventually six were taken to the *Hound*. After delays caused by bombing, a further six were saved. For some while *Hound* got alongside what remained of one of the little piers and took aboard about 100 French and Belgians.'

M.F.H. (W. H. Smith, master) also crossed.

'Upon her arrival at Dunkirk there were about eighty German raiders overhead dropping bombs on the beach 40 feet away. Troops were picked up and disembarked on to a larger vessel. They then proceeded to the Mole, and took on board about 140 troops "including a colonel" and returned to England with them.'

The lifeboats were still working, both those manned by their own crews and those manned by naval parties. *Prudential*, the Ramsgate lifeboat, which had lifted superbly all through Thursday, continued throughout Friday and Friday night at the work of ferrying until she had taken more than 2,000 troops off the beach either by herself or in small craft which she towed off. She had put two members of her crew on board the motor vessel *Rian* during the previous night, and she was, therefore, short-handed in this difficult work. At the beginning of operations she had had eight small craft working for her, but one by one they dropped out—some of them stranded, some of them stove in. By Friday evening there were three left out of the eight. One of them, a motor-boat named *Sunshine*, had been extremely useful, but her motor was now out of commission and she had much damage around the top-sides. However, putting two of her men in *Sunshine*, *Prudential* dropped her in to the beach at the end of 90 fathoms of veering line and then, when she was loaded, the men on the lifeboat hauled her out. The two remaining boats had to be baled with water-buckets. *Sunshine* was eventually lost through parting her tow on the way home, and as *Prudential* was damaged by splinters and had a section of her bottom stove in, there was no question of picking up the little boat again.

In the sector of the beach where the Margate lifeboat, *Lord Southborough*, was working, all the small craft from destroyers and other ships were lost in the early morning strandings, and as the beach in that area made it quite impossible for her to run herself aground to take men off, she decided to return. Even then her work was not done. On her way towards Dunkirk—she had been working very close to Nieuport—she picked up a whaler with two naval commanders and fifteen ratings on board.

'They had found the whaler on the sands,' says Coxswain Parker, 'with no gear in it and full of water, they got the water out, found enough oars on the beach to get it off the shore far enough for us to pick them up, but as the wind had freshened, blowing right on the shore, they were barely holding their own, they had no rowlocks, but had got the oars lashed to the gunwales, and had been rowing, trying to get to one of the many ships that were in the vicinity from before daylight. They were the remains of a party of 150 that had been working on the sands for four days. They were taken on board the lifeboat and their boat cast adrift. We brought them to Margate and landed them about 3 p.m. I cannot accurately say how many men we were able to get aboard the destroyer, H.M.S. *Icarus*, and the barge, but I do not believe it was less than 500. Bombs and shells were falling most of the time.'

The navy does not pass compliments easily, but there is a letter from Lieutenant-Commander E. G. Roper, R.N., First Lieutenant of H.M.S. *Icarus*, the destroyer with which *Lord Southborough* did most of her work, which reads:

'On behalf of every officer and man on this ship I should like to express to you our unbounded admiration of the magnificent behaviour of the crew of the lifeboat *Lord Southborough* during the recent evacuation from Dunkirk.

'The manner in which, with no thought of rest, they brought off load after load of soldiers under continuous shelling, bombing and aerial machine-gun fire will be an inspiration to us all as long as we live.

'We are proud to be the fellow countrymen of such men.'

Charles Cooper Henderson, the Dungeness lifeboat, which worked this day with her sisters off the beaches, was found broken down with four naval ratings on board in the small hours of June 1st off Margate, and was brought in by Margate lifeboatmen. But on the whole the R.N.L.I. were fortunate in this period. The first boat to be seriously damaged was the *Thomas Kirk Wright* which, as the result of a near miss, came back with 12 inches of water in her hold and one of the engines burnt out. The *E.M.E.D.* failed to return from her passage on June 1st and was believed lost, but reappeared on June 3rd. The R.N.V.R. lieutenant in command of her had been killed and her propeller was fouled by rope, but the servicing party at Dover cleared the trouble and got her back to Dunkirk. Many of the boats were stranded for varying periods. Sub-Lieutenant S. C. Dickinson, who was the Institute's inspector in Ireland, for example, found the *Mary Scott* on the beaches and worked her until she broke down and had to be abandoned again. She was, however, subsequently salved. At one time on June 1st three lifeboats were ashore, but all eventually returned. The *Jane Holland* on June 2nd was hit forward by a French motor-boat and then aft by a British torpedo-boat and was abandoned, but came home, being found on June 6th drifting water-logged in the Channel. Only the *Viscountess Wakefield* of Hythe was completely lost. No news was received of her after her departure from Dover, and she disappeared without trace.

In the early afternoon one of the most remarkable of all the ships that took part in this most remarkable of all sea movements, left Ramsgate—the Thames fire-float *Massey Shaw*. She was a floating fire-engine of the London Fire Brigade, built for short trips between the fire piers of the harbour areas of London River and the warehouses of the river bank, or the shipping anchored off them. A shallow-draught vessel, built to take the mud easily, she was little more than a casing for gigantic pumps. She was sent to Ramsgate primarily in the hope that she might be of some service in fighting the huge fires in Dunkirk. But before she reached, for the first time in her career, the open waters of the Channel, it was obvious that no good purpose could be served in attempting to fight the Dunkirk flames.

At 2 o'clock this afternoon, when everything that could float and move was being sent across to make the floating bridge to England, the *Massey Shaw*, with her crew of firemen on board, was ordered out. She reached Dunkirk at 7 o'clock. The harbour was full of personnel ships and her services were not required there, so she moved up the beaches three miles to the eastward of the Mole and, under Sub-Officer A. J. May and a naval sub-lieutenant, her crew of twelve London firemen worked to get men off the sands.

The motor cruiser *Quicksilver*, which had got away from her moorings within forty minutes of being requisitioned on May 29th, was taken over from Ramsgate by a naval party of two seamen in charge of Leading Seaman T. Phillips. On this first day, though she was only 31 feet in length, she brought away thirty-one men on her first trip, and she made five trips in all. Though she was on a number of occasions attacked by machine-gun fire from aircraft, she was only twice hit and had one man wounded in the leg by a splinter.

This Friday saw the very height of the effort of the little ships—and of their sacrifice. The disasters of the morning's tide were wiped out in the swift-flowing reinforcements of noon. By the late afternoon there was working off the beaches the greatest and the most fantastic concentration of the little ships that was got together in all that time. From the Wash to the coast of Cornwall the harbours had been swept clear and the floating bridge to England was rebuilt of fresh flotillas. No one who saw those little convoys slipping out to sea watched that movement without emotion. There was in the straggling lines of open boats and pleasure craft something incredibly gallant, something incredibly poignant. They were so small beside the huge sullen immensity of the calm Channel; across that water they were so tiny under the towering columns of the Dunkirk smoke.

5

The little ships were part of the pattern, but great though their work was —impossible of assessment in the courage and the hope that it brought to the long lines of men upon those desolate and dangerous sands—the wider road to safety still lay along the 5-foot plank-way of the Mole. The personnel ships worked on along that Mole. The little ships were one part of the pattern and they were another, and each was complementary to that glorious whole.

Royal Sovereign loaded until 1.30 on the morning of the 31st when she cast off and put to sea. Two hours later she picked up four survivors from a French steamer which had been bombed. Four hours after that she was off Margate pier. Always with *Royal Sovereign* one falls into the neatness of a time-table; her times, her journeys, were invariably remarkable. For this day Captain Aldis says, with his inevitable brevity:

'7.10 a.m. Arrived alongside Margate pier.
'8.30 a.m. Anchored off pier.
'6.5 p.m.   Hove-up and proceeded towards Dunkirk.
'10.10 p.m. Anchored off Dunkirk.
'10.40 p.m. Ordered by H.M. ship to La Panne. Hove-up and proceeded.
'11.15 p.m. Anchored off La Panne.'

Within less than twenty-four hours she had come back again to the loading.

St. Helier had left Dunkirk about dawn. At 7 o'clock she disembarked her load at Dover. The same evening she also was on her way back.

On May 29th the Southern Railway steamers *Hythe* and *Whitstable*, in reserve at Southampton, moved up to take the place of ships that had been lost. On the 30th they were anchored in the Downs. *Hythe's* master, Captain R. W. Morford, says:

'During the course of that day small craft ranging from motor-barges, coasting vessels, pleasure steamers continually arrived until the Roads took on an appearance never seen by us before.'

No man had seen the Roads like that 'before': no man had seen such a gathering of ships in any place in all the world before.

Her master was given—there is a faint touch of indignation in his account —'an army road map to navigate on', and orders to proceed to No. 3 beach Dunkirk and take as many troops from small boats as possible. She received her orders at 2.15 on the morning of the 31st. She was under way at 2.30. One little descriptive phrase in Captain Morford's account conveys a curious gallantry of atmosphere:

'We passed the sunken *Normannia*, her flags still flying, only her mast and funnels showing.'

'Passing close to the breakwater lighthouse,' he continues, 'a salvo of shells fell between us and the east pierhead. No damage suffered, the shells falling 200 feet inshore of the ship. Here we observed conditions on the east pier and I noticed the innermost end was clear.

'I was now at my beach and arriving in three fathoms, my draught was 12 feet. I waited for boats to embark troops. This was 6.34 a.m.

'The beach conditions were bad. Wind on shore force 3 making uncomfortable surf.

'I observed the difficulty the boats were having and as none could leave the beach I decided at 8 a.m. to enter Dunkerque. Approaching the entrance a salvo of shells fell between the pier heads and as we steamed past this position another salvo fell astern. No damage suffered.

'I swung the ship and berthed on the stone jetty at the root of the east pier and soon the troops started to board carrying badly wounded men on stretchers. Shell-fire continued; shells falling on either side of the pier, one damaging the handrail on the east side abreast of the ship, the pier is about six feet wide at this point. Bombs fell at intervals from aircraft flying in the pall of smoke over the town and fires were observed to start in many places.

'At 10.1 a.m., having on board 650 officers and men, 18 wounded, 4 French and 2 Belgian officers, the Naval Embarkation Officer decided to sail me as the shell-fire was getting more and more accurate. I could probably have taken twenty or thirty more. The holds were full but there was a little space on the forecastle head.

'On leaving the pier a number of shells fell on each side of the ship, one bursting under the starboard quarter. No damage was suffered to the ship or troops. The vessel lying ahead appeared to be damaged by this salvo.

'The voyage back to Dover was uneventful except for a distant air attack on vessels arriving and a few shells falling over apparently from our un-friendly battery. Dover was reached at 4.40 p.m. after making a detour of some miles to avoid mines laid the previous evening.

'During the passage my hands tended the wounded and provided tea, etc., to the tired but wonderfully cheerful troops, until water ran out.

'I would like to emphasize that the conduct of the whole crew was splendid throughout under most trying conditions. The engine-room staff kept a constant head of steam and the many difficult manœuvres were executed promptly. The chief engineer, Mr. J. Bamforth, showed leadership of his men by his example.

'The deck officers and men embarked the troops rapidly and filled the ship to capacity and carried stretchers from the quay. The helmsman, Able Seaman S. Walker, obeyed every order I gave him and showed skill and coolness when entering and leaving the port, when the rest of the crew had to take shelter. . . .

'When off the No. 3 beach in addition to many other craft sunk and aground our s.s. *Lorina* was observed, broken-backed and aground.'

Whitstable followed the *Hythe* an hour and a half later. At 8.20 she anchored off Bray-Dunes in 2¼ fathoms and, on the falling tide, was compelled to move offshore and re-anchor an hour and a half later. She lay there all through the morning and not until 2.30 did a boat come along-side her with troops. Captain N. Baxter, her master, was a little aggrieved at this.

'The method used,' he says, 'for embarking the troops from the beach was that the soldiers rowed off in boats until they were in water deep enough for shallow draught launches to take them in tow. The launches then towed the boats to the ships at anchor, who in turn carried the troops to a home port. Anchored off Bray besides my ship were the s.s. *Glengarriff* and H.M. destroyers, whose numbers varied between two and five. All the boats were towed to the destroyers, and it was not until 2.30 p.m., after a wait of six hours, that one boat was brought alongside. The *Glengarriff* and I both left for Dover at the same time. She had arrived at the anchorage before I did, but she only succeeded in obtaining twenty-six troops. It seemed to me very unfair that we merchantmen were kept waiting in a very dangerous position while ships armed to the teeth came in, loaded up, and departed again in an hour or so. . . .'

The criticism is an understandable one, but Captain Baxter was not in a position to see the whole picture. The destroyers were to a large extent using their own boats now in a desperate effort to make good the losses of the morning's tide. There were not enough of the survivors of Thursday's flotillas left to attend to all the ships, and the destroyers—old hands now at this gruelling work—knew where to lie for the small boats and how best to help them. Inevitably they loaded more swiftly. But it is none the less possible to sympathize with a big ship lying in that place of bitter danger, to feel with Captain Baxter the frustration of those hours.

At 3.30 the shell-fire, which had been approaching the area with the gradual

169

moving up of German forces during the morning, began to fall near the anchorage, and *Whitstable* hauled out.

King George V made another trip this day, picking up more than 700 men. *Malines* picked up about 900. There were others—many others. This day saw almost the very peak of the liftings. The average for the twenty-four hours was nearly 2,500 men per hour. Destroyers, personnel ships, small boats, the pattern was coming most magnificently together.

There were cargo ships too. The coasters' work matches with that of the big ships throughout this day. This is the story of Captain C. G. West, master of the s.s. *Nephrite*:

'The s.s. *Nephrite* was lying at anchor off Deal, loaded with military stores, and awaiting sailing orders, when about 6 a.m. I was called by the officer of the watch who reported that the examination tug was alongside. I did not feel too pleased at turning out as German planes had been over us during the night and I had been up until daylight, but the examination officer's first words cleared the atmosphere. I was ordered to proceed immediately to Dunkirk to evacuate troops, and to jettison any cargo I deemed necessary so that as many troops as possible could be embarked.

'Calling out all hands I told them what was required, and they turned to with a will stripping the hatches, and soon drums of oil and cases of cargo were going over the side.

'Meanwhile I received route instructions and fresh water for drinking purposes from the examination tug, and at 6.30 a.m. the vessel was under way proceeding through the Downs. The weather was fine and clear with practically no wind, and the sea was calm.

'After an early breakfast, which was to be our only meal of the day, I inspected the holds and decided that with a little levelling down of cargo the holds would carry a large number of troops. Decks were cleared and hatches arranged so that other troops would be able to sit above the holds, and I estimated that I would be able to carry 900 men.

'I then gave orders that food from the cargo be prepared for the reception of the troops, and cases of various foods were assembled by the galley. About 10 a.m. planes were observed but did not bother us, and soon the Belgian coast, which had been hidden by a pall of smoke, came into sight, also the sounds of violent gunfire and exploding bombs, which we had heard throughout the previous week, was becoming more intense. Ships of all sizes and descriptions were passed proceeding homewards full of troops, and soon we entered the narrow channel to Dunkirk, passing numerous wrecks. Off Dunkirk a squadron of enemy planes attacked the shipping, but quickly disappeared with our planes on their tails. Threading our way through the numerous wrecks at the harbour entrance I proceeded into the harbour against the ebb tide, and received orders to berth alongside the pier. It was now noon and soon about 200 soldiers were embarked and they quickly disposed of the food we had cooked for them. The crew were assisting in the embarkation, and were also kept busy preparing more food for the hungry troops. Several officers, including a padre and a doctor boarded, and I gave them the use of the cabin accommodation to make themselves more comfortable. The steward from now on was continuously employed in getting meals ready for the army officers who were starving, having had but one meal during the last three days. The doctor, who was Jewish, on being told there was pork in the stew, replied, "I do not care if there are dead dogs in it, I am going to have my share, it smells so good."

'About 1 p.m. I was ordered to shift alongside the s.s. *Roebuck* to avoid taking the ground, as I was drawing more than 14 feet of water. Destroyers, trawlers, and hospital ships were arriving continuously, and the embarkation of the troops and wounded proceeded without interruption, notwithstanding the efforts of the German bombers who were continually coming over the port and dropping their bombs. Lewis Gunner Mellis was continually in action with his gun and soon had some willing assistants from amongst the troops, who collected ammunition from the other troops and kept the Lewis gun trays full. About 3 p.m. I berthed alongside again, and on being asked by the pier commander when I would be ready to sail, replied, "I have come for a full load of troops, so why sail before I am full up? It only means more ships will be required."

'The commander informed me that he had to dispatch the destroyers as quickly as possible, and that I could assist the embarkation by taking troops whenever a jam occurred on the pier, so I carried on accordingly. About this time, the Germans were particularly active, and shore A.A. guns, destroyers, and ships were hitting back with everything they had. Occasionally a few shells whined overhead and fell into the harbour, but did no material damage. Numerous air battles were in progress and several machines came down, some of the pilots baling out.

'At 6 p.m. the pier was crowded with French troops, most of them keen to board the destroyers in the hope they would be landed in French ports. Observing a lot of them coming on board, having a feed and going ashore again, I had a conference with a British Army captain and a French major, and decided that if the French troops would not embark that the ship should sail. I estimated that I had 500 troops on board, about 70 of them French, and the French still refusing to embark I reluctantly cast off and steamed out of the harbour. . . .'

The s.s. *Levenwood* was one of the little coasters detailed long before the evacuation began to carry stores for the army in Flanders. She was already loaded with military stores when she was ordered across to Dunkirk to take part in the evacuation. Two miles east of the piers at noon this day she was attacked by German aircraft, and the first shell from her 12-pounder, manned by a Merchant Navy gunlayer, Mr. G. Knight, hit a German plane which was seen to crash on the dunes. The surf was still difficult and the afternoon flights of small boats were only just beginning to arrive. The rate of flow from the sands was desperately low, and a little after noon Captain W. O. Young, master of the *Levenwood*, was asked to put his ship on to the beach in a desperate attempt to speed things up. Captain Young says, simply:

'This I did and as there was a lack of small craft and a shortage of time I launched my lifeboat and with the help of all the crew embarked as many soldiers as possible.

'I continued as long as possible although the increasing surf was making it very difficult to get the lifeboat back to the ship again. As the tide was turning, I was having difficulty in holding my ship in position, but seeing the soldiers standing waist deep in the water, I encouraged my men to make one last trip to the beach. This they did, but unfortunately coming out through the surf the boat was swamped. I managed to save all the men and also the boat, the boat gear was lost.

'I got the ship off the beach safely and have landed the troops in a home port. . . .'

It sounds simple as Captain Young describes it, but it was an operaton of very considerable difficulty. Blowing the *Levenwood's* forepeak tank, he beached her in 8 feet of water. The tide was rising all the time and he had to keep steaming slow ahead and steering so as to prevent her swinging broadside on to the beach. By this means he managed to keep her less than 400 yards from the dry sand, and, sending in the chief officer with four men in a boat which they controlled by lines from the ship, they hauled men off for three hours, being bombed frequently. R. Moodey, one of her firemen, was in the water almost the whole time helping men off to the boats.

Matching *Levenwood's* effort was the work of the *Foam Queen*, a ship of about 1,000 tons in the Channel Islands trade. She crossed in the evening and, as there were no small boats available when she arrived, she was instructed by a patrol vessel to beach herself. She did this, launched her lifeboat, and sent it ashore with a grass warp. This she made fast to a lorry on the beach and used it to haul the lifeboat to and from the shore. She picked up about 100 men this way. At high water she floated off the beach and lay offshore until 3 o'clock on the following morning when she returned to Ramsgate.

6

At 9.2 in the morning the hospital carrier *St. David* sailed from Newhaven for Dover. There is something in this simple fact that has about it a magnificence, for it was the *St. David* which, in the previous afternoon, had declared that she would not sail unless escort or armament could be provided for the ships. In the signals and messages concerning this incident there is demonstrated a very genuine human sympathy on the part of the naval authorities; for the trouble with the men of the *St. David* and their captain was sheer exhaustion. From the very beginning of the Flanders campaign she had been carrying wounded. As the flow increased with the increasing battle her work became heavier, but as the enemy reached through to the coast it became, like that of her sisters, almost intolerably difficult. They were supposed to be protected, these hospital carriers—protected by custom, protected by international law, protected by common decency. Now they suffered not only the attacks of high-flying aircraft, which possibly could not identify them, not only night shelling and the casual hostilities of the thick weather, but deliberate attack, deliberately pressed home, deliberately repeated.

Yet it was not these attacks in reality which caused the momentary hesitation on the part of *St. David*. Fundamentally it was the physical exhaustion of her people. Captain Joy at midday on the 30th was given a medical certificate to say that he was not fit to proceed to sea. Early in the afternoon Captain Joy collapsed completely. The second engineer disappeared from the ship and was found suffering from loss of memory. And yet at 9 o'clock this Friday morning the ship sailed again. One night's rest was all that was necessary. She sailed again, unarmed and unescorted!

She was not alone in her difficulties. *St. Julien*'s crew were also suffering from strain. To stiffen them, and to assist these inexpressibly weary men, additional personnel were put aboard. She left very early in the morning.

'We proceeded,' says Captain L. T. Richardson, her master, 'using a different channel. By this time the crew were getting shaky and we arrived alongside at 8.58, and began loading under shell-fire (assisted by crew), shells falling about 50 feet away but no bombing.

'When we had completed our loading we left. . . . During the whole of this time the largest Red Cross flag was kept flying, and, no doubt about it, these were deliberate attacks on hospital carriers. . . .'

The work of these tired men was supplemented by others. *Lady of Mann*, though not a hospital carrier, was sent over in the morning to embark wounded from the French hospitals. Berthing about 1.30 p.m. she took on board a heavy load of casualties, many of them stretcher cases, together with a certain number of unwounded men. During this time she was constantly shelled and bombed. She had seven holes in the starboard bow close to the water-line, three of her lifeboats were damaged by splinters, and from her bridge they saw men killed by shell-fire on the decking of the Mole 30 yards ahead of them. She left about 5 p.m. for Folkestone.

The motor vessel *Scottish Co-operator* had sailed the previous evening from the Downs, and at 5.30 this morning her master, unable to get definite instructions, decided on his own responsibility to proceed into harbour. Immediately after arrival he began to lift wounded, taking aboard 50 stretcher cases, 150 walking wounded and 350 able men. Just as she was about to sail a hospital ship berthed alongside, and it was decided to transfer the wounded to her. This took forty minutes. Captain Robertson then determined to remain alongside for a further period in order to fill up with unwounded men, but with the stream that came he again picked up wounded and left finally with seven stretcher cases, making directly for Ramsgate. His ship was not hit by what Captain Robertson describes as almost continuous shell-fire, but her degaussing wires were cut and she had to go in for repairs to Sheerness.

A little after midday *St. Andrew* left Dover by herself. Reaching Dunkirk she was instructed to berth wherever she could find room. The only place available appeared to be at the Mole, and she berthed there during a heavy air raid. Later, however, she moved to another part of the harbour. Arriving at the new berth she could see a number of ambulances but, on investigation, they proved to have been heavily bombed and those that were left were either empty or loaded only with dead. The condition of the quay was such that loading would have been impossible anyway, and she moved a third time —again in the middle of a raid. Once more all hands had to turn out to carry stretchers and these now had to be carried a long distance down the narrow Mole with troops moving simultaneously to the personnel ships that were berthed alongside. The tide too was falling, and eventually *St. Andrew* had to be sent to sea to avoid grounding or hitting the wreckage of a ship that had sunk close under her stern.

'Navigation on the homeward passage was both difficult and dangerous,' says her report, 'as there were no aids to navigation and the risk of over-running the hundreds of small craft, heavily laden with troops, and which carried no lights, was very great.

'During these fourteen days very little rest was had by any of the crew— double lookouts were kept, and while at sea it was too dangerous to allow the men to use the forecastles; but all carried on with a good will.'

St. David followed the *St. Andrew* across. Approaching the French coast she was heavily bombed and much shaken by the under-water explosions. There were no berths available when she arrived off Dunkirk breakwater, and she had to stand off and on waiting for orders. During this time she was '... subjected to seven separate air attacks and on one occasion a magnetic mine fell so close ahead of the vessel that it was necessary to reverse the engines to avoid contact. Twenty minutes later another mine blew up less than 100 feet ahead of the vessel, lifting her partially out of the water.

'Later another magnetic mine dropped only four feet away from the star-board quarter, but, fortunately, this time did not explode. The splashes from the sea fell on the deck of the vessel as the mine entered the water.'

At 10 o'clock in the evening, when *St. Andrew* came out of the harbour, *St. David* went in, but could not get any answer to her signals. After making another attempt to get in at 1 o'clock, Captain Mendus (her chief officer, who had taken over the command after Captain Joy's collapse) returned to Dover. She reached there at 6 o'clock on the morning of June 1st and anchored out-side. Half an hour later a terrific explosion—presumably from a magnetic mine—occurred within twenty yards of her port quarter, and the ship was considerably damaged. There was little safety anywhere in those terrible days.

7

The destroyers worked the Mole all through the day. With them, matching them in everything, worked the big sweepers. They worked the beaches as well.

There was an early loss. The French destroyer *Siroco*, returning to Dover at high speed, was hit by a torpedo from a German E-boat and sank immedi-ately. About this time the Thames special service ship *Royal Eagle* reports that she was machine-gunned by German aircraft while on her way to Sheerness. This machine-gunning, she believes, was intended for the guidance of German E-boats, and it was almost immediately after this that *Siroco* was torpedoed three miles astern of her. Just prior to the attack on *Siroco* an E-boat had carried out an attempt on the Polish destroyer *Blyskawica*, which was still patrolling on the swept channels. This torpedo missed, but a heavy explosion took place close to *Blyskawica*'s bows. While she was searching for the E-boat she heard a second explosion some distance away and saw a high column of flame. Five or six minutes later *Blyskawica* heard the engines of the E-boat and, immediately after, sighting her dimly in the darkness, opened fire.

It is important to remember in connection with this and other actions something of the handicaps under which the patrolling destroyers—and indeed all the ships of the movement—worked in the dark hours. The water was full of small craft sailing independently. Some of them were high-speed craft. Almost any of them might have been E-boats. In the night darkness it is impossible to judge in the moment of sighting the precise size and shape of a small flat hull close to the water. The difference between an E-boat and a Thames pleasure yacht in the first instant in which she becomes apparent in the darkness—the critical instant in this tip-and-run warfare—is so small as to be negligible. All through, the destroyers and the other armed ships were sighting small craft and having to hold their fire until they could identify them. As has been said before, the swept channels were a potential paradise for the E-boat. The marvel is not that they sank ships like *Siroco* but that they sank so very few—that they did not disrupt the whole night sequence of the operation.

Siroco was a real loss. She had achieved an important reputation in the French Navy in the nine months prior to Dunkirk. In a single week in November of 1939 she was credited with the destruction of two German U-boats, one by depth charges and the second by shell-fire and subsequent depth charges. In December of the same year M. Campinchi, Minister of the Navy, announced that she had sunk a third German U-boat. *Siroco* was a medium destroyer of 1,319 tons, built in 1925.

Blyskawica lost contact with her E-boat, which had made off at high speed. She therefore turned back in the direction in which she had heard the explosion and immediately after sighted lights on the water. Steaming towards them, she found the survivors of *Siroco*, and picked up one officer and fourteen ratings. A few survivors were picked up subsequently, but, according to French sources, more than 300 of her crew and of the troops that she was carrying were lost. As a small measure of revenge aircraft of the Fleet Air Arm during the day bombed and sank an E-boat off the Belgian coast.

From the destroyers' point of view, however, the biggest problem of the day was not E-boats (which, despite the astonishing difficulties, were kept under control), but the shortening of the beach line. The withdrawal to the frontier line, though in a measure it made the army's task simpler, complicated that of the navy. La Panne beach had been of great service, but it had now to be abandoned. No destroyers or other ships could hope to lie at anchor for the long period necessary for loading, under direct observation of medium and heavy guns at short range. We had to withdraw to the Bray beaches, and even there the position was filled with a new danger.

Rear-Admiral Wake-Walker had transferred early back to H.M.S. *Keith* (Captain E. L. Berthon, D.S.C., R.N.), and he examined the position as it stood. By noon the minesweeper *Hebe*, under heavy shellfire, had been forced to withdraw to Bray, and *Keith* attempted to locate the battery which was responsible. She carried out a bombardment of suspected positions, but the shell-fire continued. There was more than one battery operating. Her firing, however, had some effect, and that effect may best be judged firstly by the reduction in the shelling, and secondly by the fact that *Keith* herself became the special target of numerous German planes in the early afternoon. She managed, however, to dodge all the attacks with extraordinary skill. In the late afternoon H.M.S. *Vivacious* was loading off Bray when the fire of the German batteries again became serious and she was hit twice, suffering damage. Three men were killed and twelve wounded.

Until this period we had managed a steady supply of destroyers off the Bray beaches. The numbers varied but there were never less than two and frequently there were as many as five. Their work is admirably described earlier in this chapter in the report of Major Hutchins of *Swallow*, and it need not be dilated on here. All this activity, of course, happened within full view of any German aircraft that flew over, and it was this flagrant defiance of the theoretical possibilities that predetermined the disasters of the following day. We were, in fact, trailing our coats. Yet the situation demanded this apparent recklessness and the results justified it. All through the day a tremendous stream of men poured back across the Channel to England, and with the night the stream doubled. H.M.S. *Havant* (Lieutenant-Commander A. F. Burnell-Nugent, D.S.C., R.N.), picking up at noon members of Lord Gort's staff, passed a signal saying that very large numbers of men were to be expected on the beaches at dusk, and asking for fresh boat crews and pier masters.

Though we had no actual loss this day, the destroyers suffered the usual casualties due to damage. In addition to *Vivacious*, *Basilisk* (Commander M. Richmond, R.N.) had damaged one propeller running over submerged wreckage, and had to have the assistance of tugs before she could be turned round in the narrow channel and limp off on one engine at 15 knots. *Impulsive* (Lieutenant-Commander W. S. Thomas, R.N.) arrived at Dover with her starboard engine out of control, and the majority of the ships which had worked the beaches had at least splinter damage to report when they returned.

Malcolm, *Sabre*, *Whitehall* and *Icarus*—which once again escaped from air attack by adroit use of smoke and by elaborate zig-zagging—were amongst these ships. *Wolsey* at this period spent twenty-five hours in the outer harbour motionless under almost continuous air attack, acting as W/T link ship. About midnight her degaussing circuits were at last repaired.

Matching the destroyers the minesweepers worked ceaselessly. Of the old Dover flotilla only *Sandown* and *Medway Queen* were left. The proceedings of *Sandown* might be taken as an example of the average of the work of the sweepers this day. With her mascot, the dachshund 'Bombproof Bella' (to whom the immunity of the ship from trouble was faithfully ascribed by her crew), *Sandown* was crossing in the small hours when she picked up a signal from H.M. Drifter *Golden Gift* ashore on the Goodwins with 250 troops on board. *Sandown* anchored as close to her as the water would allow and sent her motor-boat away. In five trips she brought off the entire load of troops, and, returning to Ramsgate, disembarked them. By 11 o'clock she was ready to proceed again, and in the early afternoon reached the beaches off Bray, anchoring there. With the other ships she was shelled from the Nieuport batteries, but despite high-level and dive-bombing and the incessant shelling (which made it necessary for her to change berth on two occasions in order to throw off the range), she embarked 910 British troops, and, just before midnight—immediately after two parachute mines had been dropped near her—she got under way and returned to England.

Put baldly that day's work can be compressed into a few words. The telling of it as it happened, the infinitude of anxiety and danger, the endless succession of critical moments would fill a volume.

Her remaining flotilla mate, *Medway Queen*, also crossed again on this day, working on towards the sweepers' record for the operation. She towed with her six ships' lifeboats including one from s.s. *Huntington*. Leaving Margate at 9.30, this convoy was part of the great flood of reinforcement that went on all through the evening.

To join the veterans of the sweepers, and the Harwich and Thames flotillas, fresh ships had come in this morning. They came from the Firth of Forth—the 7th Flotilla from Granton, led by the *Queen of Thanet* (Commander S. P. Herival, R.N.V.R.). *Queen of Thanet* went straight in to the beach and picked up between 300 and 400 men, disembarking them at Margate. *Brighton Queen*, using her own lifeboats, picked up 100 men, and then took in a signal from a Dutch skoot that was ashore and went to her assistance. She took off 300 troops from this vessel, and during the operation was attacked by bombers, suffering slight damage. She had, however, no casualties and duly landed her men at Margate.

H.M.S. *Whippingham*, another paddle-minesweeper, which arrived at Ramsgate at noon from Portsmouth, left before 2 o'clock at full speed for Dunkirk. She arrived off Malo beach during a violent air raid, and experiencing some difficulty, as did all the ships, in getting a fast enough flow from small craft, attempted to put her stern on to the beach. In this she failed. Between 5 o'clock and 9.30 she records three violent air raids, but at 9.30 she went into the harbour, making fast alongside the Mole. The berth was under heavy shell-fire at this time and some of her men were wounded by shrapnel or pieces of flying concrete, but the ship herself was undamaged.

There were many others and, inevitably, they suffered further loss. On this day *Devonia* was so badly damaged by aircraft attack that she had to be run ashore in a sinking condition near La Panne, and abandoned.

Of the special service ships *Golden Eagle* carried a heavy load this Friday. Arriving off Bray at 8 a.m., she worked two boats from the beaches on a whip (an endless rope). She was attacked on a number of occasions from the air, but succeeded in beating off dive-bombers with her pom-poms. Eventually however, the berth became too hot 'owing to the increasingly accurate artillery fire which worried all ships on this day, and she moved into the harbour itself. She had loaded nearly 1,500 troops when the harbour was attacked by about fifty planes, but by one of the many miracles of the operation no ships were hit.

The Fleet sweepers were again there in strength. The accounts of the small boats who worked so faithfully with them are the best record of their splendid work. And to *Hebe*, which had carried the flag of Rear-Admiral Wake-Walker on various occasions, was to come this day a fresh honour when the time came for Lord Gort's return.

8

At 6 o'clock this evening Lord Gort closed his headquarters and the story of the British Army in Flanders came to its formal ending.

There remained the rearguard.

The hour is one of formality only. There was no break in the continuity of the operation, no hesitation in the movement, no slackening in the flood of withdrawal. Lord Gort's command had shrunk from an army to less than a single corps. At 6 o'clock Major-General the Hon. H. R. L. G. Alexander took over the command of the 1st Corps, which now numbered less than 20,000 men in all. As the remainder of the B.E.F. had come inside the area of the fixed defences of Dunkirk, they now passed under the control of Admiral Abrial, who commanded both land and naval forces within the area of the city. Major-General Alexander's orders, dictated by H.M. Government, were that he should continue to assist the French in the defence of Dunkirk while continuing at the same time the evacuation of the remainder of his men, and, in discussion with Lord Gort, the night of June 2/3rd was fixed as the provisional date for the final evacuation of the rearguard.

'I stressed,' says Lord Gort, 'the importance of the French sharing equally in the facilities which were provided for evacuation.'

In point of fact, as the logs of the ships and the accounts of their masters, the stories of the small craft, show, that equality had been in progress all through this day and in some degree during the previous days, but in the middle of Friday morning a signal was made:

'The policy of H.M. Government is that both British and French troops be given equal opportunities for being evacuated in British ships and boats.'

Lord Gort was taken out in the course of the evening to the Fleet minesweeper *Hebe*. He had invited General Blanchard and General de la Laurencie to join him on the journey. They were unable to do so, but the Commander-in-Chief made arrangements for some of the staff of General de la Laurencie's 3rd Corps to sail with the staff of British G.H.Q. At 2 o'clock the following morning Lord Gort sailed for England in M.A./S.B. 6.

A chapter was ended. Fifty-nine thousand men of the British and French armies had sailed out of Dunkirk on this Friday.

CHAPTER XIII

SATURDAY, JUNE 1ST

1

The story of the last four days of Dunkirk is the story of the evacuation of the British rearguard and of the last elements of Prioux's 1st French Army. Nothing, even in the greatness of the earlier movements, matches the dogged courage, the dour endurance of these last days.

On Saturday, June 1st, the Dunkirk perimeter was a shrunken thing. On taking command of the 1st Corps Major-General Alexander went to Dunkirk to see Admiral Abrial, who informed him that his intention was to hold the perimeter until the last troops were embarked. His declared plan was for the French to stand on the sector from Gravelines to Bergues. The eastern half of the perimeter through Les Moeres to the sea was to be held by a mixed French and British Corps under General Alexander. The use of the name Gravelines is a little difficult to understand at this stage of the proceedings. Gravelines town had already been in German hands for a considerable while and no counter-attack of any importance had been launched in this direction by the French forces which held the sector nearest it. It is possible that Admiral Abrial used the name loosely meaning the Gravelines end of the line. Mardyck Fort, very much closer in to Dunkirk Mole, had already been taken by the enemy on the 29th.

According to the appendix to the Gort dispatches Admiral Abrial and General Fagalde informed Major-General Alexander that they 'intended to hold the perimeter till all the troops were embarked'. It is difficult to be quite certain precisely what was meant. To British eyes it was evident that the naval and military situations were serious 'and deteriorating rapidly. The fighting condition of the troops was now such that prolonged resistance was out of the question. . . .' Scarcity of food, supplies and, above all, the increasing shortage of ammunition, had made this inevitable.

General Alexander told the Admiral bluntly that in his opinion the front could not be maintained after the night of June 1/2nd. The naval situation was deteriorating at a rapidly increasing rate. The losses in small craft were enormous, and the loss of larger ships and of naval vessels had already become dangerous with regard to future possibilities. All the devotion of the seamen could not now materially increase the rate of flow.

It was decided at a final conference at 8 a.m. this Saturday morning—even while the naval disaster was in progress—that the eastern line would be held until midnight of June 1/2nd, thus covering what was now predominantly a French withdrawal throughout the day and the first part of the night, and that

General Alexander's troops should then withdraw to a bridgehead immediately round the town itself.

It was very plain early in the day that the enemy appreciated the situation in which the British stood almost as well as General Alexander. The enemy showed it by the viciousness and the weight of the attacks which he launched on the eastern sector of the line throughout the morning and the afternoon. At Bergues heavy attacks on Brigadier C. M. Usher's force, supported by bombing and by concentrated artillery fire, forced the garrison of the village (the 1st Loyals with other elements) to withdraw to the line of the canal north of the town. The 46th Division, the 1st Division, and the 126th Infantry Brigade of the 42nd Division were forced back north of the canal for a distance of 1,000 yards. The 50th Division had its front penetrated at various points. The fighting was bitter and casualties were considerable, but by evening the enemy appeared to have battered himself to a temporary standstill, and on the line Bergues–Uxem–Ghyvelde and thence due east to the frontier and along the frontier defences to the beach, the British held fast.

It was to the thunder of that fighting that the evacuation continued.

2

All through the Friday night the shelling had been very heavy about La Panne and in the little town itself. Our withdrawal to the frontier line between La Panne and Bray had been followed by the inevitable forward movement of the enemy's artillery, and it was apparent that the moment the doubtful cover of the night was lost ships operating in that area would have to move very far to the westward.

Meanwhile the darkness covered a multitude of tugs, motor-boats and lifeboats, and while that darkness lasted, and in the half light that followed it, they worked desperately. A quotation from the log of the master of *Sun XV*, J. J. Belton, shows something of the difficulties.

'At 12.5 a.m. on June 1st our boats left for the beach which was to rough estimation fifty yards distant, and was under continual German artillery fire of all calibres. Our boat's crew under very bad circumstances managed to ferry between seventy and eighty soldiers aboard and during this we lost all of our boats with the exception of one which eventually sank astern of the tug and was cut adrift. At 2 a.m. we hove up anchor and proceeded down the roads at slow speed. We were continually machine-gunned all the way down, but with skilful management we made the open channel without harm to tug or crew and proceeded on our way to Ramsgate.

'At 4.30 a.m., in a position three miles westerly of Ruytingen buoy, we spoke two small Government vessels, Y.C.71 and Y.C.72, both disabled with engine trouble and loaded with troops. The lieutenant in charge asked us to tow them to Ramsgate as it was very dangerous to be lying there owing to raiding aircraft; we took them in tow. . . .'

These ships had left Ramsgate (under Lieutenant Mortimer, R.N.R.) late on the Thursday night. On their arrival at the beach line they ferried off all

180

the soldiers in sight—forty-five all told—in a skiff and left a little after mid-day, Y.C.71 and a motor-boat working with them having broken down. At midnight Y.C.72 herself broke down.

Most of the tugs towing small craft had orders to get clear by daybreak. *Sun VIII* sent her boats in with instructions to fill minesweepers and, when they were full, to bring the last loads off to *Sun VIII* herself. She went so close to the beach that a little before 1 o'clock in the morning she had to shift out because she was bumping the bottom in the swell.

'At dawn,' says her master, S. Smith, 'I still had not my full quota of troops, so we waited for further boatloads. The other tugs had gone. At about 4.30 a.m. a sloop came to us and told us that Captain (D.) had ordered the *Sun VIII* to get out. We passed the lifeboats over to a sloop's motor-boat with the exception of three, which we abandoned so as not to delay our passage to the westward down Dunkirk Roads.

'The roads were littered with wrecks and abandoned vessels, the *Sun VIII* having about eight miles of this to do before putting out to sea from No. 5 buoy. During all this operation Dunkirk was being shelled and we were still having bombing attacks. The wind had come off the land which made the passage difficult owing to the smoke from the big fires west of the pierhead entrance.

'During the air attacks we replied with our twin Lewises, one each side of the bridge.

'We had about 120 troops on board.

'When we were about twenty miles out to sea from Dunkirk we had no more trouble from the air and the remainder of the passage passed without incident. . . .'

Sun IV had been anchored during the earlier part of the night off the beach and had already picked up a certain number of troops. At 2.30 a.m. the shelling came very close, and her master, C. G. Alexander, says, laconically, 'Hove up, shifted position clear of shells (we hope).' At 3.50 p.m. she left with three lifeboats in tow. An hour later she lost one boat swamped by destroyers fighting off an air attack, and while that boat was being cut adrift she was herself attacked by a plane and drove it off with the fire of her Lewis guns. A couple of hours later she lost another boat to the wash of the destroyers.

Tanga, which had towed over a string of small boats, got them back a little before 4 o'clock with 160 troops. Taking them on board, she abandoned all but one motor-boat and, under heavy shell-fire, moved away from the beach.

'When abreast of Dunkirk,' says her master, H. P. Gouge, 'we fell in with a small boat with six men in it. We stopped and picked them up, and they were the sole survivors of twenty-five from H.M. Tug *St. Fagan*, which had been bombed with her tow of three Thames barges. Two of the barges were also blown up. A mile further on we picked up barge *Pudge* with four men on board, two badly wounded, and we towed her back to Ramsgate. . . .'

At dawn the London fire-float *Massey Shaw* also pulled out with a load of sixty men, leaving the flames of Dunkirk astern of her.

Close to her the barge *Thyra* (Skipper F. W. Filley) came out of the shallows and was towed home full of troops and with the crew of the barge *H.A.C.* (Skipper R. H. Scott) (which had been towed over with her, and which had been beached on instructions) on board. *H.A.C.* was got off the next day, her cargo having been landed, and was in her turn towed back, valiantly full of men!

Once more the Belgian fishing vessels were there. The *Anna Marguerite* lifted 120 French soldiers and on her return journey picked up thirty survivors of a French cargo ship which had been sunk by a magnetic mine. The *Georges Edouard*, which was commanded by a Merchant Marine officer, picked up nearly 500 men this day, and with an earlier trip carried a total altogether of 1,007. The *Guido Gezelle* on two trips carried 403.

These small craft—the lifeboats, the motor-boats that had been towed over by the tugs, and the tugs themselves—had worked all through the hours of darkness loading larger ships. The naval-manned Dutch skoots had lifted many thousands this night. The naval drifters and trawlers, the mine-sweepers, patrol vessels and destroyers had also carried tremendous numbers.

H.M.M. *Whippingham*, for example, which had started loading about 10 o'clock the previous evening under shell-fire, estimates that she had picked up 2,700 troops by 1.30 a.m. With her sponsons only about twelve inches above the water, she cast off at that hour, struggled out between the wrecks, and got clear. Her passage back was slow, as her captain, Lieutenant Eric Reed, R.N.R., records. It was slow because she was 'very much overloaded' —so much so, in fact, that every time she altered course she took on a violent list.

With these ships worked the personnel carriers. *Royal Sovereign*, for example, which had moved down to La Panne a little before midnight, had picked up a heavy load by 2.20 a.m. and, as her sector of the beach was coming under what her master (usually very spare of words) describes as 'terrific bombarding and shelling', she pulled out and returned to Margate.

At Dunkirk itself the pier was still working steadily despite increasing shell-fire and intermittent night bombing. There were periods when it was extremely difficult, even impossible, to enter the harbour; but, broadly speaking, the flow continued astonishingly steady all night, and somehow as the men came down the·narrow pathway of the Mole there were always ships waiting to take them out. They were being sent with almost clockwork regularity from the other side.

Maid of Orleans sailed from Dover, arriving a little before dawn. Her report says, tersely, that berthing was still more difficult owing to new wrecks. As she had good gangways on board, she was instructed by the Senior Transport Officer to lie alongside and let two destroyers berth outside her and load over her. At low water the destroyers' decks—even the fo'c'sle decks—were a considerable distance from the level of the surface of the Mole.

SATURDAY, JUNE 1st

At 3.35 a.m. *Prague* left Folkestone, and from 7 o'clock onwards her master reports that she was subject to intense air attacks.

At 7.40 *Scotia* sailed from Margate Roads and half-way across, passing a returning destroyer, got the grimly humorous signal, 'Windy off No. 6 buoy'.

In an attempt to provide air cover of a sort in this mid-Channel area the cruiser H.M.S. *Calcutta* was sent out again to patrol between W and Y buoys. She worked this area for six hours, being ordered back a little after 9.30.

Beaches and pier—the work was continuous; but from the area near La Panne the boats had definite orders to get clear of the beaches before the light came, and slowly the exodus became general. To have remained in the roadstead off the little town through the sunrise would have been tantamount to suicide. Already the Germans were mounting heavy machine-guns along the sand dunes. The troops were abandoning this section of the beach and moving as rapidly as possible to the west. This was in conformity with the suggestion made originally by Major Hutchins of *Swallow* and passed with Rear-Admiral Wake-Walker's concurrence to the military authorities on shore. The eastern sections of the beach were already completely deserted. The account of the work of Captain Pim, part of which has already been quoted, says:

'By midnight all the troops which he could find were embarked and placed in ships which sailed for England. Just before midnight he went along some of the beaches to look for stragglers and was told by a staff officer that no more troops would embark from those beaches, but that it was anticipated that the beaches would be shelled and would probably be in German hands the following day. This was a correct forecast.

'He estimates that from the pontoons and beaches about 5,000 were embarked. He was impressed by the kindness that was shown to the tired soldiery in the various ships in which they were embarked and also by the fact that the military chaplains were always among the last of their respective parties to leave the beach.

'By midnight several of the motor-boats had broken down and between that and 3 a.m. complete repairs were done to these boats—a most creditable performance by the officers and ratings sent from *Excellent* and *King Alfred* to man them.

'Anchorage had to be shifted during the night as shells meant for the beaches were ricocheting over H.M.S. *Hilda*.

'Captain Pim had given an undertaking to return at dawn if anything went wrong during the night. Accordingly at 3.15 a.m. on June 1st, he sent off all the boats to search the beaches. During the next three hours he took off 250 men only, apparently stragglers. A large rearguard party marching along the beach decided to continue to Dunkirk. . . .'

But in the Malo-les-Bains sector there were still large numbers of men, and until late in the morning ships worked picking up as many as possible. The account of the experiences of Mr. Raphael de Sola, another of Captain O. M. Watts' class, who was towed across by H.M. Drifter *Strive* (Skipper J. A. Catchpole, R.N.R.) in a ship's lifeboat, gives some picture of this area.

'H.M. Drifter *Strive* dropped anchor and Mr. de Sola went ashore in the lifeboat with the three others. They were fired on by low-flying planes, but they reached the shore unhurt. There the boat was turned over by the surf and could not be righted, so the crew made for a bright light which was visible shining across the sands. It turned out to be the headlight of a deserted army lorry. Here they were again fired on by low-flying planes and they took cover behind a wrecked fishing boat, the *Rosetta*.

'They could find no troops, but there seemed a risk of being taken prisoner since gunfire sounded near at hand and several shells burst very close to them. They therefore decided to walk to Dunkirk along the beach. One of the crew suggested swimming out to the nearest ship—several were just visible. They took off their sea-boots and started swimming. They then got near to a ship, which turned out to be a paddle-steamer, aground and apparently on fire. Her davits were empty and she had been abandoned. Accordingly they swam back to the shore and came across about twenty British sailors in charge of a Paymaster-Lieutenant, R.N.R. They were trying to launch a large motor-boat which lay with two other ships' lifeboats on the beach. The motor-boat was too heavy, so they launched one of the lifeboats and got aboard. There were no oars and they chopped off the seats and used them as paddles. There were two propellers, hand-driven, but these were jammed. After a fruitless visit to the burning steamer, searching for oars, they eventually reached the minesweeper H.M.S. *Niger*.

JUNE 1ST

'In *Niger* Mr. de Sola and his companions were provided with food and dry clothes, lent by members of the crew. It was then between 3.30 and 4 a.m., and the three of them tried to get some sleep. However, soon after troops started to come aboard, most of whom had had little to eat and no sleep for the past three days. Their need was greater than his and Mr. de Sola helped to take off their equipment and to get some food. He also assisted the Surgeon-Lieutenant to bandage and dress the wounds of some of the disabled men. Afterwards he made two trips to the shore in lifeboats and helped to embark more. The regiments were chiefly the Grenadiers, the Coldstreams, the Welsh Guards, and the King's Own Scottish Borderers.

'When the sun rose the beach was seen to be covered with troops, who were being lifted in lifeboats and embarked in the many ships of all kinds lying offshore. Also on the shore were many tanks and armoured cars, which were being set on fire. During all the time German planes were circling overhead and bombing, but at daybreak R.A.F. planes appeared on the scene and attacked the enemy.

'At about 9 a.m. *Niger* got under way. . . .'

For obvious reasons, however, the period between dawn and sun-up saw a very marked slackening of the rate of flow. With dawn the Luftwaffe had come back in tremendous force and at the same time the gunners, who in the period immediately about the dawn had slackened their fire while the batteries were moved closer towards the frontier defences, began to range on targets which their observers could spot with accuracy.

It is impossible to separate the proceedings of the different classes of ship upon this day. In the swirl and stress of events that followed the rising of the sun this morning the different segments of the pattern come finally together. There is no separating naval vessel from tug, barge from motor-yacht, launch from Channel steamer. All through this day they are mingled together in an inextricable confusion of effort. The water of the Dunkirk channels, the close passages of the harbour, the long swept approaches are a wild inter-mingling of movement and of disaster.

Even while the small craft, the skoots and the minesweepers were with-drawing from the eastern beaches, fresh personnel ships and naval vessels were racing in, and with them the tugs were coming over from Ramsgate and from Dover with new tows of barges, carrying food, water and ammunition. They passed each other along the line of buoys that led to safety.

The tug *Cervia*, towing the barge *Royalty* in company with the tug *Persia* with two sailing barges, met, for example, off No. 5 buoy in the West Dun-kirk Roads a batch of about twenty Belgian motor fishermen, who bore down on them and asked the way to England.

'I heard afterwards,' says W. H. Simmons, the master of *Cervia*, 'that they all passed over the Goodwin Sands on the high water and landed their troops and refugees safely on this side. All sorts of craft were coming round the buoy all fully loaded with troops. We had to ease down many times whilst towing up Dunkirk Roads as the destroyers and cross-Channel packets were coming down from the Mole in a 20-knot procession, but we had a good tow rope and it held on.'

A mile east of Dunkirk pierhead *Cervia* slipped her tow. Skipper H. Miller of the barge *Royalty* brings into his account a fine touch of ancientry that must not be overpassed in the roar of motors and the thunder of steam.

'We were setting our topsail to carry out this operation when a large number of German planes appeared overhead and immediately started bombing and machine-gunning us.'

Having beached and abandoned his ship according to orders, he rowed out to the *Cervia*, picking up on the way a launch which had broken down and which had twenty-five soldiers on board. A little further along the beach the *Cervia* sighted the barge *Tollesbury* and offered to take off her skipper and crew, but Skipper Webb had picked up 180 soldiers already and he was taken in tow.

'At 7.20 a.m.', says *Cervia*'s master, 'we dropped our anchor and watched the barge. Soldiers began to run down the beach towards her, but guns started to bang away on the outskirts of Dunkirk, and an air-raid siren blew and the soldiers went back to shelter.'

The wail of that siren ushered in an attack which, if it had been made earlier, might have been decisive in the history of Dunkirk.

4

It was part apparently of a comprehensive scheme of assault. As the tanks and the German infantry flung themselves against our battered outposts outside Bergues and along the canals towards Les Moeres, the Luftwaffe made a synchronized attack on the shipping in the narrow roadstead. It began with an extraordinary intensity above the ships to the eastward. In the long stretch off La Panne and Malo-les-Bains at that time there were only the flotilla leader *Keith* (carrying Rear-Admiral Wake-Walker's flag), which was engaged in investigating the position to the east, the Fleet minesweeper *Skipjack*, the destroyer *Basilisk* some distance away, and a handful of tugs and small craft.

At 7.30 a.m. a very heavy force of enemy bombers—predominantly Junkers 87 dive-bombers, but with the support of twin-engined Junkers 88s, and elaborately escorted by fighters—made its appearance. There were no Allied aircraft in the air at the time, no escort for the ships in that narrow channel of destruction. The destroyers themselves, fighting against attack through almost every hour of the past days, were desperately short of ammunition. Many of them had had no time to re-ammunition in the brief spells at Dover. There was only time to discharge their troops, to take on fresh oil, and to slip and put to sea again. *Keith*, after fighting all the previous day, had two rounds of A.A. ammunition left.

At once the attacks developed on the nearest ships. There is an appalling grandeur in that scene. From behind the beaches, from the harbour, from those ships whose guns could still answer the challenge of the air, the sky was filled with the pock-marks of bursting shells, with the thin trails of tracer bullets, with the whistle and roar of projectiles. Below the sea was flecked with small plumes and big as the splinters of the shells sang down into the water. And matching them in colour, in shape, in everything but size, came the monstrous, swirling fountains of the bombs.

Keith was heavily attacked by the first wave. Twisting, turning, at the utmost speed that she could manage in the narrow waters of the roadstead, she eluded the bombs. *Cervia*'s master's account of these moments—cool, almost dour in its absence of emotion—conveys somehow a graphic picture.

'A British destroyer outside of us began to fire at the enemy planes and bombs began to fall near her as she steamed about. At full speed with her helm hard to port nine bombs fell in a line in the water, along her starboard side, and they exploded under water, heeling the destroyer over on her beam ends, but she was righted again and a sloop joined in the gunfire, also shore batteries, and as the raiders made off over towards the land they machine-gunned us and we returned the fire with our Lewis gun.

'I immediately hove up our anchor and kept the tug under way as I could see we were likely to get run down, whilst the destroyers were twisting and turning to clear the bombs. I paddled in towards the shore a bit, as I could see our crew of the barge and the soldier stevedores were rowing off in their boat towards us. I picked them up, also boat and crew of barge *Duchess* that had anchored in the roads, and then the next wave of bombers were overhead.

'Steam and smoke were coming away from the destroyer, and she began to take a list. I began to run towards her, as also did the tug *St. Abbs*, but the planes were bombing her again, intent on finishing her off, so we had to sheer away from her. Her guns were going all the time as she steamed round and round, but she stopped as she must have been hit again. She let go her anchor and swung round head on to the tide, as the crew began to take to the boats and rafts we made for her again. The bombers came over and machine-gunned the crew as they were all jumping overboard and the tug *Vincia*, which was coming in the east end of the roads, began to pick them up, and the *St. Abbs* had got alongside her starboard bow and the sloop was also going to their assistance, so I turned round to a motor-boat full of soldiers and picked them up.

'At this time I could see that another destroyer had been disabled to the west of the harbour, and a plane had just dropped a bomb on a small oil tanker astern of the *Vincia* which went up in flames. A direct hit on the stern of the sinking destroyer blew up her depth charges and we made to the sailing barge *Tollesbury* which was signalling us. We went alongside of her and were requested to tow her out of it as she had over two hundred soldiers under her main hatch. We passed the motor lifeboat *Orient IV* on to her stern and began to tow her down the Dunkirk Roads. . . .'

Actually *Keith* was damaged in the first attack, though she did not suffer a direct hit. Near misses from the stick of bombs described by *Cervia's* master jammed her rudder and she turned in small circles for some time. In the second attack, however, she was hit almost at once amidships and very near misses also damaged her side severely. She was moving at high speed and turning at the moment of impact, and she at once listed heavily to port. Enormous clouds of steam came up through the after-funnel and boiler-room casings. Still turning, she lost speed rapidly as the steam went, and in a little her captain was compelled to bring his ship to anchor. Captain Berthon, D.S.C., R.N. (who had won his decoration at Zeebrugge during the great attack on St. George's Day, 1918) had taken the place of Captain D. J. R. Simson, R.N., Captain (D.) of the 19th Flotilla, who had been killed at Boulogne on May 24th. By the time the anchor took hold *Keith* was listing almost 20 degrees to port and had no more than two feet of freeboard on that side. At this point, however, she seemed to steady up and sank no further for the time being.

Meanwhile close to her the Fleet minesweeper *Skipjack* was hit and sank almost instantly. Close off the entrance to the harbour the destroyer *Havant* was hit early in a series of attacks, and sank rapidly.

Rear-Admiral Wake-Walker, with his staff, disembarked into M.T.B. 102, which had closed *Keith* immediately after she was damaged the second time, and headed down the roadstead to call up tugs. But the tugs had already turned towards the battered ship—the Admiralty tug *St. Abbs*, the tug *Vincia* and the tug *Cervia*. Captain Pim in H.M. Skoot *Hilda* was also making his best speed towards the wreck. Before they could reach her she was hit in a third attack. This time the bombs landed in the engine-room and she heeled right over and sank almost instantly. *Hilda* picked up fifty survivors from the water including Lieutenant-General W. G. Lindsell, the Quartermaster-General, and other staff officers. The tug *Vincia* picked up 108 officers and ratings including staff officers from both British and French headquarters, and *St. Abbs*, which closed her just before she sank, took off Captain Berthon and more than 100 survivors.

Meanwhile there was no cessation in the fury of the Luftwaffe's attack. Further down the water the dive-bombers were peeling off at 10,000 feet and coming down with a terrifying snarl of their motors to within 3,000 feet of the water. While the work of rescue was in progress the destroyer *Basilisk* was bombed. *St. Abbs*, under the orders of Captain Berthon, turned towards the spot to rescue survivors. Aircraft were flying overhead all the time and a Junkers 88, at high level, let go a single bomb. By a thousand to one chance it hit the hurrying tug amidships. She disintegrated and sank, leaving Captain Berthon and the comparatively small number of men who now survived, a second time in the water.

The destroyer *Ivanhoe* was bombed almost simultaneously, but remained afloat and was taken in tow by the tug *Persia*. Within a few minutes fresh attacks took place, and a bomb, falling between *Persia* and the destroyer, cut the tow rope. Indefatigably the master of *Persia* passed the tow again and a second time she moved off.

Whitehall on her first trip—she made two trips this day—found the still-floating hulk of *Basilisk* and sank it. She was herself dive-bombed and suffered damage from near misses.

The gunboat *Mosquito* (Lieutenant D. H. P. Gardiner, R.N.), which had done magnificent work now for many days, was hit in the same period, badly damaged, set on fire, and had to be abandoned. The Fleet minesweeper *Salamander* (Lieutenant-Commander L. J. S. Ede, R.N.) was damaged and tugs were sent in search of her. There were other naval casualties, other ships damaged in this period. Rear-Admiral Wake-Walker, hurrying to Dunkirk itself in the M.T.B. which had picked him up, was dive-bombed, but not hit. All up and down the long, narrow channel of the roadstead there was havoc and the thunder of the bombs. All up and down the roadstead were the long and lamentable pools of oil which marked the new ship graves; and with them, floating on the tide, was the pitiful wreckage of smashed boats and empty rafts, of battered furnishings and splintered planks.

Within little more than an hour we had lost three destroyers, a Fleet mine-sweeper and a gunboat, and four destroyers had been damaged. Almost immediately after the French destroyer *Foudroyant* was in her turn hit by the dive-bombers and in her turn sank. Two hours of disaster—nor was it the full tally of the day.

The rate of loss was too heavy. It could not continue. There was no question of goodwill involved: it was a question entirely of ship reserves; we no longer had the ships. The loss in destroyers alone was already very nearly crippling. To the three British destroyers sunk prior to June 1st, to the three of this disastrous morning, to the many that had gone before, there had to be added the enormous tale of those, like *Ivanhoe* this day, towed home disabled and out of service for many weeks.

Rear-Admiral Wake-Walker went in in his M.T.B. to Dunkirk harbour and, landing, went to Bastion No. 32 for a conference with Admiral Abrial and Captain W. G. Tennant, R.N. At that conference it was decided that no further operations should take place in daylight along the beaches as the rate of loss had become too heavy. At 9.30 a.m. Admiral Wake-Walker re-embarked in M.T.B. 102 and left for Dover for further consultations. He was dive-bombed and machine-gunned again on the passage.

This decision was an important one. During the previous day there had been a virtual cessation of activity along the beaches for a long period, but it had been dictated more by military considerations than by naval ones. There was no question here of failure in morale. At any hour on this day ships, had they been ordered, would have gone in to any section of the beaches. The matter was one beyond the courage of men. It was a matter of the hard arithmetic of ships. We had lost in two hours the equivalent of the loss of a small campaign, the loss of a sharp naval action. With the ships had gone many of their own crews, and with them had gone very many more of the soldiers that they had picked up at such cost of courage, of effort and of life. The wastage in drowning men alone was too great to be continued.

5

Fighter Command, Coastal Command and the Fleet Air Arm worked desperately throughout the day, but here too, as with the ships, the hard arithmetic of *matériel* came in. There were simply not enough planes at any time to give continuous cover to the channels of approach, to the roadsteads, to the beaches and to the hard-pressed men of the perimeter. Hour after hour the German bombers, protected by swarms of fighters, harassed the evacuating army. Hour after hour British pilots went up to meet them. By dusk seventy-eight bombers and fighters of the enemy had been seen to crash into the sea: sixteen of our own were lost.

We used a wide variety of planes—Defiants, Spitfires, Hurricanes, Ansons, Hudsons, Swordfish. Three Ansons, reconnaissance aircraft of Coastal Command, engaged nine Messerschmitt fighters at one period of the day, flying almost at water level. They shot down two of them, possibly two more, and drove the rest away. Three Hudsons found 'a patch of sky black with Jerrys', Junkers 87s and 88s ready to dive on transports, with a dense screen of Messerschmitts above them. In thirteen minutes three dive-bombers had been shot down, two had dived out of control, and the formation was driven off. Spitfires destroyed twelve German bombers and fighters during a morning patrol, and in the afternoon went up again and shot down another six.

It was the record day for the whole course of the operations. The seventy-eight enemy aircraft destroyed established a new record for the war. And again it was not enough. The enemy also upon this day established a record for destruction from the air that was to stand until the disasters of Crete.

The view from the air was different from that of the sea. Two brief quotations from the story of a Spitfire pilot[1] will serve to illustrate that:

'Nieuport slowly appeared beneath my wings, and I turned to run back down the coast. I had just turned again at Dunkirk, and was heading back once more, when something moving on my left caught my eye. I looked round in time to see an aircraft diving down towards the shipping off the harbour. Coming hard round I dived after it, the rest of the squadron chasing after me. The aircraft flattened out over a destroyer for a moment and then turned, climbing towards the coast. As I followed there was a terrific flash below and a huge fountain of water was flung high into the air, to fall slowly back into the sea. As the disturbance subsided I saw that the destroyer had completely disappeared. So the aircraft in front of me was a Hun. A blind fury gripped me. . . .'

The bomber got clear in the cloud cover. Almost immediately afterwards, however, the pilot found a new target, attacked and damaged it, and again lost it in the cloud. After three dog-fights he turned for home short of petrol, coming down to sea level:

'A mile ahead I recognized a cross-Channel steamer. I smiled to myself, remembering the long hours I had spent on her in happier days, crossing to the Continent. She would take a good two hours more to get home now, whereas I would be there in ten minutes.

'Just as I came abreast of the ship the whole sea suddenly erupted immediately behind her, and only a few hundred yards away from me. I nearly jumped out of the cockpit with fright! I had been rudely awakened from my dreaming by a Dornier sitting at about 2,000 feet, nearly over the top of me. As I looked, four little black objects left the belly of the bomber and came hurtling down towards the ship. I turned sharply and began to climb as hard as I could, feeling absolutely wild that the Hun had given me such a fright. He looked so insolent, sitting up there throttled right back, and letting his eggs go in that deliberate fashion. Luckily for me it hadn't helped him to aim accurately, but I felt like ramming him. I was not, however, forced to dwell further on this suicidal measure, for the Hun then turned back towards the French coast and climbed away as hard as he could, pursued by bursts of A.A. fire from a cruiser a mile or so to the north-east. Looking at the cruiser I watched the flickering stabs of flame from one of her "Chicago Pianos". Though it certainly looked a wicked and deadly performance enough, I couldn't see whether the Dornier was hit or not. . . .'

[1] Squadron Leader 'B. J. Ellan', *Spitfire!* (John Murray).

6

But in spite of Rear-Admiral Wake-Walker's decision and despite the snarl of the dive-bombers and the thunder of the bombs, the work at no time ceased entirely.

S.s. *Maid of Orleans*, alongside that dangerous Mole, lay patiently while a khaki stream poured over her to the destroyers. For six hours she was a floating landing stage. Two destroyers filled up (they carried often over 1,000 men), went astern down the narrow entrance and pulled out through the bomb splashes of the channel to the open sea. In her turn *Maid of Orleans* took on her own load (she picked up 400 French troops and nearly 1,400 British), slipped and reached Dover in safety.

The destroyers *Icarus*, *Malcolm*, *Sabre* (whose people had had a brief rest while minor damage to the ship was repaired) and *Scimitar* all used the harbour this day.

S.s. *Prague*, coming in by route X, reached Dunkirk at the very height of the first attacks. Her armament was one Lewis gun and one Bren gun, but she closed the entrance and went inside. Captain Baxter's report is very clear.

'Several casualties were observed among H.M. ships,' he says, 'but we were too busy berthing the ship and later shifting across the harbour to take precise notice of what was happening in this direction. The ship finally berthed at the western side of the outer harbour, close outside the locks, and then proceeded to load about three thousand French troops it was estimated.

'Just about nine o'clock, having completed loading, the ship left for England once more and proceeded down the western roads. At the end of the channel in the vicinity of No. 6 W Buoy, the ship was subjected to a considerable amount of shell-fire from shore batteries at Gravelines. I immediately asked for utmost speed but could not zig-zag on account of narrow waters. The great majority of the shells fell short and none hit the ship.

'At 10.9 Buoy W near the Ruytingen was passed and the ship making along the homeward route towards Buoy V, another intense air attack by dive-bombers developed. Heavy fire was opened by all ships in the vicinity against these aircraft (estimated to number about half a dozen), and the ship kept continuously under helm. Suddenly an aircraft appeared out of the clouds almost directly overhead and swinging round, dived on the *Prague*.

'At this moment the *Prague* was on a steady course and I ordered hard to starboard, the aircraft released three bombs together while still at a considerable height, the bombs fell very close to the stern of the ship which was swinging to port. The force of the explosion was terrific and the ship seemed to be lifted almost out of the water.

'Although not actually hit it was evident that the ship was very badly damaged aft. The stern settled down considerably and the starboard engine had to be stopped immediately as the shaft was bumping badly. The watertight doors were closed at the time in accordance with war-time procedure, but the force of the explosion had evidently made them considerably distorted, as the ship filled up to the after engine-room bulkhead and the water rose to the level of the main deck. There was a certain amount of leakage into the engine-room through the bulkhead, but the ship's pumps managed to slow down the rate of the rising water to a reasonable amount. The only presumable casualties to personnel were one fireman missing, presumed to be blown overboard.

'From the time of the explosion (10.25) the ship was kept going ahead as fast as it was possible to do on the port engine which was the only one left in service, craft in the vicinity were warned and several naval auxiliaries agreed to stand by us and the ship slowly progressed homewards.

'It was evident, however, that the water was gaining, and such measures as getting as many troops as possible forward to ease the weight on the after part of the ship were giving only temporary respite, so I decided to try to transfer the troops while the ship was still under way so as to lose as little time as possible. H.M. Destroyer *Shikari* and a sloop and a paddle mine-sweeper whose names I was unable to obtain came alongside in turn and very skilfully managed to transfer all except a handful of troops while the ship was steaming as fast as possible towards the Downs. This being completed it was possible to concentrate all efforts on saving the *Prague* by getting into as shallow water as possible before we found ourselves unable to control the inflow of water.

'By half-past one the ship was well inside the Downs and the tug *Lady Brassey* made fast. Dover was signalled and orders were received to anchor in the Downs. On receipt of these the ship proceeded to the Small Downs and entered the Ramsgate Channel.

'Having arrived at a spot slightly north of the ruins of Sandown Castle, about a mile north of Deal, the ship was gently beached, port anchor laid out, and all active participation in the evacuation of Dunkirk ceased. . . .'

H.M.S. *Shikari* (Commander H. N. A. Richardson, R.N.) transferred under way 500 men. She then called *Queen of Thanet*, the paddle-minesweeper, to come alongside in her turn. Commander Herival asked how many troops were left on board and was told 2,000. He embarked most of these—remember both ships were moving at the best speed *Prague* could make all the time —and took them in to Margate. The corvette *Shearwater* (to which the master of *Prague* refers as a sloop) then transferred approximately 200 of the remainder and took them to Sheerness.

As *Prague* was going down the Dunkirk roadstead *Scotia* was coming in. She was a coal-burner, and in addition to the exhaustion and difficulty of the work that she was doing was the necessity to coal ship. There were no proper facilities. For the oil-burning ships there were tankers from which they could take their oil by pipe line direct. *Scotia* and the other coal-burners had to be supplied with bags and shovels and work their own coal aboard from colliers or hulks. She herself shipped 90 tons from the coal hulk *Agincourt*, then moved to Margate roads and finished bunkering from the coaster *Jolly Days*. Her whole crew took part in the work, filling bags and manhandling them to the bunkers.

SATURDAY, JUNE 1st

She completed the operation late on the Friday evening and, having left
Margate in the early morning, was two miles away from No. 6 buoy in the
Dunkirk channel (about which she had been warned) when she saw several
enemy bombers directly approaching her. She also had an armament of one
Bren and one Lewis gun, and she opened fire, but the planes kept at a very
great height. No bombs hit. A little later she saw several British planes
coming from a north-easterly direction. The enemy had disappeared, but no
sooner had our own patrol gone than they reappeared.

'We were now approaching Dunkirk,' says Captain Hughes, 'steering
inside the channel buoys so as to avoid wrecks. We were fully occupied
trying to avoid bombs, buoys, and wrecks. I had reduced speed approaching
the entrance when the bombers again dropped two bombs, one about 100 feet
from the port quarter, the other about 50 feet ahead of us. I received orders
to proceed to West Mole to embark French troops and arrived at 11 a.m.
We found Dunkirk quiet except for a few rounds fired from shore batteries.
Immediately on arriving at Dunkirk we embarked all the French troops who
were waiting on the West Mole—there were about 2,000 of them. We left at
11.25 for Sheerness. On our return trip also I had to keep close to the buoys
so as to avoid wrecks and small craft making for Dunkirk. After passing
No. 6 buoy we saw enemy bombers coming from astern. They came in
formation of fours, there were at least twelve of them. In each case they
swooped low—the two outside planes machine-gunned and the two inner
each dropping four bombs, none of which scored a hit. The second formation
of four passed over us, flying very low. The shots from their machine-guns
dropped like hail all round the bridge and funnels and in the water ahead.
One bomb struck the ship abaft the engine-room on the starboard side and
another on the poop deck starboard side. Immediately the third four swooped
over us and one of their bombs dropped down the after funnel while the
others dropped on the stern. During all this time our guns kept firing but
with no effect on the enemy. Up to then we were going on full speed and
manoeuvring with the helm. An S.O.S. had been sent out. I ordered another
to be sent, but I was informed that the wireless cabin had been shattered and
the wireless operator blown out of his room, but he had escaped injury.

'All these bombs had caused extensive damage and the ship was gradually
sinking by the stern and heeling over to starboard. I therefore gave orders to
abandon ship. The engines had been put out of action.

'We carried ten boats, but three of them had been smashed by the bombs.
The troops, being French, could not understand orders and they were rushing
the boats, which made it very difficult to man the falls—the port boats being
most difficult as the vessel was heeling over to starboard. The chief officer
had been given a revolver to use by a French officer, threatening to use this
helped matters a little. However, they obeyed my mouth whistle and hand
signs and so stood aside while the boats were being lowered.

'Commander Couch of H.M.S. Esk had received our S.O.S. He was lying
at Dunkirk at the time; he came at full speed to the rescue. By now the boat-
deck starboard side was in the water and the vessel was still going over. He

193

very skilfully put the bow of his ship close to the forecastle head, taking off a large number of troops and picking up hundreds out of the sea. Backing his ship out again, he came amidships on the starboard side, his stem being now against the boat deck, and continued to pick up survivors.

'The *Scotia* had by now gone over until her forward funnel and mast were in the water. Two enemy bombers again approached us dropping four bombs and machine-gunning those swimming and clinging to wreckage. The *Esk* kept firing and drove the enemy away. Commander Couch again skilfully manœuvred his ship around to the port side, the *Scotia* having gone over until the port bilge keel was out of the water. Hundreds of the soldiers were huddled on the bilge and some of them swam to the *Esk*, while others were pulled up by ropes and rafts.

'The bombers returned but were driven away by heavy firing from the *Esk*. I was informed by one of my crew who was on the destroyer that one of these two bombers had been brought down by the *Esk*.

'Rescue work continued. Large numbers of the troops who had climbed up on the bilge were comparatively easily rescued. Others swam to the nets attached to the destroyer where willing hands were ready to haul them up. These nets were a very great help. By this time, all who were able to help themselves had left the wreck, but there were three lying seriously wounded. One of them was a steward of the *Scotia*, the other two being French soldiers. A rope was thrown from the destroyer; I tied this around the steward and by means of a boat fall lying across the side of the *Scotia* I was able, by holding on to it, to ease the jerk into the water and against the side of the destroyer. He was very badly injured but he was very patient and never grumbled. I learn that he has since had one leg amputated. The two French soldiers were rescued in the same way. Having assured myself that everyone who was still alive had been taken off, a boat spar was swung from the *Esk* on to the *Scotia*, by which I climbed aboard the *Esk*. The destroyer landed the survivors at Dover.

'Many other survivors had been picked up by boats from another transport and other craft which were in the vicinity and were landed in different ports.

'I regret deeply to report that our final list showed twenty-eight of our crew to be missing and two others have since died in hospital, while several are lying injured in hospitals. I estimate that between two and three hundred troops must have lost their lives.

'May I warmly thank the Commander of the *Esk* for his skilful work which was the means of saving many hundreds of lives.'

With *Esk*, amongst other craft, worked the little motor-boat *Bonny Heather*. She picked up from the water the chief steward of the *Scotia* and more than forty soldiers.

'Vernon's Private Navy' was there as well. Though they were already returning heavily loaded, the three that were left of these little ships—*Fisher Boy*, *Jacketa* and *Fidget*—managed to pick up a very large number of men between them. The record of these drifters is magnificent. Though their safe load was held to be 100 men, *Silver Dawn* had crossed the Channel on one occasion with 312. In all, apart from ferrying from the beaches, they brought back 4,085 men between them. This was their last trip. One of them, *Silver Dawn*, was damaged in Dunkirk harbour on her third day, losing a propeller blade, and had not crossed for the last trip, and the *Lord Cavan*, which had remained to work in Dunkirk, had been sunk by shell-fire.

The rescues of the troops in *Prague* and *Scotia* are examples of the very highest order of seamanship. It is true that the water was calm, but beyond that there was nothing to help the men of the destroyers, the minesweepers and the small craft that went in to take off these enormous numbers of men. With *Prague* every effort was being made to save the ship as well as the men, and the complications of speed involved in that were tremendous. With *Scotia* the matter was one of time and of enemy attack, and H.M.S. *Esk* performed a rescue that, standing by itself in time of peace, would have covered the front pages of the newspapers of the world. In the greater rescue of these days it was a small thing—a paragraph, no more.

About the time of the attack on *Prague* another small convoy arrived off the coast. It consisted of the motor-barge *Sherfield*, the 'X' lighters Y.C. 63 and X. 95, and the motor-launch *Nanette II*. Under the command of Sub-Lieutenant J. D. F. Kealy, R.N., they had left Sheerness at 2.15 p.m. the previous afternoon. On the way across the leader lost contact with X. 95. At dawn they were still out of sight of land, but at 11 o'clock this morning they saw a buoy. Their one compass was, as Sub-Lieutenant Kealy's report puts it, 'irregular'. Closing the buoy they found that it was painted 'Ostend'. Ostend then had been in enemy hands for some days!

They turned westwards at once and came in to the roads off Nieuport as the battle of the morning was ending. A destroyer was in action with shore batteries and another was flaming in the fairway. A little further up they found a number of men struggling in the enormous oil slick that covered the graves of *Keith*, *Havant* and *Basilisk*. They managed to pick up a number of survivors here, and from the wreck of the s.s. *Clan MacAlister* they took off fifteen wounded men from *Keith* and other ships. Then, turning their attention to the beaches, they got off a number of men and took the load from a motor-boat filled with wounded. While this was in progress the boat was bombed and machine-gunned. Presently there was a lull, and during this Y.C. 63 and *Nanette II* put out to sea and got clear. *Sherfield* was picking up her last load when she attracted the attention of enemy planes. Sub-Lieutenant Kealy stopped his ship in the hope of being taken for a derelict, and eventually the planes sheered off. Later one dive-bombing attack was made on her without success.

In this craft there were a number of civilian volunteers, the youngest of whom was seventeen, and Sub-Lieutenant Kealy pays them a very high compliment for their fortitude and efficiency, but perhaps his best comment concerns his ratings: 'All naval members of the crews acted as expected.'

These small craft got away, but another of Rear-Admiral Taylor's little vessels *Iote* (Sub-Lieutenant R. H. C. Amos, R.N.V.R.) had to be abandoned when, in attempting to rescue two of her crew, she ran aground and smashed her rudder.

The disasters of the morning did not stop the flow of the personnel ships. About 10 o'clock *St. Helier* sailed from Dover. She reached Dunkirk in the middle of the afternoon with an air attack from sixteen planes in progress. The problem of dealing with the wounded was acute at this time and Captain Pitman was asked to wait and load stretcher cases which were then being brought down towards the harbour. At 6 o'clock she shifted from her berth at the Mole to the quay and, while she was shifting, was shelled. Two projectiles hit the docking bridge. Only slight damage was done, however, and the sole casualty was the second mate, who was slightly wounded. The *St. Helier* lay alongside altogether for seven hours all through that hectic afternoon. By 10 o'clock she had embarked forty stretcher cases and filled up all her available space with troops, and at 10.15 p.m. she left the berth. For thirty minutes thereafter she was shelled by coastal batteries, most of the shells passing over the ship, but all dropping close.

Royal Daffodil and *King George V* both crossed, *Royal Daffodil* bringing back 1,600 Frenchmen.

At 1.15 p.m. *Royal Sovereign* left for Dunkirk for the second time that day. Her work on this, as on other days, is beyond praise. In the small hours she had been picking up men off the beaches under heavy fire—within less than twelve hours she was returning! At 3.20 she was under fire again, attacked and bombed by enemy aircraft. Half an hour later she was again attacked, violent avoiding action just saving her. Immediately after she came under heavy fire from the enemy positions at Gravelines. It was Hobson's choice now whichever channel the ships attempted. *Royal Sovereign* turned back. The measure of the German opposition lies in that fact. Her record was one of the finest of all those of the personnel ships throughout the operation—but she turned back. Her master says, tersely, 'As two ships appeared to be blocking channel returned to Margate for instructions.'

Lady of Mann left Dover about 7.30. Under cover of the first darkness she made the passage safely and reached Dunkirk a little after 11 p.m.

Maid of Orleans slipped out from the Admiralty Pier at 8.30 in the evening. *Maid of Orleans* was perhaps the outstanding ship of the 'cross-Channel' fleet. Her work throughout the operation was magnificent: in six trips she lifted 5,319 men. The behaviour of her officers and crew was superb. The utter disregard that this unarmed ship showed for the almost intolerable dangers of the work and the limitless endurance of her people, give her a high place in the record of famous ships.

At 8.30 p.m. she moved out from the Admiralty Pier and within ten minutes was in collision with the destroyer *Worcester* (Commander J. H. Allison, R.N.). *Worcester* had been damaged by bombs earlier in the day. She had been towed most of the way across the Channel and then her engineers, working in the crippled engine-room, had managed to get her under her own steam again. She was slipping thankfully into port now when the two ships met with a tremendous crash. But there were many tugs and small craft available. Men thrown into the water were picked up and both ships were towed into harbour. *Maid of Orleans*, however, was so damaged as to be unable to continue her voyage. She had done most gallant work. *Worcester* also was finished as far as Dunkirk was concerned, and she too had matched the very highest traditions of her Service. In the six trips which she had made, two of them under very heavy attack from the enemy, she had brought back 4,350 men.

S.s. *Tynwald* should have sailed from Folkestone about this time, but the exhaustion and the difficulties attendant upon it amongst the crews of some of the personnel ships was spreading. *Tynwald* had completed three hard voyages, carrying something like 4,500 men away, but on this evening she failed to sail. Her master stated that his men had been continually on their feet for a week, that his officers were completely exhausted, and that he himself had had only four hours' rest in the whole course of the week and was unfit for further duty.

Malines and *Ben-My-Chree* were in the same condition. Both ships failed to sail on this night. Relief crews were sent for for *Tynwald* and *Ben-My-Chree*.

7

And with the personnel ships, despite the decision of the Admirals, the little ships went on with the work. There were some that had left at dawn on this morning. There were some that left a little after 9 o'clock, before the news of the disasters filtered through to Ramsgate. But even when the news came through there were others that went across. The previous day, as is demonstrated by the account of *Minotaur*, it was clear that rumour was spreading swiftly along the little ports of England. All that night the windows in Ramsgate and along the Kentish coast had shaken with the thunder of the Dunkirk guns and the crash of the bombing. The men who went this morning had no need of the news of the 8 o'clock disasters to convince them of the dire necessities of the situation, to warn them of its heavy dangers. Not many men went to Dunkirk without the knowledge that they were thrusting into the most dangerous area of water that the sea had known for a generation. There were few who shirked that thrusting, few who turned back.

About this time in the naval records there begin to creep in little remarks: 'Sub-Lieutenant So-and-So, against orders, attempted to go over.' . . . 'Yacht So-and-So, though told she was too slow, started out and was turned back by the drifters.' News of the morning disasters, as it filtered through to the serried boats in Ramsgate harbour and along the quays and piers of Folkestone, of Dover, of Deal, of Margate and Sheerness and Southend, seems only to have raised the temper of those who waited for fresh orders.

At dawn from Ramsgate a little convoy of eight boats, including *Westerly*, *Naiad Errant* and *White Heather*, moved off for Dunkirk. The description of Able Seaman Samuel Palmer is perhaps the best individual description by any member of the lower deck who took part in the beach work through this time. Palmer was a 'Westoe'. He came to Ramsgate with a draft from the Royal

Naval Barracks, Devonport, where he had been serving for some time past as a member of the Plymouth City Patrol. He was a 'stripey', a three-badge man, and held the Long Service and Good Conduct medals, but he was still an Able Seaman. His account is simple, and graphic with the simplicity of the 'Old Navy'.

'The adventure began with a sudden draft from Devonport to Ramsgate. For one night at Ramsgate I was billeted with other seamen in the Fun Fair Ballroom, and the next day action began. I was told off with another seaman, two ordinary seamen and two stokers, to take over two motor-yachts, the *Naiad Errant* and the *Westerly*. Being the senior hand, I detailed one seaman, an ordinary seaman, and one stoker to take charge of the *Westerly* and took the remainder on board the *Naiad Errant* with me. I thought she looked the better of the two boats.

'I had the petrol and fresh-water tanks filled and took on provisions. During the day I was told that a rendezvous had been made for eight boats outside the breakwater at 4 o'clock the next morning. At the time appointed we were there, finding other boats of the same type, waiting for the order to move. We moved into "line ahead", the *Naiad Errant* being second, and were off for Dunkirk. *Westerly* was with us when we began but what became of her I don't know, for I never saw her again.

'About three miles outside Dunkirk I saw a plane burst into flames and come tumbling out of the sky, with it a dark object which I took to be the pilot. As he landed in the water I made my way over to him and fished him out with my boat hook, but as he was dead and a German at that, I pushed him off and got on my way.

'A few minutes later I saw a French destroyer doing about 25 to 30 knots,[1] making her way into Dunkirk. I took my eyes off her for a minute or two and then glanced back, but there was nothing there. She must have had a direct hit from a bomb and sunk within a few minutes. I made my course over to where she had gone and picked up her survivors, which altogether numbered only about twenty. Those I picked up I put on board a French tug which happened to be in the vicinity, and once more carried on into Dunkirk.

'Eventually I arrived off the beach where the swarms of soldiers were gathered, and at the same time one of our big ships came and anchored close inshore. Three of our little convoy of eight had arrived. The first immediately filled with soldiers and carried on back to England. The second went aground. My first job was to ferry soldiers from the beach to the big ship, and I made a number of trips. Then I tried to tow the boat that had run aground off the beach but the young seaman with me got the tow rope around my propellers, the result being that I had to give the job up and that my own ship ran aground. All around there was ceaseless activity and, jumping over the side, I gave a hand carrying the wounded soldiers to the big ship's skiff which had been launched.

'When he knew what had happened the captain of this ship ordered me to

[1] This was the *Foudroyant*.

go on board his ship with my crew and we swam out to her, but the swift-running tide had not finished with us yet. Soon after we had clambered aboard the big ship, she too ran aground. It must have been about 2 or 3 o'clock in the afternoon then, and during the period we had to wait for the flood tide to come up and take us off, Jerry's bombers came over several times, bombing the ships and machine-gunning the soldiers on the beach. We were lucky not to be hit, for we had only the soldiers' Bren guns to defend us.

'The captain would not let me go when I asked him if I could return to my own ship, but by now some Tommies had parked themselves in the *Naiad Errant* and, after clearing the tow rope from the propellers, had got her engines going. The tide was coming in fast—it must have been between 7 and 8 o'clock (I had put my watch out of action swimming) and the rising water floated the ship, also my boat. I waved to the soldiers and made gestures to them to bring her alongside, which they managed to do, although the ship was well under way.

'I sang out to my crew to come down with me, but they did not show up and there was no time to argue. Both the ship and my boat were under way, so just as the *Naiad Errant* came alongside I jumped down alone, and got her clear of the ship, which promptly increased her speed and went towards England.

'The *Naiad Errant* was packed full. I glanced back at the petrol tank gauges and saw that they registered half-full. There was nothing to do but to scrounge some more. A boat was moored in the fairway and I reckoned she would be fair game. As luck would have it she was full of petrol in two-gallon tins, so I fisted six of them and put them in my tanks. Just as I thought we were all set for home—the engines gave out! I could not get back to the boat that was moored and we began to drift on to the pier which Jerry was bombing and shelling. To make matters worse I was right in the fairway, liable to be run down by ships coming in and going out. Darkness was fast approaching.

'With no engineer on board, and me without the slightest knowledge of engines, I had to hope that the soldiers could get her going again. The engineers among them got to work. The others I ordered to break up both the cabin doors and use the pieces as paddles in order to keep a little way on the boat and prevent her from running on to the pier. Although they were dead tired they put all they knew into it and so we managed to keep a little way on the boat and keep her in a safe position. About this time I began to shiver and got very cold as it got dark, for I had on the same togs that I had been swimming in. I was still wet through. Then one of the soldiers tapped me on the shoulder. He handed over a flask, asking me to drink. I did. It was rum, and it certainly put warmth and fresh life into me.

'The soldiers tinkered with the engine in the darkness and it must have been between 10 and 11 o'clock at night when there was a clamour of excitement. They had got the starboard engine going! I told them to "drop everything" and leave the port engine and I would get them over to England all right on the one engine, which gave me about 5 to 6 knots. I counteracted the pull of the one engine with the wheel.

'Because the main channel between Dunkirk and Ramsgate was crowded with ships that night, and I stood a big chance of being run down in the blackness, I decided to try and make Dover and keep clear of the main channel of shipping. We chugged steadily through the night. About 3 o'clock in the morning—still on the wheel and in my wet clothes—my eyes got a bit shaky through looking down into the compass bowl all the time (the compass I had was a grid steering compass and I didn't know a darned thing about it except that it had eight points on it—north, north-east, east, south-east south, south-west, west, and north-west). However, I felt confident that I should reach Dover, for I knew the geography of the coast—so I asked a soldier to take the wheel whilst I looked out into the night to give my eyes a rest. I had been looking round for about five minutes when something seemed to tell me that we were not going in the right direction, so I immediately went down and had a look at the compass—to find that we were steaming due *east*, back to Dunkirk again!

'Well, I couldn't blame the soldier. He was half asleep anyway, and seamanship is not his job after all, so I took over the wheel. . . . Just after dawn I struck Dover dead centre and then followed the coast up to Ramsgate, arriving there at eleven and I put the soldiers ashore on the pier. . . .'

White Heather was abandoned. *Westerly* was damaged and her people were rescued later.

Another convoy left about 9.30. Between the two there were a number of individual sailings. In the convoy was the Isle of Wight ferry *Fishbourne* towed by the tugs *Prince*, *Princess* and *Duke*. The *Sun III* had four barges astern of her—*Ada Mary*, *Haste Away*, *Burton* and *Shannon*. She had great trouble with barges breaking adrift, and *Duke* was detached from *Fishbourne* to pick up *Haste Away* and *Ada Mary*. By 2.30 p.m. they were close in to Dunkirk. Air attacks were heavy again at this time, and it was eventually decided that *Fishbourne* should return to Ramsgate. The barge tows meanwhile had got well ahead of her, and in the middle of the afternoon reached position a little north of Dunkirk during the inevitable air attack. But the master of *Duke*, B. P. Mansfield, records that this attack was split up by our own fighter aircraft.

About this time *Duke* sighted a lifeboat adrift off the Outer Ruytingen buoy with about forty soldiers and one naval rating. They picked up half of these and the rest went aboard *Sun III*, which was still in company with them with her two barges. An officer, who was in charge of the party, told the master of *Sun III*, F. W. Russell, that other boats had also put out to sea, and it was decided to make a search of the area. About 4.20 they sighted a lifeboat from the destroyer *Basilisk* with a midshipman and eleven seamen, whom they took aboard. A little after 5 aircraft signalled them to alter course towards the south and, following the signals, they sighted two more lifeboats. One of these was picked up by *Sun III*. The other, which contained eleven Spaniards and a single Canadian soldier, was picked up by *Duke*. By this time *Sun III* had almost 150 men on board and, having signalled to a plane asking if it could see any more boats in the area and received a negative reply, the tugs returned to Ramsgate.

Half an hour after they had left Ramsgate the yacht *Sundowner* began her crossing. *Sundowner* belonged to Commander C. H. Lightoller, D.S.C., R.N.R. (Retd.), who, as senior surviving officer of the *Titanic*, had been the principal witness at the inquiry into that disaster. She was a biggish craft, approximately 60 feet with a speed of 10 knots, and with the assistance of his son and a Sea Scout, Commander Lightoller had taken her out of Cubitt's Yacht Basin at Chiswick on May 31st and had dropped down the river to Southend as part of a big convoy of forty boats which had mustered at Westminster. At dawn on June 1st he left Southend with five others and, reaching Ramsgate, was instructed in the casual manner of those days to 'proceed to Dunkirk for further orders'. His charts, he says, were somewhat antiquated, and he was fortunate enough to be able to obtain a new set. At 10 o'clock he left by the route laid down. His account of the voyage is clear and detailed.

'Half-way across we avoided a floating mine by a narrow margin, but having no firearms of any description—not even a tin hat—we had to leave its destruction to someone better equipped. A few minutes later we had our first introduction to enemy aircraft, three fighters flying high. Before they could be offensive, a British destroyer—*Worcester*, I think—overhauled us and drove them off. At 2.25 p.m. we sighted and closed the 25-foot motor-cruiser *Westerly*; broken down and badly on fire. As the crew of two (plus three naval ratings she had picked up in Dunkirk) wished to abandon ship— and quickly—I went alongside and took them aboard, giving them the additional pleasure of again facing the hell they had only just left.

'We made the fairway buoy to the Roads shortly after the sinking of a French transport with severe loss of life. Steaming slowly through the wreckage we entered the Roads. For some time now we had been subject to sporadic bombing and machine-gun fire but as the *Sundowner* is exceptionally and extremely quick on the helm, by waiting till the last moment and putting the helm hard over—my son at the wheel—we easily avoided every attack, though sometimes near lifted out of the water.

'It had been my intention to go right on to the beaches, where my second son, Second Lieutenant R. T. Lightoller, had been evacuated some forty-eight hours previously; but those of the *Westerly* informed me that the troops were all away, so I headed up for Dunkirk piers. By now dive-bombers seemed to be eternally dropping out of the cloud of enemy aircraft overhead. Within half a mile of the pierheads a two-funnelled grey painted transport had overhauled and was just passing us to port when two salvoes were dropped in quick succession right along her port side. For a few moments she was hid in smoke and I certainly thought they had got her. Then she reappeared still gaily heading for the piers and entered just ahead of us.

'The difficulty of taking troops on board from the quay high above us was obvious, so I went alongside a destroyer (*Worcester* again, I think) where they were already embarking. I got hold of her captain and told him I could take about a hundred (though the most I had ever had on board was twenty-one). He, after consultation with the military C.O., told me to carry on and get the troops aboard. I may say here that before leaving Cubitt's Yacht Basin, we had worked all night stripping her down of everything movable, masts included, that would tend to lighten her and make for more room.

'My son, as previously arranged, was to pack the men in and use every available inch of space—which I'll say he carried out to some purpose. On deck I detailed a naval rating to tally the troops aboard. At fifty I called below, "How are you getting on?" getting the cheery reply, "Oh, plenty of room yet." At seventy-five my son admitted they were getting pretty tight—all equipment and arms being left on deck.

'I now started to pack them on deck, having passed word below for every man to lie down and keep down; the same applied on deck. By the time we had fifty on deck, I could feel her getting distinctly tender, so took no more. Actually we had exactly 130 on board, including three *Sundowners* and five *Westerlys*.

'During the whole embarkation we had quite a lot of attention from enemy planes, but derived an amazing degree of comfort from the fact that the *Worcester*'s A.A. guns kept up an everlasting bark overhead.

'Casting off and backing out we entered the Roads again, there it was continuous and unmitigated hell. The troops were just splendid and of their own initiative detailed look-outs ahead, astern, and abeam for inquisitive planes as my attention was pretty wholly occupied watching the steering and passing orders to Roger at the wheel. Any time an aircraft seemed inclined to try its hand on us, one of the look-outs would just call quietly, "Look out for this bloke, skipper," at the same time pointing. One bomber that had been particularly offensive, itself came under the notice of one of our fighters and suddenly plunged vertically into the sea just about fifty yards astern of us. It was the only time any man ever raised his voice above a conversational tone, but as that big black bomber hit the water they raised an echoing cheer.

'My youngest son, Pilot Officer H. B. Lightoller (lost at the outbreak of war in the first raid on Wilhelmshaven) flew a Blenheim and had at different times given me a whole lot of useful information about attack, defence and evasive tactics (at which he was apparently particularly good) and I attribute, in a great measure, our success in getting across without a single casualty to his unwitting help.

'On one occasion an enemy machine came up astern at about 100 feet with the obvious intention of raking our decks. He was coming down in a gliding dive and I knew that he must elevate some 10 to 15 degrees before his guns would bear. Telling my son "Stand by", I waited till as near as I could judge, he was just on the point of pulling up and then "Hard a-port". (She turns 180 degrees in exactly her own length.) This threw his aim completely off. He banked and tried again. Then "Hard a-starboard", with the same result. After a third attempt he gave it up in disgust. Had I had a machine-gun of any sort, he was a sitter—in fact there were at least three that I am confident we could have accounted for during the trip.

SATURDAY, JUNE 1st

'Not least of our difficulties was contending with the wash of fast craft, such as destroyers and transports. In every instance I had to stop completely, take the way off the ship and head the heavy wash. The M.C. being where it was, to have taken one of these seas on either the quarter or beam would have at once put paid to our otherwise successful cruise. The effect of the consequent plunging on the troops below, in a stinking atmosphere with all ports and skylights closed, can well be imagined. They were literally packed like the proverbial sardines, even one in the bath and another on the W.C., so that all the poor devils could do was sit and be sick. Added were the remnants of bully beef and biscuits. So that after discharging our cargo in Ramsgate at 10 p.m., there lay before the three of us a nice clearing-up job.

'Arriving off the harbour I was at first told to "lie off". But when I informed them that I had 130 on board, permission was at once given to "come in" (I don't think the authorities believed for a minute that I had 130), and I put her alongside a trawler lying at the quay. Whilst entering, the men started to get to their feet and she promptly went over to a terrific angle. I got them down again in time and told those below to remain below and lying down till I gave the word. The impression ashore was that the fifty-odd lying on deck plus the mass of equipment was my full load.

'After I had got rid of those on deck I gave the order "Come up from below", and the look on the official face was amusing to behold as troops vomited up through the forward companionway, the after companionway, and the doors either side of the wheelhouse. As a stoker P.O., helping them over the bulwarks, said, "God's truth, mate! Where did you put them?" He might well ask. . . .'

An hour after *Sundowner*'s departure the trawler *Kinder Star* sailed for Dunkirk with the yacht *Windsong* and five other small craft. By the middle of the afternoon they were off the beaches, but heavy air attacks developing again, *Windsong* and some of the others turned back. Her owner, G. L. Dalton, says in a description:

'We were on the point of making for the beach when we were heavily raided by dive-bombers, one large salvo just missing our trawler. We were ordered to cut adrift and make back, it was every man for himself.'

It was in the late afternoon, however, that the small-boat movement became important again. In the stream of little craft that set out from about 5.30 onwards with instructions to make their arrival after dark were many of the little ships that had gone before. It began with motor-boats and open launches; it continued with drifters and trawlers that overpassed the little craft and reached the beaches before them. And they in their turn were followed by the bigger ships.

Rear-Admiral Wake-Walker himself left in M.A./S.B. 10, and at 7.45 berthed alongside in Dunkirk harbour in readiness to take charge of the flood of the little ships. He made contact with Major-General Alexander at the Bastion. The scheme for evacuation this night was for the personnel ships and destroyers to use the harbour while the Fleet minesweepers, the paddle-minesweepers, all shallow draught ships, and the legion of tugs and small craft worked from the strip of beach a mile and a half long east of Dunkirk Mole. The evacuation from the beaches was to end at 3 o'clock in the morning and from the harbour half an hour later.

With this flood went the *Massey Shaw* on her second trip, under Lieutenant G. Walker, R.N.V.R., carrying a naval landing party to work on the beaches, but still with three members of her fire brigade crew on board. She ferried more than 500 men out to the bigger ships.

The tugs were going with the flood also. *Empire Henchman*, which had left Dunkirk at 3 o'clock in the morning, went back again this evening towing a barge with provisions and ammunition; but in the late afternoon she was stopped by a naval drifter which told her it was impossible to enter before dark. While she was dodging about in the narrow channel she was heavily attacked by dive-bombers, and her master, J. E. Fishe, says grimly:

'Fortunately neither the tug nor the barge was hit, but the terrific explosions of the bombs which were falling very closely all round the tug, which was in shallow water, resulted in violent concussions, which caused fractures to connections of our fuel oil tanks, and serious leakages of oil into the bilges with risk of fire; also serious damage was done to the tug's electrical installation, pumps and compasses'.

The point he makes is an important one. Hardly any ship which went to Dunkirk—even of those which made only a single trip—failed to suffer damage from the violent shock of bomb explosions transmitted through water. That damage was not apparent on the outside. It consisted in many cases of fractures of cast-iron fittings at inlet points on the ships' hulls, of pipe fractures, of bearings thrown out of true, of a hundred and one minor pieces of auxiliary machinery put out of action. Ships came limping back to Dover at times utterly unfit for another trip but without a scratch on their plating to show for it. *Empire Henchman* on this occasion was compelled to return.

The tug *Tanga* went across for the second time that day with four boats, and got to Dunkirk just after dark.

The tug *Sun*, which had picked up twenty boats at Tilbury landing-stage, took them to Ramsgate, and left there again with a launch and two lifeboats in tow at 5.30 p.m. The launch took forty British soldiers off the beach. The party was in charge of a naval commander who asked H. R. Cole, the master of the tug, if he was acquainted with Dunkirk.

'I replied that I was a little, having been in the I.W.T. in the last war. We hove anchor, and went in the harbour, and took on board about fifty French and Belgian soldiers off the pierhead, including one lieutenant-colonel of the Belgian Army. Came out of the harbour, and anchored off. Shortly afterwards our launch came off with more soldiers, and we left Dunkirk with 173 soldiers, 28 naval ratings, and my own crew of 7—208 persons in all. . . .'

Sun IV went over about the same time with two boats in tow. On the way over she piloted the R.N.L.I. lifeboat *E.M.E.D.* to Dunkirk, and at 9.30 p.m. her master records—laconically as always—'Arrived. Shifting berth in harbour all night (Brock's benefit).' She picked up 112 men of the B.E.F.

and, towing *E.M.E.D.* (whose naval coxswain had been killed by shrapnel), with thirty-nine men and a lifeboat also crowded, moved back to Dover.

The motor-launch *Lady Cable* made her first trip in this movement and claims to have brought off about 550 men in seven trips from the beaches to the bigger craft, coming home eventually with a full load to Dover.

Mr. T. Towndrow, Scoutmaster of the Mortlake Sea Scouts (whose account of *Minotaur*'s proceedings has already been given), joined the tug *Fossa* as *Minotaur* could not cross again, and formed part of the crew of one of the motor-boats, *Jeanette*, which she towed.

'Our job,' he says, 'was to run in to the Mole and bring off soldiers to load up the *Fossa*. In running into the harbour the motor-boat's steering cable broke and no means of repairing it could be found. In the meantime, the *Fossa* had herself got into the Mole and filled up with soldiers. Steaming out, she picked us up and took us in tow together with an open naval motor-cutter laden with French soldiers which was only making three or four knots under its own power. The tug proceeded out of Dunkirk harbour, but ran aground and was unable to get off.

'I transferred to the naval cutter which cast off to make its own way back. The officer in charge of the cutter had no charts, and it was soon apparent from the course he was steering that he did not know his course back. He admitted that this was so, and readily agreed to let me take the helm. He said he had intended following the general stream of boats going back, but had lost them in the darkness. We made very slow progress, and dawn came when we were about half-way back.

'We eventually made Ramsgate about 10.30 in the morning, having taken over ten hours to get back. On landing I was annoyed at being taken for a survivor until I realized how dirty and scruffy I must have looked.

'I later heard that the tug *Fossa*, which had grounded, had its soldiers taken off and was abandoned, later receiving a direct hit from a Jerry plane. . . .'

In the same stream of boats went *Rummy II*, a twin-screw motor-launch. She had been taken down to the sea by Lieutenant H. Simouth Willing of the Twickenham Sea Cadet Corps. At Ramsgate she was given a naval crew, but Lieutenant Simouth Willing continued with her and reached Dunkirk under shell-fire. *Rummy II* had taken over two lifeboats and Lieutenant Simouth Willing went in with these to bring troops away. His own boat brought off about 140 men on this night. The pulling boats, though at times towed off by power craft, had very serious difficulties with the strong tides which ran here, and they were instructed to return to whatever ship was available. Lieutenant Simouth Willing, however, says proudly:

'We found the tug we were serving after a long row under heavy fire, and I was pleased to report my crew by name for steadiness under close fire.'

Another new-comer on this day was H.M.S. *Portsdown*. She was a medium-size paddle-steamer, hurriedly commissioned at Sheerness, with a naval crew captained by Sub-Lieutenant R. H. Church, R.N.R., with, as first lieutenant, Sub-Lieutenant M. V. H. Caplat, R.N.V.R. *Portsdown* was not degaussed.

She had no armament, and she still had the white paintwork of peace-time. On the voyage over they had time on their hands so they camouflaged the ship. They built a dummy A.A. gun amidships. They covered the white paintwork where they could with brown and black canvas. They draped the wheelhouse with kapok and cork life-jackets as a thin protection against splinters. And at 1 o'clock that evening they slowed and dropped anchor off Dunkirk.

Almost immediately a salvo of shells landed, the nearest one ten feet from the ship; a second salvo to port amidships. They hove up and moved two cables, and dropped anchor again. The next salvo was about 50 feet astern. Eventually, after trying the harbour, they anchored in a fresh position off the beach and sent away their two 15-foot boats. One of these made three trips, the other four. By that time the second boat was so damaged that, as she was landing her men on the port sponson, she sank. As boatwork was rapidly getting impossible, Sub-Lieutenant Church put his ship's nose on to the beach and held her there until the ebb set in, loading all the time. Motorboats were helping to feed her during this period and one large boat brought off altogether something like 500 men. The remaining boat was blown out of the water by a shell as *Portsdown* was changing position again, but the paddle-steamer herself was not hit; and at 4 o'clock, with the light growing, she left for England.

A little west of Dunkirk breakwater she sighted a French vessel aground with approximately 1,000 troops on board. Taking off the majority of these, she towed the Frenchman off the bank. Further on she sighted a motor-boat that had helped her earlier in the night and took twenty-five men off her. The boat herself refused a tow and headed for the English coast by herself. Still further along she encountered a motor lighter in difficulties. On board it were Commander Clouston and the naval pier party, which was returning for a rest to Dover. The lighter was abandoned and *Portsdown* brought Commander Clouston home. She had some little difficulty in finding 'home' owing to defective compasses, but half-way across the Channel H.M.S. *Calcutta* came to her assistance with information as to her position and the line of the buoys, and she reached Ramsgate in safety.

The old stagers were still carrying on. H.M.M. *Medway Queen* was over again, having left for Dunkirk at 9.30. With the ships' boats which she towed again, was Mr. R. B. Brett, and his account of his experiences forms an interesting counterpart to that of Mr. de Sola on the previous night. One of the first points that he makes is that he saw one of the crew of the *Medway Queen*, a pensioner R.N., calmly fishing over the stern while the *Medway Queen* was lying off the Mole waiting for her turn to go in.

'When told that there were no fish about and that, if there were, they were dead, he sang out, "You never can tell, sir. I might catch a bloody Boche helmet."'

Brett took his boat in until she had almost grounded and then, being the tallest man on board, waded ashore calling out, "I want sixty men!" For some time he received no reply. Then, he says:

'I sighted a causeway about eight feet wide heading out into the water. To my surprise I found it to be a perfectly ordered straight column of men about six abreast, standing as if on parade. When I reached them a sergeant stepped up to me and said, "Yes, sir. Sixty men, sir?" He then walked along the column, which remained in perfect formation, and detailed the required number to follow me.'

Brett was asked two questions by many of the men. One was 'How far is the boat?' which was easy enough to answer, and the other was 'Where is our Air Force?' The answer to that was more difficult. It was not easy to explain to men who had been bombed and machine-gunned for days on end in a narrow demilune of country, that, had it not been for the self-sacrifice and daring of the handful of fighter aircraft that we had available, Dunkirk would have been nearly impossible. For very much of their time these fighters raided out of the view of the men on the beaches and on the perimeter, trying to intercept the German raids and break them up before they reached the area. The question was an obvious—indeed an inevitable—one, but it did less than justice to the efforts of Fighter Command.

A footnote to the stoicism of Mr. Brett's 'human pier' is his account of a blinded man. His hand was placed in Mr. Brett's and he was led to the boat and told that he was being taken to safety. He said, simply, 'Thanks, mate', and followed patiently and wordlessly into the deep water.

During this period—the afternoon while the small boats were beginning their voyages for the great lifting of the night—the tally of losses grew. The paddle-minesweeper *Brighton Queen*, making her second run (she had only arrived the previous day) lifted 600 French and Algerian troops. She had reached the end of the narrow channel when she became the target for a concentrated bombing attack. After a number of misses she was hit in the stern and badly holed. Almost immediately it became apparent that she was sinking. Meanwhile a trawler is recorded as having been sunk in the fairway near No. 5 buoy, the trawler *Jacinta* was stranded on the Mole, and ships of every possible kind were limping, damaged, back to the shelter of the Downs.

8

It was more than obvious that daylight operations were impossible. Messages show that clearly in the early evening. About 8 o'clock Vice-Admiral Ramsay informed the Admiralty in a telegram that began 'Things are getting very hot for ships' that he had directed that in future no ships should sail during daylight and that evacuation or transports would cease the following morning at 3 o'clock. With regard to the general progress of the evacuation, he said:

'If the perimeter holds will complete evacuation to-morrow (Sunday) night including most French. General concurs.'

Later in the evening he informed Major-General Alexander that casualties to shipping were now being caused by heavy artillery, and finally at midnight a long message said that as all the channels to Dunkirk were now under fire of German batteries, and a new battery had come into action suspending

SATURDAY, JUNE 1ST

traffic on the last remaining daylight route, he asked permission 'to withdraw all forces at 3 a.m. until the following night'.

The position was more than serious. In the day-to-day record of the operation it is perhaps difficult to picture the cumulative effect of the loss, but by this midnight, of the main transporting force—the cross-Channel personnel ships and the destroyers—the personnel ships had lost eight sunk and eight so seriously damaged as to be unfit for further service; the destroyers had lost six, in addition to *Wessex* (sunk off Boulogne), and had more than a score damaged in greater or lesser degree. The loss of *Foudroyant* to aircraft (described in the proceedings of *Naiad Errant* earlier in this chapter) brought the total of French destroyers sunk during Operation 'Dynamo' to three, to which must be added the four destroyers sunk earlier in the preliminary operations off the Dutch, Belgian and French coasts. In addition to these, five big paddle-minesweepers and one Fleet sweeper—all capable of carrying enormous loads of men—had gone, a number of others were damaged, and there were tremendous losses amongst the smaller craft.

Right down to the M.T.B.s attacks from the air caused damage. M.T.B. 68, for example, had to return to Dover for repairs, having been attacked from the air on her fourth trip.

With the ship losses were losses of men. There were many cases in which, owing to the heroic work of rescue ships and tugs, loads of weary soldiery were taken off in safety, but loss of life was heavy both amongst the crews of the ships and amongst the troops. This Saturday had been a day of absolute disaster, and it was impossible that the rate should be allowed to continue.

Despite the devoted efforts of the handful of R.A.F. fighter planes, despite the work of Coastal Command and the Fleet Air Arm, it was clearly impossible to maintain continuous cover over the embarkation area and over the swept channels, and it needed only an hour's gap to repeat the holocaust of the morning.

The loss in carrying power itself was an important item in the calculations of the Admiralty. The s.s. *Prague*, for example, though she had not sunk, was out of action, and *Prague* was one of the two biggest ferry steamers in the world. A 4,200-ton ship, her carrying capacity was colossal. The s.s. *Scotia* was a 3,500-ton ship, also a giant among the cross-Channellers. The excellent prevision of the Ministry of Shipping had so organized its reserves that at no time was there a break due to shortage of ships, but it was clear that the rate of loss could not continue indefinitely. The decision was a wise one. It was also a necessary one.

There is a grim comment on all these things in a comparatively simple movement that was initiated in the middle of the evening. At 9.55 the tugs *Challenge, Ocean Cock, Crested Cock, Fairplay I, Sun VII, Sun XI* and *Sun XII* received orders 'to proceed over as far as possible to Dunkirk and pick up anything'!

In view of these matters it is necessary to record that, to the eternal credit of the seamen of Britain, of Belgium and of France, 66,000 men this day were brought to safety.

CHAPTER XIV

SUNDAY, JUNE 2ND

1

On the morning of Sunday, June 2nd, a chaplain of the British Expeditionary Force celebrated Holy Communion on the beach at Malo-les-Bains. Five times before the service ended his congregation of men of the weary rearguard were scattered by low-flying aircraft. In that simple service is expressed much of the spirit and the gallantry of these last days. At the beginning of the evacuation no man had felt secure but, as the days went on and the miracle of the narrow pathway of the Mole grew, men allowed themselves hope.

But in these last days the pressure of the Germans was very hard. There was never an hour when any man could have said with certainty that the pincers would not close at last, that the tanks would not break through Bergues and come up the main road to the little town, that the old fortifications—hopelessly outmoded in this new warfare—would not yield, that the uncertain, nebulous canal by Mardyck would not fall. And yet men still stood by hope and by faith.

The day was fine.

It is impossible to draw a hard line now between one day and the next, for more than ever the evacuation had become a thing of the night. The vital hours were those between dusk and dawn, and on this day the flood of small craft—tugs, lifeboats, motor-boats and the rest—that had started from Ramsgate in the middle afternoon of Saturday—worked without break past midnight into the dark small hours of Sunday morning. There is a picture of the Mole this night by an officer on the staff of Rear-Admiral Wake-Walker that is worth quoting.

'The night was very calm, with the lightest of breezes from the southward —just sufficient to drift the huge pall of smoke over the harbour and beaches and give us excellent protection against air attack without detracting much from the ground visibility.

'Among the many vivid impressions made upon my mind during this very vivid week, one of the most dramatic was the picture by night of the eastern arm of the harbour lit up in silhouette by the huge flames behind it to show the never-ending stream of weary men moving seawards. Sometimes they hurried into a tired run, sometimes just plodded blindly on towards safety. At other times they were packed stationary on the narrow parapet waiting for the next ship to berth. The men who were embarking now were those who had borne the brunt of the fighting: the rearguard of the B.E.F. who, after three weeks of continuous battle, could still march in perfect order on to the pier—ay, and some of them even sing too. It was a never-to-be-forgotten sight to watch a famous regiment as it embarked that night. These men, and the fine French troops who followed them on the next two nights, were the heroes who defended Dunkirk to the last and made all this astounding evacuation possible.

'There was a good deal of shelling on the harbour and pier to-night and on the beaches and ships lying off them as well. I do not think it did a great amount of damage, and the pier itself was not hit, though a trawler was sunk in the harbour. It seems little less than a miracle that this five-foot wide wooden pathway, along which so many tens of thousands walked to safety, should have remained intact to the very end. The last ships left Dunkirk at dawn at 3 o'clock and all but a handful of the B.E.F. was away.'

That last handful of men held fast on the Bergues–Ghyvelde line, and through the night the Germans seemed content with artillery action and the work of their remorseless bombers. In the Saturday night and in the few hours before dawn on the Sunday morning what was left of the 46th Division, the 1st Division and the 126th Infantry Brigade was taken aboard the ships, and there were left at 3 a.m., according to Major-General Alexander's account, only 3,000 men, mainly of infantry units, but with twelve anti-tank and seven anti-aircraft guns. There were still many French, but French ships in some numbers were now working with our own: personnel ships as well as a handful of naval craft, drifters and a large number of very gallant fishermen —crabbers from St. Malo, Dieppois from the Channel grounds, many even of those who had withdrawn from this area, in accordance with the earlier orders, to the region of Brest.

The day, from the point of view of the sea, divides itself automatically into two sections—the morning darkness and the early night. In the morning darkness the ships that had crossed with the late flights of Saturday worked on.

H.M.S. *Calcutta* went out again in the small hours to cover the morning flow in approximately the same area as the previous day. She immediately became the target for enemy aircraft and three separate attacks were made upon her. She sustained slight damage from near misses.

The destroyers once more were carrying the heaviest loads. To offset something of the disasters of the previous morning, damaged ships were coming back again into service. With the night flight on the Saturday evening H.M.S. *Whitshed* had crossed with three other destroyers, coming back after making good the damage she had received at Boulogne. H.M.S. *Keith* had been the first of the battered Boulogne destroyers to get back into service, but now she was lost. *Vimiera* and *Venetia* were too badly knocked about for temporary repairs. *Vimy*, *Windsor*, *Venomous* and *Wild Swan* were already active.

Whitshed berthed at 1 o'clock against the concrete of the outer nose of the Mole. As she made fast her ropes the pier was empty. Her captain, Commander E. R. Condor, R.N., left his ship and went down the pier. A little way down it he found a bicycle lying up against a post, and on this he rode down to the town. There was damage at various points. At one place the decking of the Mole had gone completely and the gap was bridged by a ship's gangway. At other points there were shell holes patched with any material available. At the far end there was another area of damage, and he had to dismount to circumvent it.

Just beyond this he met a naval pier party and was told that troops would be coming at any moment. He went on past the pier party, and in a warehouse a few hundred yards further down found a number of exhausted French and Belgian troops. These he stirred into wakefulness, and sent them down the pier. There was an air attack on at the time, but he was busy hunting. A little further he found a party of British Tommies in command of a sergeant. Their officers had brought them down as far as the pier and gone back to round up more men. These he took back with him.

The destroyers were taking incredible risks in stowing the vast quantities of men they lifted. It is recorded that *Whitshed* had first unshipped her mess tables and cleared all possible movable gear on the lower deck, but now she opened compartments that normally were shut in danger areas, leaving the watertight doors open throughout the ship in order to make 'living spaces'. Having taken approximately 1,000 men on board by these heroic measures, *Whitshed* sent a berthing party down to take the ropes of the succeeding destroyers as they came in and, as soon as these were berthed, pulled out stern first between the breakwaters, listing heavily with the weight of men, and got clear.

Her commanding officer's search is typical of many of the efforts made by naval officers in this time. Whenever there was a break in the flow a party from the ships would search. It is on record that *Malcolm's* navigator marched through the streets of Dunkirk playing a set of bagpipes as a summons to the weary men. There is no evidence on record as to the skill with which he played them.

In these hours the first section of the gallant rearguard of the British Army that had so long held the eastern sector of the perimeter was coming down to the beaches and to the Mole. Conditions in the burning town were appalling as always, and the movement was much delayed. At 2.25 a.m. a signal was made which indicated that, owing to the congestion on the Mole due to French movements, it was essential to embark the majority of these men from the beaches—this was an hour and a half after *Whitshed* had restarted the flow. It was then anticipated that large numbers could not arrive until after the time set for the abandonment of operations for the night. The reaction of Dover was immediate and forthright. It is contained in a simple signal which said: 'Endeavour to embark rearguard from beach remaining after 3 a.m. if necessary.' The wording is simplicity itself. In actual fact it was the acceptance of a challenge. The events of the previous morning were still very vivid in the minds of Vice-Admiral Ramsay and the Dover Command. Yet, if the men could not be got down to the beach before dawn, the navy was still prepared to wait until after dawn to take them.

Codrington, Icarus—she was making the last of her six trips—*Sabre* were amongst the old hands who were back again.

The small ships too worked on. The tug *Tanga*, for example, which had arrived the previous evening at 10.30, was still lying off as dawn began to break under the dark thundercloud of the oil tanks. She had slipped four boats and none of them had returned to her, but boats from other ships—the boats of the half-tide fleet—had come off, bringing ninety British troops and eighty Frenchmen, and at 3.30 she was ordered to 'clear out and run for it'. She picked up one disabled motor-boat and left.

Crested Cock and *Ocean Cock*, *Sun VII* and *Sun XII*, who had crossed as part of the rescue team in the late evening of Saturday, hunted in the darkness for five hours around Dunkirk and in the channels between the shoals, and found nothing. They had been sent over specifically for rescue work. Visibility on this night was bad. The normal signals of distress could not be used. Ships for the most part went in darkness, or switched on dim navigation lights only when the press of traffic threatened disaster. There were no rockets to call them up, no flares were burned except in the last, most dire necessity.

Most of the rescue tugs found nothing, but at 2 a.m. *Sun XI* broke out of line. J. R. Lukes, her master, says:

'I saw small lights and someone with a very dim morse light. Put tug hard a-starboard and found large Government lighter broken down full of wounded and troops. 2.30 took lighter in tow, arrived 6.30 a.m. Berthed lighter, terrible sight.'

He had picked up the last of the survivors of H.M. Tug *St. Abbs*, who were the last survivors of H.M.S. *Keith*. Captain Berthon, with about sixty men in all, had got clear of *St. Abbs* as she disintegrated after the bomb hit. He swam for a long time, and in that period the group was passed by a small camouflaged yacht which failed to see the men struggling in the water. Otherwise nothing that floated came near them. This was at the very worst period of the air attack. Eventually Captain Berthon got to shore. The lighter in which he essayed to bring home some of his people broke down, and he was drifting helplessly when *Sun XI* saw that faint morse light and ended his odyssey. Of the crew of *Keith* three officers and thirty-three men were lost. There is no record of the number of rescued army officers and men who were lost also.

And while the tugs worked the small boats worked also. They toiled in circumstances of increasing difficulty. The language problem alone, now that the French predominated along the beaches, was enormous. It was impossible to explain to inland Frenchmen the intricacies of small-boat handling on a falling tide. Amongst certain units discipline had broken down, and it was equally hard without an absolute command of the language to stop them from rushing the boats and settling them firmly into the sand. It was impossible to stop late-comers jumping into overloaded boats. There were not a few cases of small craft that left the beach and sank as soon as they reached deep water and the tumultuous wash of the destroyers.

And there was with the Babel of tongues a Babel of order and counter-order, of rumour and counter-rumour. It was believed in the 'Dynamo Room' that there was fifth column activity in being. Signals were sent out to

Force K stating that false information and false orders to return were being given to the inshore units. It is possible that this was so, but it is also possible that in the awful confusion of those dark hours rumour flooded upon exhaustion, apprehension crowded upon lack of knowledge. Every possible effort was made by Rear-Admiral Wake-Walker and his devoted staff to keep ships and boats and men and beach parties informed; but it would have required a dozen police boats, a hundred staff officers, to have kept that navy of the improvisation ordered and orderly. The small-boat work of Dunkirk succeeded upon the initiative of individuals. Where it failed—as in some cases in all those hundreds it was bound to fail—it failed upon the initiative of individuals. That was a part of the price that had to be paid for triumph.

The great bulk of those of the small boats that still floated, and were still capable of progressing under their own steam, left in accordance with definite orders at zero hour. The French continued loading a little later than our own ships. A British battalion which had marched from Bergues through the night reached the end of the Mole as the last British personnel ship, already fully loaded, cast off for home. The battalion turned and marched off the Mole against the line of the French who still marched down to their own ships. In a little that line ceased also. Those who were left dug themselves into a canal bank on the outskirts of the town and lay there till night. A handful got a derelict boat and paddled themselves out to a French drifter which brought them across. Another unit, which had fired its last round of ammunition and destroyed its guns and material, was also turned back from the Mole end. There was a goodly congregation for the Eucharist.

But these three hours of the early morning saw close on 15,000 men lifted from Mole and beach to join the return flow, the ebb of the great tide of rescue taking the ships back to the ports of England. *Naiad Errant* was amongst them, and *Massey Shaw*, which, after bringing off ten boatloads through the night, sailed with forty-six troops on board. With these went the tugs bringing back what remained of their strings of barges, lifeboats and skiffs; and mingled with them the drifters, the trawlers, the paddle-mine-sweepers; and, studding the stream, huge in the half-light, the cross-Channel steamers and the destroyers. Evacuation was suspended. The frantic channels quieted, the sea became almost empty.

2

The men who had marched from the Mole end could dig themselves in; the men on the perimeter were entrenched: but there remained the problem of the wounded. There were many of them. The losses of the perimeter fighting had been heavy, and despite the devoted work of the R.A.M.C., despite the gallantry of the white-painted hospital carriers, it had not been possible to get them all away. On this Sunday morning there were many seriously wounded men in dire need of evacuation. Yet the hospital carriers had been the target for constant attack. Already the crews of two of them had made their protest, had asked for armament and escort, had been refused it in the harsh need of the hour, and gallantly had gone back into the hell of the channels again.

But, after the disasters of Saturday morning, it was considered imperative that other steps should be taken, and at 10.30 a.m. the British official wireless made a signal *en clair* to the German authorities. It said:

'Wounded situation acute and hospital ships to enter during day. Geneva Convention will be honourably observed and it is felt that the enemy will refrain from attacking.'

The Southern Railway steamer *Worthing*, which had been taken over at the beginning of the war for service as a hospital carrier, was lying in the Downs. Two hours after the broadcast she received orders from the N.O.I.C., Ramsgate, and at 12.55 p.m. she left for Dunkirk at 20 knots. At 2.32 p.m. she made the enemy attack signal. Captain C. G. G. Munton, her master, says:

'Twelve aircraft were sighted dead ahead and were immediately recognized as enemy aircraft. One of them detached, dived at me, and commenced machine-gunning my ship. I increased to 24 knots and put my helm hard a-starboard. The enemy aircraft then attacked with nine bombs of heavy calibre. As the ship was then swinging very fast on her helm the bombs fell on the starboard quarter and port bow and one amidships off the starboard side. Two of the bombs fell within three or four feet.

'Concussion was very violent and some pipe castings were broken in the engine-room, permitting water to enter, but this was quickly remedied. Some superficial damage is sustained and as we are making a slight amount of water in the fore hold and chain locker I surmise the plates are started on port bow. There were, at the time, no other ships in sight with the exception of two sailing barges.

'Wind was N.E. 2.3. Visibility very good and at the time I was carrying all the marks and signs of a hospital ship according to Geneva Convention and this was without a shadow of doubt, a deliberate and sustained attempt to destroy a hospital ship. . . .

'I would bring to your notice the exemplary conduct and loyalty of all personnel on board.'

The Geneva Convention had been repeatedly flouted throughout the evacuation as it had been flouted on countless occasions before. On this day, however, the attack was more despicable even than upon these earlier occasions. It was made in flagrant, open contempt of the appeal that had been sent out.

Simultaneously with the orders to *Worthing*, *Paris* of the same line received orders to sail at 3 o'clock. At 2.30 p.m. the wireless operator of *Paris* intercepted *Worthing*'s attack message, and immediately afterwards the message saying that she was believed to be making water and was returning at full speed. The master of *Paris* made an immediate signal to the shore asking if, in view of this attack, he was to carry out his previous orders. At 4.48 p.m. he was instructed by radio message to proceed. 'I at once weighed anchor and proceeded to Dunkirk.' This simple sentence in Captain Biles' report represents perhaps the whole spirit of Dunkirk—the spirit of gallantry, of defiance of known and obvious danger that possessed and lifted up the men who did that work.

'I at once weighed anchor . . .'

Dispassionately, without rancour, Captain Biles continues his account.

'Between the North Goodwins lightship and W buoy we ran into thick fog, but approaching W buoy the fog cleared. In the close vicinity of W buoy three enemy aircraft approached from the landside. From my own observation two of these circled round. I immediately gave the order to "Hard to starboard" the wheel, but before the effect of this order operated, two planes dropped bombs very close to the ship, the explosions causing steam pipes to burst in the engine-room and putting machinery and lighting out of action. Also No. 2a lifeboat was blown inwards lifting the foremost davit out of its socket.

'As the ship was out of all control, I ordered lifeboats to be swung out and lowered to boat deck level, and part of the personnel to take their stations in the boats.

'The carpenter sounded the wells, and reported that the ship was not making water. On the strength of this, I decided to keep the remainder of the crew aboard, in the hope of a rescue ship being able to tow me back to Dover.

'Immediately after the bombing, the wireless operator sent an A.A.A. message by the emergency set, as the mains set was blown to pieces. We also hoisted the distress signal—fired rockets, and hoisted ensign upside down. About fifty minutes later, a flight of about fifteen enemy planes approached from the same direction, three of which broke off, circled the ship, and dropped about ten bombs. One of these either went through the bows of No. 2b boat or the force of the explosion blew the bows right off, throwing all the occupants into the water. The ship was severely shaken and damaged by the effects of the explosions of these bombs.

'Remaining lifeboats were immediately lowered and sent to the rescue of those that were in the water. No. 4b boat when lowered into the water, immediately swamped as part of her side was blown in. Myself, the chief officer, and Quartermaster Capps were left on board.

'A naval speed-boat approached about this time and took us off. We then went to No. 4b boat which was swamped and took the occupants off her into the speed-boat. As the ship was so badly damaged, and there were a number of casualties from the bombing, and anticipating another attack, I decided to abandon ship. The speed-boat picked up all lifeboats and towed us until we met the tug *Foremost 87*, when all personnel were transferred to her and boats cast adrift. The tug then proceeded to Dover, and landed everyone there.

'During the whole of these operations, I wish to stress the behaviour of my officers and crew. The discipline was excellent, every performance being carried out with calmness and precision. At no time was any panic shown.'

It is perhaps useless to rail against the German mentality that permitted of endless breaches against the simple dictates of humanity. The Geneva Convention was ratified by a German Government when the leaders of the Nazi Government were children. It had been subscribed to by every German Government that succeeded it from the war-thirsty Government of Wilhelm II, through the Left wing of the Weimar Republic to the onset of the Nazi school of thought. It had been consistently broken by two at least of those Governments. This was only a logical climax to the series of assaults in the early days before Operation 'Dynamo' began. It was to be, as the war went on, a climax among climaxes. Others of the hospital carriers that took part in what was perhaps the most gallant work that ships of their kind have ever done were to sink off every front under the barbarity of the Nazi air. The wilful callousness of these things is beyond description. It should not be beyond punishment.

3

The command at Dover and at Dunkirk had planned for a resumption of evacuation this day at dusk, and dusk was fixed at 9.30. There is a signal from Major-General Alexander which requested 'the maximum number of transports again for British and French at 9.30 p.m.' The maximum number went.

The day was not entirely without shipping in the close waters off Dunkirk, but the few movements were isolated and almost accidental. But in the wider waters all through the day the search for survivors, for small craft broken down, for missing ships, went on. And with it went on the work of patrol, the work that was essential to guard against E-boat and submarine attack and fresh laying of mines.

We suffered loss in this. The anti-submarine trawler *Spurs* was bombed and damaged early in the afternoon. The destroyer *Vanquisher* (Lieutenant-Commander W. C. Bushell, R.N.), working near her, closed to the rescue, but found that she could proceed under her own steam. As the evening flow started these patrols pushed further and further south and east to cover the line of its approach. At 4.15 p.m. the anti-submarine trawler *Blackburn Rovers* was hit by a torpedo from a submarine and sank between S and T buoys. An hour and a half later the anti-submarine trawler *Westella* was hit in her turn and sank in the same area. Three survivors from the *Blackburn Rovers* were picked up by Stoker Banks with the motor-boat *Pauleter*. Banks was nearing the end of his run now. He made altogether some eight trips across and brought back approximately 400 Allied troops.

The main flow began actually with the movement of slow boats in the middle of the afternoon. The earliest of the little convoys to leave was one of four tugs—*Sun IV* towing four motor-boats, *Sun XI* towing four more, *Fairplay I* towing a string, *Foremost 87* towing the R.N.L.I. lifeboats *Cecil and Lilian Philpott* and *Thomas Kirk Wright*. Owing to mishaps due to parting of the tow line and other causes the convoy split up on the way. It was overtaken also by other vessels.

This day the Belgian fishing vessels met with heavy loss. The *Getuigt Vor Christus* was sunk in collision with a patrol boat in Dunkirk. *Onze Lieve*

Vrouw Van Vlaanderen was sunk by shell-fire with a cargo of munitions and supplies on board. But to offset these things the *Lydie Suzanne* lifted ninety-eight men; the *Pharaïlde* (which had sailed from Dover with food and munitions) discharged her cargo, picked up forty French soldiers, and then went to help two British ships which had been bombed and sunk, and saved eighty-two British soldiers and three seamen: the *Zwaluw* picked up 225 soldiers together with ten from a destroyer, and on the way home rescued three French soldiers from a canoe and seven from a pontoon.

The *Massey Shaw* crossed again this day, sailing at 6.40 p.m., still under the command of Lieutenant Walker, but with eight of her own crew on board. She found no troops on the beach and Lieutenant Walker took her up the harbour, leaving finally at 3.15 a.m.

Marsayru also was again working the beaches to-day, and at one time, the nearest ship being about 2½ miles away, she was attacked by four Messerschmitts who machine-gunned her ineffectually for half an hour from a height of more than 2,000 feet. At the end of the half-hour three Hurricanes came in sight and the Messerschmitts left at speed. *Marsayru* took off altogether in her various crossings some 400 French soldiers.

Sub-Lieutenant D. C. Williams, R.N.V.R., sailed in command of *Kitcat* about the same time, but became separated from his convoy and went in to work independently.

The motor-boat *Blue Bird* crossed under the command of Lieutenant-Colonel H. T. B. Barnard, who had made two previous attempts to get across, the first having failed at Lowestoft owing to engine defects, the second through excess of volunteers at Sheerness. This day, however, he got away from Sheerness with a mixed crew of yachtsmen and ratings and, touching at Ramsgate, left a little after eight in the evening in company with H.M. Skoot *Rika*. *Blue Bird* closed the eastern end of the beaches but found no troops and, moving down the beach towards the base of the Mole, fouled a propeller. Shortly afterwards it was discovered that water had been put in the petrol tank.

This last mishap was a common one through the greater part of the evacuation. Water, as has been described, was being taken over for the use of the army. The available water cans of the Southern Command—and indeed of the south of England—were used up early and as a substitute petrol cans were filled and taken over. The petrol for the small craft was also stored in ordinary two-gallon cans. These were appropriately marked, but dumps got mixed on occasion—especially when refuelling was done at night—and the mixture proved disastrous to many ships.

Blue Bird was towed home by H.M. Skoot *Hilda*.

The 20-tonner *Rosaura* had a long previous history. She had crossed first on the Thursday, being brought back on the Friday by Sub-Lieutenant W. B. L. Tower, R.N. (of H.M.S. *Somali*), and on the Friday and Saturday had crossed again under his command. On the Sunday night she reached Dunkirk a little before midnight and worked, as she had done previously, ferrying men from the Mole to ships outside. During this period her propeller was fouled. It was cleared temporarily just as Sub-Lieutenant Tower received orders to leave. He decided that he had still time to fulfil a promise to some men who had been left on the jetty and, going in for the last time, picked up thirty-three French troops and three officers. At 4 o'clock in the morning he set out for Ramsgate, but when *Rosaura* was barely clear of the harbour the engine began to race and it was discovered that the propeller-shaft had broken. Efforts were made to repair it, but these failed and Sub-Lieutenant Tower decided, as it was almost light, to attempt to swim across to a small boat a mile away and try to get assistance. He reached the boat and started in towards the harbour, but was not seen again and was listed as missing. Efforts were made by his crew to make a sail of waterproof capes, but these were unsuccessful and *Rosaura* drifted helplessly all through Monday, through Tuesday, and through most of Wednesday, until on Wednesday afternoon she was sighted by an R.A.F. speed-boat searching the Channel, and her passengers and crew were taken off and brought in to Ramsgate.

Sea Roamer, a 40-foot motor-cruiser owned and commanded by Mr. J. E. W. Wheatley, also crossed this Sunday evening, with a naval party on board. They towed over a boat to work the beaches and made an independent course across the shallows of the off-lying banks. Off the harbour they were told to investigate the beaches but, though they closed to within fifty yards of the shore, they could see no signs of life in any part of the area which they examined. While they were doing this the Casino and the Kursaal were hit by incendiary bombs and went up in flames. They searched to $2\frac{1}{2}$ miles north-east of Dunkirk and then, abandoning hopes of picking up anybody from the sands, decided to inspect the wrecks offshore. Circling the first one and shouting, they were rewarded by a head popping up over the side and demanding, 'Êtes-vous Allemands ou Français?' They replied that they were English, and picked up a number of French soldiers who had reached the wreck the day before. These men said that they had seen nobody on the beach for the past twenty-four hours. As she was nearing the next wreck *Sea Roamer*'s people sighted a low, fast-looking vessel carrying, apparently, a heavy gun. There was for some little while considerable exchange of anxiety between the two ships until the new-comer turned out to be the *Massey Shaw* with her powerful fire-fighting monitor on the fore deck. Continuing the search, they worked finally down to the Dunkirk entrance where they were in collision with a destroyer. *Sea Roamer* herself was slightly damaged, but the boat she was towing was reduced to splinters and the tow-rope, suddenly freed, fouled her propeller. She was able to move slowly with the auxiliary engine, but she was eventually picked up and towed home by a paddle-steamer.

Sea Roamer, incidentally, records one of the better stories of the operation. Discussing the difficulty of persuading French troops to entrust themselves to small boats her owner says:

'The French, it seems, were not always prepared to wade out and clamber into the dinghies in the surf. A story was told me of a French officer who steadfastly refused to do this. Finally he sent a note to the anxious yacht

218

skipper. It read, "I have just eaten and am therefore unable to enter the water."'

The personnel ship *Royal Sovereign*, which had left at 6 o'clock, passed the tug convoy, and at 8 o'clock sighted the wreck of a hospital carrier. Her master says, tersely, 'Passed *Paris*, having been bombed and ship's company in lifeboats, but all very cheerful.' The tug *Foremost 87* was not far away from the wreck then, and she cast off her tow and crossed to the scene of the disaster. In the meantime, as Captain Biles describes, a naval launch had taken the lifeboats in tow. *Foremost 87* now took over the responsibility. Her master, J. Fryer, says:

'I at once gave orders to crew to get lines, etc., ready to take these survivors on board, some of whom were Sisters who were very seriously injured, also some of crew who'd been badly scalded.

'I managed to get all of the ninety-five survivors out of their boats, some of which were half full of water, on board of *Foremost 87*, and did everything to make wounded (one of whom passed away on board tug *Foremost 87*) as comfortable as I could, and then headed at full speed towards Dover.

'I had hardly altered my course when I noticed another boat full of people. I stopped engines and on nearing this boat I found that it had thirteen Spaniards aboard. I ordered these to be taken on board and kept apart from survivors of *Paris* as I was uncertain of their nationality, and I was unable to gather from them how and when they came to be in the boat I found them in.

'I headed for Dover, time being about 10.50 p.m., at full speed. Arriving at Dover pierheads eastern entrance about 3.30 a.m. on Monday, June 3rd, I received orders to proceed direct to Admiralty Pier and land survivors, this I did as soon as possible, everything being ready on shore to assist in this job of work. I kept the Spaniards on board until they were escorted ashore by armed guard, who no doubt found out more about them than I could.'

Spaniards are among the minor mysteries of Dunkirk.

Sun XV took on a naval commander at 9 p.m. on the 2nd and proceeded immediately to the assistance of *Paris*. They sighted the wreck at 11 p.m. and found her with a list to starboard. After encircling the ship to see if there were any survivors on board, they managed to pass a wire, making it fast to the mooring bits on the starboard quarter. They began to tow, but at once the wire parted, and simultaneously they were attacked by a German plane and heavily machine-gunned. As it was evident that *Paris* was sinking fairly rapidly, the attempt was abandoned, and *Sun XV* proceeded to cruise to the westward in search of other craft. At 3.45 a.m. she took in tow H.M. Drifter *Yorkshire Lass*, loaded with troops and disabled with engine trouble, but after towing her for three-quarters of an hour the drifter managed to get her engines repaired and let go the tow.

Once again tugs were sent to stand by about the entrance to Dunkirk to render assistance as and when necessary. *Foremost 22* was one of these, and in company with her, and with the skoots, the drifters and the trawlers, the motor-boats went across.

Rear-Admiral Wake-Walker left in M.A./S.B. 10 and arrived at Dunkirk at 8.30 p.m. His officers report little change in the immediate situation in the harbour save that a naval drifter had sunk alongside the pier during the day, complicating the berthing arrangements still further. The weather was clear with a northerly breeze, but M.A./S.B. 10 was only attacked once—her people called it 'a mild bombing attack on the way across'. Other ships were not so fortunate.

One of the greatest of the personal tragedies of Dunkirk happened in these hours. Commander Clouston, R.N., who had performed work beyond praise as pier master of the narrow plank way of the Mole since the very beginning of the operation, had come back to Dover in H.M.M. *Portsdown* at the end of the loading period this Sunday morning. He was returning (having discussed the situation in the 'Dynamo Room') with two of the fast R.A.F. launches, Nos. 243 and 276, which had already done good work and which were now to help in directing traffic and policing the fairways, when they were attacked by enemy aircraft. Commander Clouston's boat, No. 243, was hit and became waterlogged at once. The second boat, which was commanded by Sub-Lieutenant Roger Wake, R.N., was also hit and extensively damaged. Commander Clouston from the water waved to No. 276 to get clear before she in her turn was sunk. Some of his crew had been killed, but one officer who survived set out with him to swim to a boat they could see a couple of miles away, and the R.A.F. men endeavoured to swim to shore. The water was bitterly cold and Commander Clouston, exhausted by lack of sleep and by the endless, unremitting effort of the week, found that he could not make the distance. He turned and swam back towards the water-logged wreck of his own boat and was not seen again. The other officer, swimming for nearly three hours, reached the boat and found her to be a deserted cutter. With difficulty he boarded her, drifted for some while until he was picked up by a French trawler which had lost her way, and navigated this ship back to Ramsgate. A.C.1 B. Kernahan also turned back to the wreck, reached it and was picked up eight hours later by H.M.S. *Whitshed*.

Under Commander Clouston's guidance nearly 200,000 men had marched down the plank-way of the Mole to safety. The berthing of ships, the keeping open of the fairway, the suspension of loading during periods of extreme enemy action, all had been his responsibility. His too, in a measure, had been the responsibility for the bridging of the gaps made in the pier by enemy shell-fire. The whole maintenance of that narrow lifeline had depended upon his work and upon his spirit, and upon that of the handful of officers and ratings of the pier party under his command. His work was described by one ship's captain as 'noble'. In the fullest, the greatest sense of that ancient word his work *was* noble.

No. 276 reached Dunkirk, but she was too damaged to be of use for the work that she had been intended to perform. Sub-Lieutenant Wake, however, landed on the Mole and, in the normal tradition of the navy, took over the work that Commander Clouston had set out to do. Despite very considerable difficulties—partly arising out of the language problem—this youngster managed to keep the flow on the Mole moving. His methods at times were empirical, but since the *poilu* refused to be separated from his companions or to have his units broken up, empirical methods were necessary.

Rear-Admiral Taylor, having dispatched from Sheerness everything that would float and move, himself went to Ramsgate in the middle of Sunday afternoon. Discussing the conditions with military officers who had just arrived, he was informed that a pocket of men who had not been able to get into Dunkirk existed near Malo-les-Bains, and Admiral Taylor organized a special party to attempt to get these men away. Three skoots and a dozen fast motor-boats were selected, and sailed late in the afternoon. Commandant Anduse-Faru of the French Navy undertook to arrange for a paddle-steamer and a French ship to be off the beach, and for a number of French fishing vessels to co-operate with our own boats and ferry off troops to them and to the skoots. He was taken out to the fishing vessels to make arrangements. They had lovely names: *Ciel de France, Ave Maria Gratia Plena, Jeanne Antoine, Arc en Ciel.* They had done good work already and they were very tired, but after argument in the French fashion they went again.

The big ships did not sail, but the skoots and the line of small British craft left at the scheduled time, putting out from the crowded raft of little ships inside the crab-like claws of Ramsgate harbour one by one for the open sea. There was something almost incredibly gallant, something stirring beyond explanation in that little movement. The skoots had gone already—square, chunky, high-sided. Astern of them went out this little line of white-painted yachts, pleasure boats all of them, built for the rivers, for narrow waters, for shallow coasts. They made a straggling line as they cleared the shoals of the eastward entrance of the harbour, unkempt perhaps by naval standards, but instinct with eager courage. One thing they had common to all of them—the course on which they lay. Their bows headed straight for the vast black plume of Dunkirk that was visible even here upon that sunlit afternoon.

The personnel ships moved out later. *Royal Sovereign* was amongst the first of them, and a little after her came *Royal Daffodil, Lady of Mann, Autocarrier* and *St. Helier*. In the morning the naval authorities had informed Captain Pitman, *St. Helier's* master, that they considered that he had done enough and that they were prepared to put a naval officer in charge. Captain Pitman refused relief, but a commander and ten ratings were put on board to assist his tired crew and to help work the boats in case she was needed to take troops off the beaches.

And with that flight went *Tynwald* with her chief officer, J. Whiteway, as master; her second officer, purser, W/T operator and carpenter of her old complement, the relief crew, and a naval officer and ten ratings. She completed the round trip, making another heavy lifting.

Ben-My-Chree (also with her chief officer, T. Cain, as master), with the W/T operator, three greasers and a relief crew, sailed about the same time. Unfortunately very shortly after she took her departure *Ben-My-Chree* was in collision and the trip was abandoned.

Malines had left the area in the course of the afternoon without orders, and returned to Southampton.

Manxman, which had made three trips already, lifting 2,300 men, should have sailed at 9.15 p.m., but failed. A new crew was put on board—her engineers had stayed with the ship—and she left, but did not reach Dunkirk.

Amongst the French personnel ships that crossed this time were *Rouen* and *Newhaven*.

Again the bridge was in place, the greatest 'bridge of boats' that the world has known.

Not all these ships reached the congestion of the piers. *Royal Daffodil* was off the Ruytingen buoy just before 8 o'clock when she was attacked by six enemy aircraft. It is probable that this was a portion of the same bomber sweep which accounted for the *Paris*. She had just passed the boats of the *Paris* when the attack developed. Six heavy bombs (Captain G. Johnson of the *Royal Daffodil* describes them as 'aerial torpedoes') were dropped.

'Five of these missed, but the sixth hit the ship, passed through three decks, entered the engine-room, and went out through the starboard side before exploding just clear of the ship. The collar of the missile went through the bilge. The engines stopped and the aeroplanes machine-gunned the ship with tracer bullets, which started small fires. The ship began to make water through the hole made by the bomb and listed to starboard. Gear was shifted to the port side and the port boats were lowered to the deck and filled with water. This raised the starboard side enough to lift the hole just clear of the water line. Mr. J. Coulthard, the chief engineer, and Mr. W. Evans, the second engineer, took all the beds they could find and used them to plug the hole. Mr. Evans stood up to his neck in the water in the engine-room holding open the bilge valve while Mr. Coulthard kept the pumps going. With a diesel-engine ship this was a great risk; but the *Royal Daffodil* managed to get back to Ramsgate, with the engines running very slowly, as they had three parts of water to one of oil in their system, and was able to land all the troops she had taken on board.'

It is difficult to speak too highly of this feat. The sheer seamanship of it is beyond praise. To lift the ship's side clear out of the water needed determination and courage of a high order. The bravery of her engineers who, with the almost pathetic inadequacy of mattresses and planks, staunched that great hole in her side is superb.

I went over with Rear-Admiral Taylor at 8.45 p.m. in the 30-foot twin-screw river cruiser *White Wing*. The Admiral proposed to supervise the lifting of the pocket of men from Malo-les-Bains in person, and also to take charge of other small-boat movements through the night. *White Wing* was capable of approximately 12 knots but, owing to trouble with the starboard engine, did not make this speed all the way across. We reached Dunkirk, however, with only minor trouble from the wash of destroyers and the navigational difficulties. Our work for the night is covered in an account I wrote at the time.

'Having the Admiral on board, we were not actually working the beaches but were in control of operations. We moved about as necessary, and after we had spent some time putting small boats in touch with their towing boats, the 5·9 battery off Nieuport way began to drop shells on us. It seemed pure spite. The nearest salvo was about twenty yards astern, which was close enough.

'We stayed there until everybody else had been sent back, and then went pottering about looking for stragglers. While we were doing that, a salvo of shells got one of our troopships alongside the Mole. She was hit clean in the boilers and exploded in one terrific crash. There were then, I suppose, about 1,000 Frenchmen on the Mole. We had seen them crowding along its narrow crest, outlined against the flames. They had gone out under shell-fire to board the boat, and now they had to go back again, still being shelled. It was quite the most tragic thing I ever have seen in my life. We could do nothing with our little dinghy.

'While they were still filling back to the beach and the dawn was breaking with uncomfortable brilliance, we found one of our stragglers—a navy whaler. We told her people to come aboard, but they said that there was a white motor-boat aground and they would have to fetch off her crew. They went in, and we waited. It was my longest wait, ever. For various reasons they were terribly slow. When they found the captain of the motor-boat, they stood and argued with him and he wouldn't come off anyway. Damned plucky chap. . . .'

The white motor-boat on the beach was *Singapore* (Sub-Lieutenant J. W. Pratt, R.N.V.R.). She had run aground at 1.30 in the morning. She eventually refloated on the rising tide and left with three French officers in addition to her crew on board. On the way Sub-Lieutenant Pratt picked up two British soldiers who were 'floating around'. Wine from the Frenchmen's water-bottles brought them back to consciousness. Subsequently he took in tow three lifeboats which he found in mid-Channel, but eventually his engines broke down and he was himself taken in tow by *Kitcat*.

Commander Troup, who had accompanied Rear-Admiral Taylor from Sheerness, took over the War Department fast motor-boat *Haig* with *Marlborough*, *Wolfe* and *Swallow*. With him was the French Naval Attaché, Captain de Revoir. The four boats crossed in company with orders to act together on the other side ferrying until dawn, and then bring a final load back to England.

Commander Troup, with *Haig*, himself went into the harbour and, proceeding to the battered pier on the west side, persuaded 'with great difficulty' forty French soldiers to come off. These men were ferried to a ship in the roadstead and *Haig* went back for a second load. Bringing out thirty-nine, she was rammed by a French tug on the port beam. As the hole was a foot above the water-line, they disregarded it and went on. But less than 200 yards further a second tug altered course and rammed her, this time in the fo'c'sle, cutting half-way through the upper deck and right down the side. Commander Troup took *Haig* alongside the paddle-minesweeper *Westward Ho* which was lying off in the roadstead, and got his men out. While the disembarkation was proceeding *Westward Ho* had to go astern suddenly to avoid collision with a destroyer. The wash from her paddle flooded in through

the hole and *Haig* became almost unmanageable. As it was by this time
3 o'clock and *Westward Ho's* captain had received orders to sail, Commander
Troup decided to abandon *Haig* and return with the paddle-sweeper to
Margate. Badly damaged as she was, *Haig* was subsequently salved and got
back to Ramsgate.

The number of troops who came off the beaches this night was comparatively small. But along the Mole in the first hours there was a steady press of
men. Major-General Alexander himself came aboard Rear-Admiral Wake-
Walker's M.A./S.B. almost as soon as she arrived, to discuss the final
arrangements. He was transferred later to a destroyer. The 3,000 British
troops who remained came down the pier with the Frenchmen and embarked
in a steady stream.

St. Helier claims the honour of picking up the last of the B.E.F. Having
loaded her full complement, she pulled out of the harbour. She had now
become very difficult to manœuvre according to her master's account, and
after her return to Folkestone it was found on examination that her forepeak
was full of water and she was down by the bows. She had suffered damage
both by the collision with H.M.S. *Sharpshooter* and by the shock of near
misses during her trips across and as, for safety's sake, her crew had been
kept out of the fore part of the ship during the crossing, the trouble had not
been discovered earlier.

At midnight the last of the gallant 3,000 of the rearguard were safely off
the Mole. The epic of the 1st British Expeditionary Force was over. Major-
General Alexander, with Captain Tennant, the S.N.O., made a tour of the
harbour and of the beach in a fast motor-boat and when General Alexander
was satisfied that no British troops remained he left for England. The fighting retreat that had begun upon the River Dyle was over. The door that had
slammed in the face of the advancing Germans had slammed back upon
France and splintered.

The last of the British were gone. There remained still many French. In
some of the very remarkable criticisms that were made by politicians of
the Vichy Government since the final fall of France much was made of
this fact. Had the French High Command taken a soldier's view of the position of the northern armies even as late as the middle of the retreat, the
position would have been different. But there existed until the last days in the
mind of the French High Command the belief—or it might be the hope—that
by the sacrifice of the northern armies time might be bought, time to
reorganize the defence of France itself. Paradoxically it was the view of a
sentimentalist rather than of a realist. It was born out of the undying French
faith in gestures. The armies of the north—without ammunition, without
petrol, without food—could not have bought even time. Their lives in the
flush and flux of this campaign were worthless; but the High Command,
clinging to formulas, held them pledged to a purposeless sacrifice. The
position of Prioux's army in the days when the British decision to evacuate
was taken has a supreme illogicality. Had the mind of the French High Command appreciated the realities of the situation as Lord Gort and the British

Cabinet rightly appreciated them, the whole circumstances of Dunkirk would have been different. Had the French Navy, under the intransigent Darlan—with its considerable resources of cross-Channel vessels and of suitable small craft—co-operated with the British Navy in the early days, the position would have been easy of solution. Had it thrown its full weight into the operation even when the French troops first began to crowd the beaches calling for help, the position would have been capable of recovery. But the early vacillations, the lack of co-operation, on this midnight of June 2nd saw the Mole still crowded with Frenchmen and the roads of the town blocked behind them.

The British ships went in again to bring them off. *Royal Sovereign*, for example, picked up French troops from the west pier. When she was ready she, as her master says abruptly, 'cleared harbour with more than her complement of troops'.

Much trouble was experienced in handling ships, particularly in getting them alongside the Mole. All through the early part of the evening a combination of flood tide sweeping through the supports of the piers with the northerly wind had made it intolerably difficult to manœuvre these high-sided ships, and turning after they had cast off on completing loading was equally difficult. In the course of this a French personnel ship, the *Rouen*, went aground on the western shallows of the harbour.

The master of *Foremost 22*, C. Fieldgate (whom the doctors had allowed to return to duty), says:

'On arrival off the harbour entrance at 11 p.m., I was instructed to enter and give any assistance I could.

'Entering, we found the French s.s. *Newhaven*[1] aground, and in an attempt to get close enough to get my tow-rope aboard him, I went aground myself.

'The tide was ebbing, making it necessary for me to get off the ground immediately. I was successful in doing this and proceeded outside the harbour while another tug of less draught assisted the ship.

'I stood off the harbour entrance for a short time, then motor-boats came alongside and loaded us with French troops. By this time the situation was getting very dangerous and bombs were dropping in our vicinity so I decided that it would be wise to leave and save what troops we had. . . .'

Sun X had reached Dunkirk well after dark. She cast off her tow and was immediately requested to go in to the assistance of the *Rouen*. The tide was falling and 200 feet away from *Rouen*, *Sun X* found only ten feet of water. She drew almost ten feet. Her master, W. A. Fothergill, manœuvred his ship in a second time from a different direction, but with the same result. It was impossible to hope to shift the heavy bulk of the French cross-Channel packet and he had to abandon the attempt, but he picked up several boats loaded with men from her and took them out of the harbour. In all he embarked more than 300 men. After this he proceeded again into the harbour to assist in berthing ships alongside the Mole, and kept up this work until nearly dawn.

[1] This is probably a mistake due to the difficulty of identifying similar ships in darkness.

Sun XI also tried to free the crippled *Rouen* without success. Subsequently she was sent up the harbour to try to get off a naval sloop which had also gone aground, but could only get within two ships' lengths of her and had to back out again. On her way home 'now like a sardine tin full up everywhere with troops' she touched the sand at the top of the Ramsgate channel, but was not damaged. Her skipper ends his report of seven days in the fury of the beaches with the statement: 'Tug lost two stern lines on large lifeboats, reported same at Dover, also lost three steel helmets.'

All attempts to get *Rouen* off on that tide failed. Most of her troops were taken off, but she still remained fast on the sand, and at low water she was aground high and dry. However, both bombing and shelling failed to get her during the latter part of the night and the morning, and she eventually got clear on the next tide.

The confusion during these hours was tremendous. *Lady of Mann*, arriving at 11.45 p.m., was instructed to wait off the pier heads as it was impossible to berth her. She stood by within hailing distance for more than two hours in which time she picked up a few Frenchmen who came off in boats, and at 2 a.m. she was ordered to leave for Dover.

The *Autocarrier*, which arrived a little after 11 o'clock, managed to get alongside the outer end of the Mole, but though she waited till after midnight, no troops came out to her and she left empty.

4

H.M.S. *Whitshed* and the other destroyers had come back with the night flow, and all through the night *Whitshed* lay in the fairway off the entrance directing traffic, controlling the movement of ships in and out of the harbour, and trying to act as A.A. guardship. Around her the movement went on as the last of the B.E.F. passed out to sea and the French passed with them. The paddlers, special service ships, the skoots, the trawlers and the drifters, were back again with the big ships.

H.M.M. *Westward Ho* was amongst these, loading from small craft in the fairway. H.M.M. *Medway Queen* was there again. This was her fifth successive night. At 10 o'clock in the morning Commander Greig, R.N., Senior Officer of the 10th Flotilla, the veterans of Dover, went aboard her and offered to take over the command and to relieve the officers for the night. He was met with a flat refusal, but finally a compromise was arrived at whereby Commander Greig's party was to take the ship over until within sight of Dunkirk when her own officers would take her in. This was done. She went alongside the Mole at 1.30 and, this time using ladders which she had picked up at Dover as well as her brow, she took off 723 French soldiers. During the loading a shell hit the water so close to her that boats astern were almost swamped.

H.M.S. *Golden Eagle* made her last journey this night. She berthed finally after some difficulty at 3 a.m., but by this time the flow had ceased again and, as the block ships were about to enter, she was ordered out. Clear of the harbour it was discovered that one of the innumerable ropes that lay in the water like crowding eels had got round her port wheel. They tried to free it. By the time it had become obvious that their efforts were vain they were the only ship in the roads save a destroyer. Finally, however, they got it sufficiently clear to enable them to proceed at slow speed and *Golden Eagle* got safely away.

5

As has been said, it is difficult now to divide the days, but this dawn on Monday morning marked the end of a period in history. By the midnight which preceded it the last men of the British Expeditionary Force had been embarked and the signal had been passed by the Senior Naval Officer, Captain Tennant, R.N., 'B.E.F. evacuated'. Though we had been restricted to the hours of darkness Sunday saw 31,407 men taken off, mostly from the harbour, and our loss in contrast to the previous day was small. No important naval vessel had been sunk. We had lost two trawlers and a drifter. We had had damaged one cruiser, one destroyer and a third trawler. We had lost one hospital carrier and a second had been severely damaged.

It was not yet the end of Operation 'Dynamo', but it was the end of a period. It was not yet the end of British intervention on the continent of Europe but it was very near to it. The dive-bombers that came out over the black smoke pall of Dunkirk found again this morning an empty sea.

CHAPTER XV

MONDAY, JUNE 3RD

1

The daylight hours of Dunkirk had ceased to have an importance save to the hard-pressed troops of the French rearguard along the slowly shrinking line of the perimeter. The German opposition during these last two days was not heavy except in the attack of the small hours of Monday morning. On Sunday, when the eastern end of the perimeter was still held by the slender skeleton of the British rearguard, they had made no heavy thrust. So on this Monday also they seemed to hesitate before the final rush.

At first light we had sent over a strong bombing force—strong for those difficult days. They found no obvious targets about the perimeter, no columns of troops on the roads, no heavy concentrations of vehicles, and, switching from their search for possible attack, they changed their targets to the enemy guns of Bergues and Gravelines. The bombing was successful. For most of the day no guns fired from Bergues and the French were able to fall back slowly to the outskirts of the town. The perimeter that had begun at Nieuport and swept in a huge arc to Gravelines was shrunk now to the outer houses of the town, and throughout this day there was no procession of ships along the channels.

But there were still many men to be rescued. It is not possible, in the absence of reliable French documents, to obtain a precise picture of these hours, but it is probable that there were at least 30,000 men still in the area, and it was essential that a tremendous effort should be made to lift the last of them. The German estimate on the evening of Monday was 60,000, but this is beyond question an exaggeration. The strongest possible representations were made to the French authorities to conclude the operation by the following dawn. It must have been as obvious to them as it was to us that ammunition was by now quite exhausted and any question of holding even a bridgehead in the town itself, despite the many rumours that filtered through to England, was hopeless.

At noon the policy for the night was decided in the 'Dynamo Room' at Dover, and a signal from Vice-Admiral Ramsay to Force K and to the various officers responsible stated that personnel vessels, destroyers and paddleminesweepers would use the east pier once again as they had used it so many times in the past: the west pier in the outer port was to be used by the Fleet minesweepers, corvettes, skoots and French vessels: drifters and small craft were to go into the inner harbour, while the gunboat H.M.S. *Locust* was to lie off the entrance and take aboard men brought out to her by small craft: all ships were to leave the harbour by 2.30 on Tuesday morning, June 4th.

This decision was arrived at with the greatest possible reluctance, and the Admiralty in successive signals extended the time for personnel ships, and subsequently the time for destroyers, up to 7 o'clock in the morning provided circumstances justified the obvious risk.

Ships moved during the day carrying out patrol work as in the past week, searching for disabled craft, sweeping for mines. And in the early afternoon, even while the Germans were moving slowly up to Rosendaël, the little suburb that is actually no more than a continuation of the Dunkirk houses along the road to Furnes, the last crusade of rescue began.

The sands were almost out. There was only dust in the upper chamber of the hourglass. But there was no hesitation amongst the men of the ships.

2

The tugs were amongst the first to leave, being probably the slowest of all the vessels taking part this day. But already the 'police' of the narrow waters were there before them—the ships of Force K, the anti-submarine trawlers, the drifters that marked the control points of the channels and were there to pass messages as the ships moved across, and the minesweepers, the corvettes, the patrol vessels, and the destroyers of the anti-submarine and anti-E-boat patrols.

All through Dunkirk there was a host of naval vessels which never approached the narrows of the pier-heads. Their duty was in this patient police work, this shepherding of strays, this guarding of the channels. They were the ships that kept that frail lifeline unbroken, that protected it in low visibility and fog and the appalling navigational difficulties of the little ships, that kept down the U-boats and drove off the E-boats like flies from a wounded man.

The tug *Racia*, which had been lying off Ramsgate with a string of seventeen lifeboats, passed her boats to a *Sun* tug and took departure at 2.30 p.m. with a commander and a naval party on board. At 4 o'clock the skoot *Pascholl*, as flagship of a party of five Dutch skoots flying the White Ensign, left under the command of Lieutenant J. N. Wise, R.N.V.R., the senior officer of the party being Commander Hammond, R.N. One of the little flotilla, the *Reiger*, went aground on the Quern bank shortly after leaving.

At about 4.30 p.m. Rear-Admiral Taylor got away a convoy of motorboats in tow of tugs. He had selected about a dozen of the best slow motorboats. These were to be dropped off Dunkirk entrance by the tugs and were to proceed to the Quai Félix Faure, some little distance up the harbour, which was still in moderately good condition. He himself started with *Mermaiden*, the leading boat. The tug *Tanga* towed four of these boats; *Sun XV* four including *Letitia II*, *Madame Sans Gêne* and the Clacton lifeboat a little later; and at 5.15 p.m. *Sun IV* left with four more, together with a party of naval officers and ratings. Close on their heels the remaining fast War Department launches took off. One of these, *Marlborough*, had orders to rendezvous in mid-Channel with Admiral Taylor, and duly picked him up at 9 o'clock.

The full spate of the night's shipping was now in motion, and with these later craft were moving trawlers and drifters and paddle-minesweepers, and a number of small French vessels of one sort and another, some of them coming direct up Channel.

And astern of them, catching them up as they roared across, came the great veterans of the liftings—the cross-Channel steamers. *Autocarrier* was the first to leave, clearing at 6.15 p.m. She was followed by *Lady of Mann*. The magnificent *King George V* sailed at 6.30 on her fifth trip, and close astern of her came the French *Côte d'Argent*, also making her fifth crossing. *Canterbury* had completed her temporary repairs following the bombing of May 29th, and sailed at 6.45. *Princess Maud* had effected temporary repairs following her shelling of May 30th and she too set out a little after 8. *Royal Sovereign* began her last trip a quarter of an hour later.

And with these ships went the destroyers—*Whitshed, Sabre, Shikari, Malcolm* and *Express* among them.

3

Rear-Admiral Wake-Walker, indefatigable, crossed in M.T.B. 102. The operations were timed to start at 10.30; he was there at 10 p.m. The evening was fine and clear in the vicinity of Dunkirk, with a fresh northerly wind, and once again shipping had difficulty in coming alongside the Mole in the prevailing conditions. The naval parties on this night came over in H.M.S. *Whitshed*, but she had difficulty at first in getting alongside and her pier parties were eventually taken in by M.T.B. 102.

Whitshed had been damaged in Dover harbour in the course of the afternoon. A small ship, attempting to berth ahead of her, had misjudged her turn and rammed the destroyer. No. 3 fuel tank was holed, and it was obvious that the damage needed dockyard assistance. But the need on this last night was too great even for the consideration of repairs, and she crossed in accordance with previous orders.

Overcoming the difficulties of the swell and the cross-tide, *Whitshed*, after backing out, made a second attempt and berthed. The account of her experiences is interesting in many ways. Once again she underscores the tremendous difficulties with the inland French. This was the last night; she was one of the last ships; to many of those men it must have appeared impossible that there would be any more ships this night. Yet in this last minute of the eleventh hour her people say that they had to push, pull, cajole and bully the *poilus* on board. When she had picked up about 800 Frenchmen, *Whitshed* took on one of the last of the small British parties that remained and backed out of the harbour. As she went down the channel she passed the block ships coming in.

A number of small French fishing craft had already arrived by this time and were strung out alongside the Mole. The plan of the night had provided for their going deep into the harbour to pick men up directly from places

where the large ships could not penetrate, but the majority of them seeme
to have made fast to the nearest part of the Mole that was unoccupied an
were loading there. It took time and energy to persuade them to clear th
berths for the larger vessels.

The first personnel ship to arrive was *Lady of Mann* but, owing to pre
vailing conditions, she could not berth until very much later. The first of th
bigger ships actually to berth, apart from naval craft, was *Autocarrier*, whicl
made fast outside the pier-head at 11 o'clock.

Meanwhile Rear-Admiral Taylor had arrived in *Marlborough* and had gon
straight up through the press of small French craft to the inner harbour ir
search of the Quai Félix Faure. *Marlborough* made fast to a deserted quay
some distance up, and Admiral Taylor, with Sub-Lieutenant Karminsky as
his interpreter, went ashore to check their position. Troops were moving
along the road at the back of the quay, but it was impossible to find anyone
who knew the geography of the harbour, and invariably the reply was,
'Sorry, I'm a stranger'. Eventually, however, they ascertained that their
guess had been correct and about 11 o'clock a party of 300 French Marines
arrived. This was the detachment which Admiral Taylor had been expecting.
The motor-boats, however, had not arrived owing to delays outside the
harbour and *Marlborough* was sent down to bring them in.

During the period of waiting Sub-Lieutenant Pool, who had found a
derelict motor-cycle, persuaded it to start and carried out a private reconnaissance of the area.

Shortly after 11.30 p.m. the motor-boats arrived, and a little after a large
French trawler came up the harbour and took all the marines that they could
not load. As efforts to persuade other French troops who were moving along
the road to come off failed, Rear-Admiral Taylor decided about 2 a.m. to
withdraw. The quay was then completely deserted, and enemy machine-gun
fire was getting very close.

On moving down the harbour the French trawler slewed suddenly across
the channel. As another French ship was trying to get out near her bows,
Marlborough was headed for the space of her stern. Unfortunately the quay
had been bombed at this point and a large shoal of rubble and broken
masonry had formed. *Marlborough* scraped over this. Her hull was undamaged; but her unprotected propellers and rudder were ripped off as she
moved, and she floated helpless on the further side. They attempted to move
Marlborough with improvised paddles, but without success. A little later
M.A./S.B. 7 attempted to give them a tow, but her own engines were giving
trouble and she rammed the boat herself. Three French trawlers in succession
were hailed, but without success, and finally *Marlborough* was picked up by
the big motor-yacht *Gulzar*, which was commanded by a Dominican monk
(R.N., retired), and towed back to Dover.

Commander Troup, Rear-Admiral Taylor's assistant, had also left in
Swallow, one of the fast War Department boats, about 8 o'clock. Arriving at
10.30, he went alongside the west pier. He found much confusion there and,
appointing himself pier-master, took control. A good deal of the trouble lay

in persuading the French to break units in order to board the small boats. The organization of the French Army, with its rigid adherence to organized units, caused great difficulties throughout the period of the evacuation of French troops. The lack of initiative on the part of other ranks and a disinclination to move in anything less than companies, caused many delays and much irritation. If a small boat could not take a whole company—sometimes if a ship could not take a whole battalion—men already on board would insist on being put ashore again.

To him came *Pascholl* with the remainder of her flotilla of H.M. skoots. One of these ran aground and was eventually abandoned, but the rest took on full loads, *Pascholl* lifting 300 men. She was unable to get away for some time as she was wedged in against the quay by a destroyer which was also loading, and her captain describes the scene as chaotic: French destroyers whooping about with their sirens going, small craft moving everywhere, the personnel ships backing and filling in the fairway.

Commander Troup, with the help of Capitaine le Comte le Chartier de Sedouy (a French liaison officer), succeeded in persuading French troops that they would meet again in England and eventually had the flow moving very rapidly. From this one battered stretch of pier some thousands of troops were evacuated in the course of that night. Commander Troup had arranged for a boat to come in to collect him at 3 o'clock, and in this he arranged to take off the French General and his staff. This boat broke down, but eventually another came in; and Commander Troup's picture of the final scene is among the dramatic moments of Dunkirk. This was the last boat out in that sector of the harbour and there were still about 1,000 men remaining on the pier. They stood at attention along the length of it. The general and his staff stood about thirty feet away from them, facing them, in the faint light of the dawn with the flames bringing faces and helmets into sharp relief. The general saluted, the men returned the salute; then he turned about, climbed down into the boat and they went out at 3.20.

Meanwhile the personnel carriers were beginning to get alongside satisfactorily. *Autocarrier* berthed on the outer end. Her master, Captain C. M. Masters, picked up 712 men of all ranks very rapidly and left almost at once. *Canterbury* got alongside the Mole just on the edge of high water. After embarking 659 French troops under what Captain Harcourt calls 'great difficulties', she was ordered to leave owing to the risk of being grounded by low water.

Côte d'Argent berthed about high water, picked up a quick load of more than 1,000 men, and was away by 12.30. This was her fifth voyage. Of the four French personnel ships which took part in the operation *Côte d'Argent's* record is by far the best. She stands high in the list of the great cross-Channel ferries. Altogether she is officially credited with having brought away 4,754 men. Of the other French vessels *Côte d'Azur* was sunk early in the operation, *Newhaven* made two trips bringing away 1,400 men and *Rouen* made one trip bringing away 1,300.

Lady of Mann was alongside by 12.30, after backing and filling inside the channel for nearly two hours before she could go alongside or get anyone to take her ropes. She picked up a heavy load of troops and pulled out at 1.45 a.m. on the falling tide. *King George V* took a full load and got clear a little later. *Tynwald* made her fifth lifting, taking her usual average of over 1,500 men.

Princess Maud arrived just before midnight, and Captain Clarke's account gives a vivid picture of the urgency and congestion of this last night.

'We arrived off Dunkirk breakwater at 11.57 p.m., very close to our appointed time. We entered the pier-heads, and looked for a berth. The narrow fairway was crammed to capacity, with all varying types of ships bound in and out. Wrecks dotted the harbour here and there. The only light was that of shells bursting, and the occasional glare of the fires.

'I shouted through the megaphone to the nearest steamer alongside, "How long will you be?". They answered "A quarter of an hour". This fifteen minutes must have been a nightmare for the engineers, with having to constantly keep clear of traffic, wrecks, etc. Shells were coming from the east and west by this time, and aircraft were overhead.

'Just before half-past twelve an outward-bound transport, presumed to be the *Côte d'Argent*, struck us on the starboard bow, inflicting slight damage.

'At 12.45 a French trawler struck us on the port quarter and almost capsized herself; no damage to us.

'At 12.55 we proceeded alongside the vacated berth at the extreme end of the eastern jetty. Troops then clambered aboard all ways, no gangways available. Dogs of all kinds got aboard somehow. There was no confusion whilst a steady line of men was directed along the jetty by several members of the crew.

'At 1.40 a.m. the flow of troops thinned out, only stragglers came along. I was told that the port was going to be blocked at 2.30 a.m.

'At 1.50 we were fairly well packed, so I cast off after being told that was the last of the troops, although one other steamer was ahead loaded.

'Whilst swinging at 2.5 a shell fell in the berth we had just vacated. . . .'

Meanwhile on the other side of the harbour *Royal Sovereign* arrived at the west pier after a slight collision with an unknown ship off No. 3 buoy. She too had found dense fog for a portion of the voyage across. At 2.55 a.m. 'overladen with troops we left the pier, cutting our own forward ropes. Heavy gunfire continuously; leaving harbour saw crew of unknown vessel being rescued by small boats'.

Royal Sovereign in her six completed crossings had carried, according to Vice-Admiral Ramsay's official record of the work of the personnel vessels, 6,858 men, almost exactly a tenth of the total carried by all the cross-Channel steamers in the operation. *Princess Maud* and *Royal Sovereign* were the last of the passenger ships to leave, and with their departure a great chapter in the history of the British mercantile marine came to its magnificent close.

A naval officer writing in an official account of the operations says:

'Owing to the difficulties of berthing, the many small ships and the blockships, the harbour and harbour entrance were very congested throughout the night, but especially in the early hours. One cannot speak too highly of the way in which the masters of the personnel ships handled their large vessels in these very difficult conditions.'

4

A little after 3 o'clock the blockships came in. Though there were still a considerable number of men on shore, it had been decided after due consideration to block the harbour this night. The block itself was well up the harbour and would not interfere seriously with the use of the seaward stretch of the East Mole—the vital stretch. The memories of the use to which Zeebrugge and Ostend had been put in the last war and the cost of our repeated efforts to render them useless to the Germans were strong, and the navy was determined that no mistake should be made on this occasion.

Zeebrugge had already been blocked. On this night Commander G. H. F. Owles, D.S.O., D.S.C., R.N., in the s.s. *Pacifico*, came to Dunkirk with four blockships escorted by H.M.S. *Vivacious*. Unfortunately one of these ships, the s.s. *Gourka*, was in collision in the approach channel, a French personnel ship hitting her almost amidships. She was so badly damaged that she foundered on the edge of the fairway: her survivors were rescued by M.A./S.B. 10. The other three proceeded into the harbour, were manoeuvred with incredible difficulty in the face of the flow of the tide, the charges were blown, and they sank. A gap, however, was left owing to the non-arrival of the fourth ship.

5

The loading, however, was not yet over. The tug *Racia*, which had been stemming the tide outside the harbour until 1.30, went in at that time, got alongside the Mole and began loading troops by ladders from the quay. At 2.30 a.m. she cast off to allow H.M.S. *Shikari* to take her place. When she had got the destroyer alongside she left with her load for home at 2.45. In the Dyke channel she found a motor-boat broken down and took out its crew with one wounded soldier. About this time another destroyer passed her and 'sang out and told us to put on all the speed we could; we did'.

Sun IV, *Sun XV* and *Tanga* went in to the Mole at the same time. This was almost the very last of the loading—the last desperate effort. Already added to the bombing and the shelling light machine-gun fire from the Germans in the streets of the town was beginning to play over the harbour. *Tanga* got only thirty-seven Frenchmen when she was ordered to get clear. Crossing the Channel, she picked up a French fishing lugger and towed her in.

The Clacton lifeboat worked throughout this period bringing men from the wharves and quays of the inner harbour to the ships outside. Mr. R. W. A. Faulkner (who had come to Ramsgate and had made an abortive effort to get across in the motor-yacht *Madame Pompadour*) was with her this night, together with Mr. W. P. Trotter, and writes:

234

'The entrance was very crowded and in the darkness it was difficult to locate one's position. At first we could not see the approach to the docks due to the fact that one large ship was lying athwart the entrance, and decided to go alongside a small pier which was in a small bay to the eastward, but before we could get there found ourselves in shoal water alongside a Dutch skoot with a naval crew in charge who had also attempted to go there, and had gone ashore. We attempted to tow her off, but having only one engine in action, without success, and as we could do no good left her for a wharf where some French soldiers were waiting and took them off to one of the ships waiting outside. We made several trips picking up soldiers from the quays which were full of men marching to the ships berthed at the seaward end, and taking them to vessels lying in the roads. At 3 o'clock in accordance with our instructions we left the harbour, having taken a last load of soldiers on board, this time from somewhat higher up the dock entrance and where we experienced great difficulty in getting them to climb down the dock wall to such a small ship, and made for home. During the time we were at Dunkirk the town was being shelled but this did not cause us any great difficulty. Our passage back was uneventful except for one short burst of machine-gun fire from a low-flying aircraft just after we had left the harbour.

'About ten miles from Dunkirk we picked up an old ship's lifeboat full of soldiers, including a few wounded, who were attempting to row away from the coast, and we were able to embark them. . . .'

The Belgian fishing fleet was still represented. In these last hours *Lydie Suzanne* made her fourth crossing, but succeeded in picking up only ten men.

Letitia II (Mr. R. D. Campbell-Hart), which had crossed with Rear-Admiral Taylor's flotilla, had picked up forty French troops some distance up the harbour and, bringing them out, transferred them to H.M.S. *Locust*. She then took aboard a demolition party from *Locust* with two depth charges made into a demolition charge, and placed these on board the stranded hulk of H.M.S. *Mosquito*. *Letitia II* then withdrew and the gunboat duly disintegrated. On taking the demolition party back to *Locust*, *Letitia II* was damaged and started for home. On the way she had engine trouble and took a tow from a paddle-steamer which was also towing a motor torpedo-boat. While on tow a collision between the two boats occurred in which two men were flung into the water. *Letitia II*, cutting her tow, rescued one of these. Continued engine trouble, however, put her finally out of action, and her crew were ordered to abandon ship by the officer in charge of a tug.

Madame Sans Gêne was also part of the tug convoy. She was a late-comer to the evacuation, having left Westminster Pier in the afternoon of June 1st in charge of Mr. G. Kimber of the Dominions Office. She left Ramsgate finally at 5 o'clock on June 3rd with *Sun XV*. On the way over the tug, trying to take the kinks out of a new warp, streamed it astern. The propellers of the yachts were in neutral, spinning with the speed of the tow, and the warp, trailing aft, fouled one of the propellers of *Madame Sans Gêne* and the single screw and rudder of the yacht aft of her. The second boat had to be cut adrift and abandoned, but *Madame Sans Gêne* went on. As they approached the green-flashing buoy off Dunkirk harbour one of the two ropes parted and *Madame Sans Gêne*'s other propeller was fouled and put out of action—the rope troubles of Dunkirk persisted into the very last hours.

Mermaiden, which belonged to Lieutenant-Commander Filleul, R.N., made four trips to vessels lying off the harbour and was considerably knocked about, her decks and wheelhouse being riddled with machine-gun bullets.

Sun IV helped to berth *Malcolm* which was amongst the last destroyers to load, and left with thirty-nine 'passengers of various nationalities'. *Sun XV*, having already taken a number of men aboard from small boats, went alongside the Mole at 2 a.m. There she found that practically all the men had been embarked, and at 2.30 she also left, towing the helpless *Madame Sans Gêne*. At 4.20, six miles west of W buoy, she picked up the naval drifter *L.H.W.D.*, which had developed engine trouble, and towed her into Ramsgate. *Madame Sans Gêne*, however, had to be abandoned. She was left afloat, carrying with her the bowler hat and the umbrella with which a Civil Servant had embarked upon adventure.

There was one other small boat that came back on this day, a small motor-yacht under the command of Lieutenant Van Hamel, a submarine commander of the Royal Netherlands Navy. He reached Ramsgate in the morning, and announced to Captain Wharton of the Small Vessels Pool that he proposed to go back again that night. When he was informed that the operation was over he said that despite that he still had to go back as he had made an arrangement with a British brigadier, with whom he had worked for days along the beaches, to go back and pick him up. He was told that the Germans were already in the town. He replied that he knew that, but that his arrangement held with the brigadier that if the German advance overwhelmed the town he was to swim out to one of the wrecks lying offshore and wait aboard her until he was rescued, and that therefore he was in honour bound to go back whatever the official decisions. Captain Wharton communicated with Dover, and it was found that the brigadier had returned with one of the last of the loads.

6

The personnel ships had ended their superb story of heroism and sacrifice at 1.40 a.m., when *Princess Maud* cast off for the last time from Dunkirk Mole. The paddle-sweepers, the Fleet sweepers, the trawlers and the drifters each in their turn had made their last departure.

H.M.M. *Medway Queen*, whose name has so often cropped up in the accounts of previous nights, made her last passage. She had established the sweepers' record of seven trips, a magnificent performance. She went alongside the Mole again, and very shortly after she had made fast a shell-burst threw a destroyer lying astern of her against her stern lines, cutting them. Both ships swung out and *Medway Queen* lost her brow. Men who were at the moment coming down it managed to fling themselves aboard as it fell. Her captain, Lieutenant Cook, R.N.R., kept control of her and nursed the destroyer back into position. Almost immediately afterwards she was in trouble again, being rammed—though not seriously—by a cross-Channel steamer. She picked up 367 French troops on this trip, being considerably incapacitated by various troubles.

Malcolm completed her last trip. She had made six runs in all, having had one day off since she began the operation on the direct and personal orders of V.-A., Dover. In these six trips she had carried 6,400 men.

Sabre also completed her last trip. One of the oldest ships to take part, she had been also one of the first. Probably to her goes the honour of bringing the first full cargo of men from the beaches. She had this day the honour of being also one of the last. In ten trips—the Dunkirk record—she carried in all something over 5,000 troops. She had been damaged by bombs, she had had minor troubles of one sort and another, but throughout the whole operation ship and crew had responded magnificently to the high demands of the days. *Sabre* in years of peace had been wrecked; her engines had been submerged in salt water, yet they too stood up with her men to the gruelling need.

At 3.18 a.m. the destroyer *Express* backed out of the harbour. She had completed six trips, two to the beaches and four to Dunkirk, lifting in all 3,500 men.

Eleven minutes before H.M.S. *Shikari* had transmitted from the French Embarkation Officer a signal that—one of the very last to be sent from Dunkirk—was also one of the most dramatic. It read: 'Send two small ships or one transport stop Situation desperate stop Enemy 3 miles away stop.' And with the enemy three miles away there were no transports available now. The last ships had gone. At 3.30 she was still lying alongside the quay. Even at walking pace the enemy could have been very close, but this was a mechanized army. Three miles is a matter of minutes to light tanks or armoured cars. Only the wreckage of Dunkirk and its flames lay between the advancing Germans and the Mole. The ammunition of the French Army had been exhausted in the afternoon. The handful of men that were left were weaponless and defenceless. At 3.40 a.m., with the German machine-guns stuttering in the nearer streets, having taken every man she could get on board, the destroyer pulled out.

To *Shikari*, one of the oldest of the destroyers in service in the Royal Navy (she was built in 1919) fell the honour of being the last ship to leave Dunkirk. It was no mean honour, no small glory.

7

And with the last ships Admiral Abrial, the commander of the naval base and the fortress of Dunkirk, came away. On reaching Dover Admiral Abrial went at once to see Vice-Admiral Ramsay. In his signal to the Admiralty Vice-Admiral Ramsay stated that Admiral Abrial informed him that by the afternoon of Monday the enemy had fought their way into the suburb of Rosendaël just to the east of Dunkirk along the Nieuport road. In opposing that attack the French had used the last of their ammunition.

MONDAY, JUNE 3RD

Admiral Abrial stated further that there remained in the Dunkirk area now only unarmed troops 'and to attempt their evacuation would be endangering the ships for nothing'. His opinion, delivered formally at Dover, was that 'he considered it impossible to carry out any further evacuation'.

CHAPTER XVI

THE SEA, THE AIR AND THE LAND

1

It is always difficult for the layman to assess adequately the merits of a naval operation. From the accounts of the masters of the ships and the skippers of the little craft that have been quoted, something, however, of the difficulty, the danger and the enormous extent of the evacuation of Dunkirk may be measured.

We can measure it a little too in the failures of our enemies. In the blunt horn of the Gulf of Tunis there were left almost the number of men who were crowded in those last brutal days into the perimeter of Dunkirk. Between the 5th and the 13th of May 1943, when General Alexander sent his telegram announcing that 'we are masters of the North African shore', 248,000 German and Italian officers and men surrendered to our arms: 638 escaped. Of those 638 the majority got clear by air. A few score only threaded their way through the vigilance of the Royal Navy and the R.A.F. to reach the shores of Sicily—yet Sicily was hardly further from Cape Blanco than Dunkirk from Dover by the route that was forced on us when the Germans captured Calais.

Though the numbers were not as great, there are other comparisons along the French coast as the tide of victory swept from Normandy to Holland. Handfuls of men got clear, but they were measured in no more than handfuls. The sea routes from Cherbourg, from Brest, from Bordeaux on the one hand, from Le Havre, Dieppe, Boulogne and Calais on the other, were a pitiful graveyard of sunken E-boats, of beached and burning cargo vessels, of battered hulks of every kind. Some 300 German naval and auxiliary craft were sunk between the 6th of June and the 25th of August 1944, and in the last days of that fantastic debacle there was another fleet to follow them to disaster. The sea casualties of the Second Battle of France and the Low Countries may never be properly assessed, but they were enormous.

It is against these things that we must put Dunkirk, where from the naked beaches and the single perilous pathway of the Mole 337,000 men came to safety.

It is worth while to dissect this figure so that we may judge the magnificence of the different classes of the ships. The thirty-eight British destroyers were the mainstay of the evacuation. Never built to carry men, they brought away 91,624. There were thirty-two British and four French personnel ships; working as gallantly, they brought away 69,321. The Fleet minesweepers carried 30,942, the paddle-sweepers 18,838. The thirty Dutch skoots that sailed under the White Ensign carried another 20,284. These figures speak for themselves. Each class of ship had its own difficulties. To each the operation presented problems wildly, almost insanely, beyond its proper purpose. They overcame these problems: they defied insanity.

The figures for the French contribution are interesting in view of the statements that were made subsequently by the Vichy Government. French destroyers between them lifted 7,623 men. Eight destroyers and six sloops of the French Navy are officially recorded as having taken part in the operation. Of the four French personnel ships that are recorded as participating in Operation 'Dynamo', three lifted between them 7,454 men. Côte d'Azur was sunk early, but may also have lifted a small number. The French vessels other than personnel ships and destroyers lifted 14,026. The French share in the lifting then was just under 30,000 men. These figures are important in view of the statement made by the French Admiralty on June 4th that 300 French warships and merchant vessels of various sizes, with 200 smaller boats, had taken part in the operations.

The total of these liftings is approximately a quarter of a million. There remain something between 80,000 and 90,000 men to be accounted for. These were the load of the little ships—of the coasters that so magnificently beached themselves to bring away their heavy loads; of the trawlers, the fishing vessels and the tugs that went in to the beaches, to the Mole and to the inner harbour; of the minor war vessels, the small sweepers, the flare-burning drifters, the harbour defence vessels and the armed yachts. And above all it is the total of the little ships—that multitude of pleasure craft, more than 600 of them, of open boats and ships' lifeboats and river cruisers that brought back their astonishing loads night after night and day after day. Ninety thousand men carried in loads that varied from half a dozen to a couple of hundred: it is the most staggering measure of them all.

2

Between May 25th and June 5th 394 German planes were destroyed for the loss of 114 aircraft of the R.A.F.—a superiority of substantially more than three to one. This was the first great qualitative victory of the Allied air. It was the pattern for the Battle of Britain and for the great air defeats of Africa and the Mediterranean, of Italy and of France.

Yet all along, as with the daily record of the work of the R.A.F., it is essential to remember that it was not enough—the protection that it gave was inadequate. Whether it could have been greater is a matter for the historians of the future to decide. Unquestionably we could have put more planes over the Dunkirk area during the period of the operation. But the Air Staff had to look not only to the beaches but into the future. They had to preserve sufficient fighters to cover England in the invasion that all men thought must follow. The matter was one for a most delicate and a most difficult judgment; a balance between loss of aircraft and its possible reaction on future battles, and between loss of men and of ships and the possible reaction on land and on the sea.

The Admiralty throughout Dunkirk showed a boldness and a decision that is as fine as anything in its long and magnificent history. It counted the cost of the future submarine battles of the Atlantic then moving to a new and critical peak, and, counting them, it still found fresh destroyers to take the place of those that sank.

It is not possible to be certain that the losses of June 1st could have been avoided. It might well be that the cost in aircraft of complete protection would have been so great that the narrow margin of safety we possessed at the time of the Battle of Britain might have been dissipated. These are matters for historical speculation, and it is sufficient to say here that the margin of safety for the ships was calculated at a level desperately near disaster.

The greatest triumph of the sky was the magnificent courage, resource and skill of the handful of pilots who daily challenged the masses of the German air.

3

The British Army had made the retreat to Dunkirk possible by the stubbornness of its defence and the splendour of its discipline. The Royal Navy and the Merchant Navy together had made the evacuation possible by an unparalleled resolution.

There was still a third side to Dunkirk. It had no glory about it. It has achieved small recognition, but none the less it was an important part of the turmoil of those astonishing days. The navies brought the men of the armies to the dry land, to the decks of the piers and the stonework of the quays. After that the land took over: and somehow on the land an organization arose that dealt with the men as they landed, that fed them, gave them some means of communicating with their homes, patched the wounded, took care of the dying, and transported the fit men into the hinterland.

In its way the enthusiasm that made that possible was as remarkable as most things in the nine days. At Ramsgate the A.R.P. organizations and women's services combined to provide the canteens that met each party of men as it stumbled off the long arm of the eastern wall. They carried huge trays of cake and rolls and sandwiches, enormous cans of tea. Children carried stacks of postcards and pencils, and collected them as the men scribbled a brief message upon each. There were nurses from voluntary and official organizations that met each party to dress minor wounds or to move men more seriously hurt to improvised dressing stations in the fun fair that was called, with a strange irony, 'Merrie England'. And to keep those parties going all Ramsgate and Margate and the villages round about threw in their effort. Bread was a primary necessity. For days it was almost impossible to buy a loaf in the shops and local bakers'. Flour was commandeered and hundreds of housewives settled down, away from excitement, away from recognition, to work solidly at their ovens for days on end turning the flour into cake and biscuits.

And what happened in Ramsgate and its fellow towns, what its A.R.P. and its women's services, its clubs and its leagues did there, was done at Sheerness and Margate, at Dover and Folkestone and Newhaven.

And as the men passed through the first line, as it were, of welcome, they went into official hands again. Buses waited at the gates of the dock areas: they filed into them, an endless khaki stream, and the buses never failed them. They were taken off to the stations, and the Southern Railway took over. There again was a masterpiece of organization. Almost at an hour's notice the Southern Railway adapted its schedules to take on a stream that amounted to as many as 60,000 men a day. Normal passenger services were ruthlessly truncated. The Southern had to lift a flow that rose to nearly 70,000 men in a single day, and to take a very high proportion of them right through the complex of the London systems and up into the north of England. And one line, one of the best, was taken up almost entirely with the traffic of the wounded—the line from Newhaven through Brighton—a difficult traffic, needing much rolling stock and much care. The railways' contribution was a tremendous one. At no time did the High Command have to fear the annihilation of large numbers of men by attacks on congested areas at the ports of disembarkation. That is the measure of the 'Southern's' work.

And even along the railway there was more hospitality. Stops were arranged at varying points where the trains waited for ten minutes or a quarter of an hour and voluntary workers on the platforms passed food, tea and cigarettes into the waiting trains.

And there was still another facet of these movements. France was breaking, but she was not yet broken. The French whom we snatched out of the very hands of the Germans in the last days were desperately needed in the plans that were still being made to check the onslaught of the panzers. As fast as they were landed the French were entrained and moved westwards, clean across the main flow from the ports, to Southampton, Weymouth and Plymouth. Behind these ports concentration areas were established, and then out of our small reserve of personnel ships—cross-Channel steamers that could carry troops—we organized a repatriation service. French assistance was forthcoming, and for many days the service ran, moving men back to Brest and Cherbourg. How heavy a burden that transport involved upon our limited facilities is indicated by the fact that as many as five ships sailed in a single night from Southampton alone.

These things have small glory, but they were an integral part of Dunkirk —a necessary, a vital part.

CHAPTER XVII

THIS WAS DUNKIRK

' When a week ago I asked theHouse to fix this afternoon for a statement, I feared it would be my hard lot to announce from this box the greatest military disaster in our long history.
' I thought, and some good judges agreed with me, that perhaps from 20,000 to 30,000 men might be re-embarked, but it certainly seemed that the whole of the French First Army and the whole of the British Expeditionary Force north of Amiens and the Abbeville gap would be broken up in the field or else have to capitulate for lack of food and ammunition.
' This was the hard and heavy tidings for which I called on the House and the nation to prepare themselves a week ago.'
(RT. HON. WINSTON CHURCHILL, C.H., M.P.
House of Commons, 4th June, 1940)

Not 20,000 men but 337,131 came safe to the ports of England. This was Dunkirk. Because of these things the name of Dunkirk has passed into the English language as a synonym for deliverance.

The Germans have called it a defeat. Militarily it was a disaster—one of the great disasters in the history of war—for with it an empire fell, and the great and warlike tradition of the French people was buried in a deep and bitter dust.

It was a defeat; but out of it sprang a resurgence of national spirit that will stand for all time among the great things of history. Out of the gallantry with which the British Expeditionary Force fell back from the Dyle, unbroken, to the perimeter of the seaport town; out of the courage with which the men of the Royal Navy, the men of the Merchant Navy, the men of the fishing vessels, the small boats and the yachts went out from these shores to match their courage with that of the army along the desperate beaches, there was born a new spirit in Britain.

The stories that have been told in these pages are simple: some of them ill written, most of them hampered with that tradition of silence that belongs to the sea. They are the plain, straightforward stuff of Dunkirk, and they are, because of that, more magnificent than any dressing of these ventures in the silver and gold of words could be. What these men have written they and their crews endured, and because of what they endured 337,000 men lived to carry on the fight for freedom.

APPENDIX A

FROM HIS MAJESTY THE KING TO THE PRIME MINISTER AND MINISTER OF DEFENCE, 4TH JUNE 1940

Buckingham Palace.

I wish to express my admiration of the outstanding skill and bravery shown by the three Services and the Merchant Navy in the evacuation of the British Expeditionary Force from Northern France. So difficult an operation was only made possible by brilliant leadership and an indomitable spirit among all ranks of the Force. The measure of its success—greater than we had dared to hope—was due to the unfailing support of the Royal Air Force and, in the final stages, the tireless efforts of naval units of every kind.

While we acclaim this great feat, in which our French Allies too have played so noble a part, we think with heartfelt sympathy of the loss and sufferings of those brave men whose self-sacrifice has turned disaster into triumph.

GEORGE R.I.

FROM THE BOARD OF ADMIRALTY, 4TH JUNE 1940

The Board of Admiralty congratulate all concerned in the successful evacuation of the British Expeditionary Force and the soldiers of the Allied armies from the Dunkirk area.

Their Lordships appreciate the splendid endurance with which all ships and personnel faced the continuous attack of enemy aircraft and the physical strain imposed by long hours of arduous work in narrow waters over many days.

The magnificent spirit of co-operation between the Navy, Army, Royal Air Force and Merchant Navy alone brought the operation to a successful conclusion.

The ready willingness with which seamen from every walk of life came forward to assist their brother seamen of the Royal Navy will not readily be forgotten.

Their Lordships also realize that success was only rendered possible by the great effort made by all shore establishments, and in particular by the Dover Command, who were responsible for the organization and direction of this difficult operation.

APPENDIX A

FROM THE MINISTER OF SHIPPING TO THE MASTERS OF SHIPS OF THE MERCHANT NAVY, 17TH JUNE 1940

I write on behalf of the Government to convey to you and to the members of your Ship's Company the gratitude and admiration felt for the help freely given and the courage and endurance displayed by you all in the evacuation from Dunkirk.

This operation, in which the Merchant Navy joined as partner with the fighting services, was carried to a successful conclusion in the face of difficulties never before experienced in war.

I am proud to pay tribute to your share and that of your Ship's Company in a great and humane adventure destined to occupy a place of honour in the pages of history.

(*Signed*) RONALD CROSS,
Minister of Shipping.

APPENDIX B

OFFICIAL LIST OF SHIPS WHICH TOOK PART IN
OPERATION 'DYNAMO', 26TH MAY–4TH JUNE 1940

PART I: BRITISH SHIPS
Asterisk (*) denotes ships sunk.

A.A. CRUISER
Calcutta

DESTROYERS

Anthony	*Intrepid*	*Venomous*
*Basilisk	*Ivanhoe*	*Verity*
Codrington	*Jaguar*	*Vimy*
Esk	*Javelin*	*Vivacious*
Express	*Keith	*Wakeful
Gallant	*Mackay*	*Whitehall*
*Grafton	*Malcolm*	*Whitshed*
*Grenade	*Montrose*	*Winchelsea*
Greyhound	*Sabre*	*Windsor*
Harvester	*Saladin*	*Wolfhound*
*Havant	*Scimitar*	*Wolsey*
Icarus	*Shikari*	*Worcester*
Impulsive	*Vanquisher*	

SLOOP
Bideford

CORVETTES

Guillemot	*Mallard*	*Sheldrake*
Kingfisher	*Shearwater*	*Widgeon*

GUNBOATS

Locust   *Mosquito

MINESWEEPERS

Albury	*Emperor of India*	*Halycon*
*Brighton Belle	*Fitzroy*	*Hebe*
Brighton Queen	*Glenavon*	*Kellett*
*Devonia	*Glengower*	*Leda*
Duchess of Fife	*Gossamer*	*Lydd*
Dundalk	*Gracie Fields	*Marmion*

246

APPENDIX B

Minesweepers—contd.

Medway Queen	Queen of Thanet	Snaefell
Niger	Ross	Speedwell
Oriole	Salamander	Sutton
Pangbourne	Saltash	*Waverley
Plinlimmon	Sandown	Westward Ho
Portsdown	Sharpshooter	Whippingham
Princess Elizabeth	*Skipjack	

Minesweeping Craft

Alcmaria	John and Nora	Relonzo
Arley	John Cattling	Renascent
Botanic	Lord Burham	Restrivo
Brock	*Lord Cavan	Rewga
*Calvi	Lord Collingwood	Rig
Clythness	Lord Grey	Sarah Hyde
Chico (E.S.)	Lord Hood	Sargasso
*Comfort	Lord Inchcape	Saturn
Conidaw	Lord Keith	Silver Dawn
Dorienta	Lord Melchett	Starlight Rays
Feasible	Lord Rodney	Stella Rigel
Fidget	Lord St. Vincent	Strathelliott
Fisher Boy	Mare	Strive
Fyldea	Maretta	Swift Wing
Genius	*Nautilus	Taransay
Gula	Olivae	*Thomas Bartlett
Gulzar	Our Bairns	Thomsons
Inverforth	Overfalls	Three Kings
Jacketa	*Polly Johnson	Tweenways
Jackeve	Reed	Unicity
Jeannie Macintosh		

Anti-Submarine Trawlers

*Argyllshire	Kingston Andalusite	Spurs
*Blackburn Rovers	Kingston Olivine	*Stella Dorado
Cape Argona	Lady Philomena	*Thuringia
Cayton Wyke	Olvina	Topaze
Grimsby Town	St. Achilleus	*Westella
Kingston Alalite	Saon	Wolves

Thames Special Service Ships

*Crested Eagle	Golden Eagle	Royal Eagle

M.A./S.B.s, M.T.B.s, Etc.

D.C. Motor-boat	M.A./S.B. 10	M.T.B. 68
(ex Excellent)	M.T.B. 16	M.L. 100
M.A./S.B. 6	M.T.B. 22	M.T.B. 102
M.A./S.B. 7	M.T.B. 67	M.T.B. 107

APPENDIX B

Dover Flare-Burning Drifters

*Boy Roy
Eileen Emma
Forecast
Gervais Rentoul
Girl Gladys
*Girl Pamela
Golden Gift
Golden Sunbeam
Lord Howard
Lord Howe
Midas
Netsukis
*Paxton
Shipmates
The Boys
Torbay II
Ut Prosim
Yorkshire Lass
Young Mun

Portsmouth A/P Yachts

Ahola
Anlah
Ankh
Bounty
Caryanda
Eila II
Lahloo
Marsayru
Noneta
Seriola
Thele

Miscellaneous H.M. Ships
(small craft)

A.L.C. 5
A.L.C. 15
A.L.C. 16
A.L.C. 17
Alouette II (Echo Sounding Yacht)
*Amulree (Harbour Defence Patrol Craft)
Aronia (Yacht)
Ben and Lucy (Drifter)
Bluebird (M.B.)
Bystander (Echo Sounding Yacht)
Caleta (Harbour Defence Patrol Craft)
Chrystobel II (Harbour Defence Patrol Craft)
Dolphin's motor-boat
Evelyn Rose (Trawler)
Excellent's A/A motor-boat
Gava (Trawler)
Glala (Harbour Defence Patrol Craft)
Grey Mist (D.A.N.-laying Vessel)
*Grive (F.A.A. Yacht)
Kindred Star (Drifter)
*King Orry (Armed Boarding Vessel)
Llanthony (Examination Service Vessel)
Lormont (Armed Boarding Vessel)
Monarda (Drifter)
Mona's Isle (Armed Boarding Vessel)
St. Olaves (Rescue Tug)
Turret (A/S Yacht)
Thrifty (Drifter)
V. 4 (Vernon's pinnace)
Vella (Armed Trawler)
Vernon I
Viviana (A/S Trawler)

Dutch Skoots
(Commissioned with Naval Crews)

Abel Tasman
Aegir
Alice
Amazone
Antje
Atlantic
Bart
Bornrif
Brandaris
Caribia
Delta
Demok I
Deneb
Despatch II
Doggersbank
Fredanja
Frisco
Gorecht
Hebe
Hilda
Hondsrug
Horst (abandoned)
Java
Jutland

APPENDIX B

Dutch Skoots—contd.

Kaapfalgia	Princess Juliana	Tiny
Lena	Reiger	Tung
Oranje	Rika	Twente
Orange Yreeswijh	Ruja	Vrede
Pacific	San Antonio	Zeus
Pascholl	Sursum Corda	
Patria	Tilly	

PERSONNEL AND HOSPITAL SHIPS

Archangel	Manxman
Autocarrier	*Mona's Queen
Ben-My-Chree	Newhaven [1]
Biarritz	Nephrite (Store Ship)
Canterbury	Ngaroma
Clan MacAlister	*Normannia
Cote d'Argent [1]	Paris (Hospital)
*Cote d'Azur [1]	Prague
Dinard (Hospital)	Princess Maud
Dorrien Rose (Store Ship)	Queen of the Channel
*Fenella	Roebuck
Foam Queen	Rouen [1]
Isle of Guernsey (Hospital)	Royal Daffodil
Isle of Thanet (Hospital)	Royal Sovereign
Killarney	St. Andrew (Hospital)
King George V	St. David (Hospital)
Lady of Mann	St. Helier
Levenwood (Store Ship)	St. Julien
Lochgarry	St. Seiriol
*Lorina	*Scotia
Maid of Orleans	Tynwald
Malines	Worthing (Hospital)
Manxmaid	Whitstable

OTHER BRITISH SHIPS

Adventuress	Bat (Lighter)
Agnes Cross (Lifeboat)	Bee (Lighter)
Albatross III	Belfast
Alouette	Black Arrow
Andora	Black Java
Andora II (R.A.F. Launch)	Blackpool
Anne IV	Bobelli (Motor-cruiser)
Athola	Bonny Heather
Aura	Bonny Belle
Bail	Bournemouth Lifeboat

[1] French vessels working with British personnel ships.

B.P. One
Britannia
Bullfinch
Cabby
Canvey Queen
Caversham (M.B.)
Chamois (Lighter)
Cherfield
*Claude (Water Boat)
Commodore
Constant Nymph
Cordelia
Cornelia
C. 9 ⎱
C. 11 ⎰ (Tugs)
C.Y. 63
Dabb II
Defender
Dhoon (Trawler)
Dogger Bank
Doria (Tug)
Dreadnought II
Dreadnought III
Duchess of York
Dwarf
D. 1 ⎱
D. 4 ⎪
D. 7 ⎬ (Harbour Launches)
D. 9 ⎪
D. 16 ⎰
D.C. 715
D.G. 694
D.G. 950
Eastbourne Lifeboat
Edward Nissen
Edwina (Trawler)
Elizabeth Queen
E.M.E.D. (Motor Lifeboat)
Empress
Emprise (Harbour Launch)
Endeavour
Enterprise
Erica
Eskburn
Fair Breeze (Drifter)

Fawley (Gosport Ferry)
Ferry King (Gosport Ferry)
Fervent
Fishbourne (I.O.W. Ferry)
Foremost 22 (Hopper Barge)
Foremost 87 (Tug)
Formidable
Forsa
*Fossa
Frightened Lady
F.W. 23 (Lighter)
Galleon's Reach (Hopper)
Gay Crusader
Glenway (Barge)
Glitter II
Goliath
Gourka
Grace Darling
Grappler (Lighter)
Greater London Lifeboat
Gondia (Tug)
H. 75
Haig (W.D. Craft)
Halfway
Handy Billy
Hastings Lifeboat
Holland
Hopper 26
Hound (Lighter)
Hythe (Coaster)
Iolanthe
Iote
Irma Maria (Fishing Boat)
Jaba
Jacinta (Trawler)
James 67 (Hopper Barge)
Janis
Johanna (Eel Boat)
Jong
Jordan
Kayell
Kestrel
Kingsgate
Kitcat (Motor-boat)
Lady Brassey (Rescue Tug)

Lady Cable (Motor-boat)
Lady Sheila
Lady Southborough (Hopper Barge)
Lansdowne
Laroc
Laudania
Letitia (Smack)
Little Ann (Motor-boat)
Lotus
Louisiana
Madame Sans Gêne
Ma Joie
Malden
Malden Annie IV
Marasole
Margherita
Marlborough (W.D. Craft)
Marquis (Tug)
*Mary Rose
Mary Spearing I
Mary Spearing II
Massey Shaw (Fire Float)
Mayspear
Meander
Mermaiden (Motor Launch)
M.F.H. (Lighter)
Michael Stevens
Minekoi (Tug)
Minoru II (Motor-boat)
Minwood
Monarch
Motor-boat 42
    ,,   27B
    ,,   43 R.A.F.
    ,,   101 ,,
    ,,   102 ,,
*   ,,   243 ,,
    ,,   270 ,,
    ,,   275 ,,
M.L. 8 (W.D. Craft)
Murious
Naiad Errant
Nanette (Motor-launch)
Nelson (Motor-boat)
Nemo IV

Newhaven Lifeboat
New Prince of Wales
No. 4 ⎫
No. 101 ⎬ (Hopper Barges)
No. 102 ⎭
Ocean Breeze
Offeria
Olivia
Orient Line Motor-boat
Pauleter
Peggy IV
Pellag II
Persia (Tug)
Pigeon (W.D. Craft)
Pioneer
Prima (Tug)
Prince of Wales
Princess Freda
Princess Lily
Pudge
Queen
Queen Alexandra
Queen Boadicea II
Queen's Channel (Hopper Barge)
Queensland
Quicksilver
Qui Si Sana (Motor-boat)
Ramsgate Lifeboat
Rapide
Reda (Motor-boat)
Reliance
*Renown
Resolute
Ricas
Robert Cliff
Rosa Wood and Phyllis Lund
Rowan (Smack)
Rygate II (Yacht)
St. Abbs
St. Clears
*St. Fagan
St. Olaf
Sambra (Motor-boat)
Saviour
Scene Shifter

Scottish Co-operator
Sea Falcon
Sea Foam
Seasalter
Seine
Shamrock
Sherfield (Motor-barge)
Silicia (Coaster)
Silver Foam
*Silver Queen (Motor-boat)
Silvery Breeze
Singapore
Skylark (abandoned)
Skylark I
Skylark II
Skylark VI
Small Viking
Southend Britannia
Speedwell
Sprite (Harbour Launch)
Sultan
Sun IV ⎫
Sun X ⎬ (Tugs)
Sun XI ⎭
Swallow
S.O. One
Tanga (Tug)
Thark
Tenias
Thyforsa

Thyra
Tony
Triton
Tug XV
Two Rivers (Motor-boat)
37270
Vanguard
Vera (Motor-boat)
Viewfinder
Viking (Motor-barge)
Vincia (Tug)
Walmer Castle
Walton and Frinton Lifeboat
Warrior
Wave Queen (Motor-boat)
Wessex (Lighter)
West Cove
Westgrove
White Bear
White Heather (Motor-boat)
White Wings (Motor-boat)
Wolfe (W.D. Craft)
Wootton (I.O.W. Ferry)
W. 24 (Hopper Barge)
X. 95 ⎫
X. 134 ⎬(Lighters)
X. 209 ⎭
Y.C. 63 ⎫
Y.C. 71 ⎬ (Lighters)
Y.C. 72 ⎭

PART II: FOREIGN WARSHIPS

POLISH
Blyskawica

FRENCH

Amiens
Amiral Mouchez
Arras
Belfort
Bouclier
*Bourrasque
Branlebas
Cyclone

Diligente
Epervier
Flore
*Foudroyant
Impetueuse
Incomprise
Leopard
Marceau

Mistral
M.T.B. 24
Simoun
*Siroco
T. 112
T. 113
T. 143

DUTCH
Netherland Motor-boat M. 74

PART III: FOREIGN SHIPS, OTHER THAN WARSHIPS

Abel Dewulf
*Ambleve (Belgian Launch)
André Louis
André Marcel
Angele
Arras
Ausa
A. 5 (Belgian Patrol Craft)
A. 73 (Belgian Patrol Craft)
A.D. 389
Barbara Auguste
Belge
Bernadette de Lisieux
Besta (Dutch)
Bordeaux
Caporal Pungest
Chalutier
Chantecler (Dutch Eel Boat)
Chasse Rave
Chasseur
Chasseur 7th
Chasseur Marrie
Cods Cenade
Commandant Delage
Constant Leopold
Cor Jesu (Belgian Trawler O. 227)
Cul de France
Dame Franche
Devin Papin
Drifter 145 (Belgian)
*Duperre (French Trawler)
Dutch Daffil
Dutch M.V.M.
*Emile Deschamps
Emile Lastus
Emile Louise
*Escaut (Belgian Launch)
Fransah
Gamboul
Gaston River
Gativois
Georges Edouard (Belgian Trawler [O. 86)

Guido Gazelle (Belgian Trawler
Hdaya   [O. 225)
H. 51 (Belgian Trawler)
H. 75 (Belgian Trawler)
Ingenieur Cachin
Jean Bart
Jean Ribault
Jeune France
Jonge Jan (Belgian Trawler O. 200)
La Cere
Louise Marie
Lucien Gaigy
Lutter
Mana Elena
*Maréchal Foch (Belgian Trawler)
Meuse (Belgian Launch)   [O. 274)
Monique
Moya
M. 2 (French Trawler)
Normanville
N. 53 (Barge)
Onder Ons
O. 87 ⎫
O. 92 ⎬ (Belgian Trawlers)
O. 318 ⎭
Patrie (French Trawler)
*Pierre Marie (French Drifter)
Pinette
President Buars
Puisse Marie
Reine de Flots
Sambre (Belgian Launch)
Sarzik
*Semois (Belgian Launch)
Sideres Louise
Surcouf de Guesclin
Thérésé Louise
V.P. 19 (French Barge)
Watonprise
*Yser (Belgian Launch)
Z. 25 ⎫
Z. 26 ⎬ (Belgian Trawlers)
Z. 40 ⎭

MINISTRY OF WAR TRANSPORT LIST OF VESSELS, MASTERS AND OWNERS OF PRINCIPAL PERSONNEL
SHIPS, MERCHANT VESSELS AND TUGS WHICH TOOK PART IN OPERATION 'DYNAMO'

Name of Ship	Name of Owners	Name of Master
*Abukir	General Steam Navigation Co., Ltd.	Captain R. M. Woolfenden
Beal	Tyne-Tees Steam Shipping Co., Ltd. ..	Captain Liley
Bulfinch ..	General Steam Navigation Co., Ltd. ..	Captain H. Buxton
Clewbay ..	John Kelly Ltd.	Captain D. B. Ivor
Corinia ..	Northwest Shipping Co., Ltd. ..	Captain J. R. Hughes
Dorrien Rose ..	Richard Hughes & Co. (Liverpool) Ltd. ..	Captain W. Thompson
*Firth Fisher	James Fisher & Sons, Ltd.	Captain J. O. Roberts
Foam Queen	British Channel Islands Shipping Co., Ltd.	Captain A. T. Mastin
Gateshead ..	Tyne-Tees Steam Shipping Co., Ltd. ..	Captain J. R. Linn
Hythe	Southern Railway Co., Ltd.	Captain R. W. Morford
Levenwood ..	Joseph Constantine Steamship Line Ltd. ..	Captain W. O. Young
Lowick	Tyne-Tees Steam Shipping Co., Ltd. ..	Captain T. F. Stewart
Nephrite ..	Stephenson Clarke & Associated Companies Ltd.	Captain C. G. West, O.B.E.
Ngaroma ..	W. A. Wilson	Captain J. W. Dickenson
Sandhill ..	Tyne-Tees Steam Shipping Co., Ltd. ..	Captain E. Wilson
Scottish Co-operator	Scottish Co-operative Wholesale Society Ltd.	Captain T. S. Robertson
*Sequacity ..	F. T. Everard & Sons Ltd.	Captain J. MacDonald
Sodality ..	F. T. Everard & Sons, Ltd.	Captain W. Roberts
Westown ..	Comben Longstaff & Co., Ltd.	Captain R. A. Shanks
Whitstable ..	Southern Railway Co., Ltd.	Captain W. Baxter
Williamstown	Comben Longstaff & Co., Ltd. ..	Captain M. McInnes
*Worthtown ..	Comben Longstaff & Co., Ltd. ..	Captain R. Thomas
Tewdale	John Stewart & Co. Shipping Ltd. ..	Captain E. Jones
Teviglen	John Stewart & Co. Shipping Ltd. ..	Captain R. Thomas

Name of Ship	Name of Owners	Name of Master
Clan MacAlister	Clan Line Steamers Ltd.	Captain R. W. Mackie
Roebuck	c/o Chief Docks Manager, Great Western Railway Co., Ltd.	Captain W. Larbalestier
Kitty	Basso & Co.	Mr. W. McCondach
¹Spinel	William Robertson Ltd.	Captain R. Humphreys
Queen of the Channel	General Steam Navigation Co., Ltd.	Captain W. J. O'Dell
Royal Daffodil	General Steam Navigation Co., Ltd.	Captain G. Johnston
Royal Sovereign	General Steam Navigation Co., Ltd.	Captain T. Aldis
Mona's Queen	Isle of Man Steam Packet Co., Ltd.	Captain A. Holkham / Captain R. Duggan
Fenella	Isle of Man Steam Packet Co., Ltd.	Captain W. Cubbon
Manxman	Isle of Man Steam Packet Co., Ltd.	Captain P. B. Cowley
Tynwald	Isle of Man Steam Packet Co., Ltd.	Captain W. A. Qualtrough / Chief Officer J. Whiteway
Lady of Mann	Isle of Man Steam Packet Co., Ltd.	Captain T. C. Woods / Chief Officer T. Cain
Lorina	Southern Railway Co., Ltd.	Captain A. Light
Normannia	Southern Railway Co., Ltd.	Captain M. C. Whiting
Canterbury	Southern Railway Co., Ltd.	Captain C. Hancock
Maid of Orleans	Southern Railway Co., Ltd.	Captain A. E. Larkins / Captain G. Walker
Biarritz	Southern Railway Co., Ltd.	Captain M. H. Baker
Autocarrier	Southern Railway Co., Ltd.	Captain C. Masters
Princess Maud	London, Midland & Scottish Railway Co., Ltd.	Captain H. Clarke
Scotia	London, Midland & Scottish Railway Co., Ltd.	Captain H. W. Hughes
St. Seiriol	Liverpool & North Wales S.S. Co., Ltd.	Captain R. D. Dobb
Prague	London & North-Eastern Railway Co., Ltd.	Captain C. Baxter

¹ Ordered to Dunkirk with petrol, but did not evacuate troops.

Name of Ship	Name of Owners	Name of Master
King George V	David MacBrayne Ltd.	Captain R. E. MacLean
Lochgarry	David MacBrayne Ltd.	Captain E. MacKinnon
Killarney	Coast Lines, Ltd.	Captain R. Hughes
St. Helier	Great Western Railway Co., Ltd.	Captain R. Pitman
St. Julien	Great Western Railway Co., Ltd.	Captain L. S. Richardson
St. Andrew	Great Western Railway Co., Ltd.	Captain H. C. Bond
St. David	Great Western Railway Co., Ltd.	Captain C. Joy / Captain B. H. Mendus
Paris	Southern Railway Co., Ltd.	Captain E. Biles
Isle of Guernsey	Southern Railway Co., Ltd.	Captain F. W. Hodges
Dinard	Southern Railway Co., Ltd.	Captain P. Lewis / Captain J. A. Jones
Worthing	Southern Railway Co., Ltd.	Captain C. J. Munton
Isle of Thanet	Southern Railway Co., Ltd.	Captain A. J. Hammond

Tug	Owners	Master
Sun	W. H. J. Alexander Ltd.	H. Cole
Sun III	W. H. J. Alexander Ltd.	F. Russell
Sun IV	W. H. J. Alexander Ltd.	C. Alexander
Sun V	W. H. J. Alexander Ltd.	W. Mastin
Sun VII	W. H. J. Alexander Ltd.	G. Cawsey
Sun VIII	W. H. J. Alexander Ltd.	S. Smith
Sun X	W. H. J. Alexander Ltd.	W. Fothergill
Sun XI	W. H. J. Alexander Ltd.	J. Lukes
Sun XII	W. H. J. Alexander Ltd.	B. Mastin (Navigating Master) / A. V. Mee (Towing Master on board whole trip)

Tug	Owners	Master
Sun XV	W. H. J. Alexander Ltd.	J. Belton
Contest	Elliott Steam Tug Co., Ltd.	H. Bates
Challenge	Elliott Steam Tug Co., Ltd.	C. Parker
Fossa	Gaselee & Son, Ltd.	G. Finch
Betty	Gaselee & Son, Ltd.	G. Leeks
Crested Cock	The Gamecock Steam Towing Co.	T. Hills
Ocean Cock	The Gamecock Steam Towing Co.	A. V. Mastin
Foremost 87	Managed by W. Watkins, Ltd.	J. Fryer
Fairplay I	Managed by W. Watkins, Ltd.	S. Wright
Cervia	William Watkins, Ltd.	W. Simmonds
Doria	William Watkins, Ltd.	A. Mastin
Fabia	William Watkins, Ltd.	F. Smith
Gondia	William Watkins, Ltd.	C. Pratt
Hibernia	William Watkins, Ltd.	B. Youseman
Java	William Watkins, Ltd.	W. Jones
Kenia	William Watkins, Ltd.	W. Hoiles
Persia	William Watkins, Ltd.	H. Aldrich
Racia	William Watkins, Ltd.	C. Addison
Simla	William Watkins, Ltd.	G. Lowe
Tanga	William Watkins, Ltd.	H. Gouge
Vincia	William Watkins, Ltd.	A. Hoiles
Empire Henchman	United Towing Co., Ltd.	E. Fisher
Foremost 22	Southern Railway Co., Ltd.	{ C. L. Fieldgate { F. Holden (acting for one trip)
Lady Brassey	Dover Harbour Board	{ G. W. Blackmore { F. J. Hopgood

The Ministry of War Transport gives the following list of small craft utilized in the operation. These vessels were taken up in connection with the operation and left their home ports. Not all of them reached Ramsgate, and of those that reached Ramsgate not all reached Dunkirk. But in the confusion of the times it was impossible to keep an absolute record, and this list must stand as the basic list for the operation.

Ace	Brenart	Desiree
Ada Mary	Britannia IV	Devilfish
Adeline	*Britannic	Diamond
Advance	Brywyn	Diana Mary
Aid	*Bull Pup	Diante
*Albatross	Burgonia	Dianthus
Aljanor	Burton	*Dinky (10-foot boat)
Aloa-Oc	Cachalot	D.L.G.
Aloha	Cairngorm	Dolphin
Amity	Camellia	Doreen
*Anee (Wherry)	*Carama (15-foot punt)	Dorian
Anne	Caraid	*Doris (Wherry)
Anthony	Carmen	*Dreadnought II
Antoinette	Caronia	*Dreadnought III
Aqua Belle	Caversham	Duchess of York
Ashingdon	Cecille	Duke
Auntie Gus	Cervates	*Dumplin (Boat)
Aura	Chamois	Eastbourne Belle
Balquhain	Chantecler	*Eastbourne Queen
Barbara	Charlotte	*Edina (Wherry)
Barbill II	Chriscraft (25 feet)	Edna
Basildon	*Clara Belle (Wherry)	Edward & Mary
Bat	*Commodore	*Edwina
Bee	Constant Nymph	Elaine
Bessie	Cora-Ann	Elizabeth Green
Betty	Cordelia	Ella
*Beverley	Corsair	Elvin
Bhurana	Count Dracula	*Empress
*Black Arrow	Court Belle II	*Enchantress
Blue Bird (1)	Creole	Encourage
Blue Bird (2)	Cruiser	Endeavour
*Boat (16 feet)	Curlew	Enterprise
*Bobeli	*Cyb	Eothen
*Bonnibell	Dab II	Eric
Bonny Heather	Dandy	E.R.V.
Bou Saada	Daphne	Esperanza
Boy Billy	Dawn	Ethel Ellen
Boy Bruce	Deenar	Ethel Maud
Boy Fred	Defender	*Ex-Service Dinghy
Bread Winner	Desel II	Fairwind

Faith
Falcon II
Favourite SM 225
Fedelma II
Felicity
Ferry Nymph
Firefly
Fleet Wing
Floss Hilda
Folkestone Belle
Formosa
Fortuna
Forty Two
Fram
Francis (99B)
Gavine
Gay Crusader
Gay Fly
Gay Venture
Gertrude
Gipsy King
Girl Nancy
Girl Vine
Golden Lily
Golden Spray
*Golden Spray II
Gondolier King
Gondolier Queen
Gondolier III
Good Hope
Good Luck
Grace
Grace Darling IV
Grace Darling (E 36)
*Green Eagle
Greta
Gwenny
Handy Billie
*Hanora
Hastaway
Hawfinch
*Hazard
Heather-Bell LN 101
Henry Harris
Hilda
Hilfranor

His Majesty
Hound
Hurlingham
Idaho
Imshi
Industry
Inspiration II
Iota
*Iote
Irma
Irenic
*Island Queen
Jane Hannah
Jeff
Jetsam
Jockett II
Jong
Karina
Kayell
Kestrel R 7
King
King Fisher
Kingwood
Kintail
Kitcat
Kitty
Kongoni
Lady Cable
Lady Haig
Lady Isabelle
Lady Kay
Lady Nancy
Lady Rita
*Lady Rosebery
Lamouette
Lansdowne
*Lark
Latona
Laurel Leaf
Lavinia
Lazy Days
Leach's Romance
Leading Star
Leila 4
Lent Lily
*Letitia (1)

Letitia (2)
Liebestraum
Lijns
*Little Ann
Little Admiral LN 85
Little Mayflower
Little O' Lady
Lorna Doone
Lurline
Lydie Suzanne
Madame Pompadour
*Madame Sans Gêne
*Maid of Honour
*Ma Joie
Major
*Maldon Annie
Malvina
Marasole
Marchioness
Mare Nostrum
Margaret Mary
*Margherita
Marina
Marsayru
Mary
Mary Irene
Mary Jane
Mary Rose
*Mary Spearing
Mary Spearing II
Mata Hari
Matilda
Matoya
Mayflower
May Queen SM 270
Meander
*Medora (Wherry)
Mermaiden
Mersey
M.F.H.
Millicent D. Leach
Mimosa
*Minikoi
Minnedosa
Minoru II
Minotaur

Minx
*Miranda No. 58 boat
Miss Ming
Miss Modesty
Mizpah
M.L. 108
Moiena
Monarch
*Montague (Whaler)
*Moss Rose
Motor-boat (36 feet)
Motor-boat (30 feet)
M.T.B. M.2
Mousme
Murius
Mutt
Naiad Errant
Nancy Belle
Nanette II
Narcissa
Nautilus A
*Nemo IV
New Prince of Wales
*New White Heather
New Windsor Castle
Nin
Nirvana
No Name II
Norwich Belle
Offemia
Omega
Ona II
Oratava RX 45
Orellana
Oulton Belle
Our Lizzie
Our Maggie
Palmerston
Pandora
Papillon
Papkura
Pauleter
Pearl
*Peggy IV
Petra
Pioneer

Polly
Pride of Folkestone
Prince
Prince of Wales
Princess
Princess Freda
Princess Lily
*Princess Maud
Providence
Provider R 19
Queen
Queen Alexandra
Queen Boadicea
Queen Boadicea II
*Queen of England
Quicksilver
Q.J. & J.
Quisiana
Quest
Rapide
Rayon
Reda
Reliance
Remembrance
*Renown
Resolute
*Roberta
Robina Tenant
Rocinante
*Rosabelle
Rose
Rose LN 19
Roselyne
Rose Marie
Royal Thames
Rummy II
Ryegate II
St. Patrick
Sally Forth
Salvage Launch
Sandown
Santosy
Sarah & Emily
Satyr
Scene Shifter
Schedar

*Sea Falcon
Sea Foam
Seagull
Seagull LN 203
Sea Hawk
Sea Roamer
Seasalter
Seaschool
Sea Swallow
Seymour Castle
*Shamrock
Shannon
Sheldrake
Shunesta
Silver Foam
Silver Spray
Silver Spray LI 230
Silvery Breeze
Sinbad II
Singapore I
Singapore II
Skylark (1)
Skylark (2)
Skylark I
Skylark II
*Skylark II SM. 281
*Skylark III
*Skylark III SM 391
Skylark IV SM 5
Skylark VI
Skylark IX
Skylark X
Smiling Through
Smolt
Smuggler
Snow Bunting
Sonia
Southend Britannia
Southern Queen
*Southern Queen PL 17
South Ray
Spinaway
Spindrift
Starfish
Stonehaven
Suffolk's Rose

Summer Maid
Sundowner
*Sunshine R 13
Surrey
Sylvia
Tankerton Towers
Tarpon
Thark
*Thetis
Three Brothers
Thurn
Thyme
Tigris I
Tom Hill
Trillene
Triton
Tony LN 40
Tortoise
Two Rivers

Two Sisters
Unique
Usanco
Valerie
Vanguard
*Vanitee
Vedettes
Venture
Vera
Victoria
*Viewfinder
Viking
*Viking III
Viscount
Volante R 110
Volo
Waikakei II
Wanda
Warrior (1)

Warrior (2)
Wave Queen
Welcome
Westall
Westerley
Westward
Weymouth Queen
White Bear
White Lady
White Orchid
Whitewater
Whitewing
*Willie & Alice
Windsong
Wings of the Morning
Winmabet
Winston
Wolsey
Yola

APPENDIX C

DUNKIRK HONOURS AND AWARDS

STAFF AND SHORE PARTIES

K.C.B. (MILITARY)
  Vice-Admiral Bertram Home Ramsay, C.B., M.V.O., Flag Officer Commanding, Dover.
C.B. (MILITARY)
  Rear-Admiral William Frederick Wake-Walker, O.B.E.
  Captain William George Tennant, M.V.O., R.N.
  Captain Michael Maynard Denny, R.N.
C.B.E. (MILITARY)
  Captain (Commodore 2nd Class) Edward Glyn de Styrap Jukes-Hughes, R.N. (Retd.).
  Captain William Raigersfield Phillimore, R.N. (Retd.)
O.B.E. (MILITARY)
  Commander Robert Gordon Hood Linzee, R.N. (Retd.)
  Acting Commander Philip Brian Martineau, R.N. (Retd.)
  Lieutenant-Commander James Coverley Stopford, R.N.
  Major (Temporary) Arthur Edward Mervyn Walter, B.A., R.E.
  Captain (Temporary) Lancelot Edwin Lax Wright, R.A.
O.B.E. (CIVIL)
  James Leonard Keith, Esq., Commercial Assistant, Ministry of Shipping.
M.B.E. (MILITARY)
  Acting Inspector of Shipwrights Frederick Hercules Harvey.
B.E.M. (MILITARY)
  Acting Master-at-Arms Sidney Welfare, C/M 36212.
  Chief Petty Officer Telegraphist Alexander Arthur Lee, C/J 96386.
  Chief Shipwright Joseph William Heathcote, P/M 23064.
  Chief Engine Room Artificer Reginald Francis Fox, P/M 5545.
  Chief Stoker Herbert John Baxter, C/K 2659.
  Sick Berth Petty Officer Cecil Ernest Jelley, C/M 39618.
B.E.M. (CIVIL)
  Skilled Labourer George Victor Bonnett (Chatham Dockyard 3828).
  Acting Assistant Foreman of Storehouses Clifford James Hartfree.
D.S.O.
  Captain Eric Wheler Bush, D.S.C., R.N.
  Captain Michael Oliver Dundas Ellwood, R.N. (Retd.)
  Commander Reginald Wastell English, R.N. (Retd.)
  Commander Renfrew Gotto, R.N.
  Commander Edward Reginald Lewis, R.N. (Retd.)

APPENDIX C

Commander Guy Oakley Maund, R.N. (Retd.)
Commander Hector du Plessis Richardson, R.N.
Commander Richard Cyril Vesey Ross, R.N.
Commander Villiers Nicholas Surtees, R.N.
Acting Commander Kenneth Morland Greig, R.N. (Retd.)
Lieutenant-Commander Neville Lionel John Pisani, D.S.C., R.N. (Retd.)
Lieutenant Robert Bill, R.N.

BAR TO D.S.C.

Lieutenant-Commander John Mark Symonds Cox, D.S.C., R.N.
Lieutenant-Commander Arthur Jelfs Cubison, D.S.C., R.N. (Retd.)

D.S.C.

Lieutenant-Commander Stratford Hercules Dennis, R.N.
Lieutenant-Commander Redvers Michael Prior, R.N. (Retd.)
Lieutenant-Commander John Bruce Goodenough Temple, R.N.
Lieutenant-Commander Harold Unwin, R.N.
Lieutenant-Commander Cecil John Wynne-Edwards, R.N.
Lieutenant Christopher William Stuart Dreyer, R.N.
Lieutenant Joseph Cox, R.N.R.
Lieutenant Tom Preston Graham, R.N.R.
Temporary Lieutenant Cedric Victor Brammell, R.N.R.
Temporary Lieutenant F. L. Davies, R.N.V.R.
Sub-Lieutenant George Arthur Gabbett-Mulhallen, R.N.
Sub-Lieutenant Martin Herbert Bernhard Soloman, R.N.V.R.
Probationary Temporary Sub-Lieutenant Jack Mason, R.N.V.R.
Temporary Skipper George William Aldan, R.N.R., W.S. 1014.
Temporary Skipper Edward Frederick Dettman, R.N.R., W.S. 3306.
Temporary Skipper Alfred Manning Lovis, R.N.R., W.S. 3397.
Temporary Skipper James Henry Mugridge, R.N.R., W.S. 3018.

BAR TO D.S.M.

Able Seaman Arthur Victor Johnson, P/J 24734.

D.S.M

Petty Officer Frederick William Parker, C/J 84930.
Petty Officer Thomas A. Topley, O/J 112800.
Acting Petty Officer Ernest Wilfred Spickett, JX 128246.
Yeoman of Signals Geoffrey Piper, C/JX 132686.
Leading Seaman Hugh James Spanton, C/J 114468.
Able Seaman Walter F. Cox, R.F.R., B 22716.
Able Seaman Carl Leonard Fletcher, C/SS 10579, R.F.R., D 941.
Able Seaman Harold Fletcher, C/J 99712.
Able Seaman Charles Lawrence Montagu Foster, C/JX 135628.
Able Seaman J. L. Fraser.
Able Seaman Robert Houghton Fry, C/JX 144641.
Able Seaman William Charles Grainger, C/SSX 22139.
Able Seaman George Arthur Hall, C/J 43442, B 21047.
Able Seaman Robin Lancaster, C/JX 129630.
Able Seaman Francis H. McLaughlin, C/JX 146012.

APPENDIX C

Able Seaman Alexander C. Moore, C/JX 129026.
Able Seaman George Frederick Nixon, C/SSX 12961.
Able Seaman James G. Owen, R.F.R., B 20977.
Able Seaman Gilbert Rose, C/JX 151776.
Able Seaman Thomas Douglas David Sones, C/JX 145091.
Able Seaman John Doig Stewart, C/SSX 20706.
Able Seaman John William Swales, C/JX 152505.
Able Seaman Joseph L. Turner, C/SSX 24037.
Signalman Richard Franklyn Jones, C/JX 144282.
Signalman Joseph Mulheron, C/JX 133241.
Signalman Ernest Renfree Robinson, C/JX 145689.
Signalman Donald Wallace Simmonds, C/JX 133346.
Signalman Arthur Waters, C/JX 142009.
Signalman Ernest Reginald Savidge, R.N.V.R., P/LD/X 5433.
Sick Berth Attendant Stanley John Lively, C/SBR/X 8022.
Ordinary Seaman William J. Edward Burrows, C/JX 154411.
Ordinary Seaman Frederick William Garrott, C/JX 172487.
Ordinary Seaman Sydney V. Genner, C/JX 150954.
Ordinary Seaman Andrew McKay H. Miller, C/JX 174079.
Stoker Thornley Coltman, C/KX 88357.

MENTION IN DISPATCHES

Vice-Admiral Sir James Fownes Somerville, K.C.B., D.S.O. (Retd.)
Vice-Admiral Gilbert Owen Stephenson, C.B., C.M.G. (Commodore, 2nd Class) (Retd.)
Vice-Admiral Theodore John Hallett, C.B., C.B.E. (Commodore, 2nd Class) (Retd.)
Rear-Admiral Alfred Hugh Taylor, O.B.E. (Commodore, 2nd Class) (Retd.)
Rear-Admiral John Stewart Gordon Fraser, D.S.O. (Commodore, 2nd Class) (Retd.)
Captain Lionel George Dawson, R.N. (Retd.)
Captain John George Lawrence Dundas, R.N.
Captain John Fawcett, R.N. (Retd.)
Captain William Vesey Hamilton Harris, M.V.O., D.S.C., R.N. (Retd.)
Captain John Montagu Howson, R.N.
Captain Llewellyn Vaughan Morgan, C.B.E., M.V.O., D.S.C., R.N.
Engineer Captain John Lewis Deacon, M.V.O., R.N. (Retd.)
Surgeon Captain Arthur Rowland Fisher, R.N. (Retd.)
Commander Harold Robson Conway, R.N.
Commander Lewes George Gardner, R.N. (Retd.)
Commander Harold Pitcairn Henderson, R.N.
Commander Francis John Lambert, D.S.C., R.N. (Retd.)
Commander Robert Jocelyn Oliver Otway-Ruthven, R.N.
Commander Desmond Adair Stride, R.N. (Retd.)
Commander Frederick John Walker, R.N.
Commander Eric FitzGerald Wharton, R.N. (Retd.)

APPENDIX C

Commander Herbert James Buchanan, R.A.N.

Surgeon Commander William Gordon Caulfield Fitzpatrick, R.N.

Paymaster Commander Cecil John Leary, R.D., R.N.R.

Lieutenant-Commander William Canning Eykyn, R.N. (Retd.)

Lieutenant-Commander Bruce Balfour Junor, R.N.

Lieutenant-Commander James Whaley McLelland, R.N.

Lieutenant-Commander St. John George Hanson Pitt, R.N. (Retd.)

Lieutenant-Commander Ralph William Vernon Soper, R.N.R.

Lieutenant-Commander Robert Glen Wardrop, R.D., R.N.R. (Retd.)

Lieutenant-Commander (E) Weston Smith, R.N.

Paymaster Lieutenant-Commander John Wissett Edelsten, R.N.R.

Major Lionel Steele Wilkinson, R.M.

Lieutenant Richard Galfridus Hastings Giles Eyre, R.N.

Lieutenant Viscount Kelburn, R.N.

Lieutenant Awlan Raymond Mackewn, R.N.R.

Lieutenant Charles Edward Stocker, R.N.R.

Surgeon Lieutenant Godfrey Fraser Carey, M.B., Ch.B., M.R.C.S., L.R.C.P., R.N.V.R.

Temporary Surgeon Lieutenant George Atherton Hart, M.B., B.S., M.R.C.S., L.R.C.P., R.N.V.R.

Paymaster Lieutenant Frank Neil Brockett, R.N.R.

Sub-Lieutenant Norman Walter Albert Mann, R.N.V.R.

Temporary Paymaster Sub-Lieutenant Maxwell Kerr Hamilton, R.N.V.R.

Commissioned Signal Boatswain William Pearce, R.N. (Retd.)

Gunner (T) Richard James Archy Baker, R.N.

Chief Yeoman of Signals John William Baker, C/J 26656.

Chief Yeoman of Signals George Edward Files, C/J 14130.

Chief Yeoman of Signals Lawrence Hamer Hanson, C 229251.

Chief Yeoman of Signals Francis George Ward, C/J 31094.

Chief Electrical Artificer Edgar James Lovell, P/M 27540.

Petty Officer Edward Bastable, P/J 127305.

Petty Officer Alexander Hood Bruce Ireland, C/J 6530.

Acting Engine Room Artificer Fourth Class Hugh Duffie, R.N.R., X 2957 EA.

Stoker Petty Officer Frederick George Charman, P/KX 75070.

Sick Berth Petty Officer Wilfred Harry Groves, C/MX 48183.

Sick Berth Petty Officer Harry Munro Hawkins, C/M 37726.

Sick Berth Petty Officer (R) Rupert Arthur Lockwood, C/MX 49872.

Sick Berth Petty Officer (R) George Robert Wright, C/X 6227, R.N.A.S.B.R.

Regulating Petty Officer Francis James Phillips, C/M 39981.

Regulating Petty Officer George Stapley, C/M 39658.

Leading Sick Berth Attendant Norman Clyde Martin, C/MX 49373.

Signalman James Stanley Duffy, R.N.V.R., C/TDX 1412.

Signalman Ronald Henry Walters, R.N.V.R., C/LDX 4178.

Sick Berth Attendant (R) Alfred Bassford, R.N.A.S.B.R., C/X 8080.

APPENDIX C

Canteen Manager Francis Montague Davis, N.A.A.F.I.
Mr. William Ferguson, Acting Naval Store Officer.
Mr. Robert William Whidby Corbitt, Acting Deputy Naval Store Officer.
Mr. Donald John Woods, Deputy Armament Supply Officer.
Mr. Archibald Armytage Bakewell, Deputy Victualling Store Officer.
Acting Sergeant Geoffrey Chapman, 6208138, 1/8th Middlesex Regiment.
Private William Cecil Ernest Smith, R.A.M.C., 7520070.
Mr. George Allen Cadell.

A.A. CRUISER

Calcutta
  MENTION IN DISPATCHES
    Gunner Frederick James March, R.N.
    Signalman Harry Guy, C/JX 150713.

DESTROYERS

Anthony
  MENTION IN DISPATCHES
    Lieutenant-Commander Norman Vivian Joseph Thompson Thew, R.N.
    Lieutenant Ronald de Leighton Brooke, R.N.

Codrington
  BAR TO D.S.O.
    Captain George Frederick Stevens-Guille, D.S.O., O.B.E., R.N.
  D.S.C.
    Lieutenant Arthur Alan Whitshed Pollard, R.N.
  BAR TO D.S.M.
    Leading Seaman Douglas Nicholas, D/JX 137869.
  D.S.M.
    Able Seaman John McDonald, D/JX 173583.
    Able Seaman Frank Willcox, D/SSX 16241.
    Able Seaman Samuel John Williams, D/J 100798.
    Seaman William Beer, R.N.R., X 20873A.
  MENTION IN DISPATCHES
    Lieutenant-Commander Hugh Charles Bainbridge Coleridge, D.S.C., R.N.
    Lieutenant-Commander Peter Charles Oswald Moseley, R.N.
    Commissioned Gunner (T) Bernard Evelyn Chitty, R.N.
    Chief Petty Officer Marshall Howard Hodges, D/J 101930.
    Chief Petty Officer Telegraphist Reginald Thomas Arnold, D/J 82044.
    Chief Engine Room Artificer Harold Duckworth, D/MX 59963.
    Leading Seaman William Frederick Lionel Perry, D/JX 136417.
    Leading Seaman Reginald Charles Wilson, D/JX 136600.
    Leading Stoker Albert Loomes, D/KX 81236.
    Able Seaman Henry Bernard Robert Burns Butcher, D/JX 145695.
    Able Seaman Henry Claude Curtis, D/J 90128.

APPENDIX C

Able Seaman Wilfred Edward Green, D/SSX 19925.
Able Seaman Harry Murrell, D/J 109760.
Able Seaman Arthur Savage, D/SS 10494.
Able Seaman Richard Philip Smith, R.N.V.R., MD/X 1950.
Signalman Leslie David Ball, R.N.V.R., LD5/X 3548.

Esk
D.S.C.
Lieutenant-Commander Richard John Hullis Couch, R.N.
Lieutenant Clifford Woodruff Carter, R.N.
D.S.M.
Petty Officer Hyacinth Alec George Adam, P/JX 131408.
Acting Leading Seaman Mansell Richard Powell, P/SSX 15191.
MENTION IN DISPATCHES
Sub-Lieutenant Wilfrith Francis Chamberlain Elstob, R.N.
Chief Petty Officer Bertie Featherstone, P/J 55642.
Chief Engine Room Artificer Alfred Thomas Sidey, P/M 31294.
Acting Yeoman of Signals William Frederick Sear, P/JX 129492.
Leading Seaman Arthur Saunders, P/J 105542.
Acting Leading Seaman John Thomas Cody, P/JX 134308.
Acting Leading Seaman Gordon Simons McAully, P/J 102728.
Acting Leading Seaman Alfred Solen, P/JX 141699.
Leading Stoker Thomas William Pickersgill, P/KX 76937.
Sick Berth Attendant Edward Welch, R.N.A.S.B.R., P/SBR/X 7341.

Express
D.S.O.
Captain Jack Grant Bickford, D.S.C., R.N.
D.S.C.
Lieutenant David Hugh Maitland-Makgill-Crichton, R.N.
D.S.M.
Engine Room Artificer First Class James Barton, R.N.R., Portsmouth 32EE.
Petty Officer Maurice William Crisp, P/J 100655.
Acting Leading Seaman John Mountain, P/JX 142248.
Able Seaman Frank Stroud, P/SSX 15110.
Able Seaman Gerald Arthur Douglas Rooke, R.N.V.R., P/SD/X1781.
MENTION IN DISPATCHES
Lieutenant-Commander Denis Worth Deane, R.N.
Petty Officer Steward Arthur Victor Read, P/L 1816.
Able Seaman Edwin Cecil Holloway, P/J 98570.
Sick Berth Attendant John Yeoman, R.N.A.S.B.R., P/X 7093.

Grafton
D.S.C.
Surgeon Lieutenant Joseph Wishart Shield, M.B., B.Ch., R.N.V.R.

Grenade

D.S.C.

Gunner (T) Reginald William Clare, R.N.

D.S.M.

Leading Stoker Fred Stables, C/KX 84191.

MENTION IN DISPATCHES

Mr. Reginald James Crews, B.Sc., Schoolmaster, R.N.

Petty Officer Samuel Bennion, C/J 102723.

Petty Officer Harold Richard Emery, C/JX 144399.

Greyhound

MENTION IN DISPATCHES

Commander Walter Roger Marshall-A'Deane, R.N.

Stoker Petty Officer Emil Rothman Teichert, P/K 59694.

Leading Seaman Aubrey William Saunders, P/SSX 15620.

Leading Seaman Stanley Hayes Settersfield, P/J 102005.

Harvester

D.S.C.

Sub-Lieutenant Edmund Charles Croswell, R.N.

MENTION IN DISPATCHES

Lieutenant-Commander Mark Thornton, R.N.

Gunner (T) William George Alfred Robinson, R.N.

Havant

D.S.M.

Chief Stoker Martin Gallon, P/K 59221.

Petty Officer Steward John Lysaght, D/L 13388.

MENTION IN DISPATCHES

Lieutenant-Commander Anthony Frank Burnell-Nugent, D.S.C., R.N.

Sick Berth Attendant Albert William Keller, R.N.A.S.B.R., D/X 6785.

Icarus

D.S.C.

Lieutenant-Commander Edward Gregson Roper, R.N.

Lieutenant Derek Peel Willan, R.N.

D.S.M.

Chief Petty Officer Reginald Frank Tupper, P/J 94060.

Chief Stoker Horace Frederick Goddard, P/KX 95692.

Petty Officer Joseph William Fred Tibbles, P/J 108799.

Able Seaman Albert Thomas Williams, P/JX 154589.

MENTION IN DISPATCHES

Lieutenant-Commander Colin Douglas Maud, D.S.C., R.N.

Chief Petty Officer Telegraphist Frank Harfield, P/J 96718.

Chief Engine Room Artificer Lionel Edwin Miles, P/M 22015.

Acting Yeoman of Signals William George Giddings, P/JX 136912

APPENDIX C

Petty Officer Cook Frederick Albert Day, P/M 38606.
Able Seaman Eric Richard Ponton, P/SSX 14194.

Impulsive
D.S.M.
Able Seaman Frank William Knight, P/J 102492.
MENTION IN DISPATCHES
Lieutenant-Commander William Scott Thomas, R.N.
Leading Seaman Thomas Henry Heath, P/JX 155193.
Leading Seaman Albert George Tullett, P/JX 129610.

Ivanhoe
D.S.M.
Able Seaman James Pearce Clare, R.F.R., C/J 99666.
MENTION IN DISPATCHES
Commander Philip Henry Hadow, R.N.
Lieutenant (E) Andrew Cormac Mahony, R.N.
Chief Engine Room Artificer Richard Edward Cox, C/M 34441.
Chief Stoker Henry Joseph Prendergast, C/K 62741.
Sick Berth Attendant Eric James Littlewood Gibson, D/MX 56025.

Jaguar
D.S.C.
Lieutenant Francis Bruen, R.N.
D.S.M.
Acting Stoker Petty Officer James William Carr, D/K 63042.
Able Seaman Harold Albert Keeling, D/SSX 17807.
Boy First Class George Albert Furzer, D/JX 158564.
MENTION IN DISPATCHES
Lieutenant (E) Cyril Rothwell, R.N.
Petty Officer Frederick John Cole, D/J 110727.
Stoker Petty Officer John McCarthy, D/K 65035.
Acting Leading Seaman Walter James Whale, D/JX 134747.
Able Seaman Berty Richard Culley, D/JX 130278.
Able Seaman Frank Henry Hopwood, D/SSX 18782.
Able Seaman John Lawrence Joyce, D/SSX 20230.
Able Seaman James Kidd, R.F.R., D/SSX 13321.
Able Seaman John Edward Ratcliffe, D/SSX 21633.
Stoker First Class Jack Chadwick, D/KX 81834.
Ordinary Seaman Noel Edward Holmes Berry, D/JX 158456.
Seaman Raymond Allenby Stone, R.N.R., X 19746A.

Keith
D.S.C.
Lieutenant Charles Paynder Adams, R.N.

269

APPENDIX C

D.S.M.

Chief Yeoman of Signals Fred Laister, C/J 69665.
Acting Petty Officer Ernest Francis Standley, C/JX 137068.
Leading Seaman Eldric Ivan John Alfred Gent Joplin, C/JX 138400.
Able Seaman Thomas Fortune Asprey, C/J 114945.
Able Seaman George Edward Davies, R.F.R., C/J 86552.
Able Seaman Eric Bradley Wilkinson, C/JX 152120.
Ordinary Seaman William Thompson Moore, C/JX 171200.

MENTION IN DISPATCHES (POSTHUMOUS)

Captain David James Robert Simson, R.N.

MENTION IN DISPATCHES

Captain Edward Lyon Berthon, D.S.C., R.N.
Lieutenant-Commander Robert Stevenson Miller, D.S.C., R.N.R.
Lieutenant Robert Walker Hughes, R.N.
Lieutenant Graham James Alexander Lumsden, R.N.
Midshipman Henry Batten Poustie, R.N.R.
Chief Yeoman of Signals Fred Laister, D.S.M., C/J 69665.
Leading Telegraphist Ernest John Murray Beeley, C/JX 141015.
Able Seaman Thomas Fortune Asprey, C/J 114945.
Able Seaman Walter Tom Bowering, C/J 39899.
Able Seaman Thomas Emmett Cassidy, C/SSX 22123.
Able Seaman Ronald Charles Chalk, C/SSX 28170.
Able Seaman Daniel Fossey, C/JX 148554.
Able Seaman Robert Macaulay, R.F.R., C/J 108727.
Able Seaman William Marshall, C/SSX 28196.
Able Seaman Ian Alan Nethercott, C/SSX 28288.
Able Seaman James Wallis, C/SSX 27313.
Able Seaman George John Woodger, C/J 45802.

Malcolm

D.S.O.

Captain Thomas Edgar Halsey, R.N.

D.S.C.

Lieutenant Ian Nagle Douglas Cox, R.N.

D.S.M.

Chief Petty Officer Rowland Evan Lines, C/JX 142401.
Chief Yeoman of Signals Albert Charles Mason Shepherd, C/J 48458.
Chief Petty Officer Telegraphist Charles Henry Bycroft, C/J 65751.
Chief Engine Room Artificer Redvers Woodhead Atkinson, C/MX 47004.
Petty Officer Walter Alfred Reginald Hooper, D/JX 142642.
Yeoman of Signals Alfred Charles Halls, C/JX 129457.
Leading Seaman James Sowerby, C/JX 109521, R.F.R., B 24792
Stoker First Class William Stephen Grimmitt, C/KX 90969.

MENTION IN DISPATCHES

Captain Thomas Edgar Halsey, D.S.O., R.N.
Lieutenant David Barclay Nairne Mellis, R.N.

Lieutenant Ronald John Robertson, R.A.N. (twice mentioned).
Gunner (T) Dudley Eric Wright, R.N.
Warrant Engineer Arthur George Scoggins, R.N.
Engine Room Artificer Second Class Leslie Allan Gardener Dyer,
C/M 39382.
Petty Officer Arthur George Cooper, C/J 105794.
Petty Officer Ernest William Simpson, C/J 95860.
Petty Officer Steward George Robert Nokes, C/L 6194.
Leading Seaman William Alfred Hart, C/JX 130453.
Able Seaman William Albert Clarke, C/J 78426.
Able Seaman Frederick William Jacobs, C/J 100758, R.F.R., B23901
Sick Berth Attendant Joseph Leonard Sharp, Ch.SBR/X 6710.

Sabre

D.S.O.
Commander Brian Dean, R.N. (Retd.)
D.S.C.
Commissioned Engineer Reginald Thomas Jones, R.N.
D.S.M.
Chief Petty Officer Ernest George Dewey, C/J 104364.
Chief Engine Room Artificer Andrew Millar McOwan, C/M 18445.
Stoker Petty Officer George Albert Aitchison, C/K 61056.
Stoker First Class Reginald Arthur Powling, C/K 52210.
MENTION IN DISPATCHES
Lieutenant Norman John Parker, R.N.
Midshipman Edward Folmer Archdale, R.N.
Stoker Petty Officer Benjamin Fletcher, C/K 65982.
Acting Leading Seaman Frederick Arthur May, C/JX 141390.
Leading Steward Norman Lorraine Gilchrist, C/LX 21538.
Stoker First Class Charles Irvine, C/KX 86537.

Scimitar

D.S.C.
Midshipman Malcolm John Ball, R.N.R.
D.S.M.
Able Seaman George Pasmore, P/J 96339.
Stoker Frank Anthony Tyler, R/K 61614.
MENTION IN DISPATCHES
Lieutenant Robert Denys Franks, O.B.E., R.N.

Shikari

D.S.C.
Lieutenant-Commander Hugh Nicholas Aubyn Richardson, R.N.
D.S.M.
Leading Stoker George Alfred Browne, D/KX 81441.

APPENDIX C

Signalman William Hicks, D/JX 144358.
Ordinary Seaman George Park, D/JX 170122.

MENTION IN DISPATCHES
Lieutenant John Rees Wilson, R.N.
Ordinary Seaman Dominic Kenny, D/SSX 30221.
Ordinary Seaman William Lyons, D/SSX 30211.

Valentine
D.S.O.
Commander Herbert James Buchanan, R.A.N.
D.S.M.
Petty Officer Albert Leonard Gilbert, R.F.R., D/J 106272.
Stoker Petty Officer Russell George Chase, D/K 58542.
Stoker Second Class John Henry Fountain, D/K 100363.

MENTION IN DISPATCHES
Lieutenant Robert Morton MacFie, R.N.V.R.
Acting Gunner Stanley Frederick Burrow, R.N.
Acting Petty Officer Frederick William Thornton, C/J 99845.
Stoker Petty Officer William Henry Newton, D/K 62039.
Able Seaman Leslie Herbert Boyce, D/J 61014.
Able Seaman John Doyle, D/J 112616.
Stoker Second Class Norman Worwood, D/KX 100442.

Vanquisher
D.S.M.
Chief Engine Room Artificer Francis Henry Patrick, C/M 14987.
Leading Seaman David Anderson, C/J 107567.

MENTION IN DISPATCHES
Commander Conrad Byron Alers-Hankey, R.N.
Lieutenant Cecil William Clarence Checucci, R.N.
Lieutenant Reginald Noel Hankey, R.N.
Chief Petty Officer Frederick Arthur Calver, C/J 21929.
Petty Officer Charles Morrice, C/J 110582.
Stoker Petty Officer William King, C/K 53308.

Venetia
D.S.C.
Lieutenant-Commander Bernulf Henry de Clegg Mellor, R.N.
Sub-Lieutenant Denis Hervey Jones, R.N.R.
Commissioned Engineer Stanley Samuel Vincent, R.N.
D.S.M.
Chief Engine Room Artificer William George Edwin Stiles, D/M 38822.
Petty Officer Jeremiah Vincent Burke, D/J 115014.
Petty Officer William Henry Leece, D/JX 134292.
Able Seaman Adam Reid Henderson, D/J 36746.

APPENDIX C

MENTION IN DISPATCHES

Lieutenant Rudolf John Marc Wratislaw, R.N.
Sub-Lieutenant Edwin Arthur Owen Glynn Herring, R.N.
Acting Gunner (T) Douglas Honey, R.N.
Acting Chief Petty Officer James Frederick Ernest Wagner, D/J 102707
Chief Engine Room Artificer Second Class Frederick James Hill,
P/M 35048.
Petty Officer Preston Owen Denny, D/J 111903.
Petty Officer Robert Robertson, D/J 4291.
Acting Yeoman of Signals Arthur Herbert Hampson, D/J 112753.
Stoker Petty Officer Theodore John Hayman, D/KX 78991.
Able Seaman Bernard Craven Thomas Chapman, D/J 90057.
Able Seaman Thomas Edmund Everard Watts, D/J 13108.
Stoker First Class Charles David Beatty Watts, D/KX 99255.

Venomous

D.S.O.
Lieutenant-Commander John Edwin Home McBeath, R.N.
D.S.C.
Sub-Lieutenant Walter Reginald Wells, R.N.
D.S.M.
Ordnance Artificer Third Class Horace Hugh McGeeney, D/MX 47358.
Petty Officer Michael Joseph O'Sullivan, D/JX 132003.
Acting Petty Officer Leslie William Dagley, D/JX 127574.
Able Seaman Harold Knapton, D/JX 151137.
Able Seaman Ernest Roy Stallard, D/JX 142935.
MENTION IN DISPATCHES
Lieutenant-Commander John Edwin Home McBeath, R.N.
Lieutenant Angus Alexander Mackenzie, R.N.R.
Midshipman Alan Flockhart Esson, R.N.R.
Acting Gunner (T) Robert Knight Thomson, R.N.
Able Seaman James Edwards, D/MD/X 2534.
Able Seaman James Gilchrist Henderson, D/JX 149499.
Able Seaman William Henry Nickless, D/J 100855.
Signalman Oscar Charles Mayland, D/J 31639.

Verity

MENTION IN DISPATCHES
Lieutenant-Commander Arthur Ronald Mawson Black, R.N.
Midshipman William Campbell Neill, R.N.R.

Vimiera

D.S.O.
Lieutenant-Commander Roger Bertram Nettleton Hicks, R.N.
Commissioned Engineer Edgar Glanville Blofield, R.N.
D.S.C.
Lieutenant Reginald Lacey Caple, R.N.

APPENDIX C

C.G.M.

Chief Engine Room Artificer Second Class Frank North, C/M 11514.

D.S.M.

Chief Petty Officer Henry George Dean, C/J 28737.

Engine Room Artificer Third Class Harold Thomas Mansfield, C/MX 53899.

Stoker Petty Officer George William Tranter, C/K 55760.

MENTION IN DISPATCHES

Sub-Lieutenant Norman MacPherson, R.N.

Vimy

D.S.C.

Lieutenant Adrian Paul Wilbraham Northey, R.N.

Probationary Sub-Lieutenant Stephen Anthony Golden Godden, R.N.

D.S.M.

Petty Officer James Owen Paget, P/JX 129854.

Leading Seaman Thomas Frederick Brewerton, P/JX 166128.

Leading Seaman Frederick Martindale, P/JX 136855.

Leading Seaman Aubrey Robert Porter, P/J 54868.

MENTION IN DISPATCHES (POSTHUMOUS)

Lieutenant-Commander Colin George Walter Donald, R.N.

MENTION IN DISPATCHES

Lieutenant Adrian Paul Northey, D.S.C.

Sub-Lieutenant Robert Andrew Morgan, R.N.

Chief Stoker John Wattam, P/K 56834.

Leading Seaman Thomas Frederick Brewerton, P/JX 166128.

Leading Seaman Aubrey Robert Porter, P/J 54868.

Stoker First Class Joseph Samuel Comben, P/K 62179.

Vivacious

D.S.C.

Lieutenant Francis Peter Baker, R.N.

D.S.M.

Petty Officer Ernest Richard Meredith, P/J 95625.

Stoker John Joseph Williamson, P/KX 76409.

MENTION IN DISPATCHES

Sub-Lieutenant John Teague Gilhespy, R.N.

Commissioned Engineer John George Revolta, R.N.

Chief Stoker Charles Tanner, P/K 58508

Engine Room Artificer Third Class Cyril Ernest Strugnell. P/MX 47645.

Petty Officer William Flint, P/JX 126621.

Petty Officer Ronald Ford, P/J 106208.

Acting Yeoman of Signals John Thomas Loynes, P/JX 129983.

Petty Officer Telegraphist Albert Walter Bennett, P/JX 126535.

Sick Berth Attendant James Timothy Tomlinson, R.N.A.S.B.R., P/X 6941.

Wakeful
D.S.C.
  Commander Ralph Lindsay Fisher, R.N.

Westminster
MENTION IN DISPATCHES
  Lieutenant-Commander Aymé Arthur Carrington Ouvry, R.N.

Whitehall
D.S.M.
  Petty Officer Cecil Kenneth Souster, D/J 102935.
MENTION IN DISPATCHES
  Lieutenant-Commander Archibald Boyd Russell, R.N.
  Temporary Surgeon Lieutenant James Gorrie Brown, M.B., B.S.,
    M.R.C.S., L.R.C.P., R.N.V.R.
  Chief Petty Officer Harold Methuen Seabrook, D/J 43574.
  Chief Engine Room Artificer William Alfred Frederick Luke,
    D/M 37041.
  Officers' Steward First Class William Smith, D/L 824.
  Leading Telegraphist Wallace Eugene Breton, D/JX 135520.
  Able Seaman George Frederick Sims, D/J 111989.

Whitley
D.S.C.
  Lieutenant Commander Guy Neville Rolfe, R.N.
D.S.M.
  Chief Engine Room Artificer Second Class Jesse Pearce, P/M 36622.
  Petty Officer Thomas Martin McMahon, P/BD/X 785.
  Petty Officer Norman Victor Robinson, P/J 112893.
  Able Seaman Herbert Francis Clark, P/J 97656.
MENTION IN DISPATCHES
  Leading Telegraphist Anthony Walter Story, P/JX 140026.
  Able Seaman William Arthur Halsey, P/J 54128.

Whitshed
D.S.O.
  Commander Edward Reignier Conder, D.S.C., R.N.
D.S.C.
  Lieutenant (E) Albert Valentine English, R.N.
  Probationary Temporary Surgeon Lieutenant David William Pugh,
    M.B., B.S., M.R.C.S., L.R.C.P., R.N.V.R.
D.S.M.
  Acting Yeoman of Signals John Wilson, P/JX 132176.
  Acting Engine Room Artificer Fourth Class Edward William Jacobs,
    P/MX 51759.

Able Seaman Reginald Harry James Barnard, P/JX 146417.
Able Seaman Richard O'Neill, P/JX 150241.
Ordinary Seaman Norman Henry Stringer, R.N.V.R., SD/X 1423.

MENTION IN DISPATCHES
Lieutenant Samuel Richard Le Hunte Lombard-Hobson, R.N.
Sub-Lieutenant Peter Lin Keith Needham, R.N.
Chief Petty Officer William Nathaniel Head, P/J 35888.
Petty Officer Walter Henry Homewood, P/J 111612.
Leading Seaman Frederick Charles Caplin, P/JX 163780.
Stoker First Class Daniel Tildesley, P/K 20012.
Ordinary Seaman John Duff Woods, P/JX 169753.

Wild Swan

D.S.C.
Lieutenant Moses James Lee, R.N.
D.S.M.
Chief Petty Officer Horace Fletcher, T.C., P/J 55657.
Chief Engine Room Artificer Second Class John Pullen, P/M 1577.

MENTION IN DISPATCHES
Lieutenant-Commander John Leslie Younghusband, D.S.C., R.N.
Sub-Lieutenant Harry Guy Vere, R.N.
Midshipman Leslie Willougby Green, R.N.R.
Commissioned Engineer Cecil John Charles Derbyshire, R.N.
Acting Yeoman of Signals Charles William Greig Burton, P/JX 134134.
Leading Seaman John Callaghan, J 11777.
Leading Telegraphist Robert Charles Edward Clement, P/J 80581.
Able Seaman Alexander John MacDonald, D/J 98930.
Able Seaman Joseph Eric Weston, P/JX 156937.

Winchelsea

D.S.C.
Lieutenant-Commander William Alan Frank Hawkins, R.N.
D.S.M.
Engine Room Artificer Fourth Class Joseph Edric Whitenstall, P/MX 57728.
Leading Seaman Walter George Harold Last, P/JX 132139.

MENTION IN DISPATCHES
Chief Petty Officer Rupert Armstrong, P/J 104917.
Chief Engine Room Artificer Cecil John Rhodes, P/M 28822.
Able Seaman Peter Frederick Byford, P/JX 135124.

Windsor

MENTION IN DISPATCHES
Commander Peter Douglas Herbert Raymond Pelly, R.N
Surgeon Lieutenant Peter Neale Shutte, R.N.V.R.

Wivern

D.S.C.

Commander William Charles Bushell, R.N.

D.S.M.

Chief Petty Officer Otto Ian Hamilton Elphick, P/J 53291.
Petty Officer Thomas William Thorp, C/JX 135052.
Sick Berth Attendant Harold Peacock, P/SBR/X 8001.
Seaman Donald Buchanan, R.N.R., X10119B

MENTION IN DISPATCHES

Lieutenant John Wychard Harbottle, R.N.
Sub-Lieutenant Sydney Evelyn Pritchard, R.N.
Midshipman Douglas David George Roberts, R.N.
Petty Officer Gilbert Henry Line, P/J 111957.
Petty Officer Charles Edward Walder, P/J 106198.

Wolsey

D.S.C.

Lieutenant-Commander Colin Henry Campbell, R.N.
Gunner Frederick William Benoy, R.N.

D.S.M.

Electrical Artificer First Class Kenneth Simpson, C/MX 45564.
Acting Leading Seaman Dennis Philip Arthur Gilbert, C/JX 151519.
Telegraphist John Greer Graham, P/SSX 17539.

MENTION IN DISPATCHES

Lieutenant George Blackler, R.N.
Acting Petty Officer Claude Leslie Williams, C/JX 128094.
Leading Seaman Cyril Hammond Mackenzie, C/J 101310.
Able Seaman Thomas Fox, C/SSX 12418.
Able Seaman George William Ncicho, C/SSX 24070.
Stoker First Class William Reginald Gordon Jones, C/KX 92890.

Worcester

D.S.O.

Commander John Hamilton Allison, R.N.

D.S.C.

Lieutenant Frederick Greville Woods, R.N.

D.S.M.

Chief Petty Officer Francis Withington, C/J 8739.
Chief Engine Room Artificer Sidney Arthur Wilkins, P/M 18465.
Leading Seaman John William Flattery, P/JX 131896.
Leading Seaman Arthur Charles Godden, P/JX 129206.

MENTION IN DISPATCHES (POSTHUMOUS)

Sub-Lieutenant Neville Lyon Humphreys, R.N.
Able Seaman John Edward Reynolds, P/JX 147968.
Stoker First Class Thomas Moscrop, P/KX 83677.

APPENDIX C

Surgeon Lieutenant Francis Whitwell, M.B., B.S., M.R.C.S., L.R.C.P., R.N.V.R.

Engine Room Artificer Second Class Ronald William Brenton, P/MX 46507.

Petty Officer Benjamin Matthews, P/J 3593.

Petty Officer Ronald Laurence Motteram, P/JX 129270.

Petty Officer Horace William Smith, P/J 108414.

Leading Seaman John Leonard Brown, P/JX 138751.

Leading Stoker Charles William Morris, P/KX 81034.

Able Seaman Edward Gair, P/SSX 15905.

Ordinary Seaman Bert Marston, P/JX 175182.

Stoker Second Class Ralph Kearvell, P/KX 99946.

Sloop

Bideford

D.S.O.

Surgeon Lieutenant John Jordan, M.B., B.Ch., R.N.

D.S.C.

Lieutenant-Commander John Hugh Lewes, R.N.

D.S.M.

Stoker Petty Officer Charles William Donnelly, D/K 59925.

Cook Albert Victor Hockin, D/MX 58549.

Mention in Dispatches

Signalman Charles Raymond Craig, D/JX 141848.

Corvette

Kingfisher

D.S.M.

Stoker First Class Frederick Frank Beer, C/KX 86684.

Mention in Dispatches

Lieutenant-Commander George Anthony Mayhew Vaughan Harrison, R.N.

Leading Seaman Patrick John Ball, C/SSX 15444.

Able Seaman Stanley Collie, C/SSX 21361.

Able Seaman Ambrose Bernard Harkin, D/JX 128450.

Able Seaman Thomas Oswald Pigg, C/JX 142167.

Able Seaman Ronald Henry Shipp, C/JX 126720.

Able Seaman Edwin George Webster, C/JX 127168.

Signalman Stanley Thompson, C/JX 133505.

Gunboats

Locust

D.S.C.

Lieutenant-Commander Ackroyd Norman Palliser Costobadie, R.N.

APPENDIX C

MENTION IN DISPATCHES
Lieutenant John Arundell Holdsworth, R.N.
Signalman Harold Oscar Carter, C/SSX 17317.
Signalman Eric Ernest Roden, C/J 103654.

Mosquito
D.S.C.
Lieutenant Denis Harold Palmer Gardiner, R.N.
Sub-Lieutenant Eric Sidney Flint, R.N.R.
C.G.M.
Acting Leading Seaman Ronald Thirlwall, C/JX 139421.
D.S.M.
Stoker Petty Officer William Edward White, C/K 64353.
Able Seaman Cecil Arthur Leonard Hirschfield, C/J 100099.
MENTION IN DISPATCHES (POSTHUMOUS)
Lieutenant Anthony Hugh Mainwaring, R.N.
MENTION IN DISPATCHES
Surgeon Lieutenant Noel Louis Fox, M.B., B.Ch., R.N.
Chief Petty Officer George Albert Sawyer, C/J 46680.
Acting Petty Officer Telegraphist James Riddell, C/JX 132853.

MINESWEEPERS

Albury
D.S.C.
Lieutenant-Commander Colin Henry Corbet-Singleton, R.N.
D.S.M.
Acting Leading Stoker Frank Putt, D/KX 84370.
Canteen Manager Alfred Harris.

Dundalk
D.S.M.
Seaman William Tilley Elmslie, R.N.R., X 19014A.
MENTION IN DISPATCHES
Lieutenant-Commander Frederick Arthur Ivone Kirkpatrick, R.N. (Ret.)

Fitzroy
D.S.C.
Midshipman Ian Kinloch Bryce, R.N.R.
D.S.M.
Signalman Frederick Froggatt, C/JX 144084.
Signalman Dick Minter, C/JX 155114.
Stoker First Class Walter Albert Worman Ward, C/KX 97894.
Ordinary Seaman Gordon Harry Hawkins, C/JX 168509.
MENTION IN DISPATCHES
Lieutenant-Commander Reginald Arthur Forbes, R.N.
Sub-Lieutenant David Alexander Shaw, R.N.

Leading Seaman Lionel Arthur Aspen, C/J 108791.
Leading Seaman John Cole, D/J 48211.
Leading Stoker Edward Collison, C/KX 78651.

Glenavon
MENTION IN DISPATCHES
Seaman Arthur George Farrow, LT/JX 179655.

Glengower
D.S.C.
Acting Commander Michael Anthony Ormus Biddulph, R.N.
D.S.M.
Able Seaman Jeremiah Fleming, D/JX 140199.
Fireman Trimmer Thomas Nieva, T 124.
MENTION IN DISPATCHES
Leading Seaman John Richard Darby, D/JX 139835.
Able Seaman Leonard Travers, D/JX 133219.

Gossamer
D.S.M.
Petty Officer Edward William Higgs, C/JX 133416.
Assistant Cook (O) Thomas Henry Ward, C/MX 59579.
MENTION IN DISPATCHES
Petty Officer Steward Arthur Hockney, C/L 14824.

Halcyon
D.S.O.
Commander Eric Perceval Hinton, M.V.O., R.N.
D.S.C.
Sub-Lieutenant John Francis Worthington, R.N.V.R.
D.S.M.
Stoker Petty Officer John Henry Salmon, D/K 66881.
Able Seaman Clarence Edward Jarnet, D/J 95955.

Hebe
D.S.M.
Chief Petty Officer Stanley Freeman Piggott, P/J.15784
MENTION IN DISPATCHES
Engine Room Artificer Third Class Harold Brickwood Biles,
P/MX.47301.

Kellett
D.S.M.
Ordinary Seaman James Frederick Shiret, C/JX.168490.
MENTION IN DISPATCHES
Commander Reginald Cecil Hasket-Smith, R.N.

Engine Room Artificer Fourth Class George Harry Redmond,
  C/MX 49208.
Leading Telegraphist Edward Hatch, C/JX 138717.

Leda
D.S.M.
  Chief Engine Room Artificer George Bertram Head, P/M 34498.
  Petty Officer John Collins, P/J 90457.
MENTION IN DISPATCHES
  Lieutenant William McKee, R.N.R.

Lydd
MENTION IN DISPATCHES
  Lieutenant-Commander Rodolph Cecil Drummond Haig, R.N.

Medway Queen
D.S.C.
  Lieutenant Alfred Thomas Cook, R.N.R.
  Sub-Lieutenant John David Greaves, R.N.R.
D.S.M.
  Petty Officer Alfred Ernest Crossley, C/J 103237
  Petty Officer Henry Joseph McAllister, C/J 16046.
  Seaman Kenneth Roy Olly, R.N.R., X 20348A.
MENTION IN DISPATCHES
  Second Engineer Thomas Irvin, T 124.
  Fireman John Develand Connell, T 124.

Niger
D.S.C.
  Lieutenant Robert Peverell Hichens, R.N.V.R.
D.S.M.
  Leading Seaman Clive Frederick Mane Cooper, C/JX 137062.
MENTION IN DISPATCHES
  Commander St. John Cronyn, R.N.

Oriole
MENTION IN DISPATCHES
  Sub-Lieutenant John Crosby, R.N.V.R.

Portsdown
MENTION IN DISPATCHES
  Sub-Lieutenant Richard Hepworth Church, R.N.R.
  Engine Room Artificer Third Class Henry White, P/MX 51366.
  Stoker Petty Officer William Ramel, P/KX 87522.
  Leading Signalman Percy Alfred Kent, P/JX 137932.
  Ordinary Seaman Arthur Thomas Burton, P/JX 182142.

Princess Elizabeth

D.S.C.

Lieutenant Cecil John Carp, R.N.V.R.
Temporary Sub-Lieutenant James Tomkin, R.N.V.R.

D.S.M.

Petty Officer Henry George Coalbran, P/JX 127274.
Fireman Stoker Godfrey Ernest Baker, T 124.

Queen of Thanet

D.S.M.

Fireman William Frederick Mitchell, T 124.

MENTION IN DISPATCHES

Acting Commander Sidney Peck Herival, R.N.V.R.
Chief Petty Officer Arthur Nelson Goldsmith, C/J 27799.
Signalman John Albert Williamson, R.N.V.R., LD/X 4036.

Ross

D.S.C.

Lieutenant Kenneth Arthur Gadd, R.N.R.

D.S.M.

Leading Signalman Edwin Charles Atkins, P/JX 152931.
Ordinary Seaman Theo Norman Pasfield, P/JX 176952.

Salamander

D.S.O.

Lieutenant-Commander Lionel James Spencer Ede, R.N.

D.S.C.

Commissioned Engineer Thomas Kirby Reynolds, R.N.

D.S.M.

Engine Room Artificer First Class Charles Henry Andrew, D/M 28768.
Stoker Petty Officer Thomas Rochford, D/K 61034.
Able Seaman Arthur Dane Trevor Benyon, D/JX 142424.
Stoker First Class Henry Joseph Thompson, D/KX 93732.

MENTION IN DISPATCHES

Leading Signalman James Thomas, D/JX 135962.
Leading Stoker Albert Hussey, D/K 62678

Saltash

D.S.M.

Stoker First Class Brian Gaughan, C/KX 79268.

Skipjack

D.S.M.

Leading Seaman Murdo Macleod, R.N.R., 5849 D.

Speedwell
D.S.C.
   Lieutenant Robert Archibald Vallings, R.N.R.
D.S.M.
   Chief Petty Officer Albert William Cobley, C/J 22075.
   Leading Seaman Stanley Robert Holden, C/J 106164.
   Able Seaman James Thomas Kesby, C/J 87250.
MENTION IN DISPATCHES
   Lieutenant-Commander Frederick Richard Guy Maunsell, R.N. (Retd.)

Sutton
D.S.O.
   Acting Commander Grenville Mathias Temple, R.N.
D.S.C.
   Sub-Lieutenant William Geoffrey Hewitt, R.N.V.R.
D.S.M.
   Petty Officer Harold Beasley, C/J 93287.
   Acting Stoker Petty Officer Albert George Dollery, P/KX 80017.
MENTION IN DISPATCHES
   Acting Chief Engine Room Artificer Allerton Bywater, P/M 39426.

Whippingham
D.S.M.
   Chief Mechanician Second Class Frederick Arthur Ford, P/K 21534.

MINESWEEPING CRAFT
Clythness
D.S.C.
   Skipper Walter Frederick Salenius.
D.S.M.
   Engineman George Alfred Day, LT/KX 102500.

Conidaw
D.S.C.
   Skipper Reginald G. Snelgrove
D.S.M.
   Signalman Thomas Horton Bailey, R.N.V.R., C/LD/X 3929.
MENTION IN DISPATCHES
   Sub-Lieutenant J. M. Thompson, R.N.V.R.
   Chief Engineman Joseph H. Stanley
   Deck Hand Norman Clive Watts

Dorienta
D.S.C.
   Skipper William Francis Reynolds, R.N.R.

D.S.M.
Engineman William Hunter Kennedy, R.N.R., X 369 EU.
MENTION IN DISPATCHES
Stoker John Pirie, R.N.R., X 10415 S.
Stoker James Shone, LT/KX 107502.
Engineman James Smith.

Feasible
D.S.M.
Engineman Aubrey August Storr, R.N.R., X 6082.

Gula
D.S.M.
Seaman George Guyan Mearns, LT/JX 179790.

Gulzar
D.S.M.
Coxswain Edward J. S. Woodhead, T 124.
Deckhand Peter Blake, T 124.
MENTION IN DISPATCHES
Ordinary Signalman Victor Albert Leslie Shallis, LD/X 4505.
Cook George Henry Cliefe, T 124.
Deckhand Charles E. Baldry, T 124.

Jeannie Macintosh
D.S.M.
Seaman Allan Morrison, R.N.R., X 7184 C.

John and Norah
D.S.M.
Stoker Reginald Whiteley, LT/KX 100149.

John Cattling
D.S.C.
Temporary Lieutenant Guy St. Clair Rideal, R.N.V.R.
D.S.M.
Seaman William Mills, LT/JX 179732.
Second Hand Charles Bruce Adams, LT/JX 173276.
MENTION IN DISPATCHES
Petty Officer Telegraphist Sydney Montague Williams Pepper,
C/J 3348.
Engineman William Walter Jefferies, LT/KX 101234.

Lord Grey
D.S.C.
Temporary Lieutenant John Adhemar Simson, R.N.V.R.

APPENDIX C

D.S.M.
Engineman Ivan William Lennox, LT/X 399 ET.
MENTION IN DISPATCHES
Probationary Skipper William John Tiller.

Lord Rodney
MENTION IN DISPATCHES
Captain Robert Durrant, Master.

Mare
MENTION IN DISPATCHES
Commander John Williams Damer Powell, D.S.C. (Bar), R.N.R. (Retd.)

Maretta
MENTION IN DISPATCHES
Sub-Lieutenant Montague Reginald Mills, R.N.V.R.

Reed
D.S.C.
Skipper George Hattan, R.N.R.

Sargasso
MENTION IN DISPATCHES
Lieutenant Charles C. L. Gaussen, R.N.V.R.

Strive
MENTION IN DISPATCHES
Skipper Henry Arthur Catchpole, R.N.R.

Swift Wing
D.S.M.
Second Hand John William Crawford, LT/JX 173174.

Three Kings
MENTION IN DISPATCHES
Skipper Arthur Victor Long, R.N.R.

THAMES SPECIAL SERVICE SHIPS

Crested Eagle
D.S.M.
Able Seaman George Frend, C/J 95190.
MENTION IN DISPATCHES
Lieutenant-Commander Bernard Ralph Booth, R.N.R.
Engineer Lieutenant Ewart Jones, T 124.
Chief Steward John Frank Gooch, T 124.

APPENDIX C

Able Seaman Frederick James Slack, C/J 93546, R.F.R., B 21781.
Able Seaman George Tilbury, C/SS 7850, R.F.R., B 17336.
Ordinary Seaman Frank Arthur Victor Pattrick, C/JX 171302.

Royal Eagle

D.S.O.
Commander Edward Cawdron Cordeaux, M.B., M.R.C.S., L.R.C.P., R.N. (Retd.)

D.S.M.
Chief Petty Officer Percy Simeon Thomas Munn, C/J 10033.

Mention in Dispatches
Lieutenant-Commander Edward Frederick Allen Farrow, R.N.R.
Ordinary Seaman Hugh Watson Miller, C/JX 170010.

M.A./S.B.s, M.T.B.s, Etc.

M.T.B. 68

Mention in Dispatches
Lieutenant Ralph Kenneth Livingstone Walker, R.N.V.R.
Leading Seaman Percy Ward, D/JX 134801.
Able Seaman Sydney Walter Davey, D/JX 146839

M.T.B. 102

D.S.M.
Engine Room Artificer Third Class George William Hyman, P/MX 49826.
Able Seaman Albert Richard Carver Stephens, P/JX 131369.

Mention in Dispatches
Lieutenant John Cameron, R.N.V.R.

M.T.B. 107

Mention in Dispatches
Chief Petty Officer Maurice John Driver, R.N.R., 6134 D.
Leading Seaman Alfred Peter Dawkins, P/SSX 17291.
Leading Stoker Charles William Thomas Murrin, P/KX 82587.

Dover Flare-burning Drifters

Boy Roy

D.S.M.
Engineman Harry Spicer Sharman, LT/KX 105182.

Forecast

Mention in Dispatches
Skipper George William Brown, R.N.R.
Seaman Robert Harold Hardy, LT/JX 181737.

Golden Gift
D.S.M.
    Seaman Cook Reginald George Arthur Remblance, LT/JX 181854.

Golden Sunbeam
D.S.M.
    Seaman Joseph Allen Peters, LT/JX 180429.

Lord Howe
D.S.C.
    Skipper William H. Pollock.
D.S.M.
    Seaman William Edward Jonathan Bullen, LT/JX 181821.
MENTION IN DISPATCHES
    Second Hand Thomas Herbert Christian, LT/JX 187326.

Midas
D.S.C.
    Skipper Herbert Holden, R.N.R.
D.S.M.
    Seaman William Omar Blowers, LT/JX 181818.
    Second Hand James Bettess, LT/JX 187267.

Paxton
D.S.M.
    Second Hand Sydney Rose, LT/JX 185667.

Shipmates
D.S.M.
    Second Hand Herbert Cuthbertson, LT/JX 1858584.

The Boys
D.S.C.
    Skipper Andrew Buchan, R.N.R.
MENTION IN DISPATCHES
    Seaman George Fred Mathews, R.N.P.S., LT/JX 185264.

Yorkshire Lass
D.S.M.
    Seaman Samuel William George Bauldry, LT/JX 181750.
    Stoker John Joseph Collins, LT/KX 105201.

PORTSMOUTH A./P. YACHTS

Ahola
MENTION IN DISPATCHES
    Petty Officer Hubert Horace Hollands, P/J 20594.
    Able Seaman Francis Harold Finch, P/SSX 23237.

APPENDIX C

Ankh
D.S.M.
>Able Seaman Walter Frank Lunn, P/JX 166227.
>Yacht Engineer F. Barter.

Bounty
D.S.M.
>Able Seaman Ernest Fenton, P/JX 145044.
>Able Seaman Holborn Gerald Hayles, C/JX 140933.
>Ordinary Signalman William Arthur Denny, TD/X 1790.
>Engineer Albert Ferris.

Caryanda
D.S.M.
>Acting Petty Officer Herbert Henry Smith, P/JX 125648.
>Able Seaman Thomas William Schofield, P/J 26827.

Eila II
Mention in Dispatches
>Petty Officer Charles Sydney Smith, P/J 14350.
>Able Seaman Kenneth Freer Marriott, P/SSX 23766.
>Mr. Thomas McDermott Weir, Yacht Engineer.

Lahloo
Mention in Dispatches
>Lieutenant John Vander Ould, R.N.V.R.
>Mr. Donald Brewer, Yacht Engineer.

Marsayru
D.S.M.
>Skipper G. D. Olivier.
Mention in Dispatches
>Mr. C. Coggins, Engineer

Seriola
D.S.C.
>Sub-Lieutenant Thomas Ellison Godman, R.N.V.R.

Thele
D.S.M.
>Chief Petty Officer Arthur Henry Herbert Gutsell, P/J 28475.

Miscellaneous H.M. Ships
Alouette II
D.S.M.
>Seaman Frederick Herbert Wyatt, R.N.V.R., LD 9/1806.

APPENDIX C

Second Hand John Malcolm Fenwick, LT/JX 185753.

Bystander
C.G.M.
Seaman Cook Jesse Harry Herbert Elton, LT/JX 180250.

Chrystobel II
Mention in Dispatches
Lieutenant Hubert Edward Wigfull, R.N.V.R.
Ordinary Seaman John Philip Charles Mead, LT/JX 193106.

Grive
D.S.C.
Sub-Lieutenant John Kenneth Barton Miles, R.N.V.R.
Mention in Dispatches (Posthumous)
Captain The Honourable Lionel John Oliver Lambert, D.S.O., R.N.
(Retd.)

King Orry
D.S.O.
Commander Jeffrey Elliott, R.D., R.N.R.

Llanthony
D.S.C.
Sub-Lieutenant Robert Walter Timbrell, R.C.N.
D.S.M.
Ordinary Seaman Jack Randle, P/JX 182172.

Lynx
D.S.M.
Yeoman of Signals James Collins, C/J 69513.

Mona's Isle
D.S.O.
Commander John Charles Keith Dowding, R.D., R.N.R.
D.S.M.
Petty Officer Leonard Bertram Kearley-Pope, R.N.R., D 5762.

St. Abbs
D.S.M.
Leading Steward Edmund Samuel Lawrence, P/L 8649.

St. Olaves
Mention in Dispatches
Skipper Henry Forrester, R.N.R.

Semois
D.S.C.
Temporary Sub-Lieutenant Geoffrey Ross Weller, R.N.V.R.
D.S.M.
Chief Petty Officer David Edward Ford, C/JX 163828.
Acting Leading Stoker John Francis Nolan, C/KX 87092.
MENTION IN DISPATCHES
Petty Officer Arthur Edland, C/J 77078.
Seaman Churchill.

Watchful
D.S.C.
Lieutenant Alexander Harper Turner, R.N.V.R.

SKOOTS

Amazone
D.S.M.
Ordinary Seaman Vincent Wakeham, P/JX 194588.
MENTION IN DISPATCHES
Lieutenant-Commander Lawrence Henry Phillips, R.N.

Brandaris
MENTION IN DISPATCHES
Commander Charles Euman, R.N. (Ret.)

Doggersbank
D.S.C.
Lieutenant Donald Terry McBarnet, R.N.
D.S.M.
Engine Room Artificer Fourth Class Eric Matt Horne, C/MX 62572.

Fredanja
MENTION IN DISPATCHES
Lieutenant-Commander Kenneth Warden Stewart, R.N.
Petty Officer Thomas Alfred Willing, P/J 100988.
Engine Room Artificer Fourth Class Jack Stanley Ambrose, P/MX 65337.

Hilda
D.S.O.
Lieutenant Archibald Gray, R.N.
D.S.C.
Sea Cadet Lieutenant Harry Simouth-Willing.
BAR TO D.S.M.
Acting Petty Officer Leonard Charles Curd, D.S.M., C/JX 155644.
D.S.M.
Able Seaman George Leslie Edwin Godfrey, C/JX 144633.

APPENDIX C

Hondsrug
D.S.C.
Lieutenant Frederick Thomas Renny, R.N.R.
D.S.M.
Petty Officer James Potts, D/J 92186.

Lena
MENTION IN DISPATCHES
Leading Seaman Lauchlan Maclean Watt Gibb, D/J 64311.

Patria
D.S.M.
Leading Seaman Willie Hagger, P/J 95873.

Reiger
MENTION IN DISPATCHES
Lieutenant Alexander Tyson, R.N.

Twente
D.S.O.
Lieutenant-Commander Humphrey Gilbert Boys-Smith, R.N.R.
D.S.M.
Leading Seaman Reginald William Legg, D/J 107221.
Able Seaman George Henry Baker, D/SSX 27349.

Zeus
MENTION IN DISPATCHES
Petty Officer Francis Herbert Franklin, P/J 96765.

PERSONNEL AND HOSPITAL SHIPS

Biarritz
D.S.C.
Mr. James Lang Crockart, Engineer.
MENTION IN DISPATCHES (POSTHUMOUS)
Fireman Albert Phillips.
MENTION IN DISPATCHES
Captain William Hay Baker, Master.

Canterbury
D.S.C.
Captain Charles Archibald Hancock, Master.

Dinard
MENTION IN DISPATCHES
Mr. John William Ailwyn Jones, Chief Officer.
Mr. Norman Smith, Chief Engineer.
Mrs. A. Goodrich, Stewardess.

APPENDIX C

Dorrien Rose
D.S.C.
  Captain William Thompson, Master.
  Mr. Terence O'Hanlon, Mate.
  Mr. Bernard Murphy, Chief Engineer.
D.S.M.
  Lewis Gunner T. W. Watson.
  Able Seaman J. O'Rawe.
  Ordinary Seaman W. Barrett.
  Fireman A. Gilson.
MENTION IN DISPATCHES
  Mr. James Steward, Second Engineer.
  Mr. Paddy McFadden, Boatswain.
  Able Seaman T. Barrett.
  Able Seaman John Upperton.
  Ordinary Seaman Clifford Barrett.
  Fireman Ali Khan.
  Fireman Abdul Mohand.

Isle of Guernsey
D.S.C.
  Captain Ernest Leonard Hill, Master.
  Mr. David Douglas Robb, Chief Engineer.
D.S.M.
  Able Seaman John Fowles.
MENTION IN DISPATCHES
  Mr. Reginald Frederick Pembury, Chief Officer.

Killarney
MENTION IN DISPATCHES
  Captain Richard Hughes, Master.

King George V
D.S.C.
  Captain Robert McCallum McLean, Master.
  Mr. William McGregor, Chief Engineer.
D.S.M.
  Able Seaman Donald Joseph McKinnon.

Lady of Mann
MENTION IN DISPATCHES
  Captain Thomas C. Woods, Master.

Levenwood
D.S.C.
  Captain William Oswald Young, Master.

D.S.M.
Merchant Navy Gunner George Knight.
Fireman Robert Moody

Lochgarry
MENTION IN DISPATCHES
Captain Ewen Mackinnon, Master.

Lord Rodney
MENTION IN DISPATCHES
Captain William Josiah Penny, Master.

Maid of Orleans
D.S.C.
Captain Gordon Dyer Walter, Master.
Mr. George Frederick Tooley, Second Engineer.
D.S.M.
Quartermaster Henry Russell.

Mona's Queen
D.S.C.
Captain R. Duggan.
MENTION IN DISPATCHES
Chief Petty Officer Telegraphist Ernest John William Amos, C/J 24627.
Chief Petty Officer Telegraphist George Frederick Oliver Bloyce, C/240081.

Nephrite
D.S.M.
Acting Able Seaman Albert Edward Mellis, C/LDX 5187.
MENTION IN DISPATCHES
Captain Cyril Gilford West, O.B.E., Master.

Ngaroma
MENTION IN DISPATCHES
Captain John William Dickinson, Master.

Prague
D.S.C.
Captain Clifford Rowland Baxter, Master.
Mr. Walter Ernest Oxenham, Chief Engineer.
D.S.M.
Boy Frederick William John Rusby.

Princess Maud
MENTION IN DISPATCHES
Captain Henry Clarke, Master.

APPENDIX C

Roebuck
MENTION IN DISPATCHES
Captain Wilfred Yvon Larbalestier, Master.

Royal Daffodil
D.S.C.
Captain George Johnson, Master.
Mr. Arthur Patrick Joseph Paterson, Chief Officer.
Mr. Joseph Wilfred Coulthard, Chief Engineer.
D.S.M.
Donkeyman Albert Delamain.
MENTION IN DISPATCHES
Mr. John Bingham Woodhouse, Second Officer.
Mr. William Leonard Evans, Second Engineer.

Royal Sovereign
D.S.C.
Captain Thomas Aldis, Master.
Mr. Andrew Sinclair, Chief Engineer.
D.S.M.
Chief Steward Thomas Edward Manser.

St. Andrew
MENTION IN DISPATCHES
Captain Herbert Cecil Bond, Master.

St. Helier
D.S.C.
Captain Reginald Richard Pitman, Master.
Mr. Hubert Donald Freeman, First Officer.
Mr. Frank Edward Martin, Second Officer.
D.S.M.
Quartermaster Clarence Jack Walkey.

Scotia
D.S.C.
Captain William Henry Hughes, Master.

Tynwald
D.S.C.
Captain John Henry Whiteway, Master.
Mr. Allan Watterson, Second Officer.
Mr. Charles Powell Mason, Radio Officer.
D.S.M.
Seaman Thomas Gribbin.

APPENDIX C

MENTION IN DISPATCHES
Mr. William Edward Lister, Purser.
Carpenter John Gawne.
Donkeyman Arthur James Allen.

OTHER BRITISH SHIPS

Alouette
MENTION IN DISPATCHES
Sub-Lieutenant Reginald Edward Lee, R.N.V.R.

Aura
MENTION IN DISPATCHES
Sub-Lieutenant Michael Adam Anthony Chodzko, R.N.V.R.

Bonny Heather
BAR TO D.S.C.
Lieutenant Charles Waterland Read, D.S.C., R.N.R.

Constant Nymph
D.S.M.
Mr. Basil Arthur Smith.

Dwarf
D.S.M.
Petty Officer George Albert Coussens, P/J 7788.

Erica
MENTION IN DISPATCHES
Shipwright Second Class Charles Robert Greenwood, P/M 8899.

Fervent
MENTION IN DISPATCHES
Mr. Douglas Kirkaldie, Coxswain.

Foremost 87
D.S.C.
Captain James Fryer, Master.

Haig
MENTION IN DISPATCHES
Mr. Reginald Walter, First Engineer..

Hopper Barge 24
MENTION IN DISPATCHES
Captain H. F. Boyce, Master.

APPENDIX C

Java
D.S.M.
Seaman Harry Griffith.
MENTION IN DISPATCHES
Mr. Victor Smith, Mate.

Kestrel
MENTION IN DISPATCHES
Mr. James Henry Spain, Third Engineer.

Lady Brassey
MENTION IN DISPATCHES
Captain Frederick John Hopwood, Master.

Lady Southborough
MENTION IN DISPATCHES
Captain A. M. Poole, Master.

Laroc
MENTION IN DISPATCHES
Captain George Beaumont Butler, Master.
Mr. Jack Lynn, Mate.
Mr. Raymond Crane, Engineer.
Deck Hand Leonard Lynn.
Steward H. A. E. Frost.

Lighter X 209
MENTION IN DISPATCHES
Captain R. G. Banks, Acting Master.

Little Ann
D.S.M.
Mr. A. D. Divine.

Massey Shaw
D.S.M.
Sub-Officer Aubrey John May, London Fire Brigade.
MENTION IN DISPATCHES
Lieutenant Geoffrey Frank Walker, R.N.V.R.
Fireman Henry Albert William Ray, Auxiliary Fire Service.
Fireman Edmund Gordon Wright, Auxiliary Fire Service.

Mermaiden
D.S.M.
Leading Stoker William Alfred Stanley Horne, R.F.R.
MENTION IN DISPATCHES
Petty Officer Frederick John Norton, D/217022.

APPENDIX C

Motor Boat 275
D.S.M.
    Able Seaman Leo Frederick Strand, C/J 69009.

Naiad Errant
D.S.M.
    Able Seaman Samuel Palmer, D/JX 148052.

Newhaven Lifeboat *Rosa Wood and Phyllis Lund*
D.S.M.
    Able Seaman William James Morris, P/JX 126097.
    MENTION IN DISPATCHES
    Stoker First Class Percy William Spray, P/KX 87052.
    Ordinary Seaman Thomas Edgar Whyte, R.N.V.R., CD/X 133.

Ocean Breeze
    MENTION IN DISPATCHES
    Lieutenant Victor Alexander Christian Henry George De Mauny,
    R.N. (Retd.)

Pauleter and *Marasole*
D.S.M.
    Stoker First Class Douglas Thomas Banks, C/KX 86174.

Princess Lily
    MENTION IN DISPATCHES
    Probationary Temporary Sub-Lieutenant Kenneth Egremont Anson
    Bayley, R.N.V.R.

Queensland
D.S.M.
    Deck Hand W. Absolom.
    Deck Hand M. Hains.

Rapide
D.S.C.
    Sub-Lieutenant John Cambridge Clarke, R.N.V.R.

Rosaura
    MENTION IN DISPATCHES (POSTHUMOUS)
    Sub-Lieutenant William Bernard Lyulph Tower, R.N.

Skylark
    MENTION IN DISPATCHES
    Probationary Temporary Sub-Lieutenant Marwood John Richard Yeat-
    man, R.N.V.R.

APPENDIX C

Swallow
D.S.C.
Sub-Lieutenant William Ronald Williams, R.N.

MENTION IN DISPATCHES
Mr. Frank Cherry, Third Engineer (Able Seaman).
Able Seaman Henry Charles Herring Hay.

Triton
D.S.C.
Lieutenant Robert Hunter Irving, R.N.R.

Walton and Frinton Lifeboat
MENTION IN DISPATCHES (POSTHUMOUS)
Temporary Lieutenant Reginald Hounsham Mead, R.N.V.R.
MENTION IN DISPATCHES
Petty Officer Telegraphist William Henry Cooley, P/J 93203.
Able Seaman James Laurence MacManus, P/SSX 14756.

Yser
MENTION IN DISPATCHES
Acting Petty Officer William Henry Atkin, C/JX 149919.

INDEX

A.5, 163
Abbeville, 16–17, 19, 22, 26, 28–30, 32, 243
Abdy Beauclerk, 132
Abrial, Admiral, 22, 57, 178–9, 189, 237–8
Ahukir, 74–6, 80, 83
Adam, Lieutenant-General Sir Ronald, 22, 57, 71
Ada Mary, 200
Admiralty, 29, 33, 35–6, 52, 62, 88, 103, 114, 133, 159, 207–8, 229, 237, 240, 244; Small Vessels Pool, 24, 33, 36, 61–2, 73, 137, 146
L'Adroit, 43
Advance, 72–3, 101–3
Aegir, H.M. Skoot, 160
Agincourt, 192
Aidie, 155
Ailwyn-Jones, Captain J., 92
Albury, H.M.M., 112
Aldis, Captain T., 92, 167
Aldrich, H., 136
Alers-Hankey, Lieutenant-Commander C. B., 107
Alexander, C. G., 181
Alexander, Major-General the Hon. H. R. H. L., 178–80, 203, 207, 210, 216, 224
Allen, Sub-Lieutenant S. C., 101
Allison, Commander J. H., 196
Ambleve, 112
A.M.C.3, 151
Amos, Sub-Lieutenant R. H. C., 195
Anderson, Lieutenant J., 111
Andora II, 131
Anduse-Faru, Commandant, 221
Annaheim, Paymaster-Captain E. C., 62
Anna Marguerite, 182
Anthony, H.M.S., 123, 141
Arc en Ciel, 221
Archangel, 36, 65
Armed boarding vessels, 69, 99, 113, 248. See also under names of individual ships
Armitage, Lieutenant R. S., 113
Autocarrier, 221, 226, 230–2
Ave Maria Gratia Plena, 221

Baker, Captain W. H., 64
Banks, Stoker D. T., 100, 131, 216
Barbara Jean, 155
Barges, 36–7, 54, 100, 133, 136, 151, 154–6, 160–1, 165, 185–6, 200, 204, 213, 250. See also under names of individual ships
Barlone, D., 60
Barnard, Lieutenant-Colonel H. T. B., 217

Barrell, Allen, 101, 123
Bartlett, Sir Basil, 77–9, 105–6
Basilisk, H.M.S., 151, 176, 186, 188, 195, 200
Bat, 131–2, 164
Baxter, Captain B., 82, 119, 191
Baxter, Captain N., 169
B.B.C. broadcast, 33–4
Beal, 83, 90–1
Beatrice Maud, 156
Bee, 131, 164
Belgian Army, 13–16, 18–23, 26, 29, 47, 53, 57, 71, 83
Belgian ships, 30, 50, 112, 137, 253. See also Fishing boats
Bell, Sub-Lieutenant, 150
Bellamy, B. E., 35
Belton, J. J., 180
Ben-My-Chree, 197, 221
Berthon, Captain E. L., 176, 187–8, 212
Best, Captain Digby, 37
Besta, H.M. Skoot, 160
Betts, A., 72
Biarritz, 36, 64
Bickford, Captain J. G., 109
Bideford, H.M.S., 113, 136, 141–2
Biles, Captain, 214–15, 219
Black Arrow, 100–1
Blackburn Rovers, H.M. Trawler, 216
Blackmore, G. W., 43, 142
Blanchard, General, 18, 20, 22–3, 53, 57, 88, 178
Blockships, 234
Blows, Sub-Lieutenant R. E., 112
Blue Bird, 217
Blyskawica, 68, 107–8, 175
Bobelli, 100–1
Bonham, Sub-Lieutenant W. G. H., 101
Bonny Heather, 124–5, 194
Booth, Lieutenant-Commander B. R., 98
Bornrif, H.M. Skoot, 160
Boulogne, 19–20, 22, 24, 26, 30, 36–8, 45–7, 58
Bourrasque, 132, 141
Bowles, Commander, 125
Boyle, Commander R. C., 83
Bray-Dunes, 27, 65, 79, 84, 106–9, 113, 117–18, 138, 141, 145, 161, 169, 176–7, 180
Brest, 41, 210, 242
Brett, R. C., 206–7
Brighton, 101, 242
Brighton Belle, H.M.M., 85–6
Brighton Queen, H.M.M., 177, 207
Britannic, 161–2

INDEX

Dover Command, see Vice-Admiral Sir Bertram Ramsay

Drew, Nicholas, see Robert Harling

Drifters, 11, 25, 36, 55, 65, 69, 112, 151, 161, 194–5, 213, 226–30, 236, 247–8. See also under names of individual ships

Duchess, 155, 187

Duchess of Fife, H.M.M., 110–11, 142

Duggan, Captain R., 55

Duke, 200

Dungeness, 166

Dutch Army, 14, 29, 75

Dutch ships, 30, 37, 133, 137, 253. See also Coasters and Skoots

'Dynamo Room', 31–2, 61, 212, 220, 228

Easter, Skipper W. H., 155

E-boats, 32, 39, 41, 53, 74, 76, 105–6, 140, 174–5, 216, 229

Ede, Lieutenant-Commander L. J. S., 188

Edge-Partington, Sub-Lieutenant T. K., 138

Edward Z. Dresden, 132

Edwards, D. H., 35

Efford, 49

Elbe, 50

Ellen Mary, 101

Elliott, Commander Jeffery, 99

Ellis, W. F., 155

Elizabeth Green, 100, 131

E.M.E.D., 132, 166, 204–5

Empire Henchman, 143, 204

Ena, 156

Endeavour, 159

Esk, H.M.S., 109, 112, 117, 138, 140, 193–5

Ethel Everard, 151, 155

Eve, 137

Ewart-Wentworth, Lieutenant-Commander M. W., 140

Excellent, H.M.S., 183

Express, H.M.S., 109, 140, 230, 237

Fagalde, General, 57, 179

Fairplay I, 208, 216

Farrow, Lieutenant-Commander E. F. A., 114

Faulkner, R. W. A., 234

Fenella, 97–8, 113

Ferry Nymph, 125

Fidget, H.M. Drifter, 113, 194

Fieldgate, C., 142, 225

Filleul, Lieutenant-Commander, 156, 236

Filley, Skipper F. W., 182

Filley, Skipper J. F., 156

Finbow, Skipper F., 155

Firth Fisher, 43

Firth of Forth, 33, 139, 177

Fishbourne, 200

Fishe, J. E., 204

Fisher, Captain J., 35–6, 62, 160

Fisher, Commander R. L., 141

Fisher Boy, H.M. Drifter, 113, 194

Fishing boats, 25, 125, 159–60, 240, 249–52. See also under names of individual ships; Belgian, 131, 163, 182, 216–17, 235, 253; French, 11, 210, 221, 234, 253

Fleet Air Arm, 175, 189, 208

Flushing, 32, 39

Foam Queen, 150, 172

Folkestone, 25–6, 197, 242

Force K, 55, 110, 213, 228–9

Foremost 22, 142–3, 219, 225

Foremost 87, 120, 136, 142, 151, 215–16, 219

Foremost 101, 161

Fossa, 205

Fothergill, W. A., 225

Foudroyant, 188, 198, 208

Franks, Lieutenant R. D., 84

Fraser, Captain G., 161

Freeman, Commander V. P., 62

French Army, 12–24, 29, 41, 43, 47, 53, 57, 60, 87–8, 116–17, 144, 178–9, 210, 224–5, 228, 231–2, 237, 242–4

French Navy, 36, 41, 88, 103–4, 210, 221, 225, 231–2, 237, 240, 244, 252. See also Admiral Abrial and Destroyers

French ships (excluding warships), 36, 41, 43, 88, 103–4, 116, 150, 182, 198, 206, 210, 213, 220, 228, 230–1, 233, 240, 244, 253. See also Personnel ships

Frightened Lady, 100–1

Fryer, J., 136, 219

Furse, Leading Seaman Norman, 137

Gaffney, Lieutenant H. C., 111

Gallant, H.M.S., 69, 84, 107

Gallipoli, 10–11

Gandell, Commodore W. P., 37

Gardiner, Lieutenant D. H. P., 188

Garside, Sub-Lieutenant E. T., 131

Georges Edouard, 182

German Army, 16, 19–20, 22, 26, 32, 44, 53, 55, 57, 61, 63–5, 71, 81, 87–9, 96, 117, 119, 121, 136, 140, 142–7, 151, 156–8, 161, 168, 171, 173, 176–7, 180, 182–3, 186, 191, 196, 207, 209–10, 233–4, 236–7

German Navy, 32, 39, 41. See also E-boats and Submarines

Getuigt vor Christus, 216

Gilda, 131

Gipsy King, 72, 161–2

Glengariff, 169

Glenway, 150, 155–6

Glitter II, 100–1

Golden Eagle, H.M.S., 111, 114, 177–8, 226–7

Golden Gift, H.M. Drifter, 177

Golden Lily, 100, 138

Golden Spray, 161–2

Goldeve, 51

Goliath, 50

Gondia, 49, 142

Goodrich, Mrs., 121–2

Gordon, Commander R. C., 107

Gorecht, H.M. Skoot, 160

301

221, 236, 240, 248–52. See also under names of individual ships
Yarmouth, 68, 132
Y.C. 63, 195
Y.C. 71, 180–1
Y.C. 72, 180–1
Yewdale, 63–4, 83, 90–1

Yewglen, 64
Yorkshire Lass, H.M. Drifter, 219
Young, Captain W. O., 171–2

Zeebrugge, 19, 30, 41, 234
Zwaluw, 163, 217